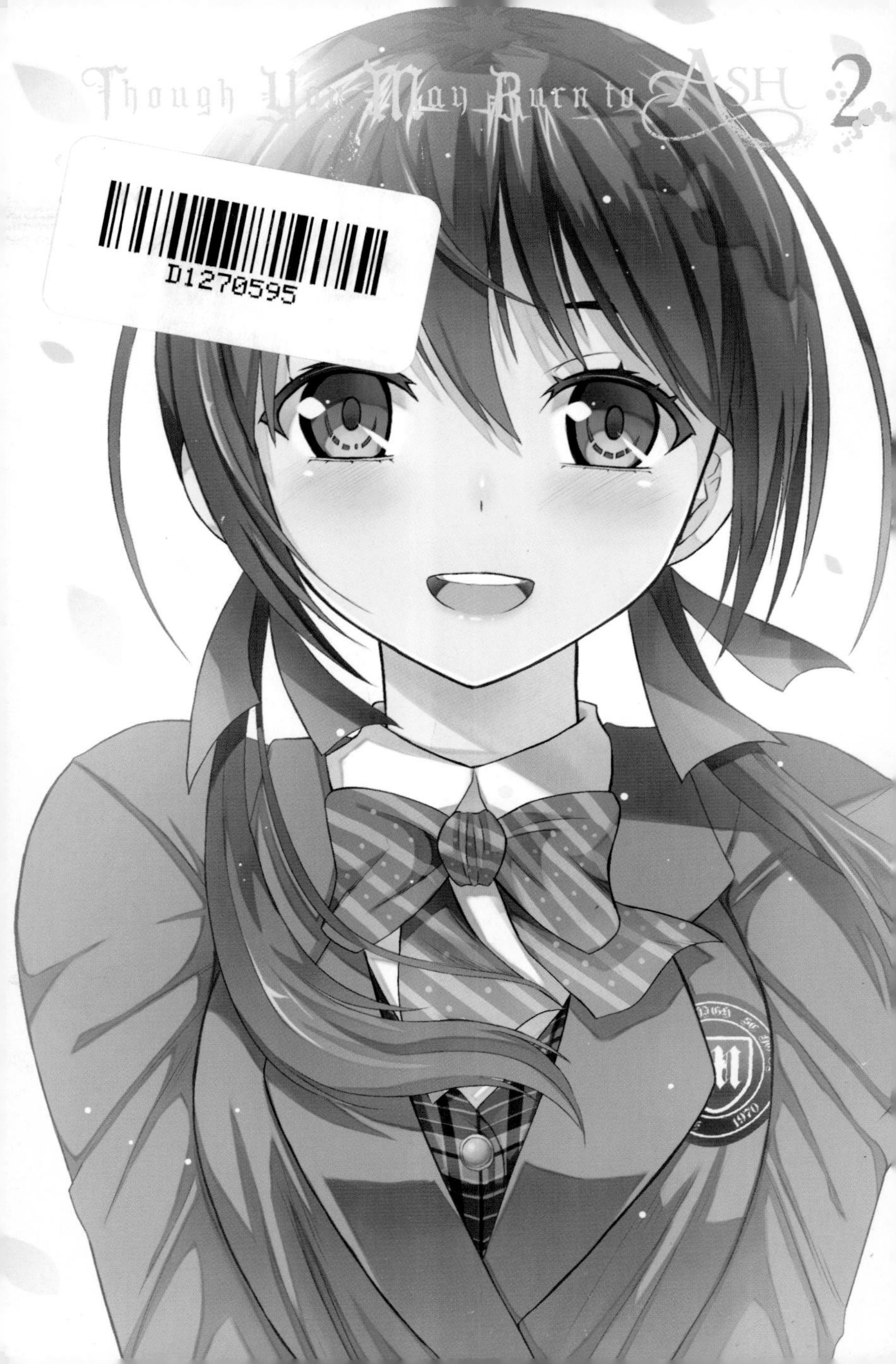
Though You May Burn to ASH 2

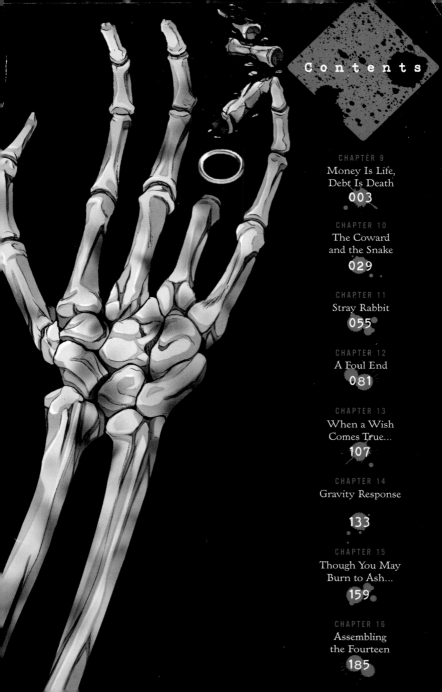

Contents

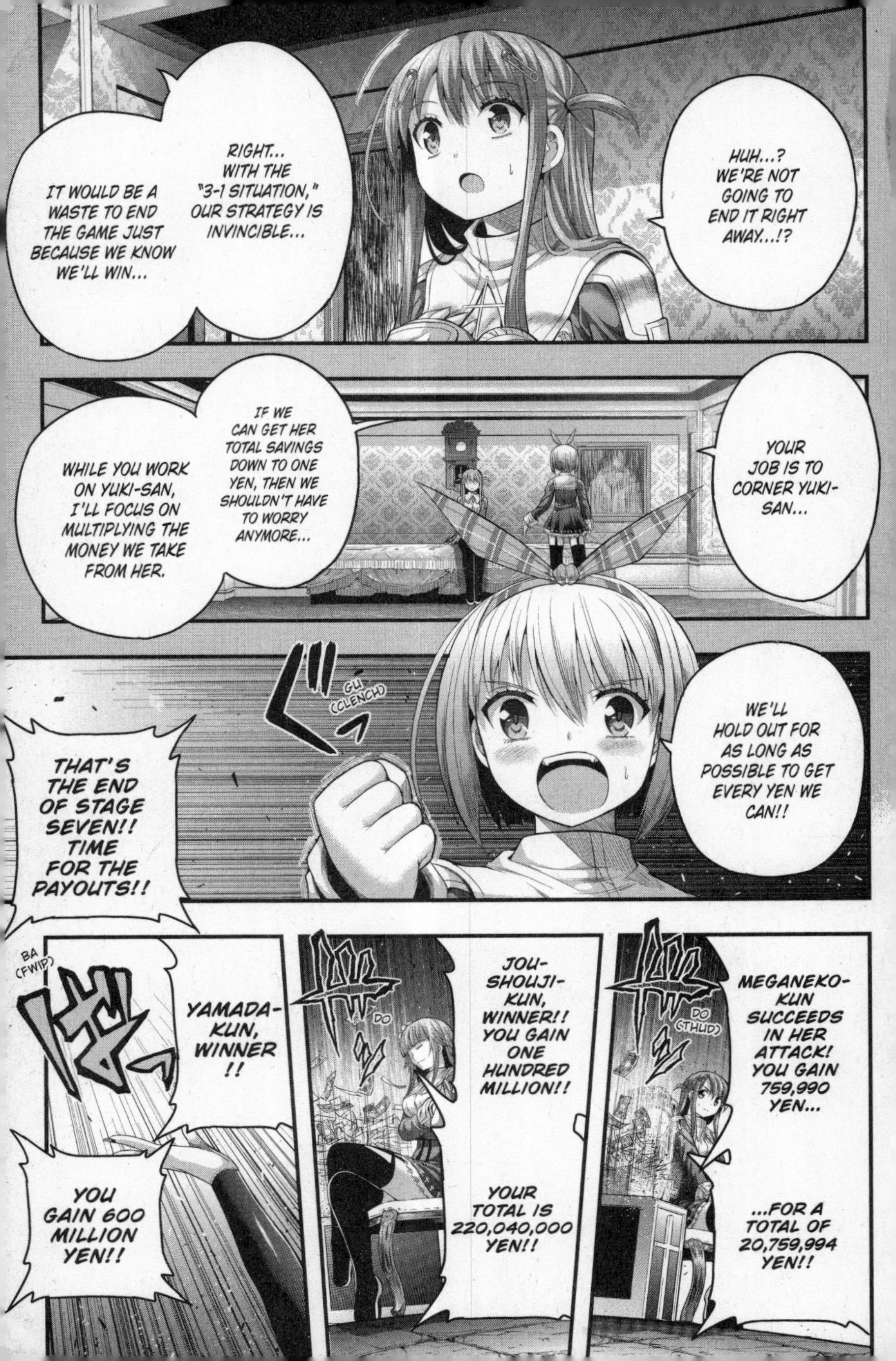
HUH...? WE'RE NOT GOING TO END IT RIGHT AWAY...!?
RIGHT... WITH THE "3-1 SITUATION," OUR STRATEGY IS INVINCIBLE...
IT WOULD BE A WASTE TO END THE GAME JUST BECAUSE WE KNOW WE'LL WIN...
YOUR JOB IS TO CORNER YUKI-SAN...
IF WE CAN GET HER TOTAL SAVINGS DOWN TO ONE YEN, THEN WE SHOULDN'T HAVE TO WORRY ANYMORE...
WHILE YOU WORK ON YUKI-SAN, I'LL FOCUS ON MULTIPLYING THE MONEY WE TAKE FROM HER.
WE'LL HOLD OUT FOR AS LONG AS POSSIBLE TO GET EVERY YEN WE CAN!!
GU (CLENCH)
THAT'S THE END OF STAGE SEVEN!! TIME FOR THE PAYOUTS!!
MEGANEKO-KUN SUCCEEDS IN HER ATTACK! YOU GAIN 759,990 YEN...
DO (THUD)
...FOR A TOTAL OF 20,759,994 YEN!!
JOU-SHOUJI-KUN, WINNER!! YOU GAIN ONE HUNDRED MILLION!!
DO
YOUR TOTAL IS 220,040,000 YEN!!
BA (FWIP)
YAMADA-KUN, WINNER!!
YOU GAIN 600 MILLION YEN!!

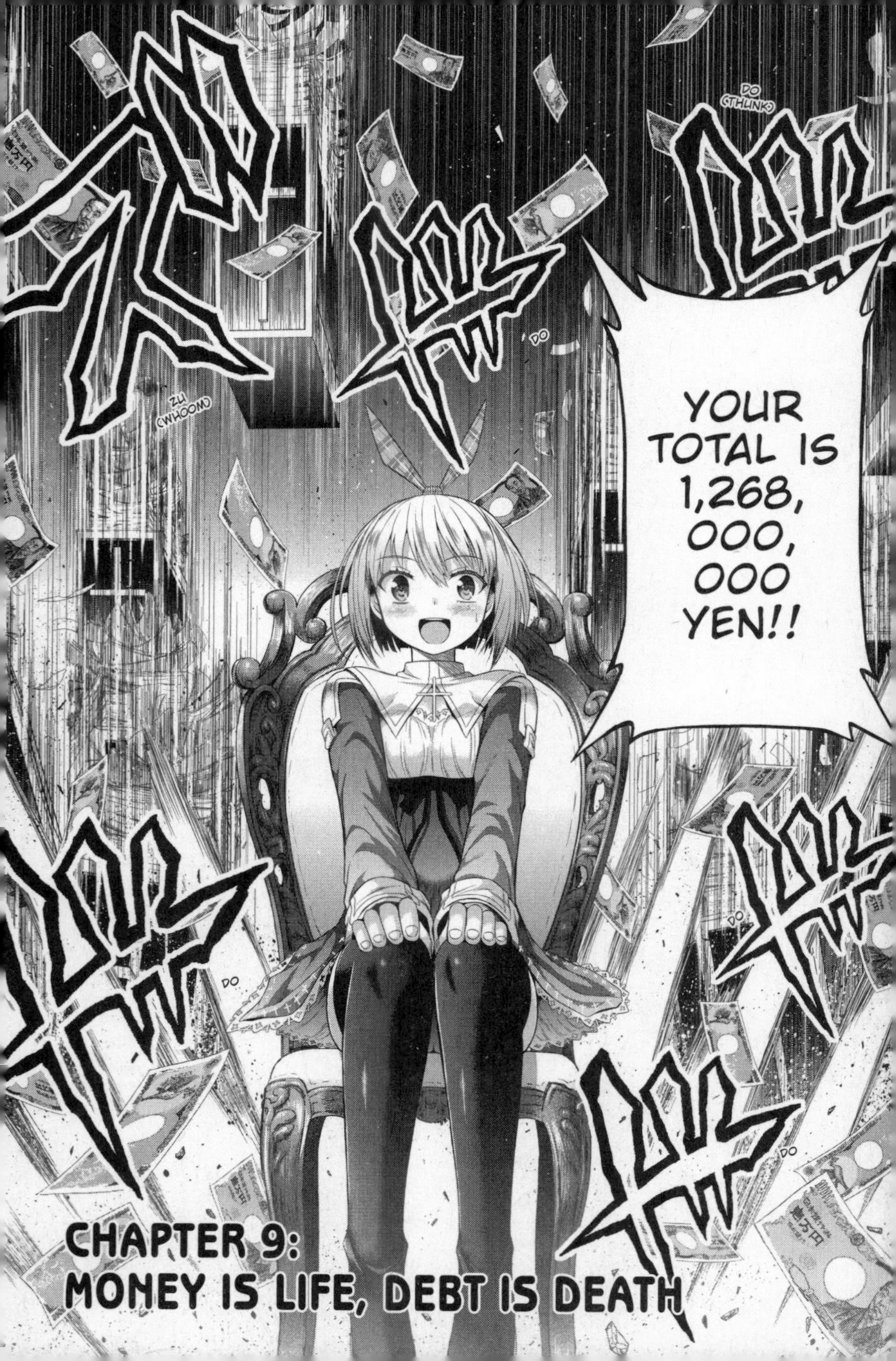
DO (THUNK)
YOUR TOTAL IS 1,268, 000, 000 YEN!!
DO
ZU (WHOOM)
DO
DO
DO
CHAPTER 9:
MONEY IS LIFE, DEBT IS DEATH

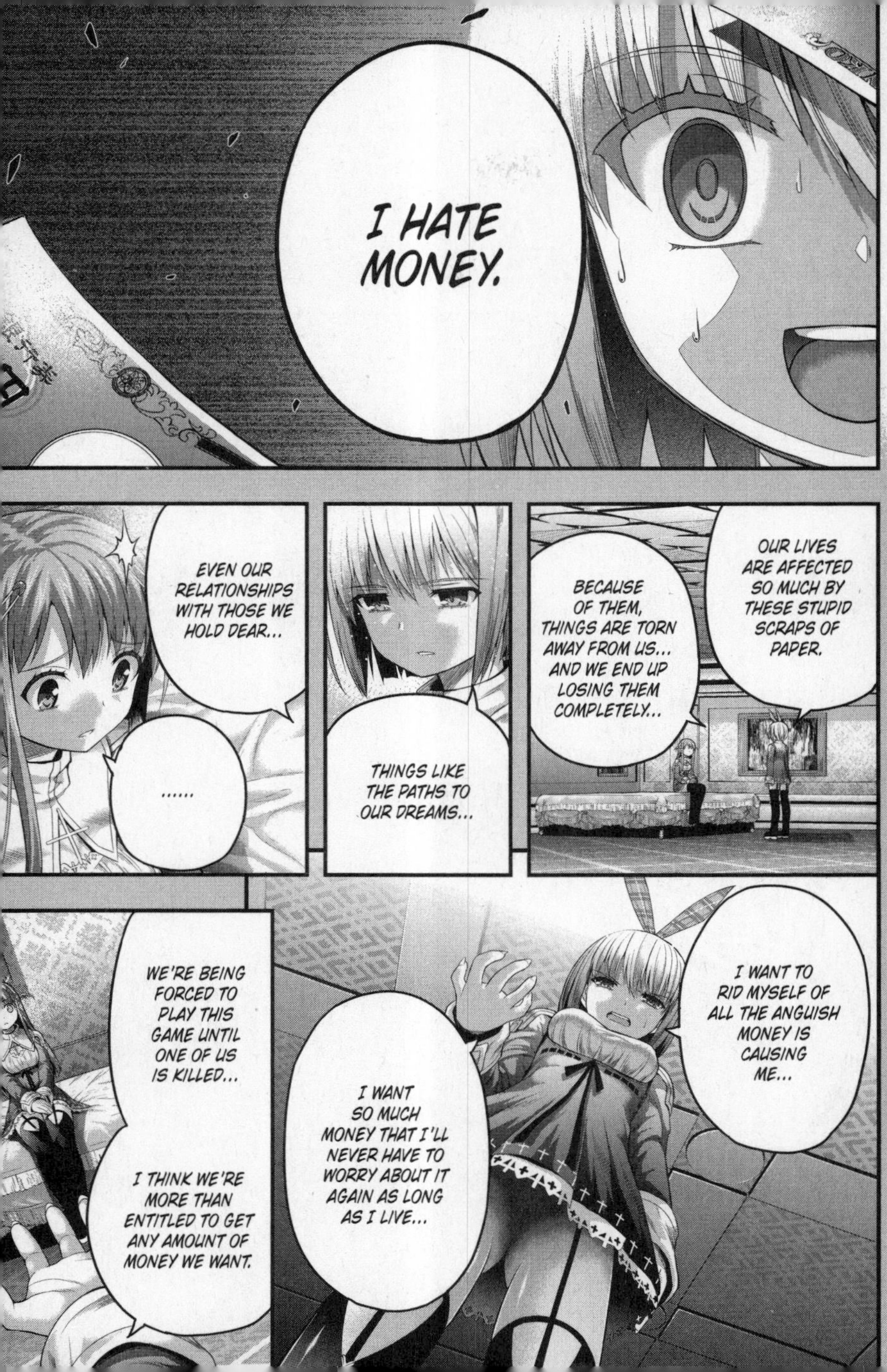
I HATE MONEY.
OUR LIVES ARE AFFECTED SO MUCH BY THESE STUPID SCRAPS OF PAPER.
BECAUSE OF THEM, THINGS ARE TORN AWAY FROM US... AND WE END UP LOSING THEM COMPLETELY...
THINGS LIKE THE PATHS TO OUR DREAMS...
EVEN OUR RELATIONSHIPS WITH THOSE WE HOLD DEAR...
......
I WANT TO RID MYSELF OF ALL THE ANGUISH MONEY IS CAUSING ME...
I WANT SO MUCH MONEY THAT I'LL NEVER HAVE TO WORRY ABOUT IT AGAIN AS LONG AS I LIVE...
WE'RE BEING FORCED TO PLAY THIS GAME UNTIL ONE OF US IS KILLED...
I THINK WE'RE MORE THAN ENTITLED TO GET ANY AMOUNT OF MONEY WE WANT.

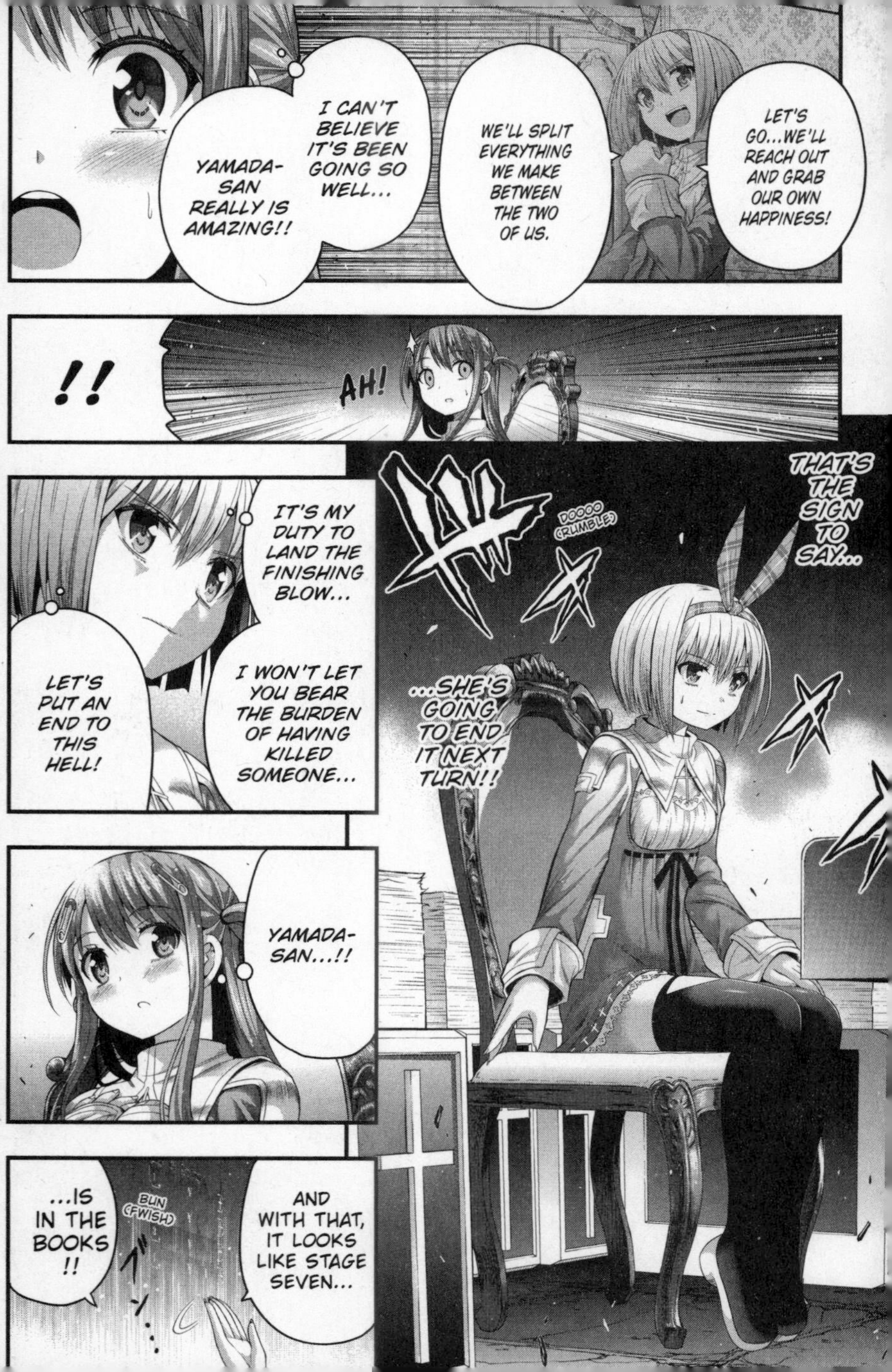
LET'S GO...WE'LL REACH OUT AND GRAB OUR OWN HAPPINESS!
WE'LL SPLIT EVERYTHING WE MAKE BETWEEN THE TWO OF US.
I CAN'T BELIEVE IT'S BEEN GOING SO WELL...
YAMADA-SAN REALLY IS AMAZING!!
AH!
!!
THAT'S THE SIGN TO SAY...
DOOOO (RUMBLE)
...SHE'S GOING TO END IT NEXT TURN!!
IT'S MY DUTY TO LAND THE FINISHING BLOW...
I WON'T LET YOU BEAR THE BURDEN OF HAVING KILLED SOMEONE...
LET'S PUT AN END TO THIS HELL!
YAMADA-SAN...!!
AND WITH THAT, IT LOOKS LIKE STAGE SEVEN...
BUN (FWISH)
...IS IN THE BOOKS!!

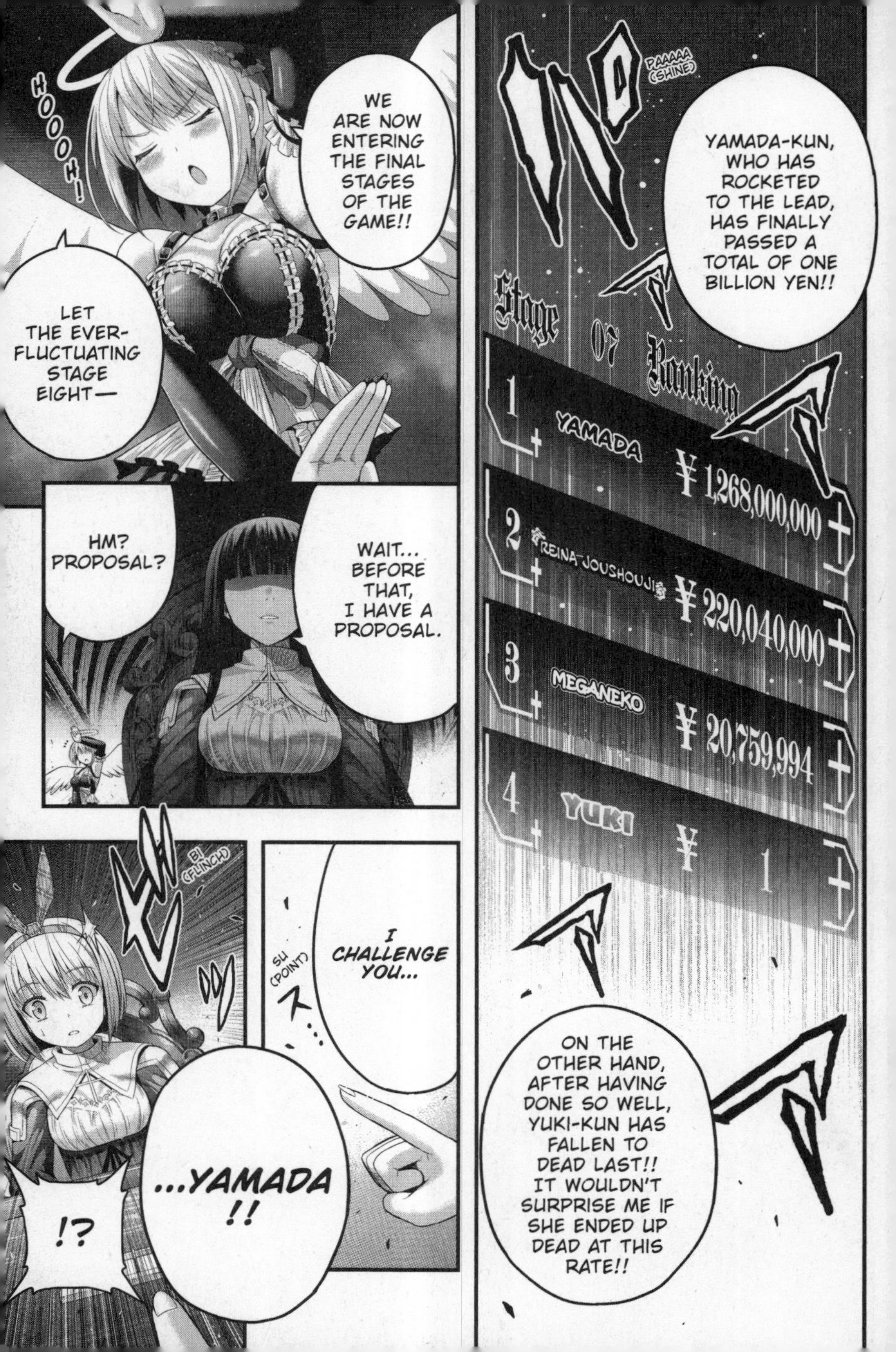
PAAAAA (SHINE)
YAMADA-KUN, WHO HAS ROCKETED TO THE LEAD, HAS FINALLY PASSED A TOTAL OF ONE BILLION YEN!!
Stage 07 Ranking
1 YAMADA ¥1,268,000,000
2 REINA JOUSHOUJI ¥220,040,000
3 MEGANEKO ¥20,759,994
4 YUKI ¥1
ON THE OTHER HAND, AFTER HAVING DONE SO WELL, YUKI-KUN HAS FALLEN TO DEAD LAST!! IT WOULDN'T SURPRISE ME IF SHE ENDED UP DEAD AT THIS RATE!!
WE ARE NOW ENTERING THE FINAL STAGES OF THE GAME!!
HOOOOH!
LET THE EVER-FLUCTUATING STAGE EIGHT—
WAIT... BEFORE THAT, I HAVE A PROPOSAL.
HM? PROPOSAL?
I CHALLENGE YOU...
SU (POINT)
...YAMADA!!
BI (FLINCH)
!?

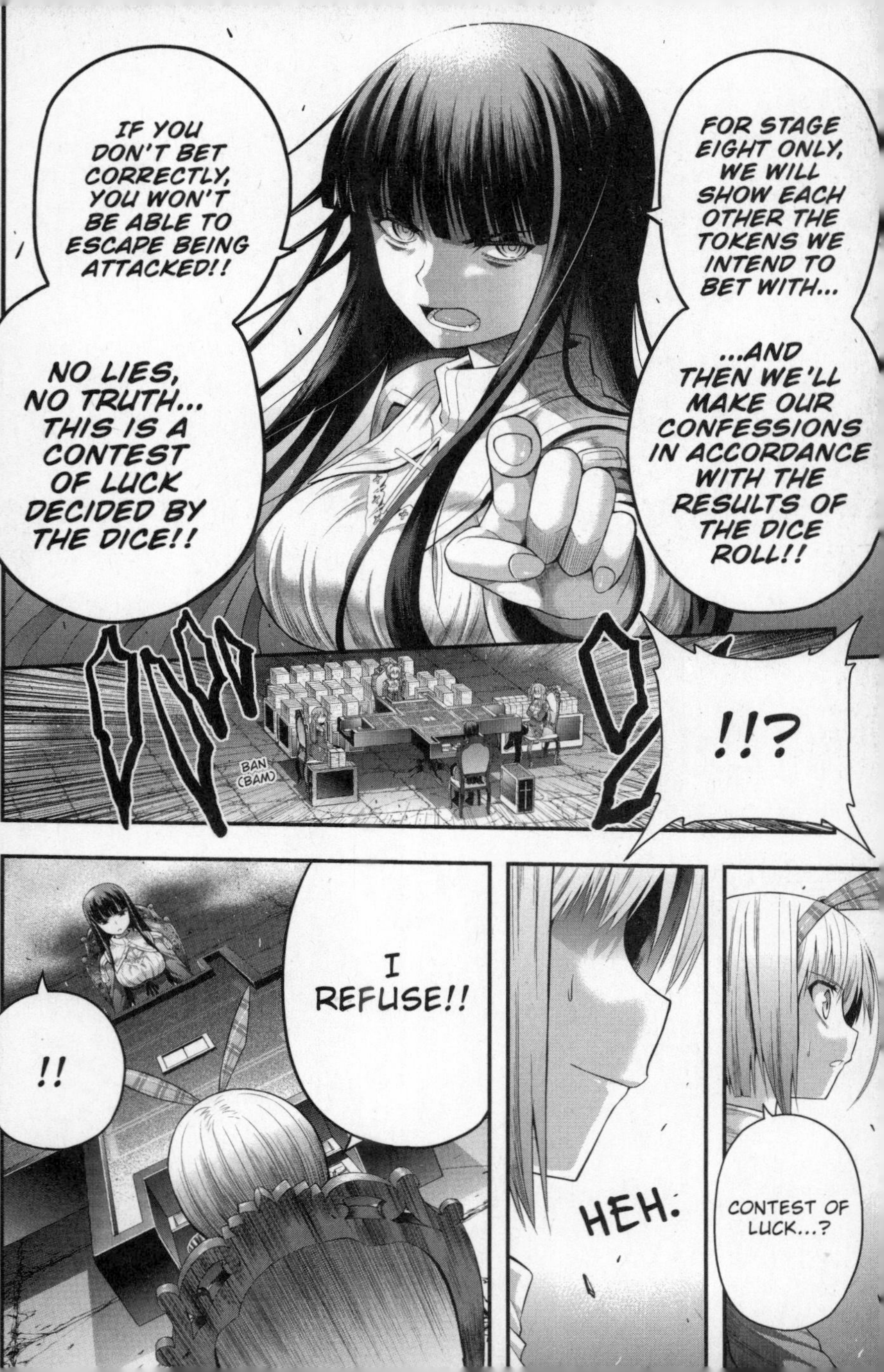
FOR STAGE EIGHT ONLY, WE WILL SHOW EACH OTHER THE TOKENS WE INTEND TO BET WITH...
...AND THEN WE'LL MAKE OUR CONFESSIONS IN ACCORDANCE WITH THE RESULTS OF THE DICE ROLL!!
IF YOU DON'T BET CORRECTLY, YOU WON'T BE ABLE TO ESCAPE BEING ATTACKED!!
NO LIES, NO TRUTH... THIS IS A CONTEST OF LUCK DECIDED BY THE DICE!!
!!?
BAN (BAM)
CONTEST OF LUCK...?
HEH.
I REFUSE!!
!!

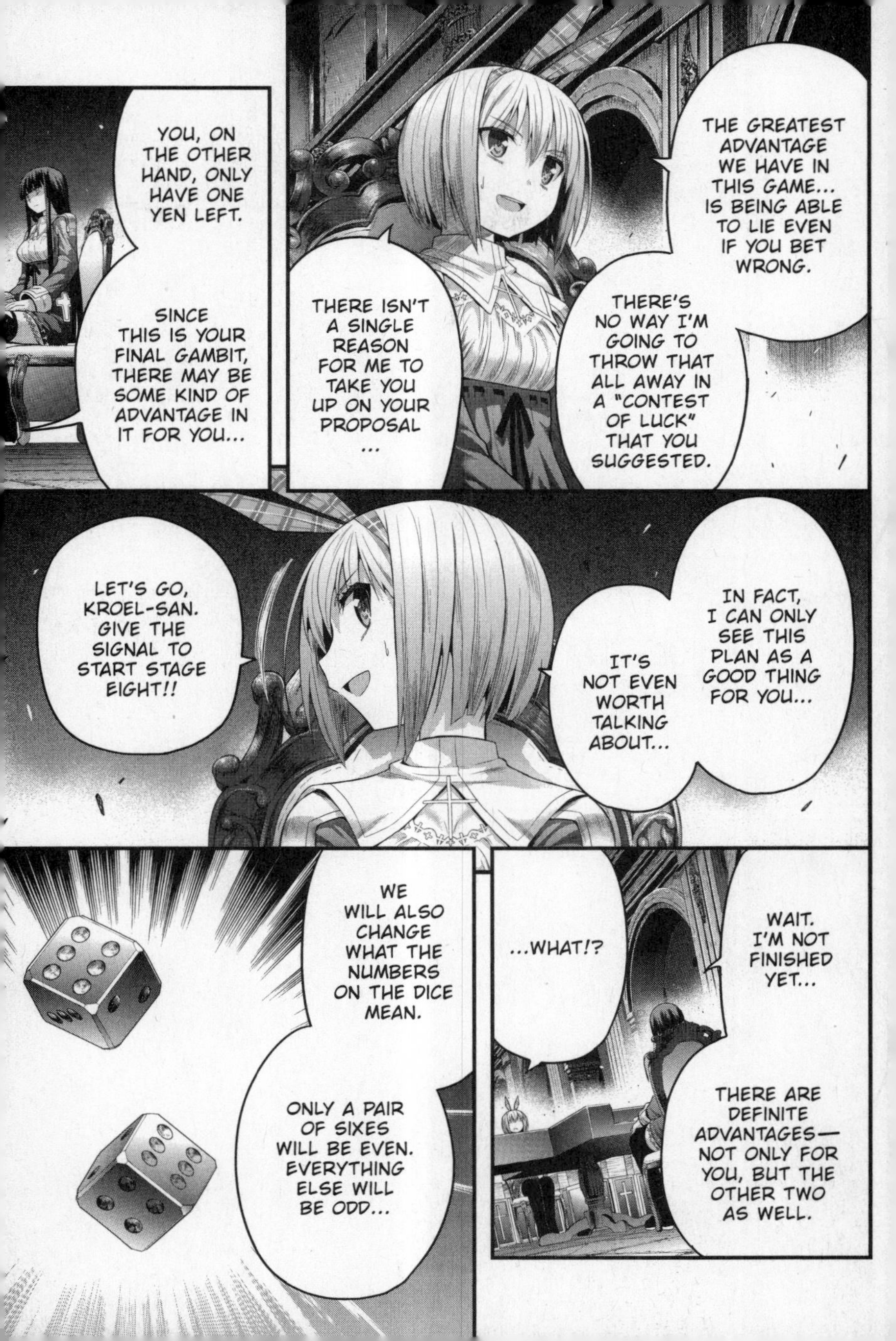
THE GREATEST ADVANTAGE WE HAVE IN THIS GAME... IS BEING ABLE TO LIE EVEN IF YOU BET WRONG.
THERE'S NO WAY I'M GOING TO THROW THAT ALL AWAY IN A "CONTEST OF LUCK" THAT YOU SUGGESTED.
THERE ISN'T A SINGLE REASON FOR ME TO TAKE YOU UP ON YOUR PROPOSAL ...
YOU, ON THE OTHER HAND, ONLY HAVE ONE YEN LEFT.
SINCE THIS IS YOUR FINAL GAMBIT, THERE MAY BE SOME KIND OF ADVANTAGE IN IT FOR YOU...
IN FACT, I CAN ONLY SEE THIS PLAN AS A GOOD THING FOR YOU...
IT'S NOT EVEN WORTH TALKING ABOUT...
LET'S GO, KROEL-SAN. GIVE THE SIGNAL TO START STAGE EIGHT!!
WAIT. I'M NOT FINISHED YET...
...WHAT!?
THERE ARE DEFINITE ADVANTAGES—NOT ONLY FOR YOU, BUT THE OTHER TWO AS WELL.
WE WILL ALSO CHANGE WHAT THE NUMBERS ON THE DICE MEAN.
ONLY A PAIR OF SIXES WILL BE EVEN. EVERYTHING ELSE WILL BE ODD...

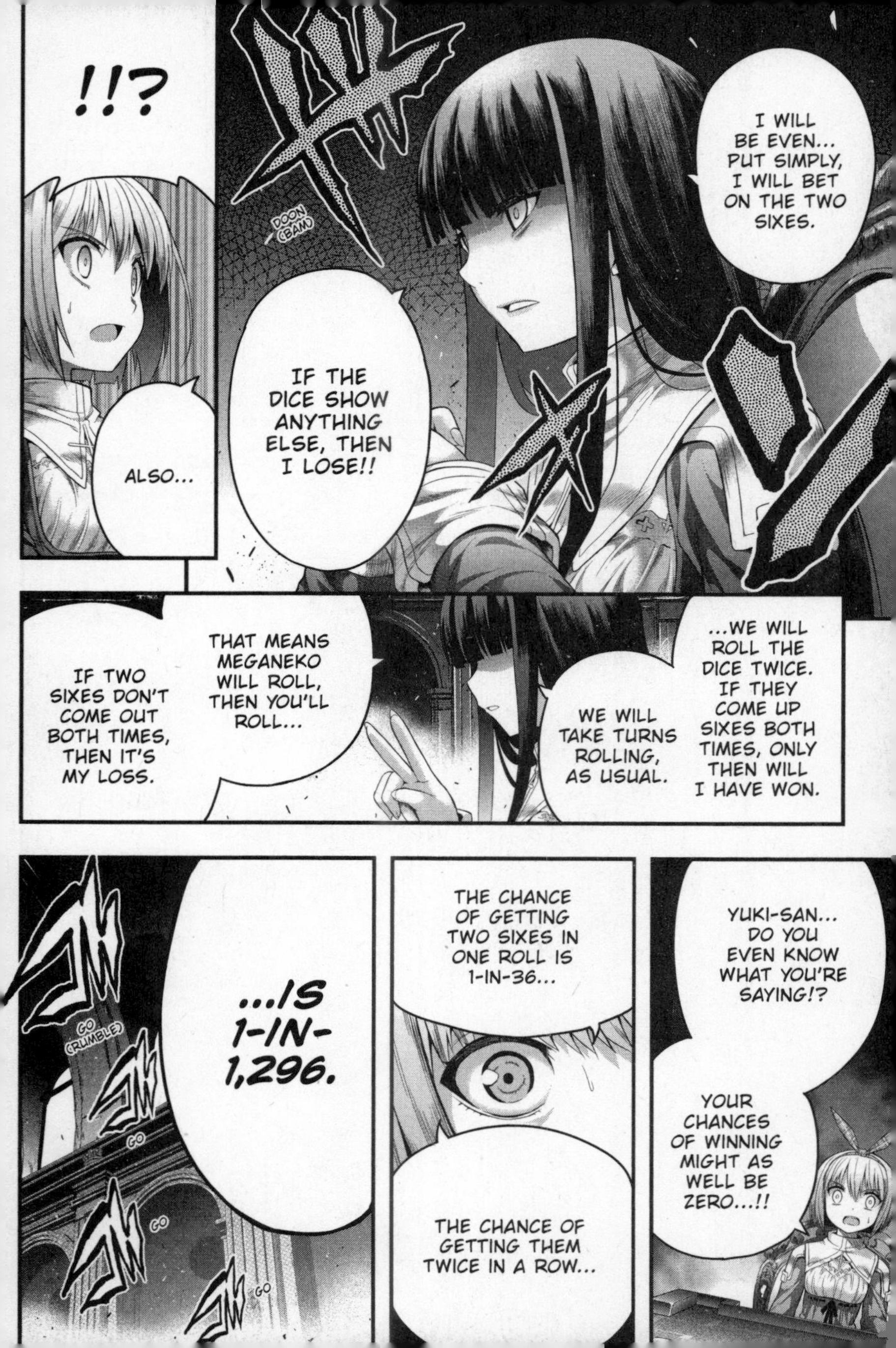
I WILL BE EVEN... PUT SIMPLY, I WILL BET ON THE TWO SIXES.
DOON (BAM)
IF THE DICE SHOW ANYTHING ELSE, THEN I LOSE!!
!!?
ALSO...
...WE WILL ROLL THE DICE TWICE. IF THEY COME UP SIXES BOTH TIMES, ONLY THEN WILL I HAVE WON.
WE WILL TAKE TURNS ROLLING, AS USUAL.
THAT MEANS MEGANEKO WILL ROLL, THEN YOU'LL ROLL...
IF TWO SIXES DON'T COME OUT BOTH TIMES, THEN IT'S MY LOSS.
YUKI-SAN... DO YOU EVEN KNOW WHAT YOU'RE SAYING!?
YOUR CHANCES OF WINNING MIGHT AS WELL BE ZERO...!!
THE CHANCE OF GETTING TWO SIXES IN ONE ROLL IS 1-IN-36...
THE CHANCE OF GETTING THEM TWICE IN A ROW...
...IS 1-IN-1,296.
GO (RUMBLE)
GO
GO
GO

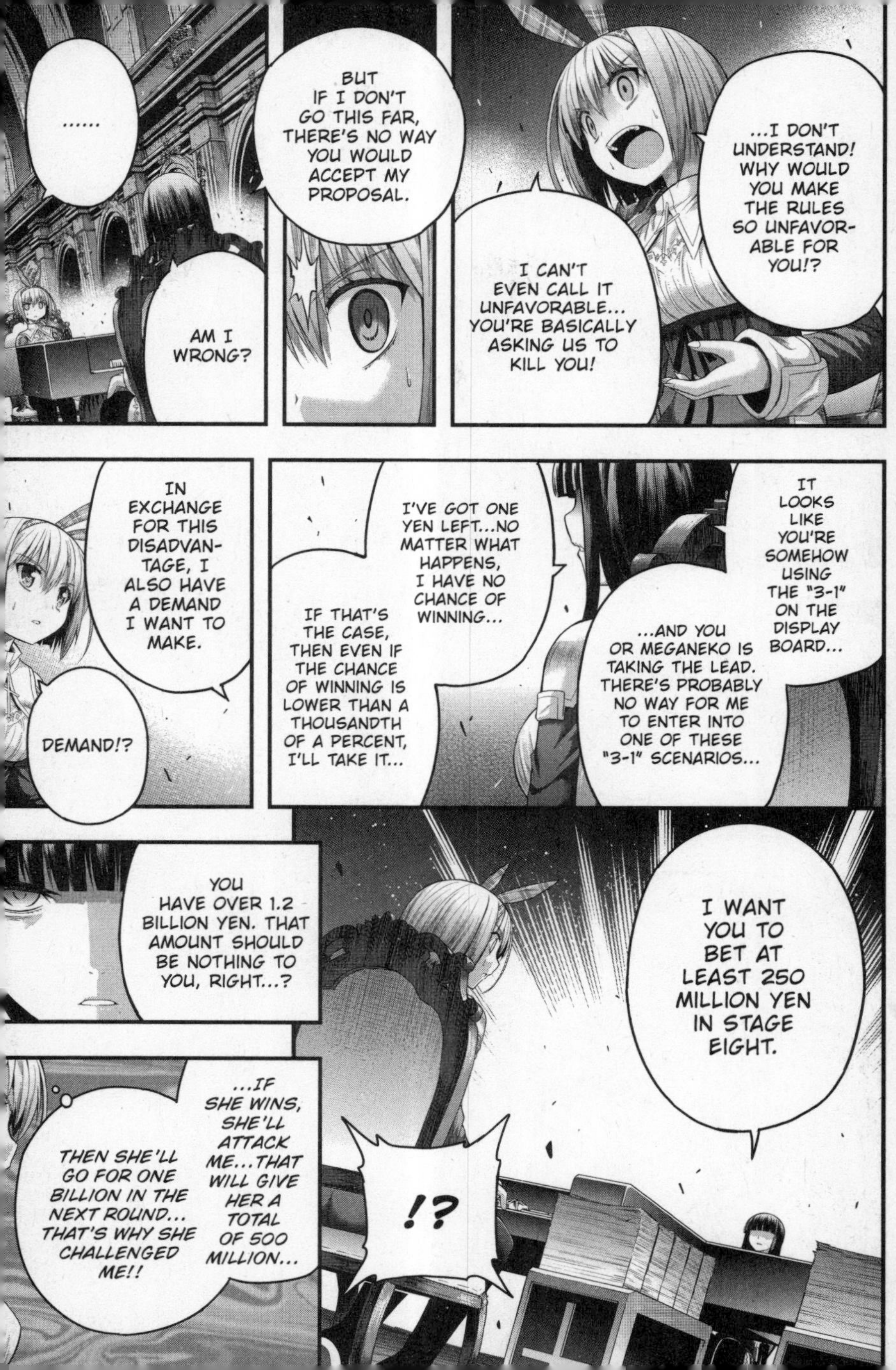
...I DON'T UNDERSTAND! WHY WOULD YOU MAKE THE RULES SO UNFAVORABLE FOR YOU!?
I CAN'T EVEN CALL IT UNFAVORABLE... YOU'RE BASICALLY ASKING US TO KILL YOU!
BUT IF I DON'T GO THIS FAR, THERE'S NO WAY YOU WOULD ACCEPT MY PROPOSAL.
......
AM I WRONG?
IT LOOKS LIKE YOU'RE SOMEHOW USING THE "3-1" ON THE DISPLAY BOARD...
...AND YOU OR MEGANEKO IS TAKING THE LEAD. THERE'S PROBABLY NO WAY FOR ME TO ENTER INTO ONE OF THESE "3-1" SCENARIOS...
I'VE GOT ONE YEN LEFT...NO MATTER WHAT HAPPENS, I HAVE NO CHANCE OF WINNING...
IF THAT'S THE CASE, THEN EVEN IF THE CHANCE OF WINNING IS LOWER THAN A THOUSANDTH OF A PERCENT, I'LL TAKE IT...
IN EXCHANGE FOR THIS DISADVANTAGE, I ALSO HAVE A DEMAND I WANT TO MAKE.
DEMAND!?
I WANT YOU TO BET AT LEAST 250 MILLION YEN IN STAGE EIGHT.
!?
YOU HAVE OVER 1.2 BILLION YEN. THAT AMOUNT SHOULD BE NOTHING TO YOU, RIGHT...?
...IF SHE WINS, SHE'LL ATTACK ME...THAT WILL GIVE HER A TOTAL OF 500 MILLION...
THEN SHE'LL GO FOR ONE BILLION IN THE NEXT ROUND... THAT'S WHY SHE CHALLENGED ME!!

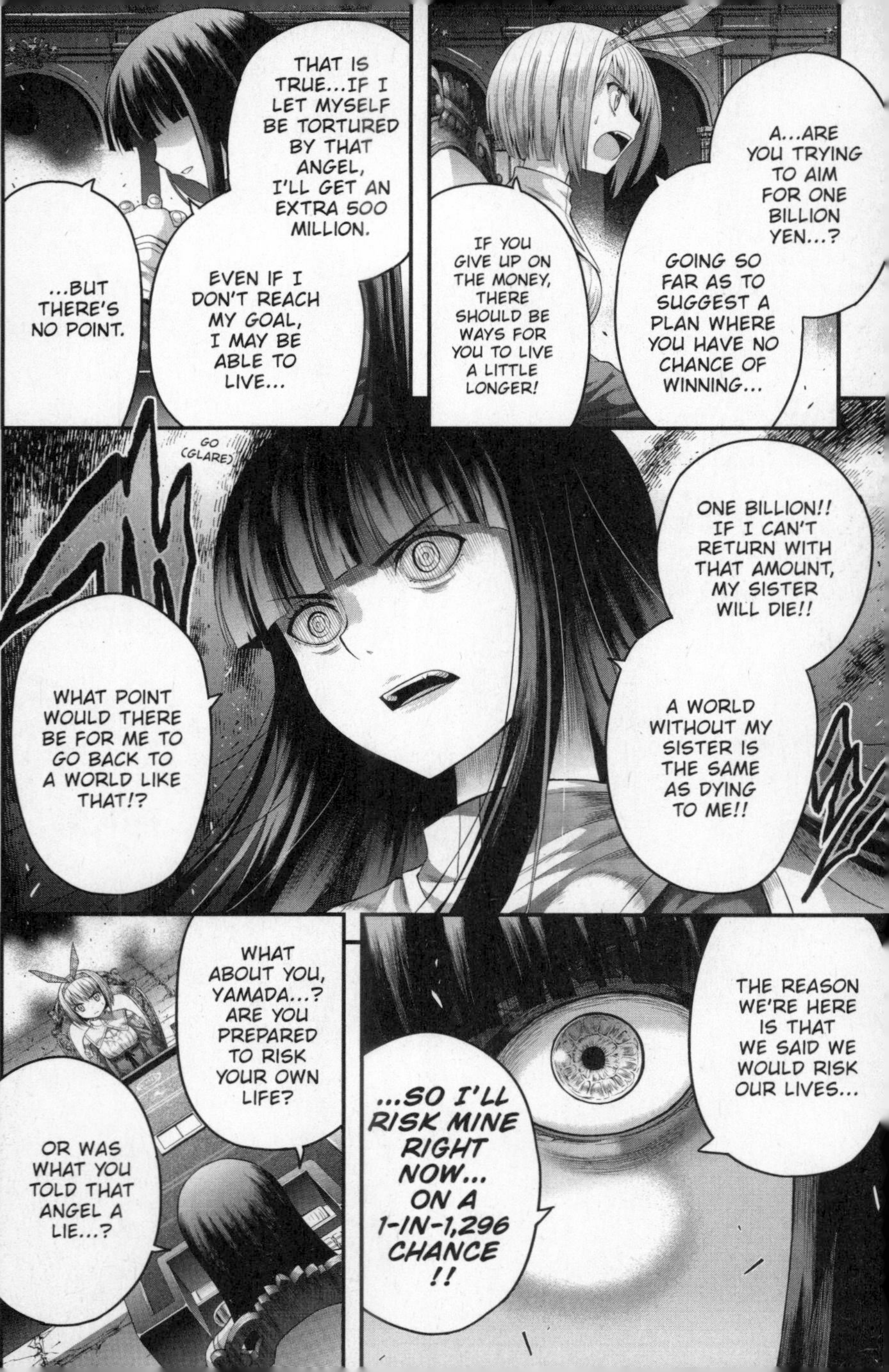
A...ARE YOU TRYING TO AIM FOR ONE BILLION YEN...?
GOING SO FAR AS TO SUGGEST A PLAN WHERE YOU HAVE NO CHANCE OF WINNING...
IF YOU GIVE UP ON THE MONEY, THERE SHOULD BE WAYS FOR YOU TO LIVE A LITTLE LONGER!
THAT IS TRUE...IF I LET MYSELF BE TORTURED BY THAT ANGEL, I'LL GET AN EXTRA 500 MILLION.
EVEN IF I DON'T REACH MY GOAL, I MAY BE ABLE TO LIVE...
...BUT THERE'S NO POINT.
ONE BILLION!! IF I CAN'T RETURN WITH THAT AMOUNT, MY SISTER WILL DIE!!
A WORLD WITHOUT MY SISTER IS THE SAME AS DYING TO ME!!
GO (GLARE)
WHAT POINT WOULD THERE BE FOR ME TO GO BACK TO A WORLD LIKE THAT!?
THE REASON WE'RE HERE IS THAT WE SAID WE WOULD RISK OUR LIVES...
...SO I'LL RISK MINE RIGHT NOW... ON A 1-IN-1,296 CHANCE!!
WHAT ABOUT YOU, YAMADA...? ARE YOU PREPARED TO RISK YOUR OWN LIFE?
OR WAS WHAT YOU TOLD THAT ANGEL A LIE...?

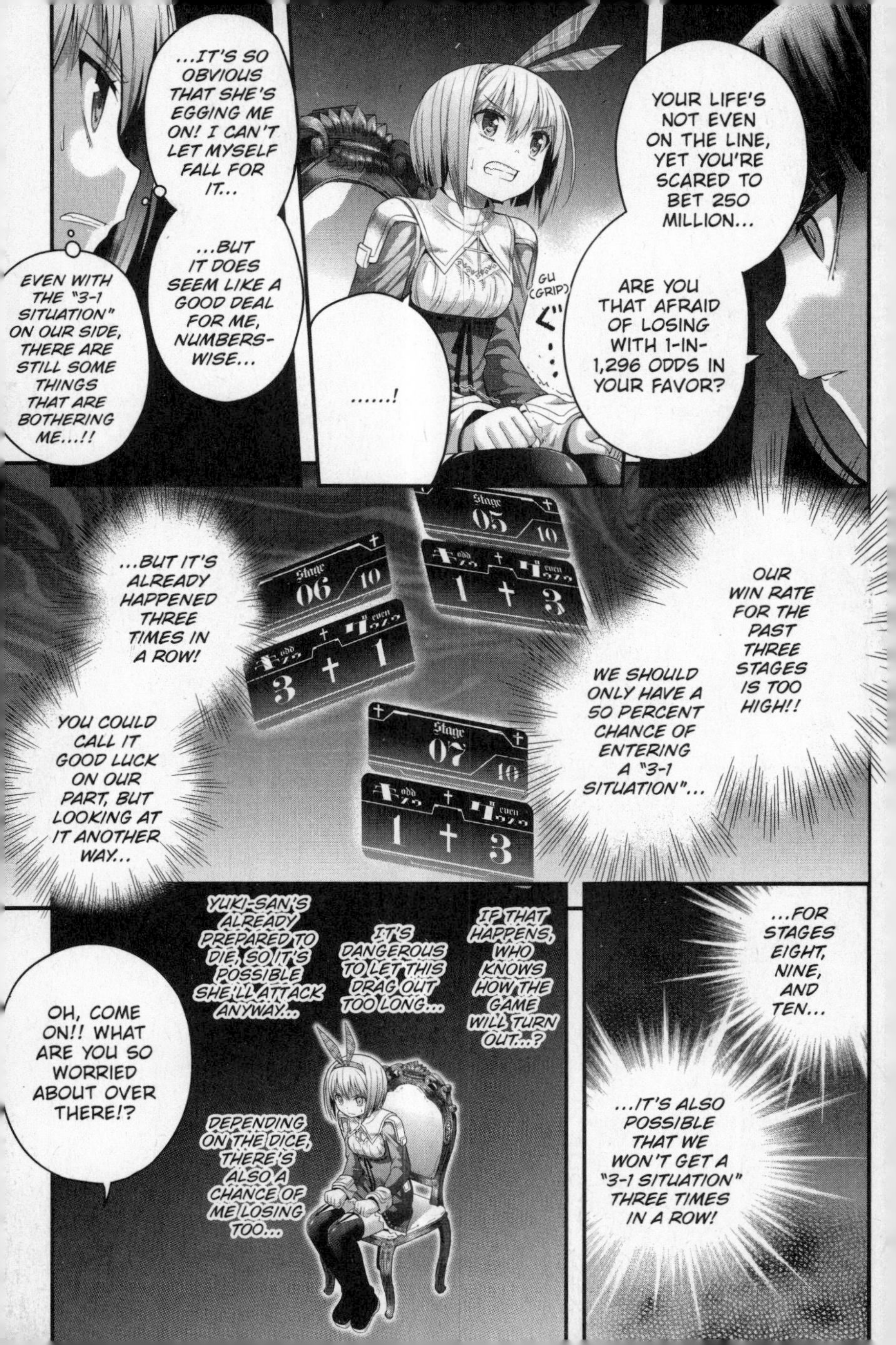
YOUR LIFE'S NOT EVEN ON THE LINE, YET YOU'RE SCARED TO BET 250 MILLION...
ARE YOU THAT AFRAID OF LOSING WITH 1-IN-1,296 ODDS IN YOUR FAVOR?
GU (GRIP)
......!
...IT'S SO OBVIOUS THAT SHE'S EGGING ME ON! I CAN'T LET MYSELF FALL FOR IT...
...BUT IT DOES SEEM LIKE A GOOD DEAL FOR ME, NUMBERS-WISE...
EVEN WITH THE "3-1 SITUATION" ON OUR SIDE, THERE ARE STILL SOME THINGS THAT ARE BOTHERING ME...!!
OUR WIN RATE FOR THE PAST THREE STAGES IS TOO HIGH!!
WE SHOULD ONLY HAVE A 50 PERCENT CHANCE OF ENTERING A "3-1 SITUATION"...
Stage 05 10
1 + 3
Stage 06 10
3 + 1
Stage 07 10
1 + 3
...BUT IT'S ALREADY HAPPENED THREE TIMES IN A ROW!
YOU COULD CALL IT GOOD LUCK ON OUR PART, BUT LOOKING AT IT ANOTHER WAY...
...FOR STAGES EIGHT, NINE, AND TEN...
...IT'S ALSO POSSIBLE THAT WE WON'T GET A "3-1 SITUATION" THREE TIMES IN A ROW!
IF THAT HAPPENS, WHO KNOWS HOW THE GAME WILL TURN OUT...?
IT'S DANGEROUS TO LET THIS DRAG OUT TOO LONG...
YUKI-SAN'S ALREADY PREPARED TO DIE, SO IT'S POSSIBLE SHE'LL ATTACK ANYWAY...
OH, COME ON!! WHAT ARE YOU SO WORRIED ABOUT OVER THERE!?
DEPENDING ON THE DICE, THERE'S ALSO A CHANCE OF ME LOSING TOO...

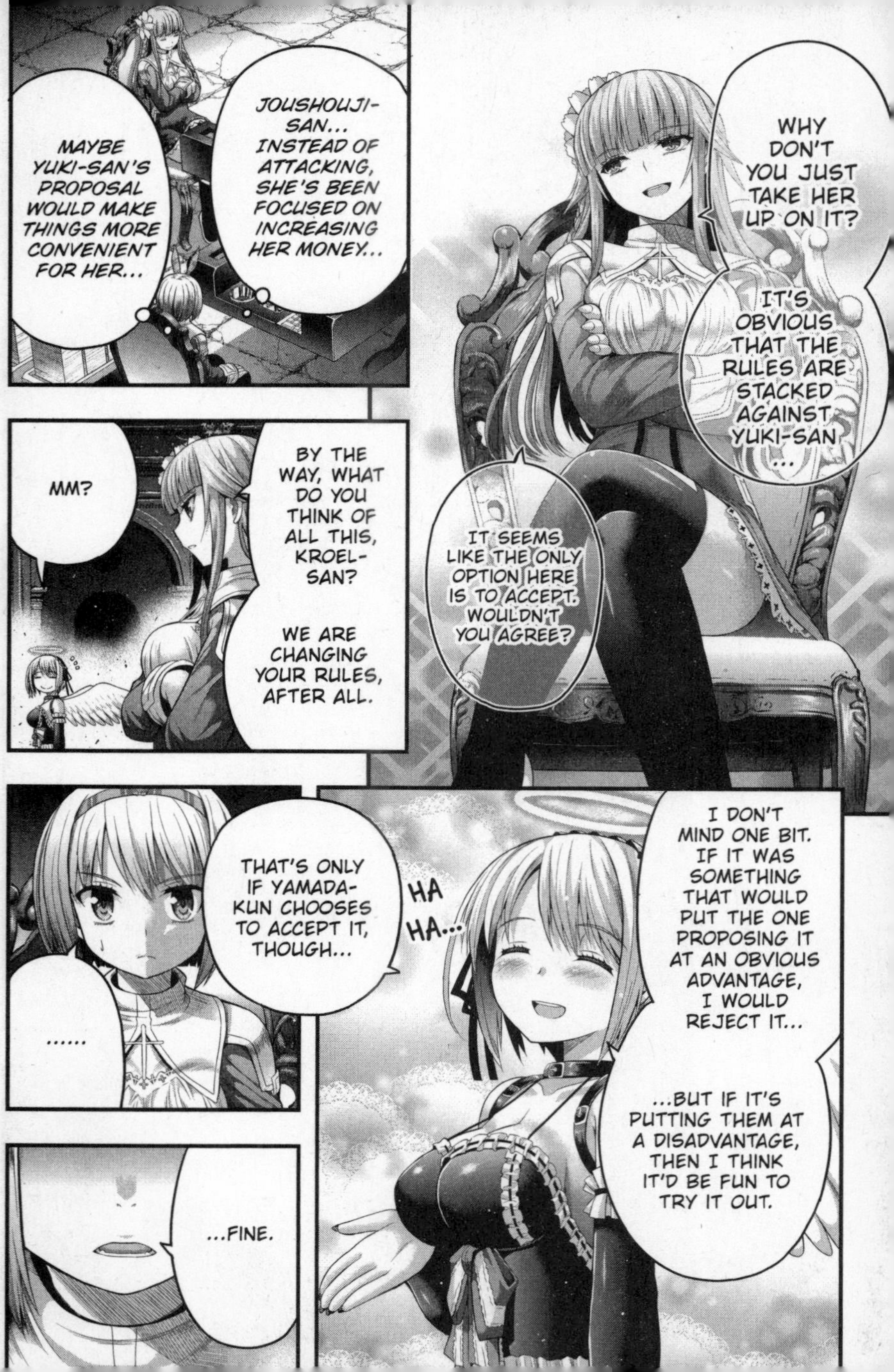
WHY DON'T YOU JUST TAKE HER UP ON IT?
IT'S OBVIOUS THAT THE RULES ARE STACKED AGAINST YUKI-SAN...
IT SEEMS LIKE THE ONLY OPTION HERE IS TO ACCEPT. WOULDN'T YOU AGREE?
JOUSHOUJI-SAN... INSTEAD OF ATTACKING, SHE'S BEEN FOCUSED ON INCREASING HER MONEY...
MAYBE YUKI-SAN'S PROPOSAL WOULD MAKE THINGS MORE CONVENIENT FOR HER...
BY THE WAY, WHAT DO YOU THINK OF ALL THIS, KROEL-SAN?
MM?
WE ARE CHANGING YOUR RULES, AFTER ALL.
I DON'T MIND ONE BIT. IF IT WAS SOMETHING THAT WOULD PUT THE ONE PROPOSING IT AT AN OBVIOUS ADVANTAGE, I WOULD REJECT IT...
HA HA...
...BUT IF IT'S PUTTING THEM AT A DISADVANTAGE, THEN I THINK IT'D BE FUN TO TRY IT OUT.
THAT'S ONLY IF YAMADA-KUN CHOOSES TO ACCEPT IT, THOUGH...
......
...FINE.

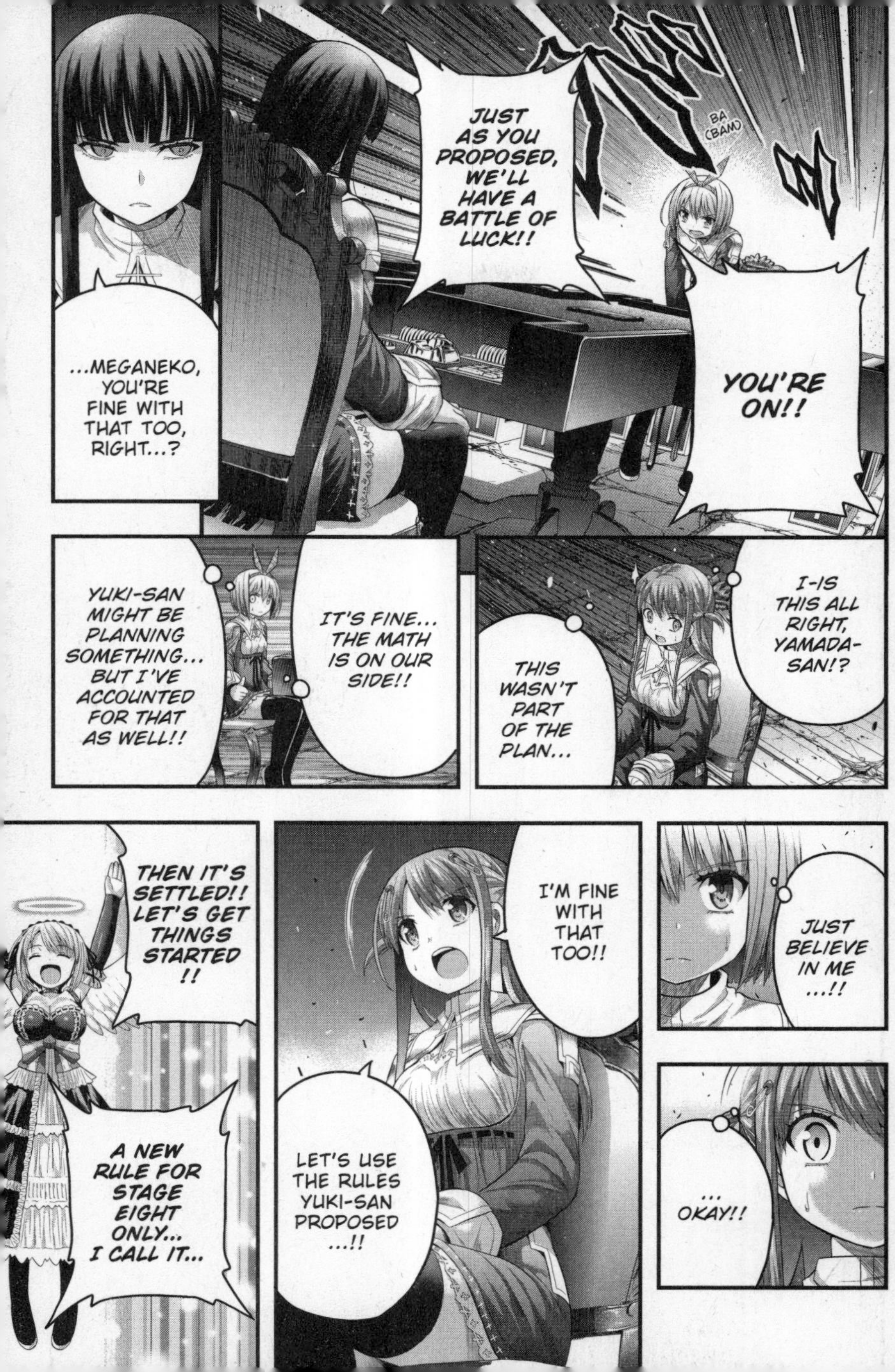
JUST AS YOU PROPOSED, WE'LL HAVE A BATTLE OF LUCK!!
BA (BAM)
YOU'RE ON!!
...MEGANEKO, YOU'RE FINE WITH THAT TOO, RIGHT...?
I-IS THIS ALL RIGHT, YAMADA-SAN!?
THIS WASN'T PART OF THE PLAN...
IT'S FINE... THE MATH IS ON OUR SIDE!!
YUKI-SAN MIGHT BE PLANNING SOMETHING... BUT I'VE ACCOUNTED FOR THAT AS WELL!!
JUST BELIEVE IN ME ...!!
... OKAY!!
I'M FINE WITH THAT TOO!!
LET'S USE THE RULES YUKI-SAN PROPOSED ...!!
THEN IT'S SETTLED!! LET'S GET THINGS STARTED !!
A NEW RULE FOR STAGE EIGHT ONLY... I CALL IT...

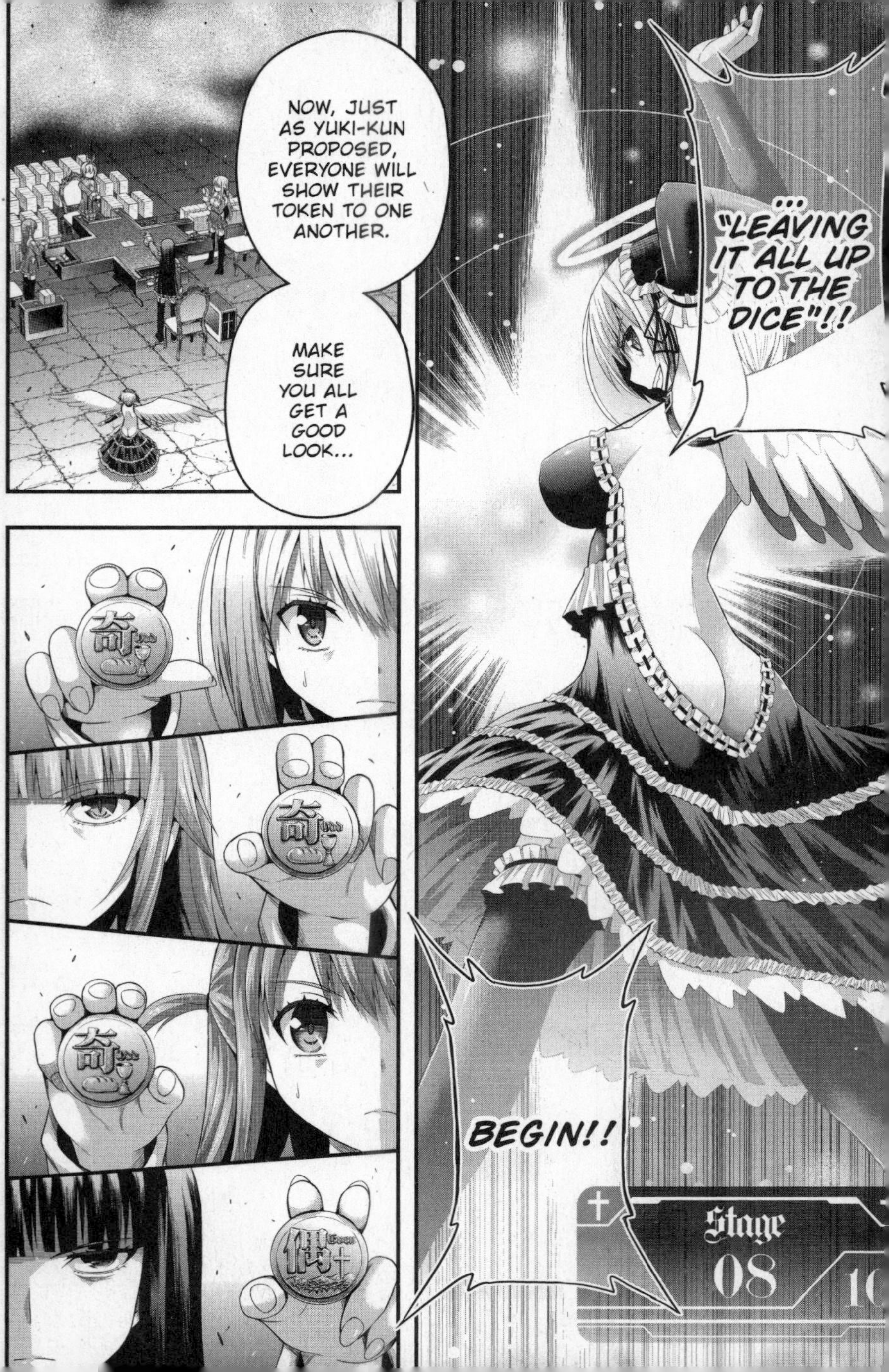

..."LEAVING IT ALL UP TO THE DICE"!!
BEGIN!!
Stage
08
NOW, JUST AS YUKI-KUN PROPOSED, EVERYONE WILL SHOW THEIR TOKEN TO ONE ANOTHER.
MAKE SURE YOU ALL GET A GOOD LOOK...

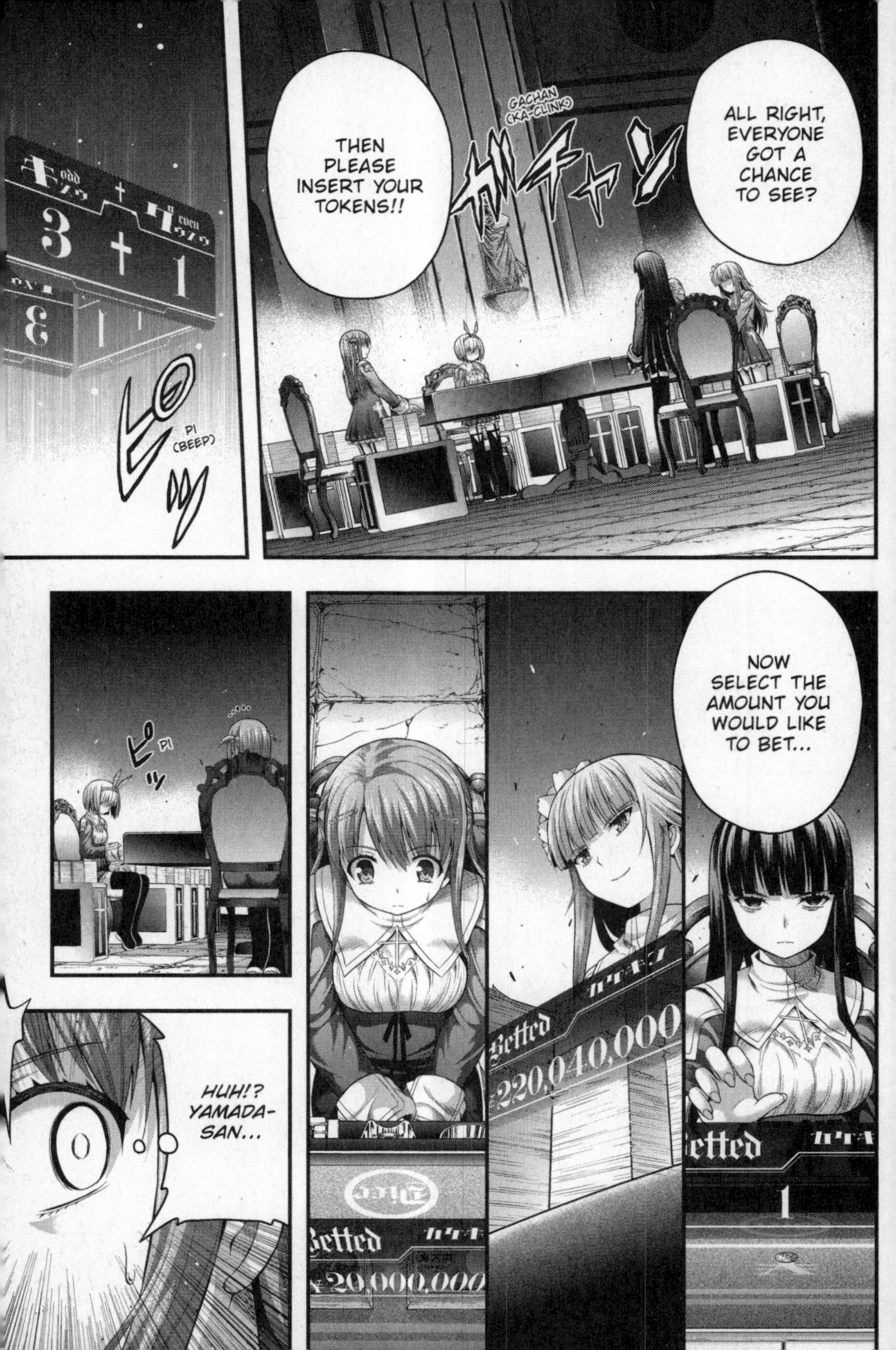
ALL RIGHT, EVERYONE GOT A CHANCE TO SEE?
GACHAN (KA-CLINK)
THEN PLEASE INSERT YOUR TOKENS!!
odd
even
PI (BEEP)
NOW SELECT THE AMOUNT YOU WOULD LIKE TO BET...
Betted
1
Betted
¥220,040,000
Betted
¥20,000,000
PI
HUH!? YAMADA-SAN...

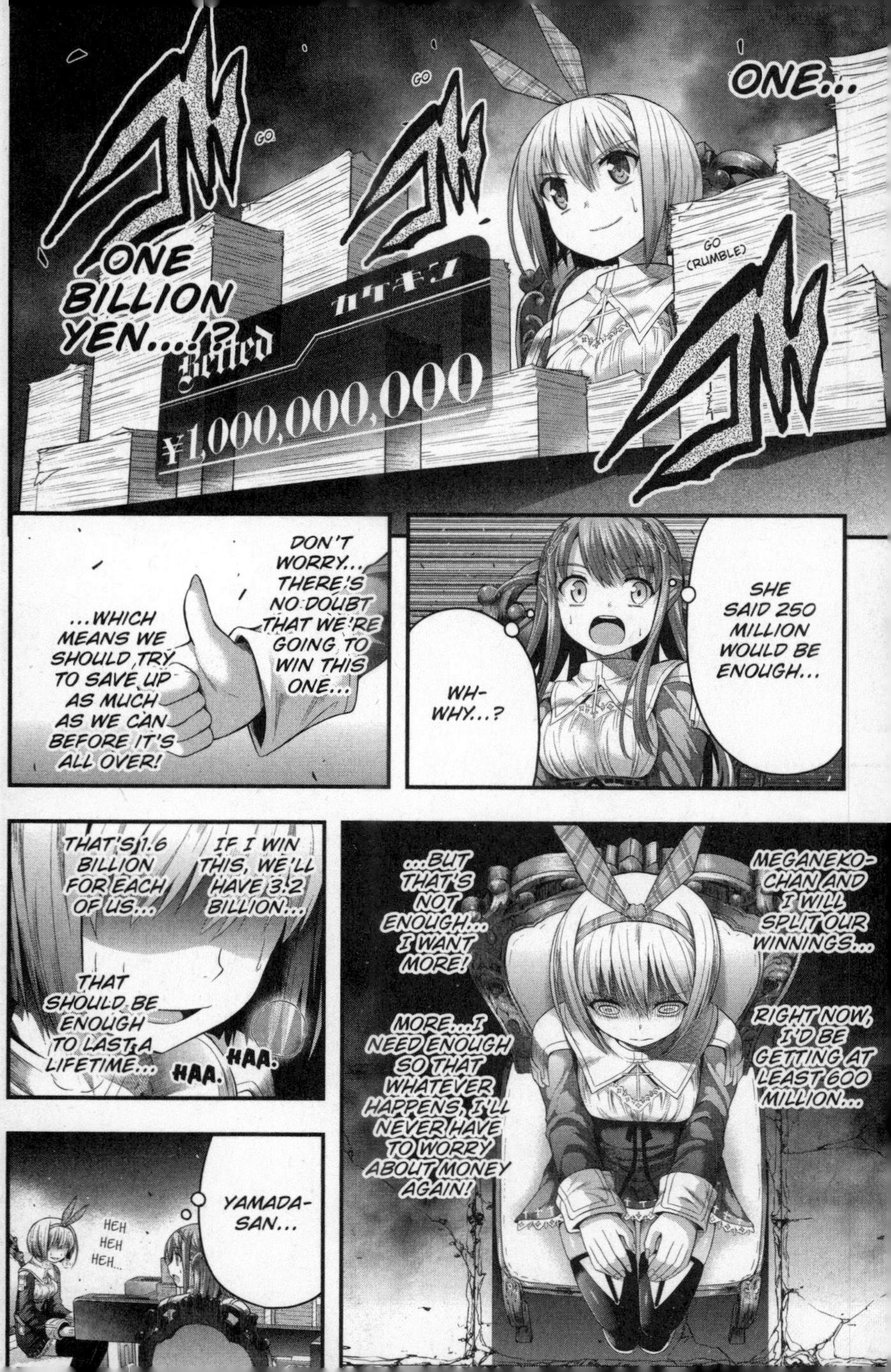
ONE...
GO (RUMBLE)
GO
GO
ONE BILLION YEN...!?
カケキン
Betted
¥1,000,000,000
SHE SAID 250 MILLION WOULD BE ENOUGH...
WH- WHY...?
DON'T WORRY... THERE'S NO DOUBT THAT WE'RE GOING TO WIN THIS ONE...
...WHICH MEANS WE SHOULD TRY TO SAVE UP AS MUCH AS WE CAN BEFORE IT'S ALL OVER!
MEGANEKO-CHAN AND I WILL SPLIT OUR WINNINGS...
RIGHT NOW, I'D BE GETTING AT LEAST 600 MILLION...
...BUT THAT'S NOT ENOUGH... I WANT MORE!
MORE... I NEED ENOUGH SO THAT WHATEVER HAPPENS, I'LL NEVER HAVE TO WORRY ABOUT MONEY AGAIN!
IF I WIN THIS, WE'LL HAVE 3.2 BILLION...
THAT'S 1.6 BILLION FOR EACH OF US...
THAT SHOULD BE ENOUGH TO LAST A LIFETIME...
HAA.
HAA.
YAMADA-SAN...
HEH HEH HEH...

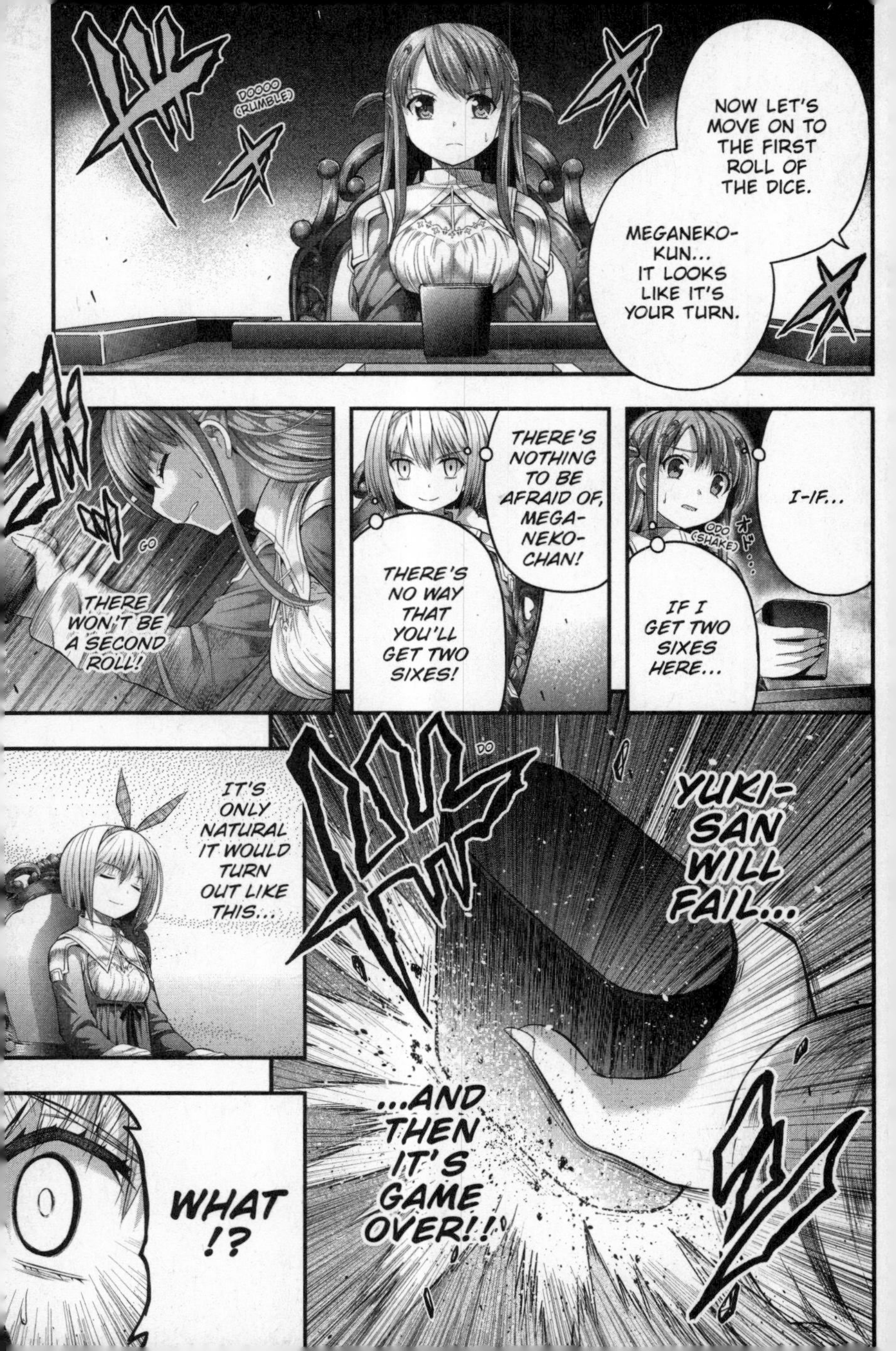
DOOOO (RUMBLE)
NOW LET'S MOVE ON TO THE FIRST ROLL OF THE DICE.
MEGANEKO-KUN... IT LOOKS LIKE IT'S YOUR TURN.
I-IF...
ODO (SHAKE)
IF I GET TWO SIXES HERE...
THERE'S NOTHING TO BE AFRAID OF, MEGA-NEKO-CHAN!
THERE'S NO WAY THAT YOU'LL GET TWO SIXES!
GO
THERE WON'T BE A SECOND ROLL!
DO
YUKI-SAN WILL FAIL...
...AND THEN IT'S GAME OVER!!
IT'S ONLY NATURAL IT WOULD TURN OUT LIKE THIS...
WHAT!?

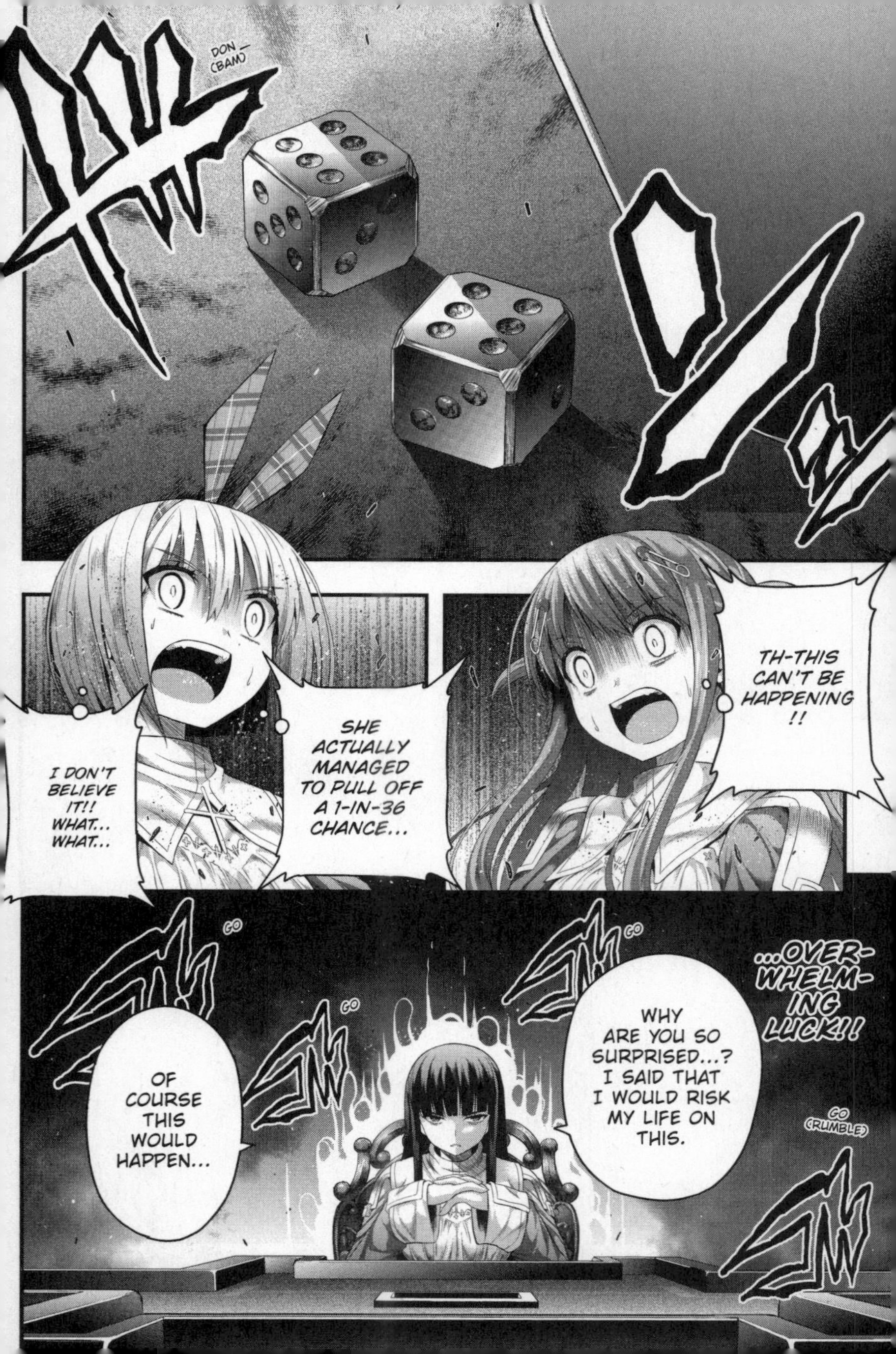
DON (BAM)
TH-THIS CAN'T BE HAPPENING!!
SHE ACTUALLY MANAGED TO PULL OFF A 1-IN-36 CHANCE...
I DON'T BELIEVE IT!! WHAT... WHAT...
...OVER-WHELM-ING LUCK!!
GO
WHY ARE YOU SO SURPRISED...? I SAID THAT I WOULD RISK MY LIFE ON THIS.
GO (RUMBLE)
GO
OF COURSE THIS WOULD HAPPEN...
GO

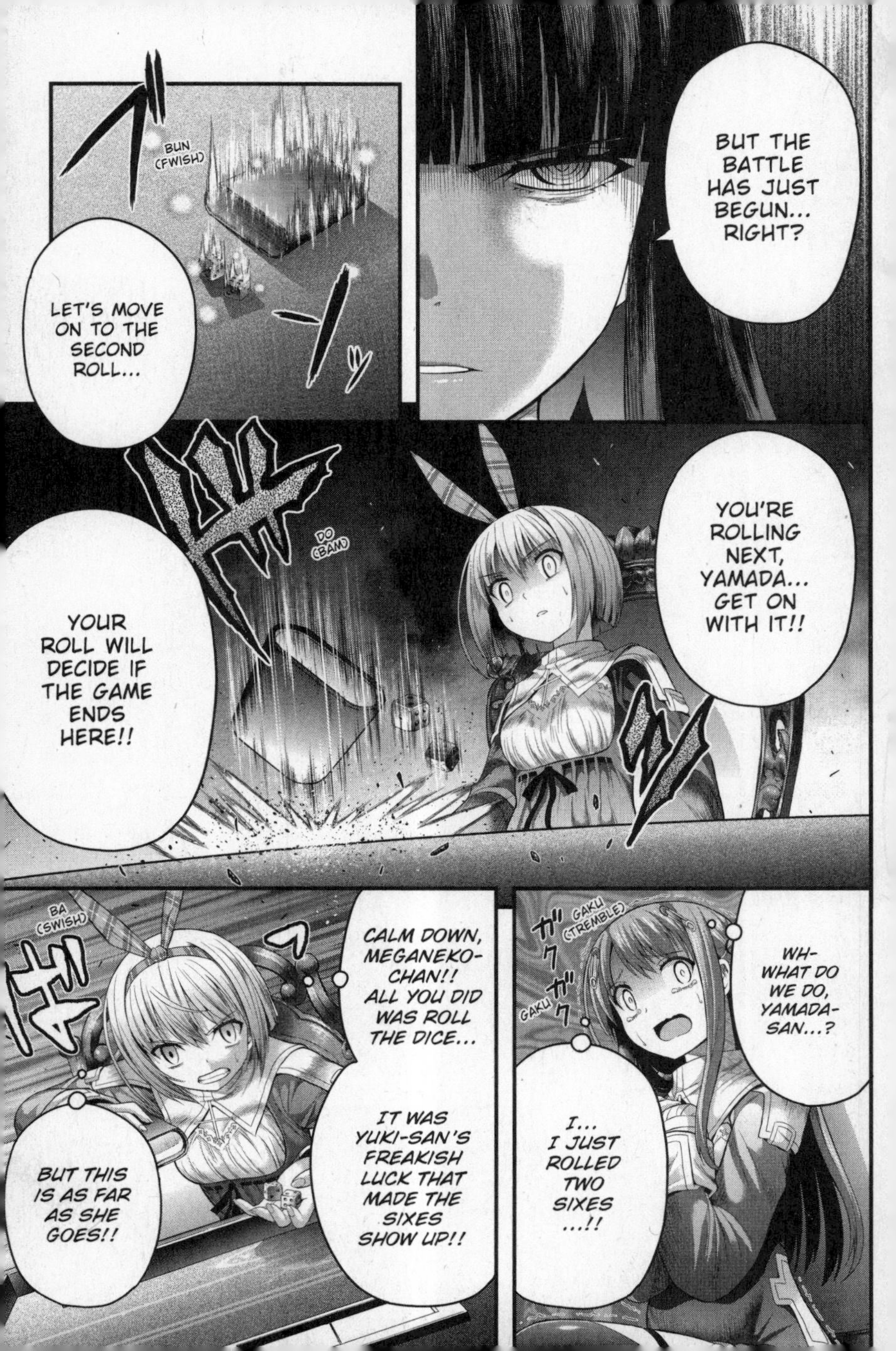

BUT THE BATTLE HAS JUST BEGUN... RIGHT?
BUN (FWISH)
LET'S MOVE ON TO THE SECOND ROLL...
YOU'RE ROLLING NEXT, YAMADA... GET ON WITH IT!!
DO (BAM)
YOUR ROLL WILL DECIDE IF THE GAME ENDS HERE!!
GAKU (TREMBLE)
GAKU
WH-WHAT DO WE DO, YAMADA-SAN...?
I... I JUST ROLLED TWO SIXES ...!!
BA (SWISH)
CALM DOWN, MEGANEKO-CHAN!! ALL YOU DID WAS ROLL THE DICE...
IT WAS YUKI-SAN'S FREAKISH LUCK THAT MADE THE SIXES SHOW UP!!
BUT THIS IS AS FAR AS SHE GOES!!

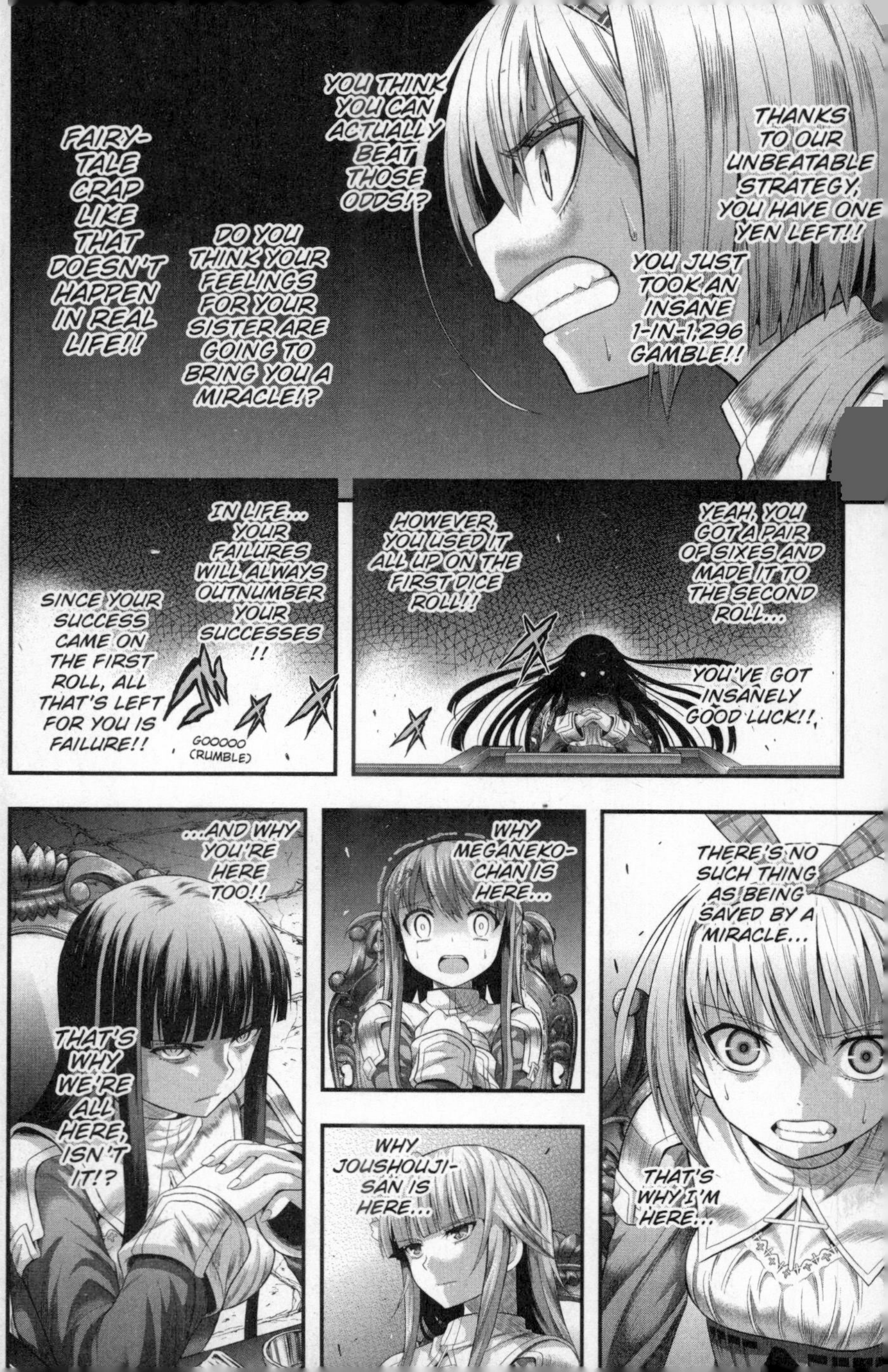
THANKS TO OUR UNBEATABLE STRATEGY, YOU HAVE ONE YEN LEFT!!
YOU JUST TOOK AN INSANE 1-IN-1,296 GAMBLE!!
YOU THINK YOU CAN ACTUALLY BEAT THOSE ODDS!?
DO YOU THINK YOUR FEELINGS FOR YOUR SISTER ARE GOING TO BRING YOU A MIRACLE!?
FAIRY-TALE CRAP LIKE THAT DOESN'T HAPPEN IN REAL LIFE!!
YEAH, YOU GOT A PAIR OF SIXES AND MADE IT TO THE SECOND ROLL...
YOU'VE GOT INSANELY GOOD LUCK!!
HOWEVER, YOU USED IT ALL UP ON THE FIRST DICE ROLL!!
IN LIFE... YOUR FAILURES WILL ALWAYS OUTNUMBER YOUR SUCCESSES!!
SINCE YOUR SUCCESS CAME ON THE FIRST ROLL, ALL THAT'S LEFT FOR YOU IS FAILURE!!
GOOOOO (RUMBLE)
THERE'S NO SUCH THING AS BEING SAVED BY A MIRACLE...
THAT'S WHY I'M HERE...
WHY MEGANEKO-CHAN IS HERE...
WHY JOUSHOUJI-SAN IS HERE...
...AND WHY YOU'RE HERE TOO!!
THAT'S WHY WE'RE ALL HERE, ISN'T IT!?

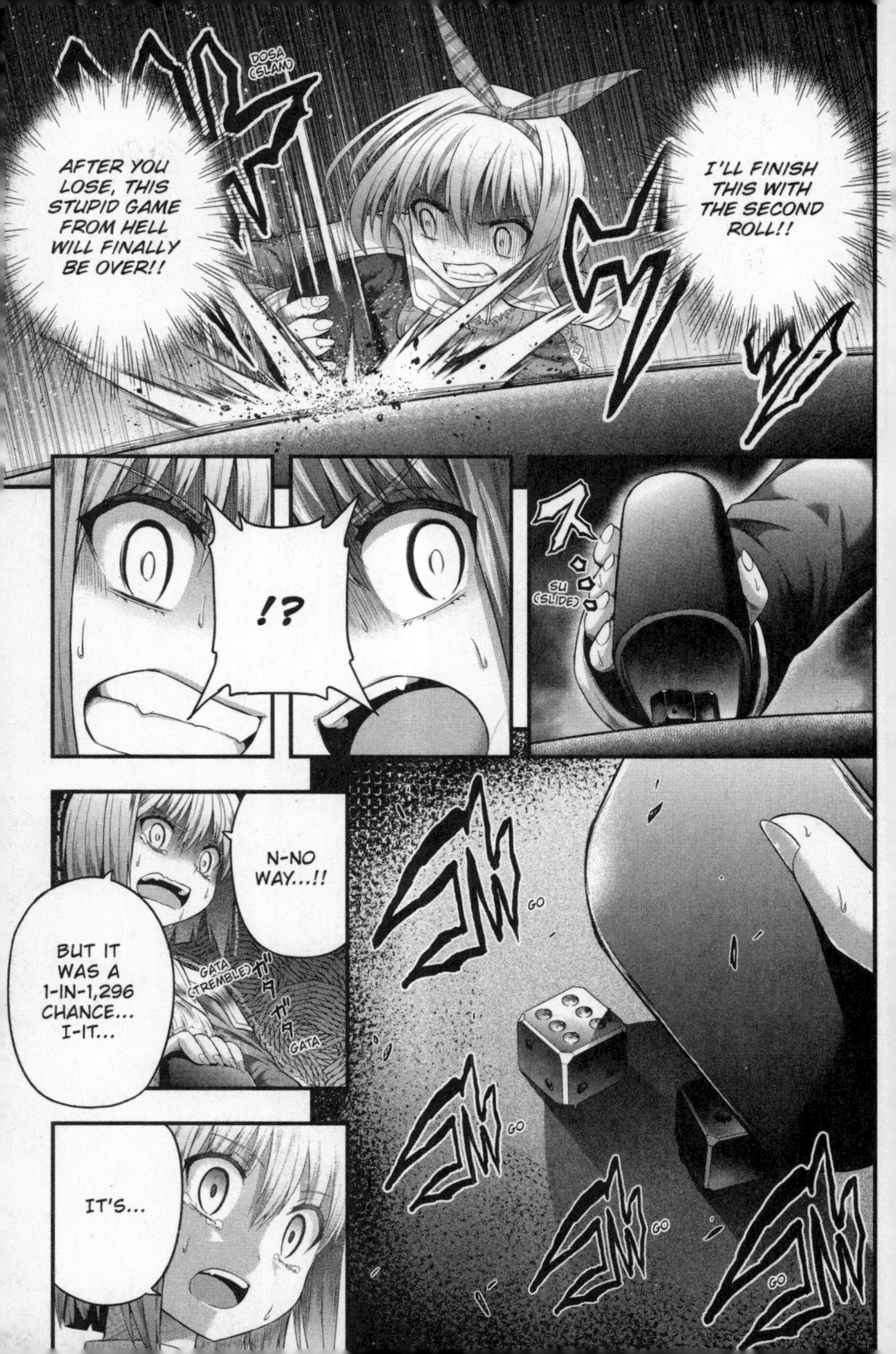
I'LL FINISH THIS WITH THE SECOND ROLL!!
DOSA (SLAM)
AFTER YOU LOSE, THIS STUPID GAME FROM HELL WILL FINALLY BE OVER!!
SU (SLIDE)
!?
GO
GO
GO
GO
N-NO WAY...!!
BUT IT WAS A 1-IN-1,296 CHANCE... I-IT...
GATA (TREMBLE)
GATA
IT'S...

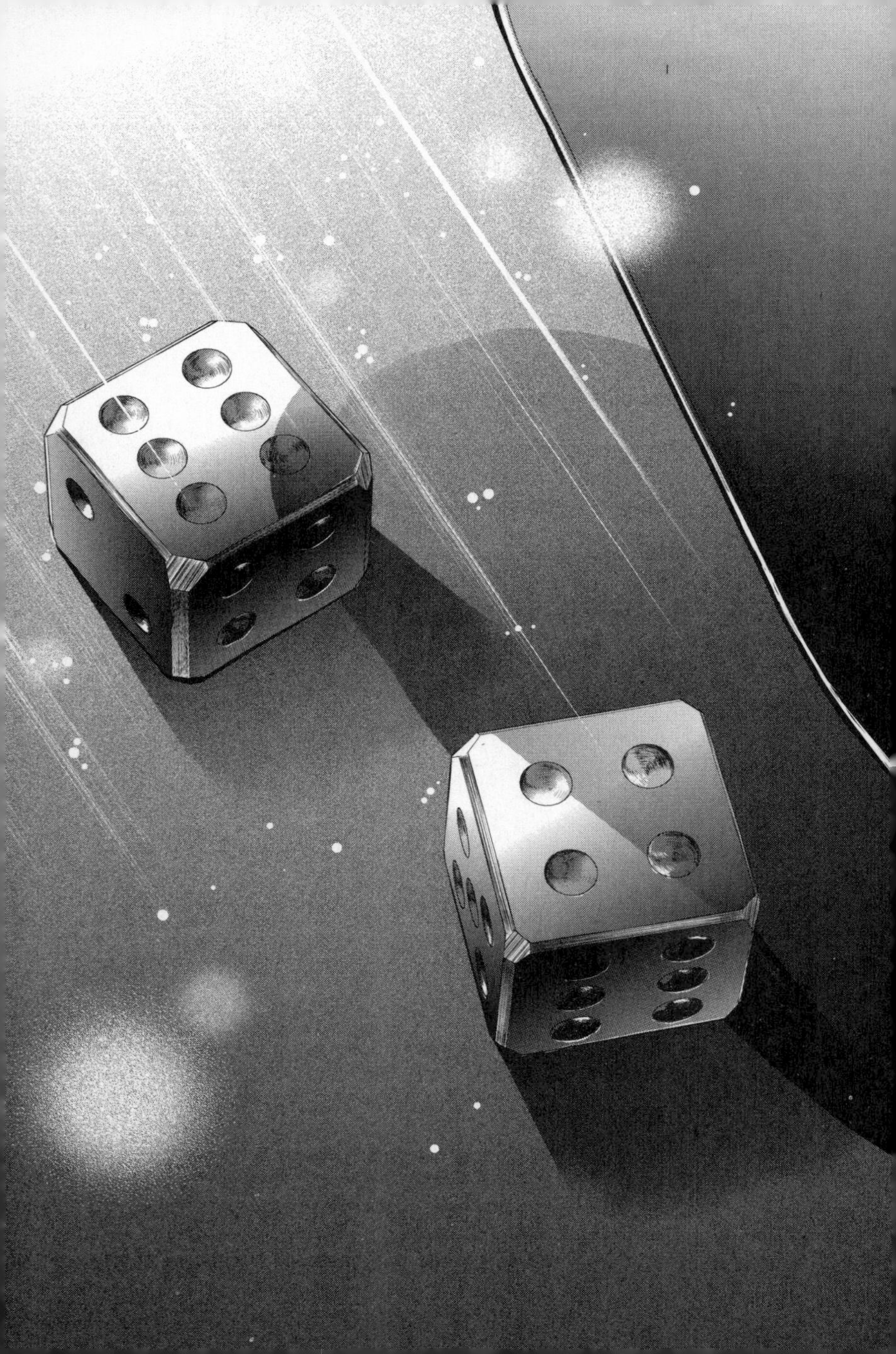

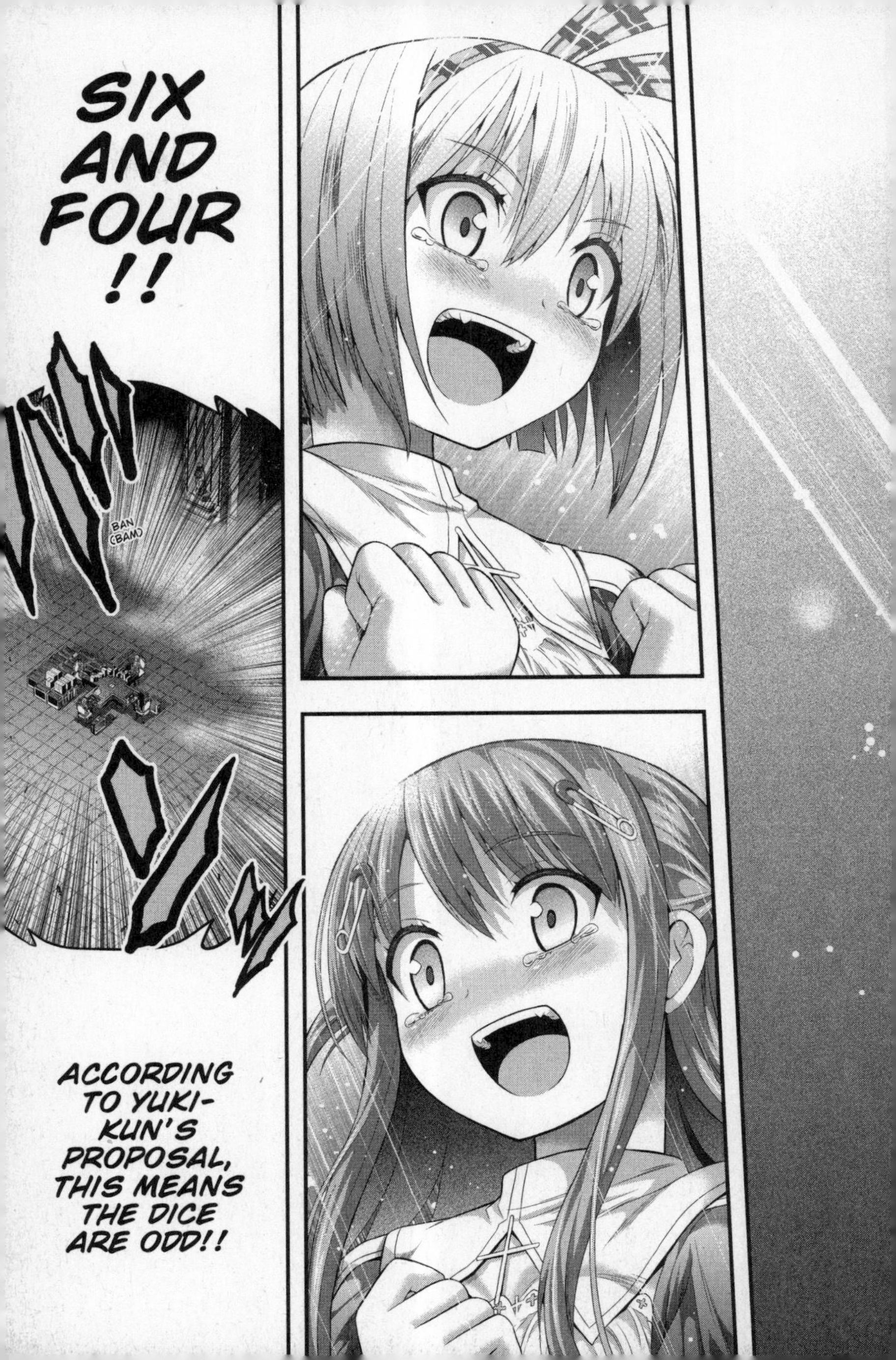
SIX AND FOUR!!
BAN (BAM)
ACCORDING TO YUKI-KUN'S PROPOSAL, THIS MEANS THE DICE ARE ODD!!

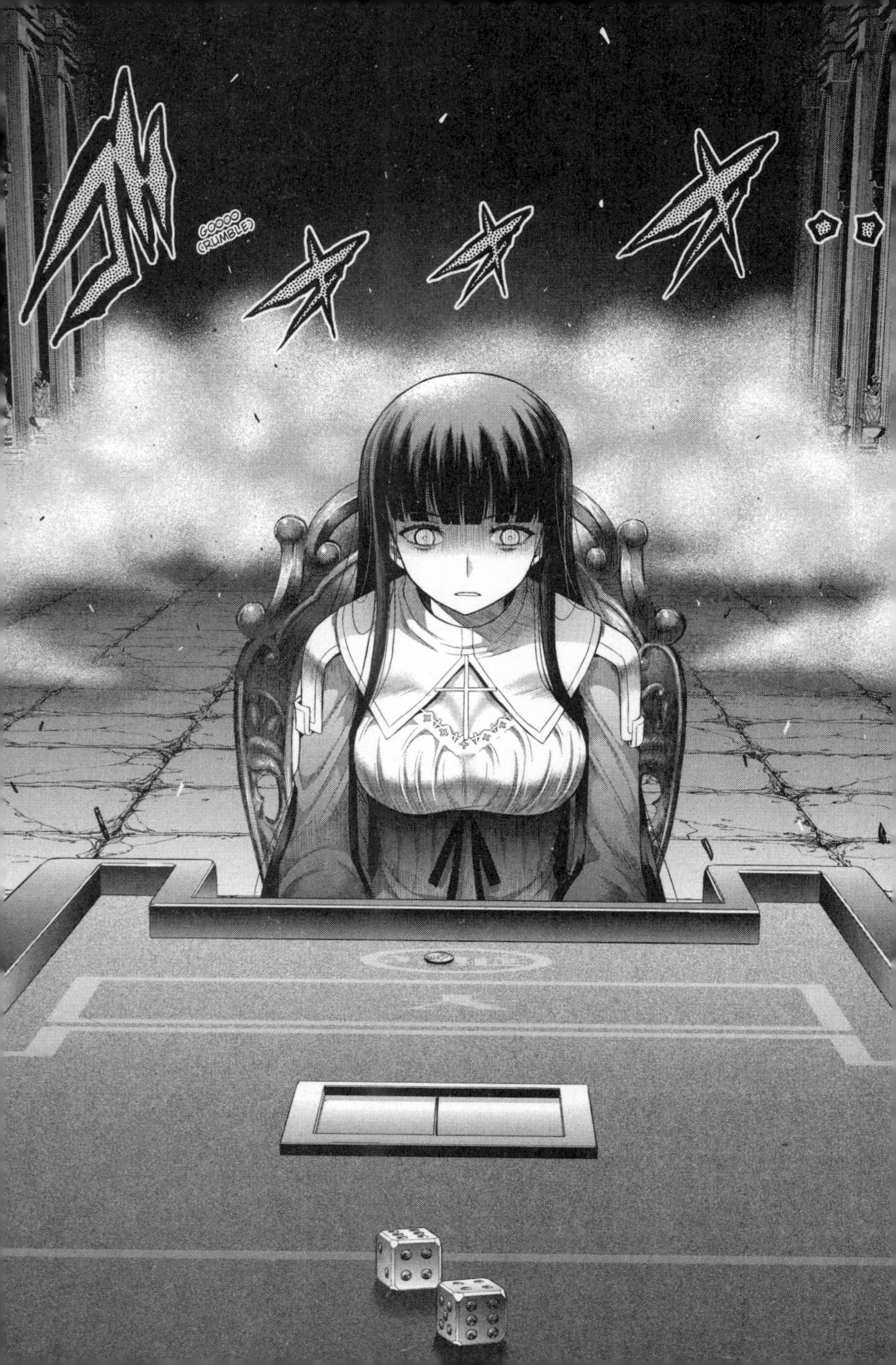
GOOOO (RUMBLE)

Though You May Burn to Ash

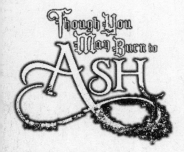

Though You May Burn to Ash

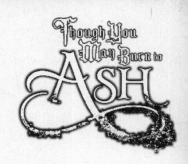

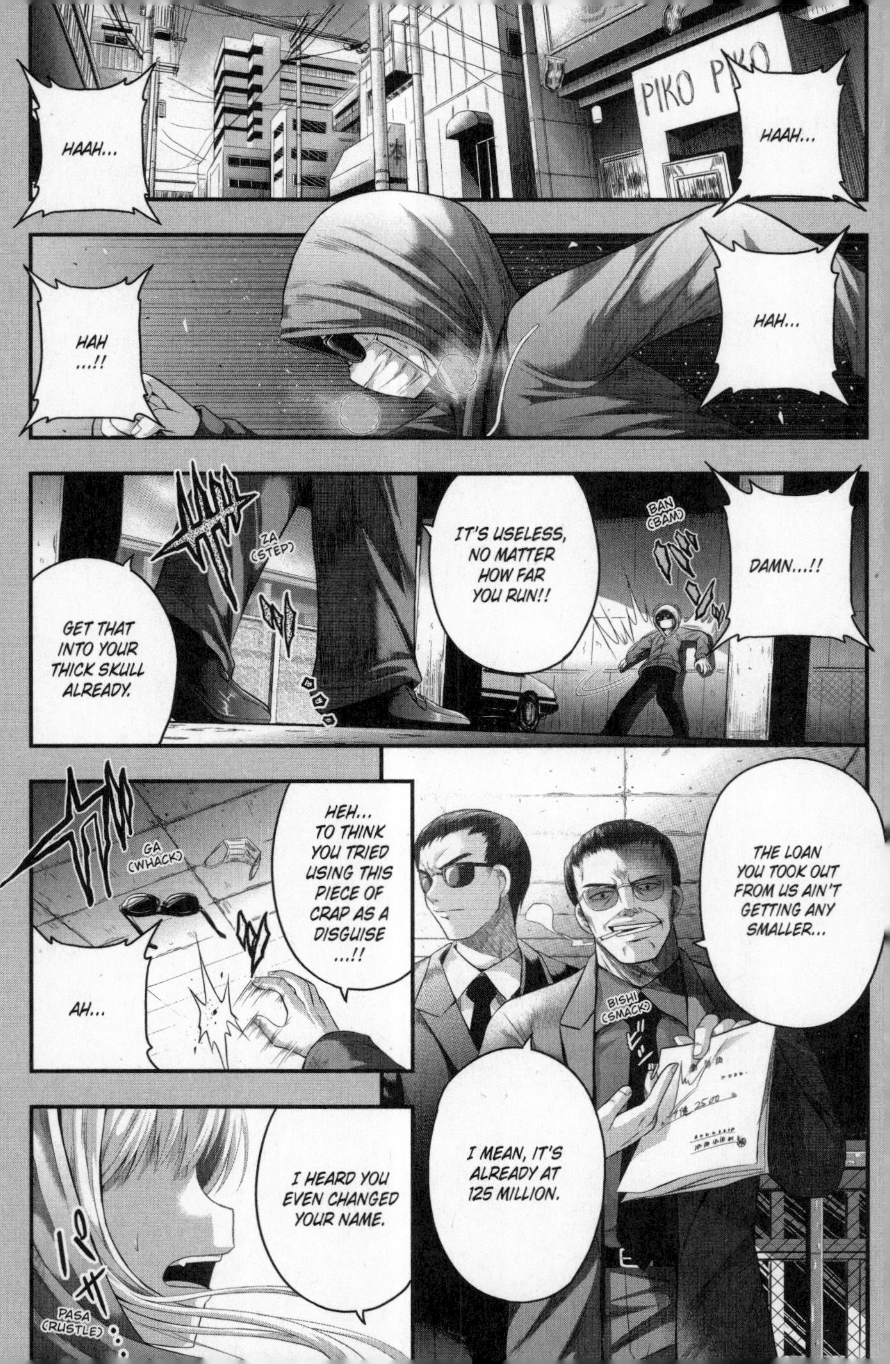
HAAH...
HAAH...
HAH...
HAH ...!!
DAMN...!!
BAN (BAM)
IT'S USELESS, NO MATTER HOW FAR YOU RUN!!
ZA (STEP)
GET THAT INTO YOUR THICK SKULL ALREADY.
THE LOAN YOU TOOK OUT FROM US AIN'T GETTING ANY SMALLER...
BISHI (SMACK)
I MEAN, IT'S ALREADY AT 125 MILLION.
HEH... TO THINK YOU TRIED USING THIS PIECE OF CRAP AS A DISGUISE ...!!
GA (WHACK)
AH...
I HEARD YOU EVEN CHANGED YOUR NAME.
PASA (RUSTLE)

CHAPTER 10: THE COWARD AND THE SNAKE

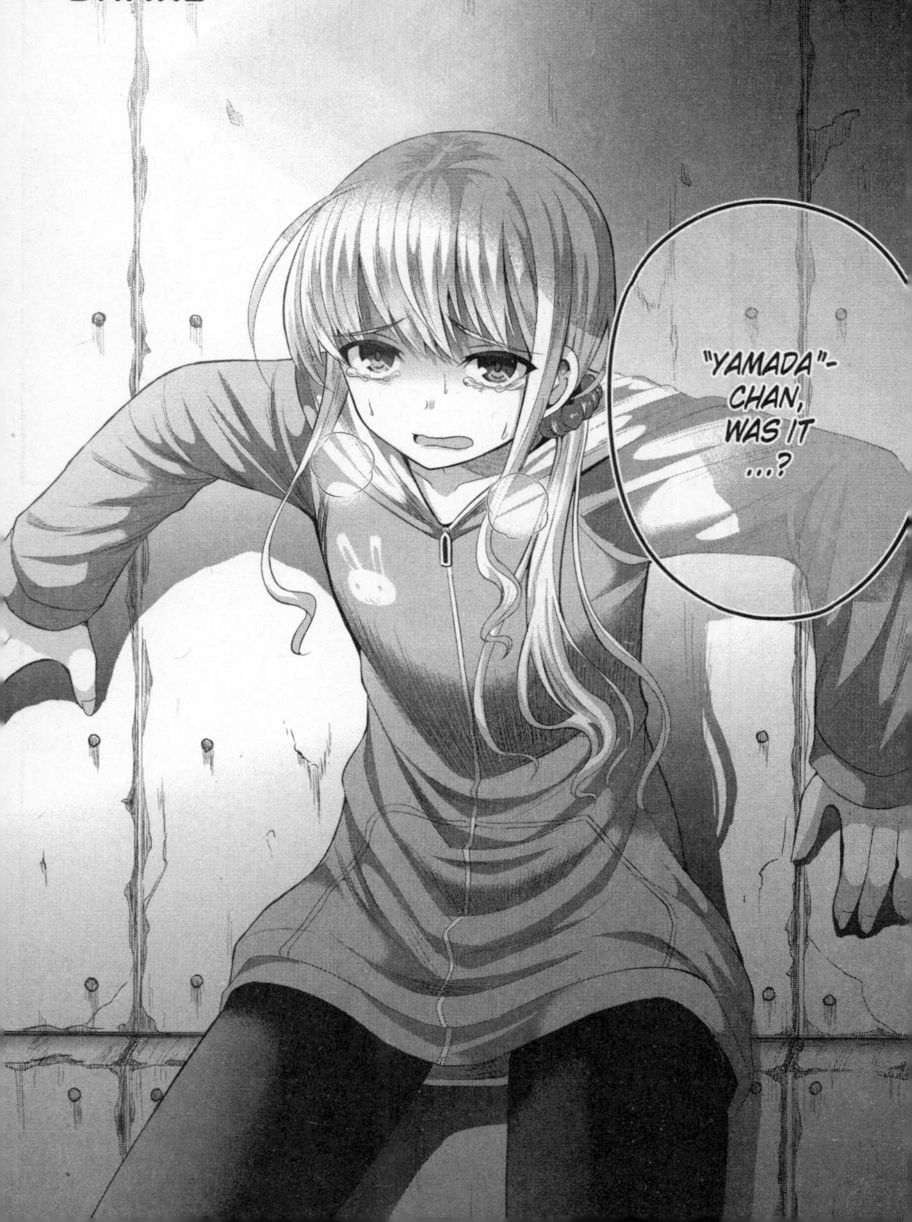
"YAMADA"-CHAN, WAS IT ...?

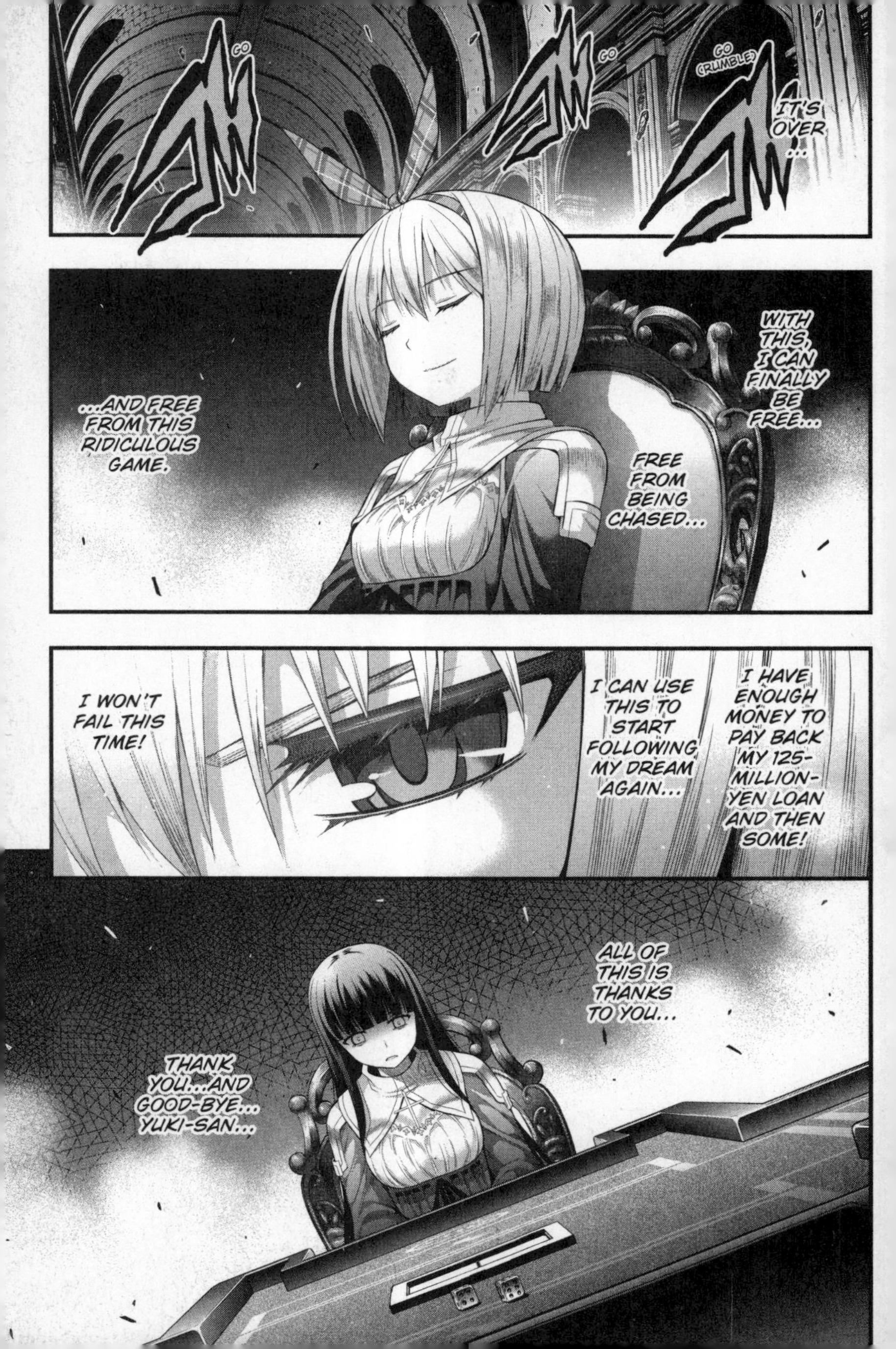
GO (RUMBLE)
IT'S OVER...
GO
GO
WITH THIS, I CAN FINALLY BE FREE...
FREE FROM BEING CHASED...
...AND FREE FROM THIS RIDICULOUS GAME.
I HAVE ENOUGH MONEY TO PAY BACK MY 125-MILLION-YEN LOAN AND THEN SOME!
I CAN USE THIS TO START FOLLOWING MY DREAM AGAIN...
I WON'T FAIL THIS TIME!
ALL OF THIS IS THANKS TO YOU...
THANK YOU...AND GOOD-BYE... YUKI-SAN...

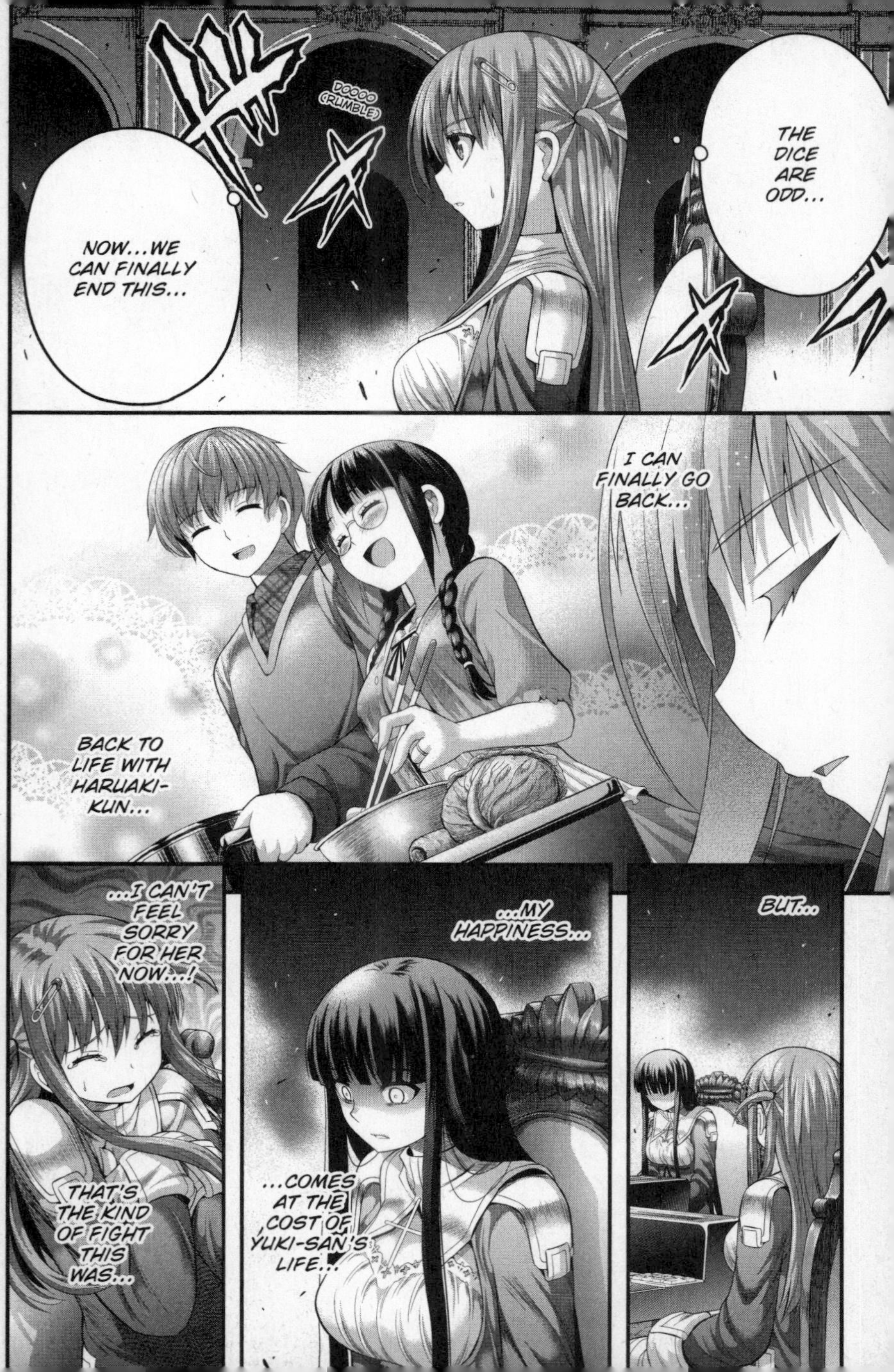
THE DICE ARE ODD...
DOOOO (RUMBLE)
NOW...WE CAN FINALLY END THIS...
I CAN FINALLY GO BACK...
BACK TO LIFE WITH HARUAKI-KUN...
BUT...
...MY HAPPINESS...
...COMES AT THE COST OF YUKI-SAN'S LIFE...
...I CAN'T FEEL SORRY FOR HER NOW...!
THAT'S THE KIND OF FIGHT THIS WAS...

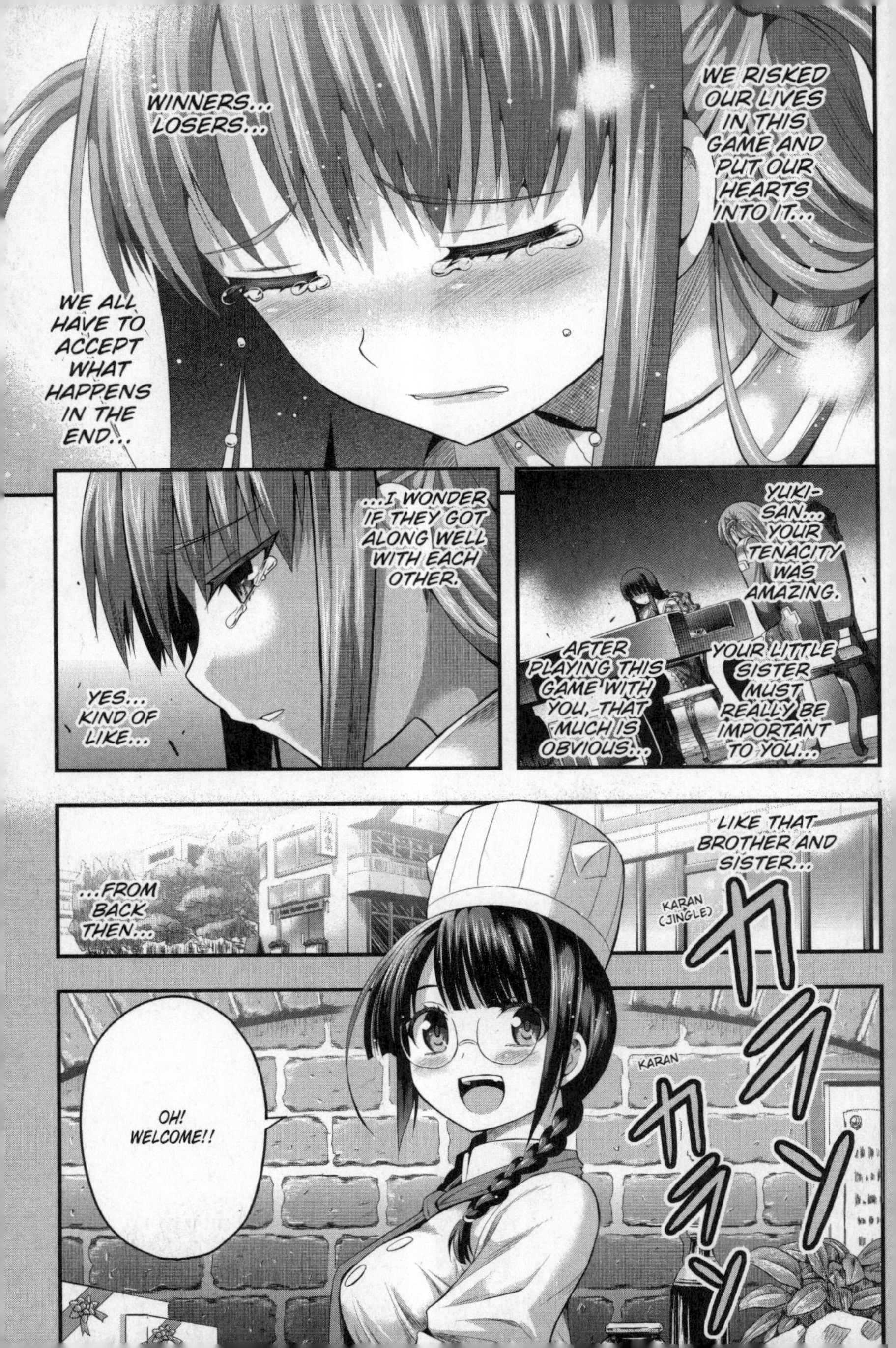
WE RISKED OUR LIVES IN THIS GAME AND PUT OUR HEARTS INTO IT...
WINNERS... LOSERS...
WE ALL HAVE TO ACCEPT WHAT HAPPENS IN THE END...
YUKI-SAN... YOUR TENACITY WAS AMAZING.
YOUR LITTLE SISTER MUST REALLY BE IMPORTANT TO YOU...
AFTER PLAYING THIS GAME WITH YOU, THAT MUCH IS OBVIOUS...
...I WONDER IF THEY GOT ALONG WELL WITH EACH OTHER.
YES... KIND OF LIKE...
LIKE THAT BROTHER AND SISTER...
KARAN (JINGLE)
...FROM BACK THEN...
KARAN
OH! WELCOME!!

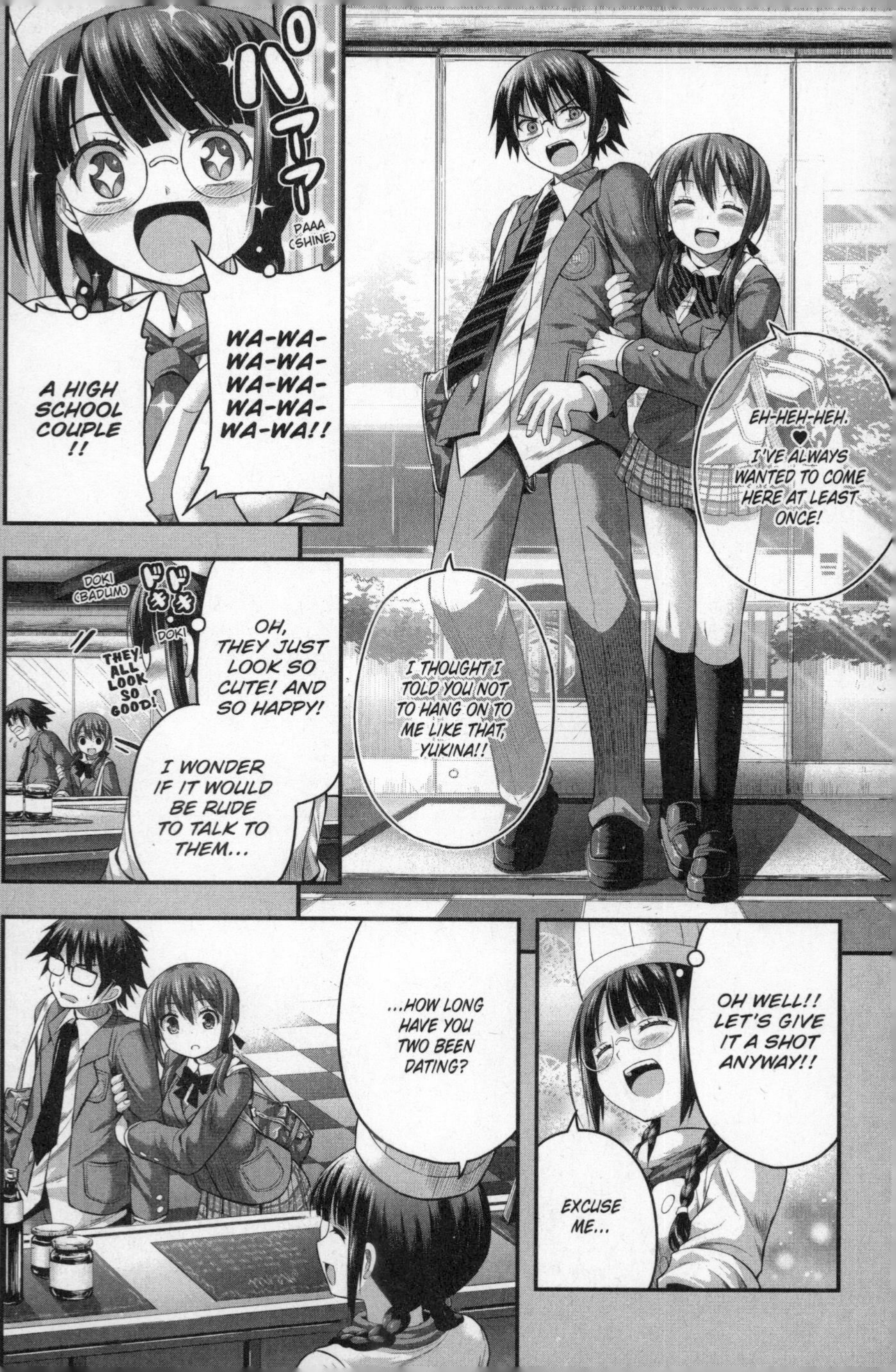
EH-HEH-HEH. ♥ I'VE ALWAYS WANTED TO COME HERE AT LEAST ONCE!
I THOUGHT I TOLD YOU NOT TO HANG ON TO ME LIKE THAT, YUKINA!!
PAAA (SHINE)
WA-WA-WA-WA-WA-WA-WA-WA-WA-WA!!
A HIGH SCHOOL COUPLE !!
DOKI (BADUM)
DOKI
OH, THEY JUST LOOK SO CUTE! AND SO HAPPY!
THEY ALL LOOK SO GOOD!
I WONDER IF IT WOULD BE RUDE TO TALK TO THEM...
OH WELL!! LET'S GIVE IT A SHOT ANYWAY!!
EXCUSE ME...
...HOW LONG HAVE YOU TWO BEEN DATING?

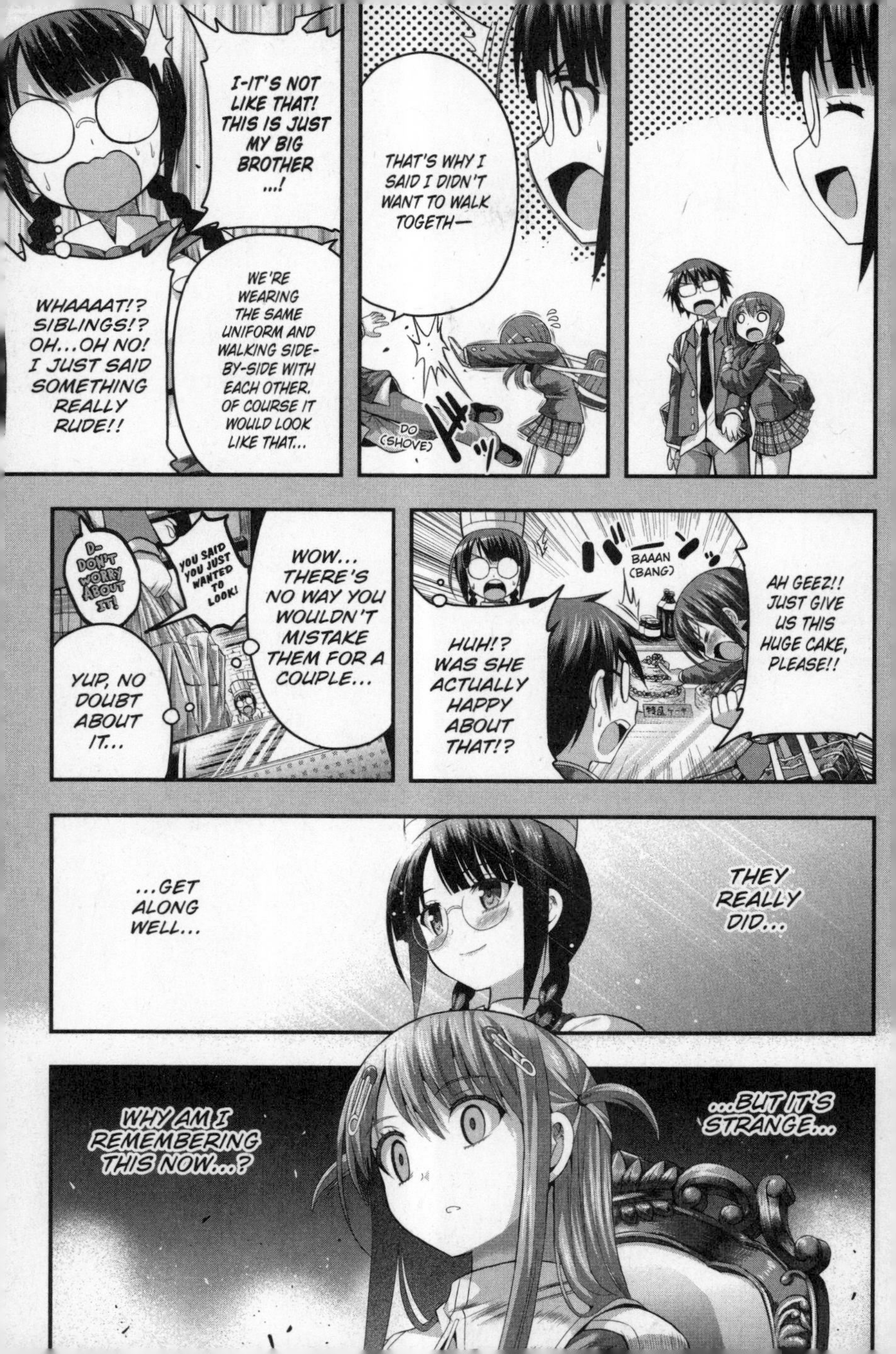
THAT'S WHY I SAID I DIDN'T WANT TO WALK TOGETH—
DO (SHOVE)
I-IT'S NOT LIKE THAT! THIS IS JUST MY BIG BROTHER ...!
WE'RE WEARING THE SAME UNIFORM AND WALKING SIDE-BY-SIDE WITH EACH OTHER. OF COURSE IT WOULD LOOK LIKE THAT...
WHAAAAT!? SIBLINGS!? OH...OH NO! I JUST SAID SOMETHING REALLY RUDE!!
BAAAN (BANG)
AH GEEZ!! JUST GIVE US THIS HUGE CAKE, PLEASE!!
HUH!? WAS SHE ACTUALLY HAPPY ABOUT THAT!?
WOW... THERE'S NO WAY YOU WOULDN'T MISTAKE THEM FOR A COUPLE...
YOU SAID YOU JUST WANTED TO LOOK!
D-DON'T WORRY ABOUT IT!
YUP, NO DOUBT ABOUT IT...
THEY REALLY DID...
...GET ALONG WELL...
...BUT IT'S STRANGE...
WHY AM I REMEMBERING THIS NOW...?

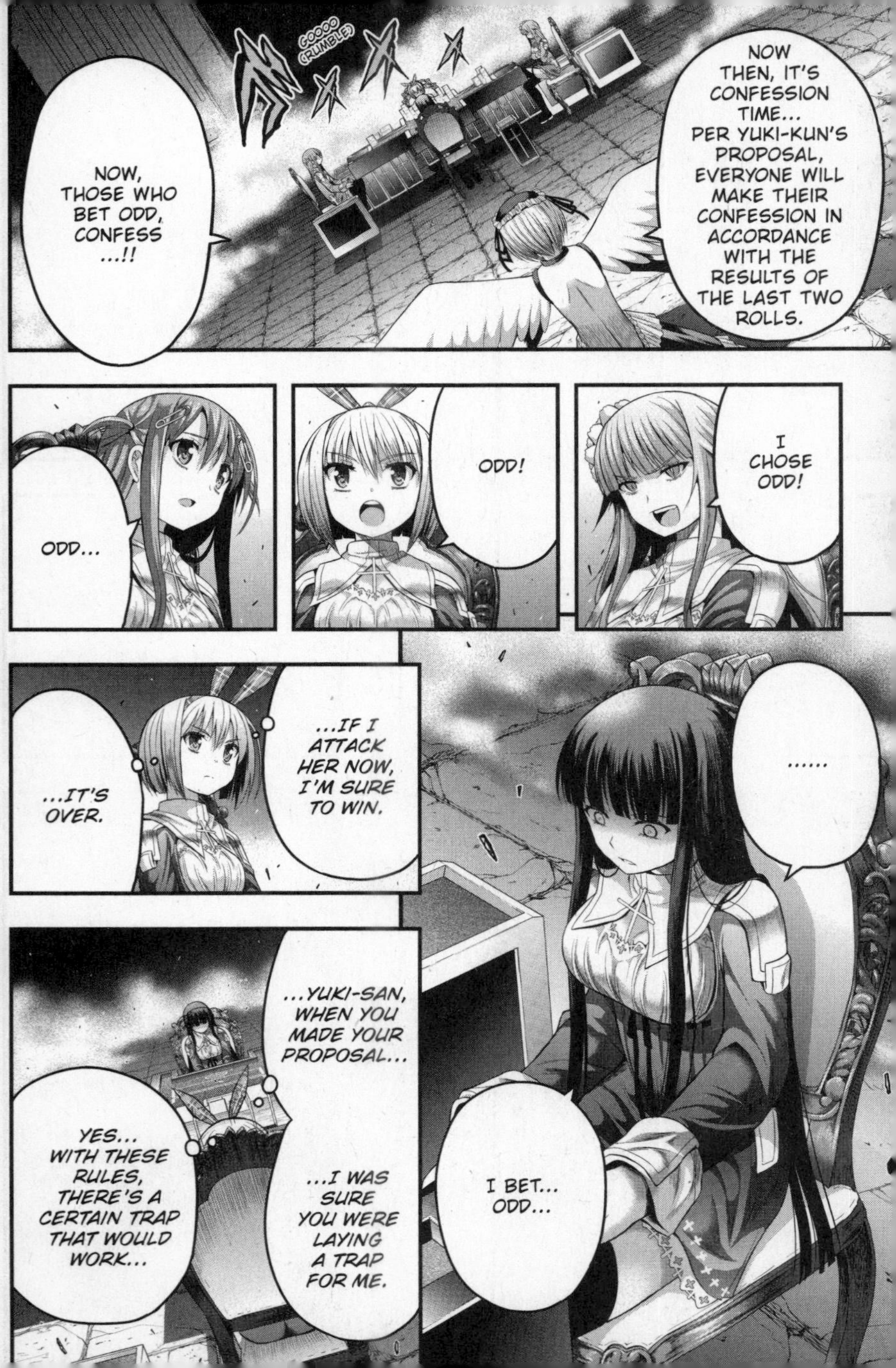
NOW THEN, IT'S CONFESSION TIME... PER YUKI-KUN'S PROPOSAL, EVERYONE WILL MAKE THEIR CONFESSION IN ACCORDANCE WITH THE RESULTS OF THE LAST TWO ROLLS.
GOOOO (RUMBLE)
NOW, THOSE WHO BET ODD, CONFESS ...!!
I CHOSE ODD!
ODD!
ODD...
......
I BET... ODD...
...IF I ATTACK HER NOW, I'M SURE TO WIN.
...IT'S OVER.
...YUKI-SAN, WHEN YOU MADE YOUR PROPOSAL...
...I WAS SURE YOU WERE LAYING A TRAP FOR ME.
YES... WITH THESE RULES, THERE'S A CERTAIN TRAP THAT WOULD WORK...

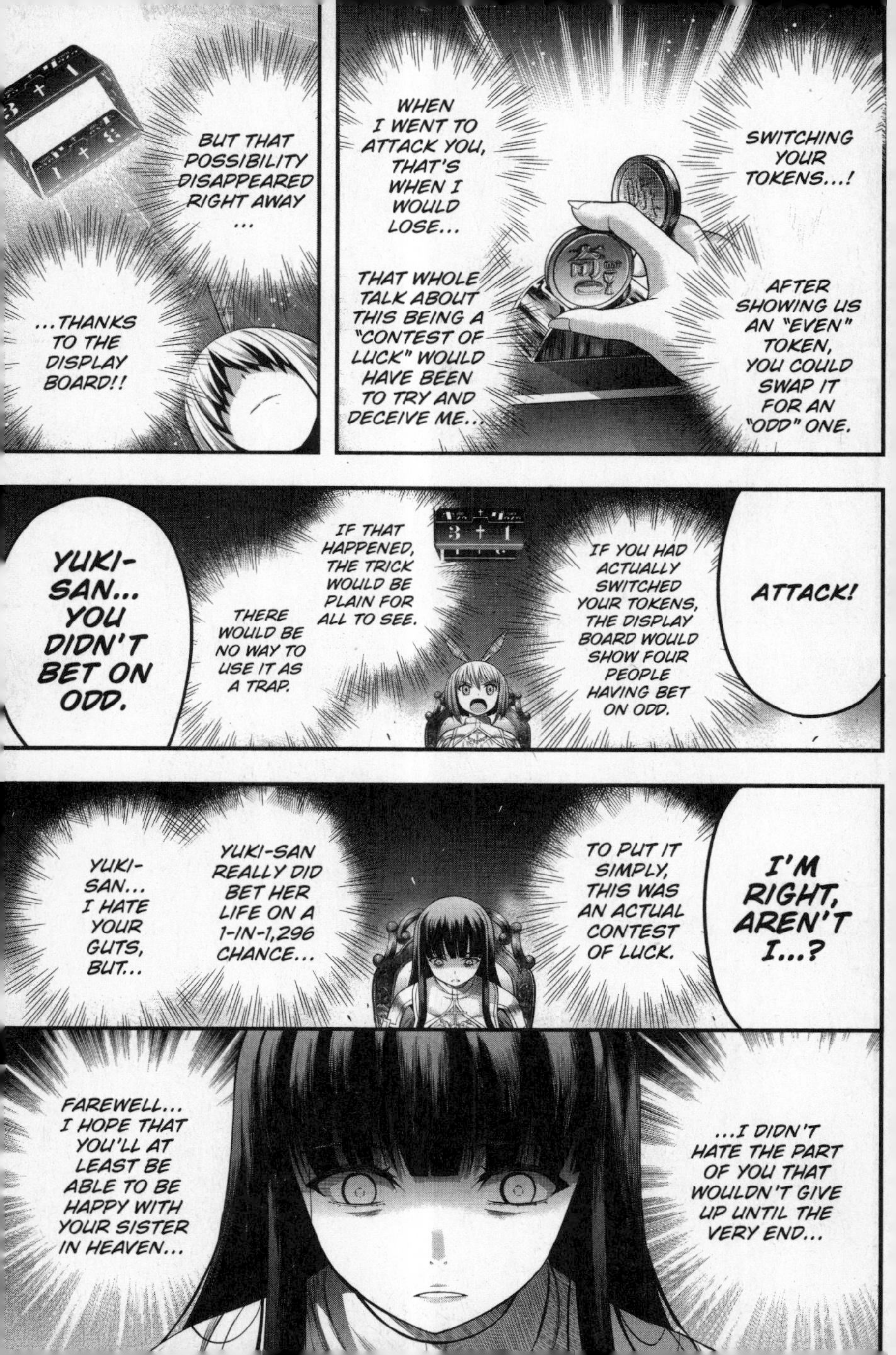
SWITCHING YOUR TOKENS...!
AFTER SHOWING US AN "EVEN" TOKEN, YOU COULD SWAP IT FOR AN "ODD" ONE.
WHEN I WENT TO ATTACK YOU, THAT'S WHEN I WOULD LOSE...
THAT WHOLE TALK ABOUT THIS BEING A "CONTEST OF LUCK" WOULD HAVE BEEN TO TRY AND DECEIVE ME...
BUT THAT POSSIBILITY DISAPPEARED RIGHT AWAY...
...THANKS TO THE DISPLAY BOARD!!
ATTACK!
IF YOU HAD ACTUALLY SWITCHED YOUR TOKENS, THE DISPLAY BOARD WOULD SHOW FOUR PEOPLE HAVING BET ON ODD.
IF THAT HAPPENED, THE TRICK WOULD BE PLAIN FOR ALL TO SEE.
THERE WOULD BE NO WAY TO USE IT AS A TRAP.
YUKI-SAN... YOU DIDN'T BET ON ODD.
I'M RIGHT, AREN'T I...?
TO PUT IT SIMPLY, THIS WAS AN ACTUAL CONTEST OF LUCK.
YUKI-SAN REALLY DID BET HER LIFE ON A 1-IN-1,296 CHANCE...
YUKI-SAN... I HATE YOUR GUTS, BUT...
...I DIDN'T HATE THE PART OF YOU THAT WOULDN'T GIVE UP UNTIL THE VERY END...
FAREWELL... I HOPE THAT YOU'LL AT LEAST BE ABLE TO BE HAPPY WITH YOUR SISTER IN HEAVEN...

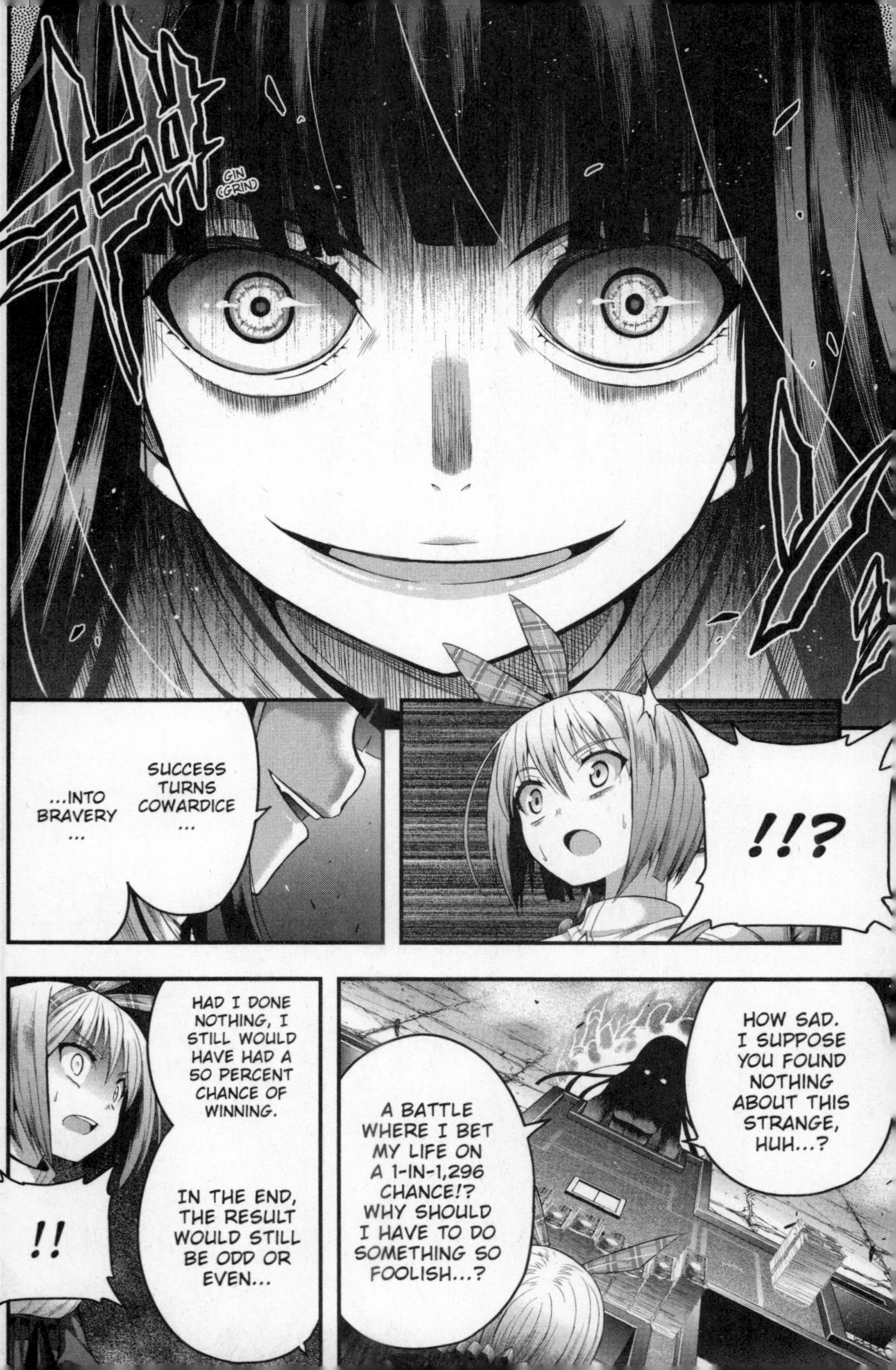
GIN (GRIN)
!!?
SUCCESS TURNS COWARDICE...
...INTO BRAVERY...
HOW SAD. I SUPPOSE YOU FOUND NOTHING ABOUT THIS STRANGE, HUH...?
A BATTLE WHERE I BET MY LIFE ON A 1-IN-1,296 CHANCE!? WHY SHOULD I HAVE TO DO SOMETHING SO FOOLISH...?
HAD I DONE NOTHING, I STILL WOULD HAVE HAD A 50 PERCENT CHANCE OF WINNING.
IN THE END, THE RESULT WOULD STILL BE ODD OR EVEN...
!!

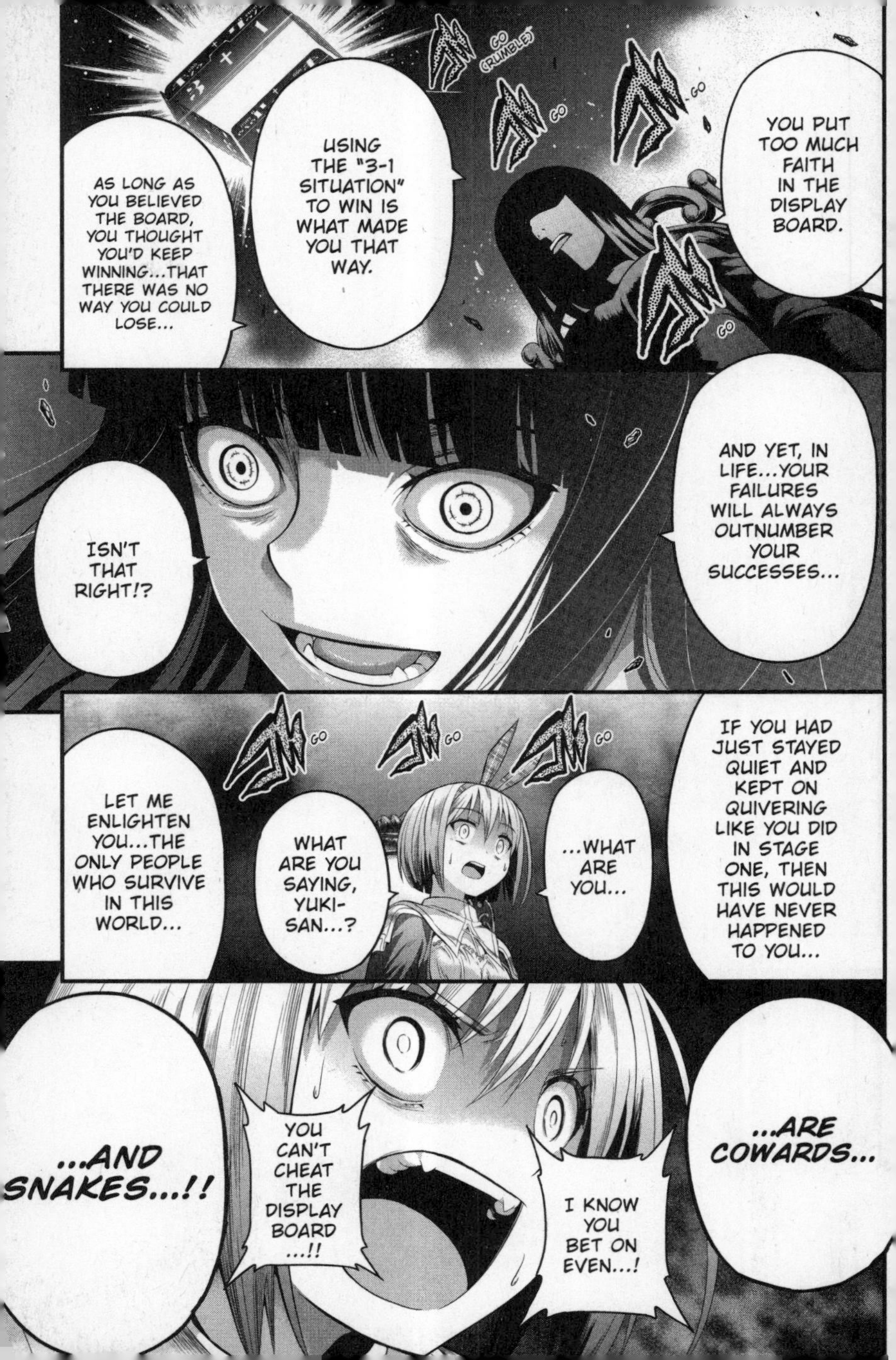
YOU PUT TOO MUCH FAITH IN THE DISPLAY BOARD.
GO
GO (RUMBLE)
GO
GO
USING THE "3-1 SITUATION" TO WIN IS WHAT MADE YOU THAT WAY.
AS LONG AS YOU BELIEVED THE BOARD, YOU THOUGHT YOU'D KEEP WINNING...THAT THERE WAS NO WAY YOU COULD LOSE...
AND YET, IN LIFE...YOUR FAILURES WILL ALWAYS OUTNUMBER YOUR SUCCESSES...
ISN'T THAT RIGHT!?
IF YOU HAD JUST STAYED QUIET AND KEPT ON QUIVERING LIKE YOU DID IN STAGE ONE, THEN THIS WOULD HAVE NEVER HAPPENED TO YOU...
GO
GO
GO
...WHAT ARE YOU...
WHAT ARE YOU SAYING, YUKI-SAN...?
LET ME ENLIGHTEN YOU...THE ONLY PEOPLE WHO SURVIVE IN THIS WORLD...
...ARE COWARDS...
I KNOW YOU BET ON EVEN...!
YOU CAN'T CHEAT THE DISPLAY BOARD ...!!
...AND SNAKES...!!

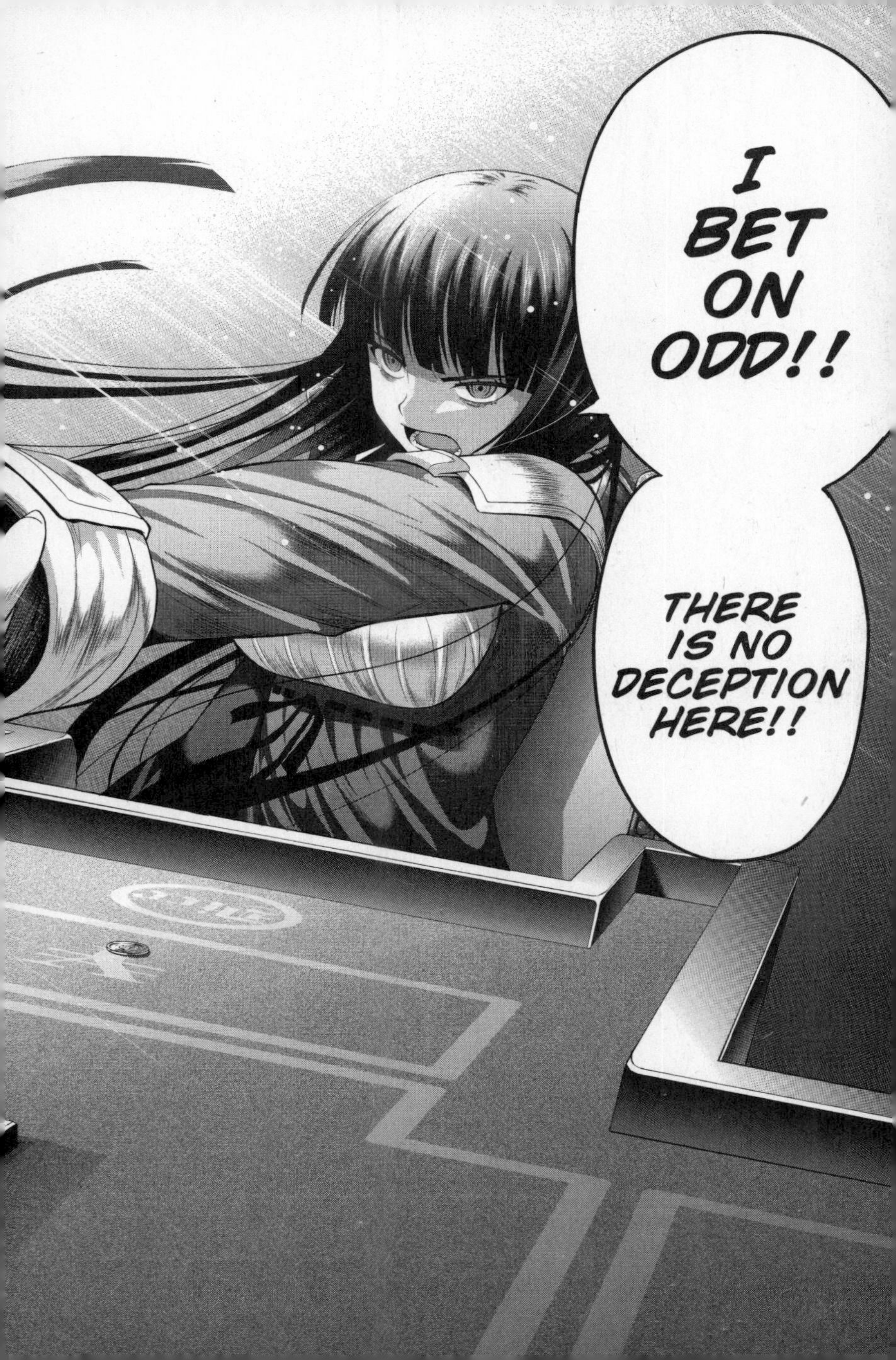
I BET ON ODD!!
THERE IS NO DECEPTION HERE!!

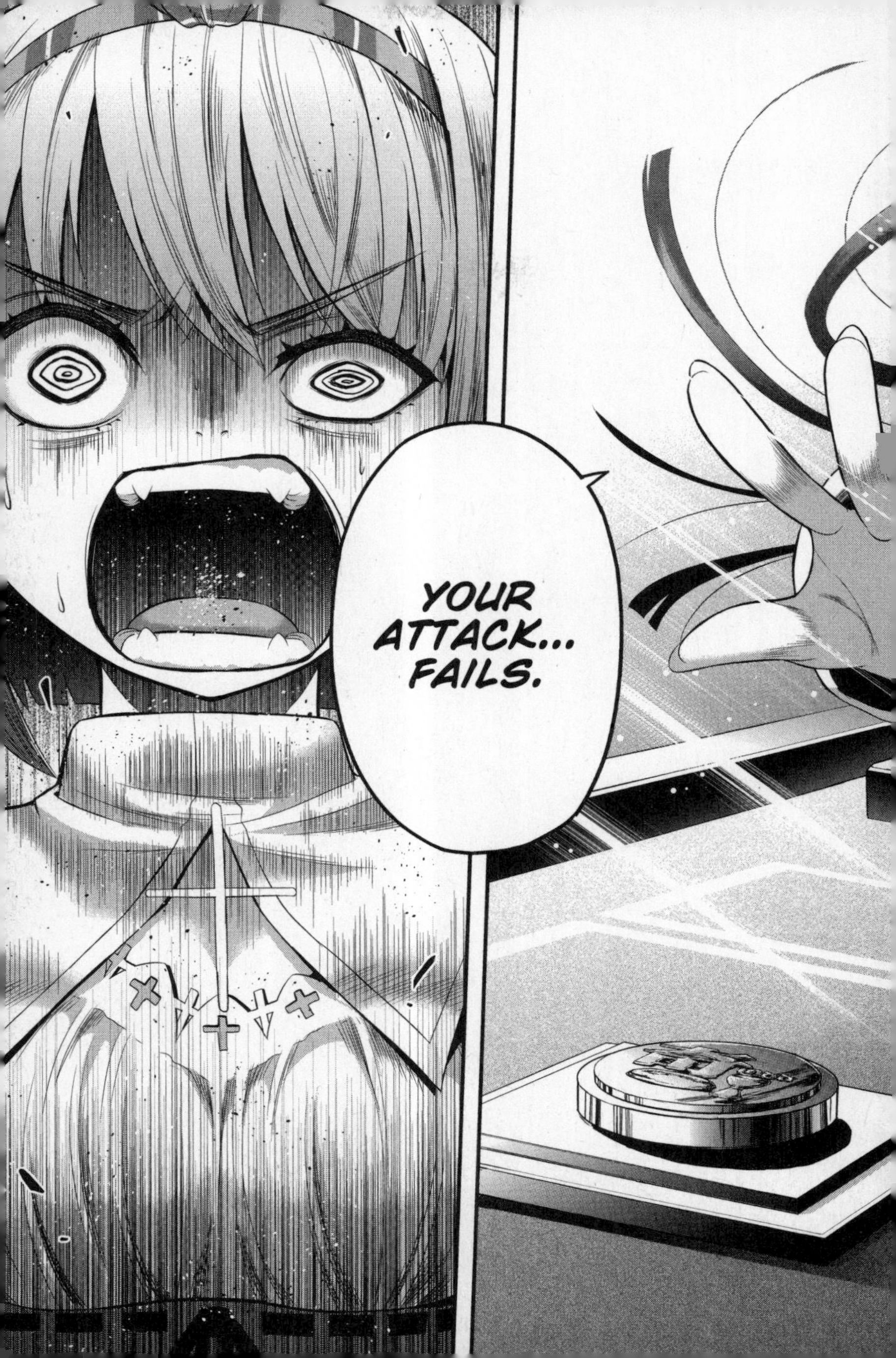
YOUR ATTACK... FAILS.

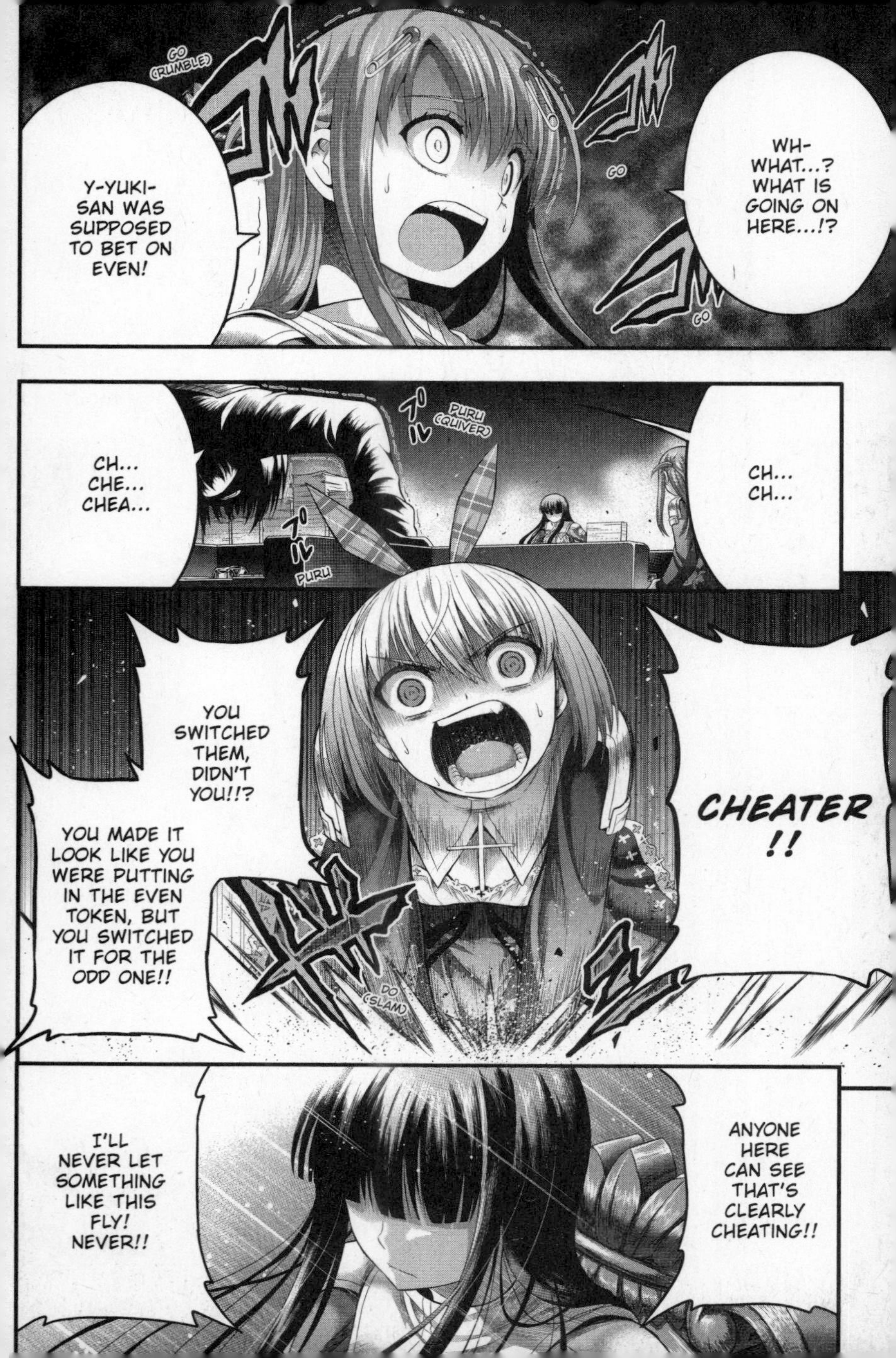
WH- WHAT...? WHAT IS GOING ON HERE...!?
GO (RUMBLE)
GO
GO
Y-YUKI-SAN WAS SUPPOSED TO BET ON EVEN!
CH... CH...
PURU (QUIVER)
PURU
CH... CHE... CHEA...
CHEATER !!
YOU SWITCHED THEM, DIDN'T YOU!!?
YOU MADE IT LOOK LIKE YOU WERE PUTTING IN THE EVEN TOKEN, BUT YOU SWITCHED IT FOR THE ODD ONE!!
DO (SLAM)
ANYONE HERE CAN SEE THAT'S CLEARLY CHEATING!!
I'LL NEVER LET SOMETHING LIKE THIS FLY! NEVER!!

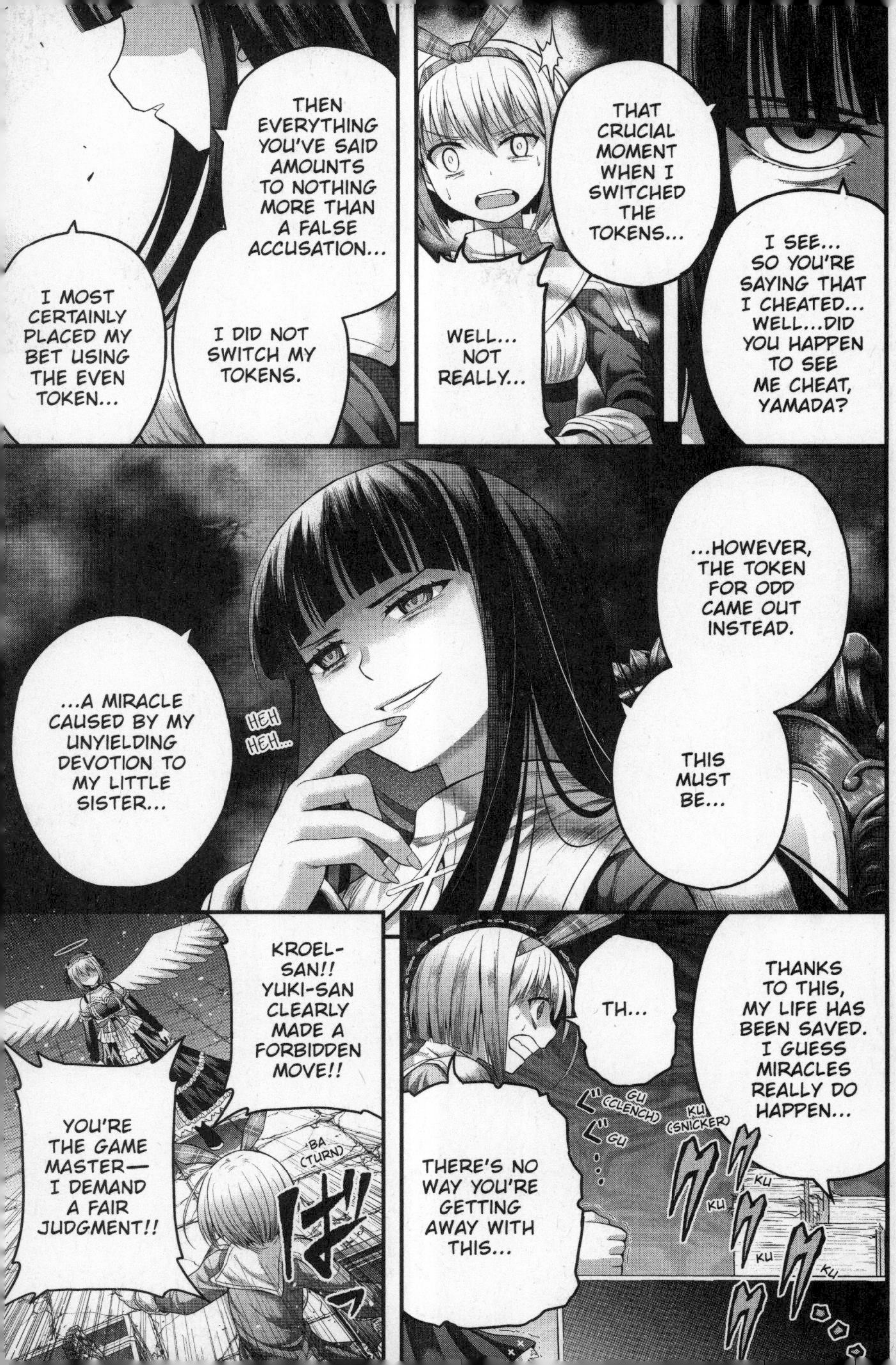
I SEE... SO YOU'RE SAYING THAT I CHEATED... WELL...DID YOU HAPPEN TO SEE ME CHEAT, YAMADA?
THAT CRUCIAL MOMENT WHEN I SWITCHED THE TOKENS...
WELL... NOT REALLY...
THEN EVERYTHING YOU'VE SAID AMOUNTS TO NOTHING MORE THAN A FALSE ACCUSATION...
I DID NOT SWITCH MY TOKENS.
I MOST CERTAINLY PLACED MY BET USING THE EVEN TOKEN...
...HOWEVER, THE TOKEN FOR ODD CAME OUT INSTEAD.
THIS MUST BE...
HEH HEH...
...A MIRACLE CAUSED BY MY UNYIELDING DEVOTION TO MY LITTLE SISTER...
THANKS TO THIS, MY LIFE HAS BEEN SAVED. I GUESS MIRACLES REALLY DO HAPPEN...
KU (SNICKER)
KU KU KU KU
TH...
GU (CLENCH) GU
THERE'S NO WAY YOU'RE GETTING AWAY WITH THIS...
KROEL-SAN!! YUKI-SAN CLEARLY MADE A FORBIDDEN MOVE!!
BA (TURN)
YOU'RE THE GAME MASTER— I DEMAND A FAIR JUDGMENT!!

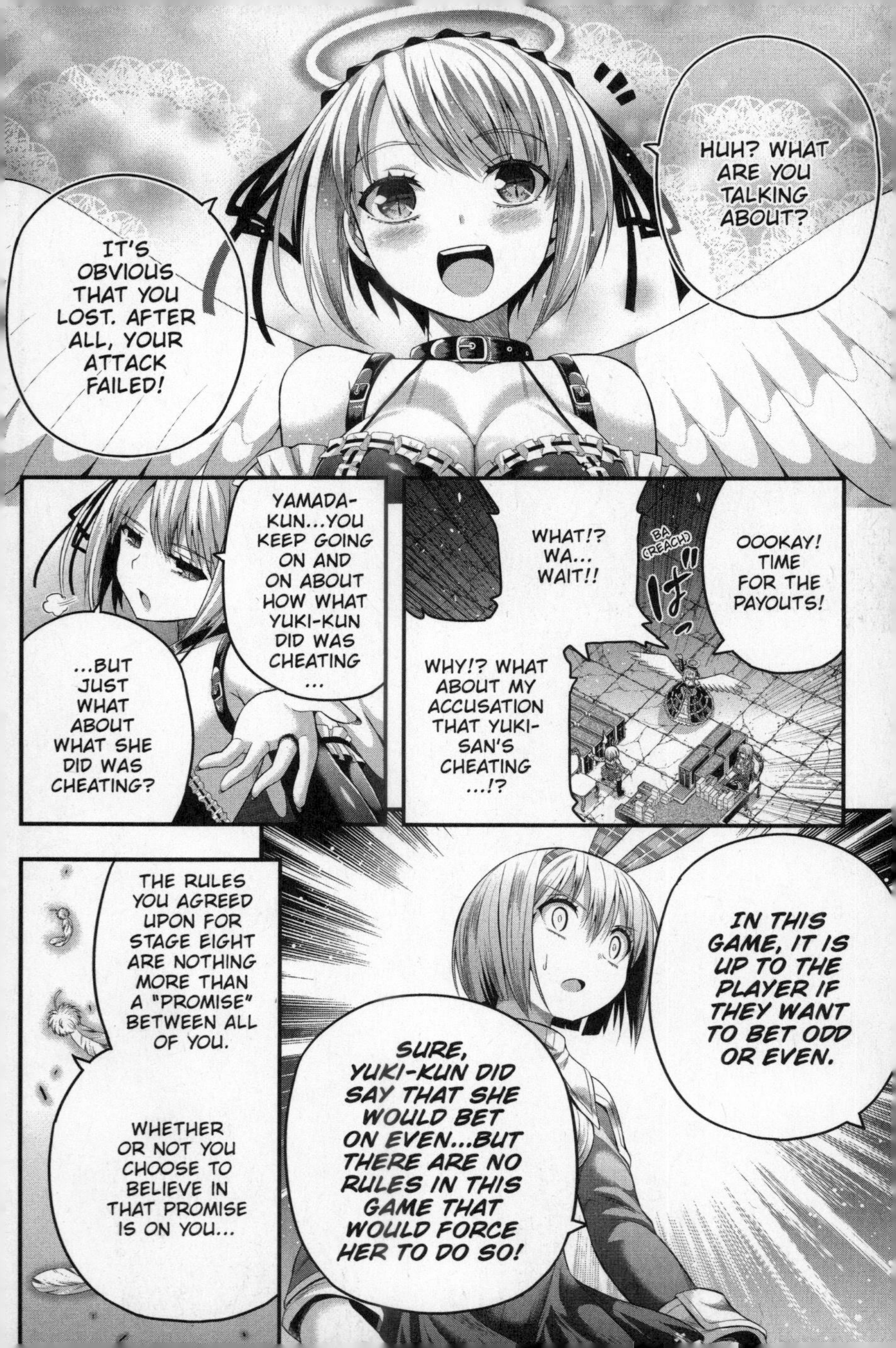
HUH? WHAT ARE YOU TALKING ABOUT?
IT'S OBVIOUS THAT YOU LOST. AFTER ALL, YOUR ATTACK FAILED!
OOOKAY! TIME FOR THE PAYOUTS!
BA (REACH)
ばっ
WHAT!? WA... WAIT!!
WHY!? WHAT ABOUT MY ACCUSATION THAT YUKI-SAN'S CHEATING ...!?
YAMADA-KUN...YOU KEEP GOING ON AND ON ABOUT HOW WHAT YUKI-KUN DID WAS CHEATING ...
...BUT JUST WHAT ABOUT WHAT SHE DID WAS CHEATING?
IN THIS GAME, IT IS UP TO THE PLAYER IF THEY WANT TO BET ODD OR EVEN.
SURE, YUKI-KUN DID SAY THAT SHE WOULD BET ON EVEN...BUT THERE ARE NO RULES IN THIS GAME THAT WOULD FORCE HER TO DO SO!
THE RULES YOU AGREED UPON FOR STAGE EIGHT ARE NOTHING MORE THAN A "PROMISE" BETWEEN ALL OF YOU.
WHETHER OR NOT YOU CHOOSE TO BELIEVE IN THAT PROMISE IS ON YOU...

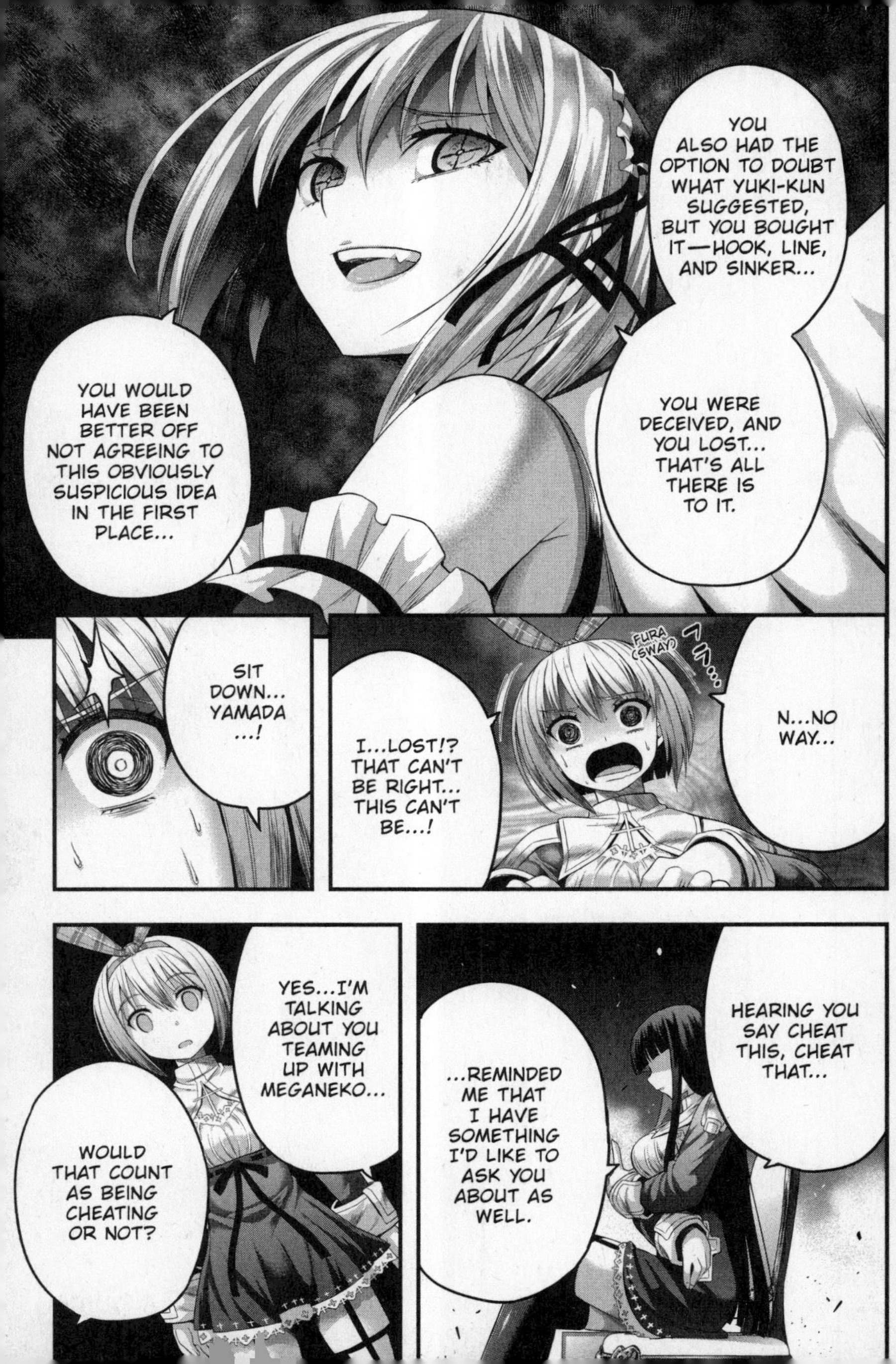
YOU ALSO HAD THE OPTION TO DOUBT WHAT YUKI-KUN SUGGESTED, BUT YOU BOUGHT IT—HOOK, LINE, AND SINKER...
YOU WERE DECEIVED, AND YOU LOST... THAT'S ALL THERE IS TO IT.
YOU WOULD HAVE BEEN BETTER OFF NOT AGREEING TO THIS OBVIOUSLY SUSPICIOUS IDEA IN THE FIRST PLACE...
N...NO WAY...
FURA (SWAY)
I...LOST!? THAT CAN'T BE RIGHT... THIS CAN'T BE...!
SIT DOWN... YAMADA ...!
HEARING YOU SAY CHEAT THIS, CHEAT THAT...
...REMINDED ME THAT I HAVE SOMETHING I'D LIKE TO ASK YOU ABOUT AS WELL.
YES...I'M TALKING ABOUT YOU TEAMING UP WITH MEGANEKO...
WOULD THAT COUNT AS BEING CHEATING OR NOT?

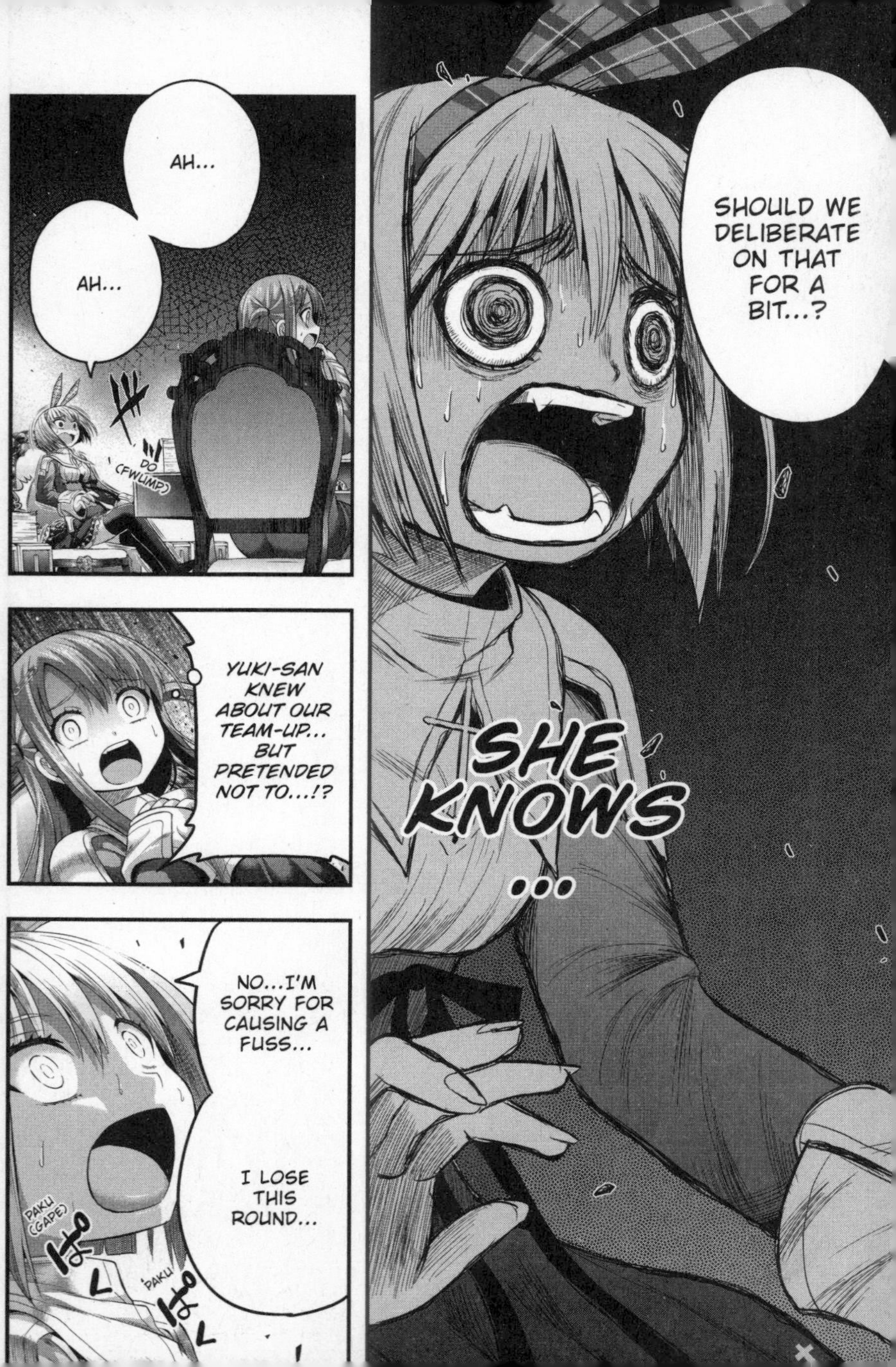
SHOULD WE DELIBERATE ON THAT FOR A BIT...?
SHE KNOWS...
AH...
AH...
DO (FWUMP)
YUKI-SAN KNEW ABOUT OUR TEAM-UP... BUT PRETENDED NOT TO...!?
NO...I'M SORRY FOR CAUSING A FUSS...
I LOSE THIS ROUND...
PAKU (GAPE)
PAKU

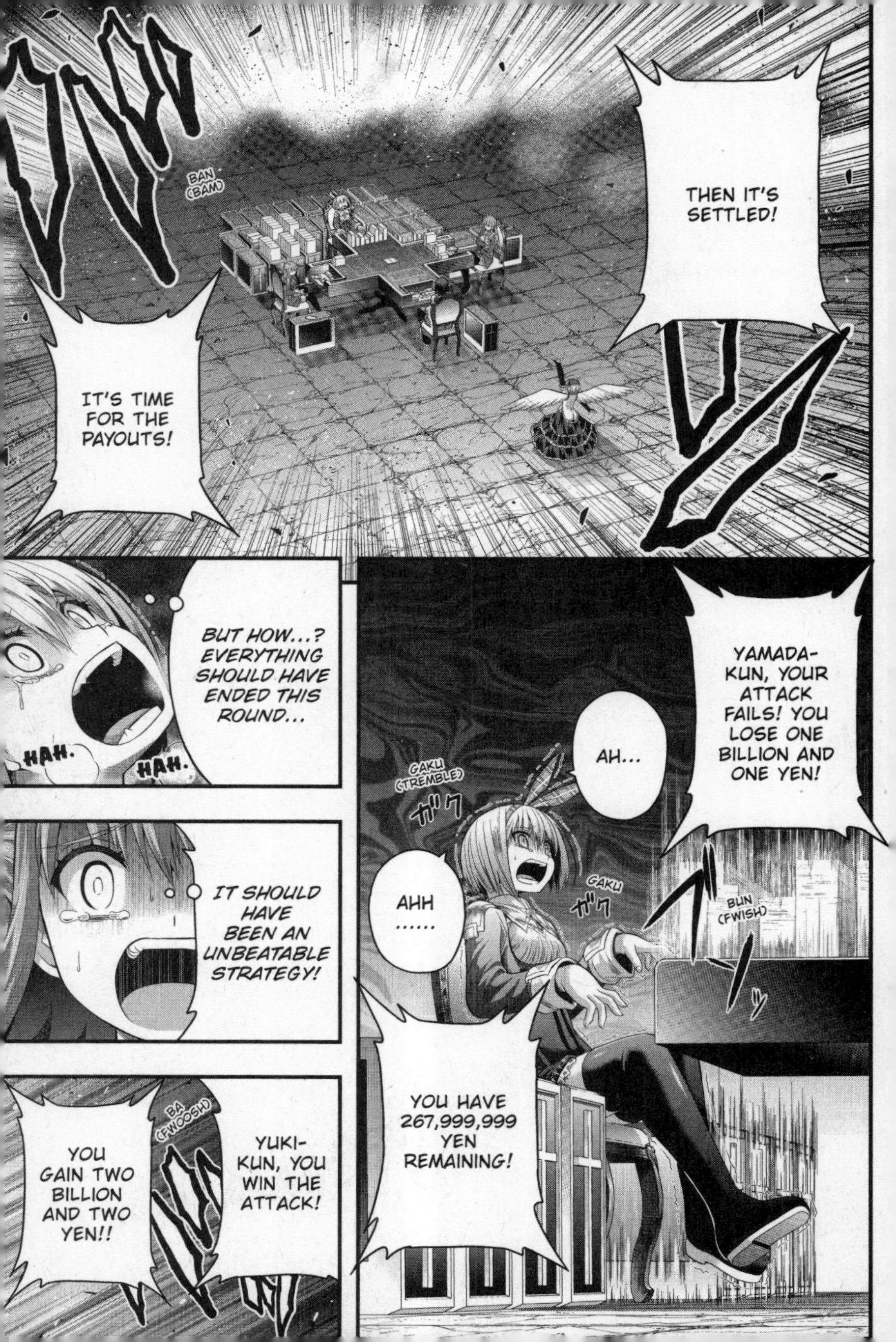
THEN IT'S SETTLED!
BAN (BAM)
IT'S TIME FOR THE PAYOUTS!
YAMADA-KUN, YOUR ATTACK FAILS! YOU LOSE ONE BILLION AND ONE YEN!
AH...
GAKU (TREMBLE)
AHH ......
GAKU
BUN (FWISH)
YOU HAVE 267,999,999 YEN REMAINING!
BUT HOW...? EVERYTHING SHOULD HAVE ENDED THIS ROUND...
HAH.
HAH.
IT SHOULD HAVE BEEN AN UNBEATABLE STRATEGY!
YUKI-KUN, YOU WIN THE ATTACK!
BA (FWOOSH)
YOU GAIN TWO BILLION AND TWO YEN!!

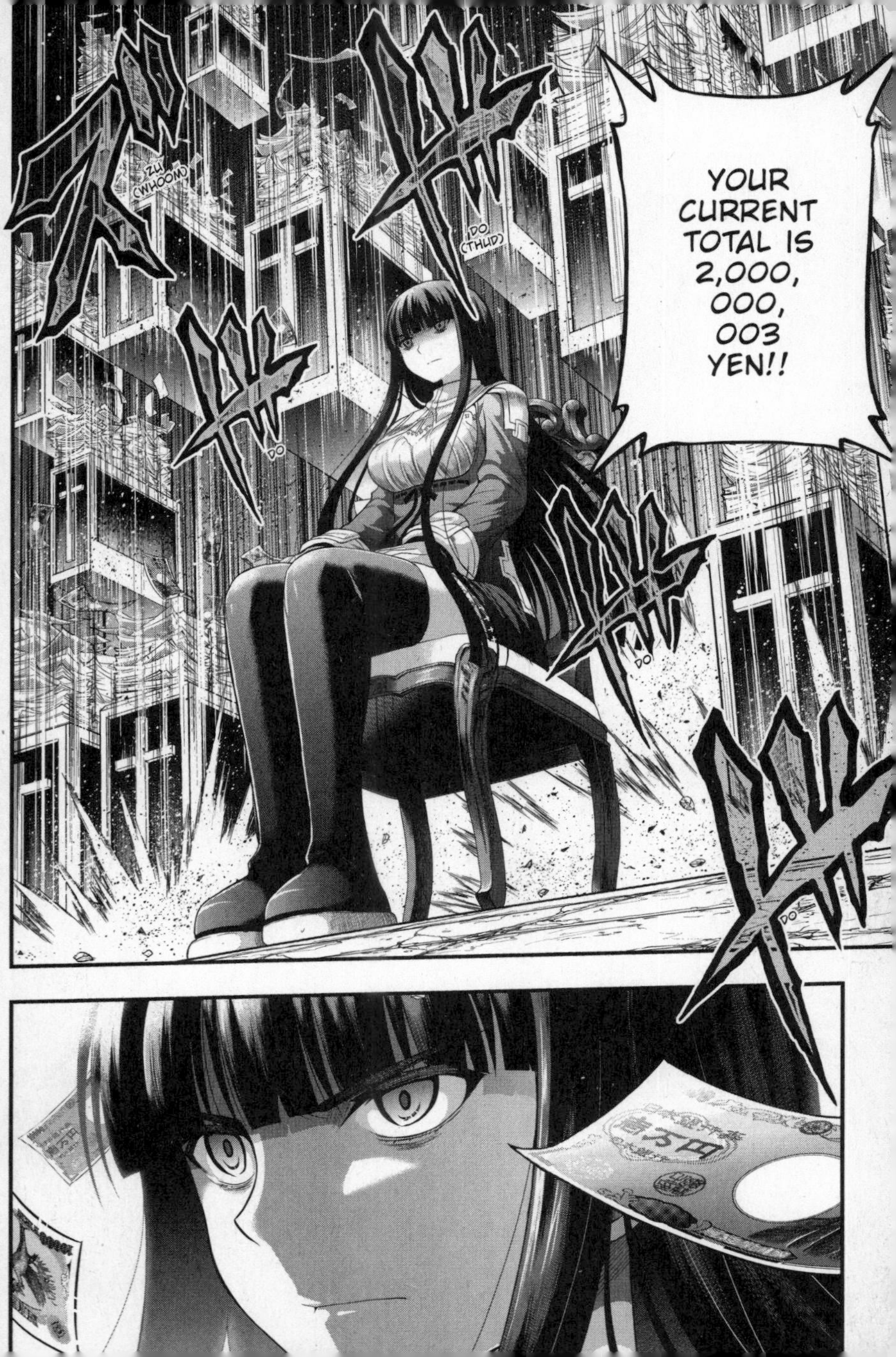
YOUR CURRENT TOTAL IS 2,000,000,003 YEN!!
DO (THUD)
ZU (WHOOM)
DO
DO
DO

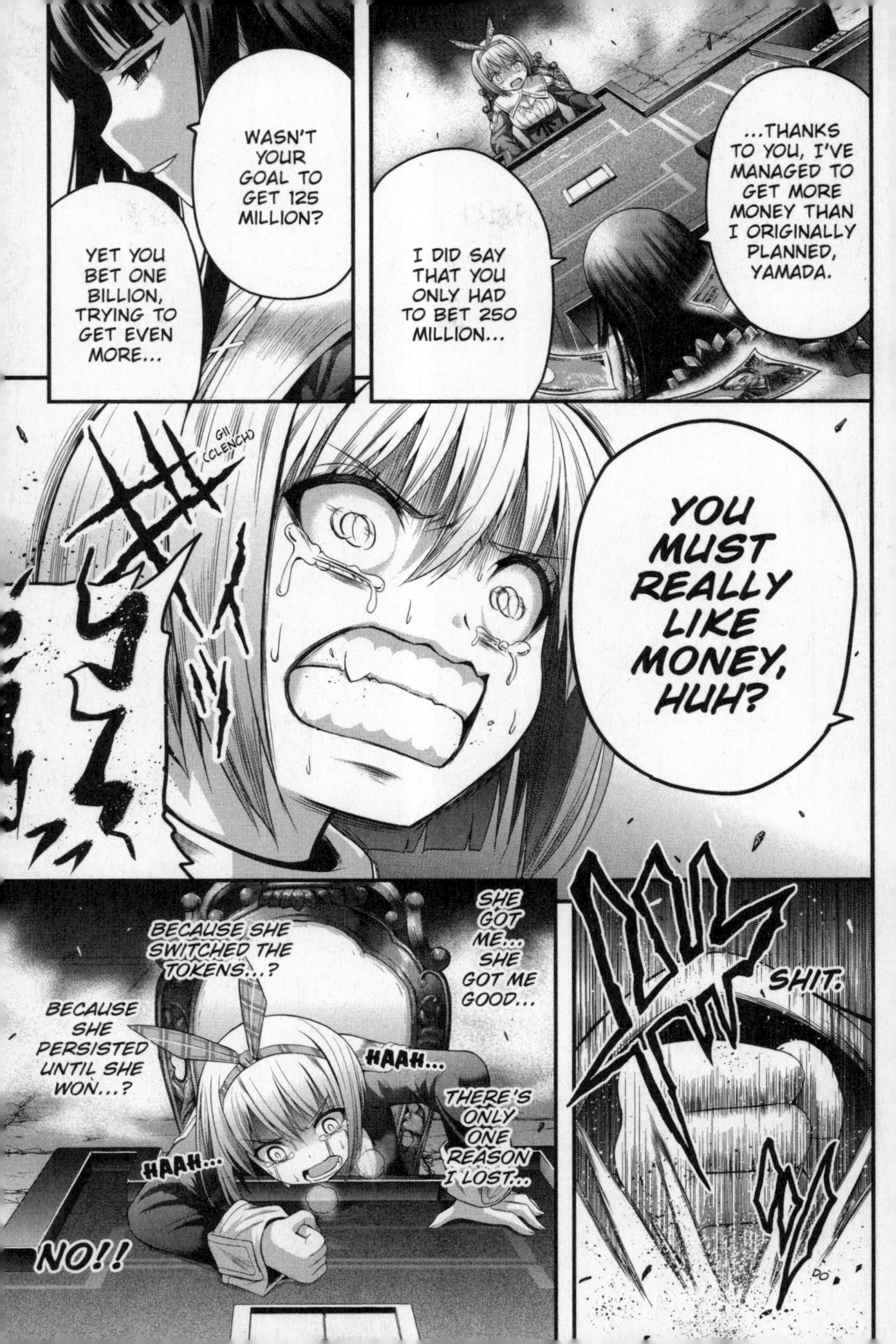
...THANKS TO YOU, I'VE MANAGED TO GET MORE MONEY THAN I ORIGINALLY PLANNED, YAMADA.
I DID SAY THAT YOU ONLY HAD TO BET 250 MILLION...
WASN'T YOUR GOAL TO GET 125 MILLION?
YET YOU BET ONE BILLION, TRYING TO GET EVEN MORE...
YOU MUST REALLY LIKE MONEY, HUH?
GII (CLENCH)
SHIT.
DO
SHE GOT ME... SHE GOT ME GOOD...
BECAUSE SHE SWITCHED THE TOKENS...?
BECAUSE SHE PERSISTED UNTIL SHE WON...?
HAAH...
THERE'S ONLY ONE REASON I LOST...
HAAH...
NO!!

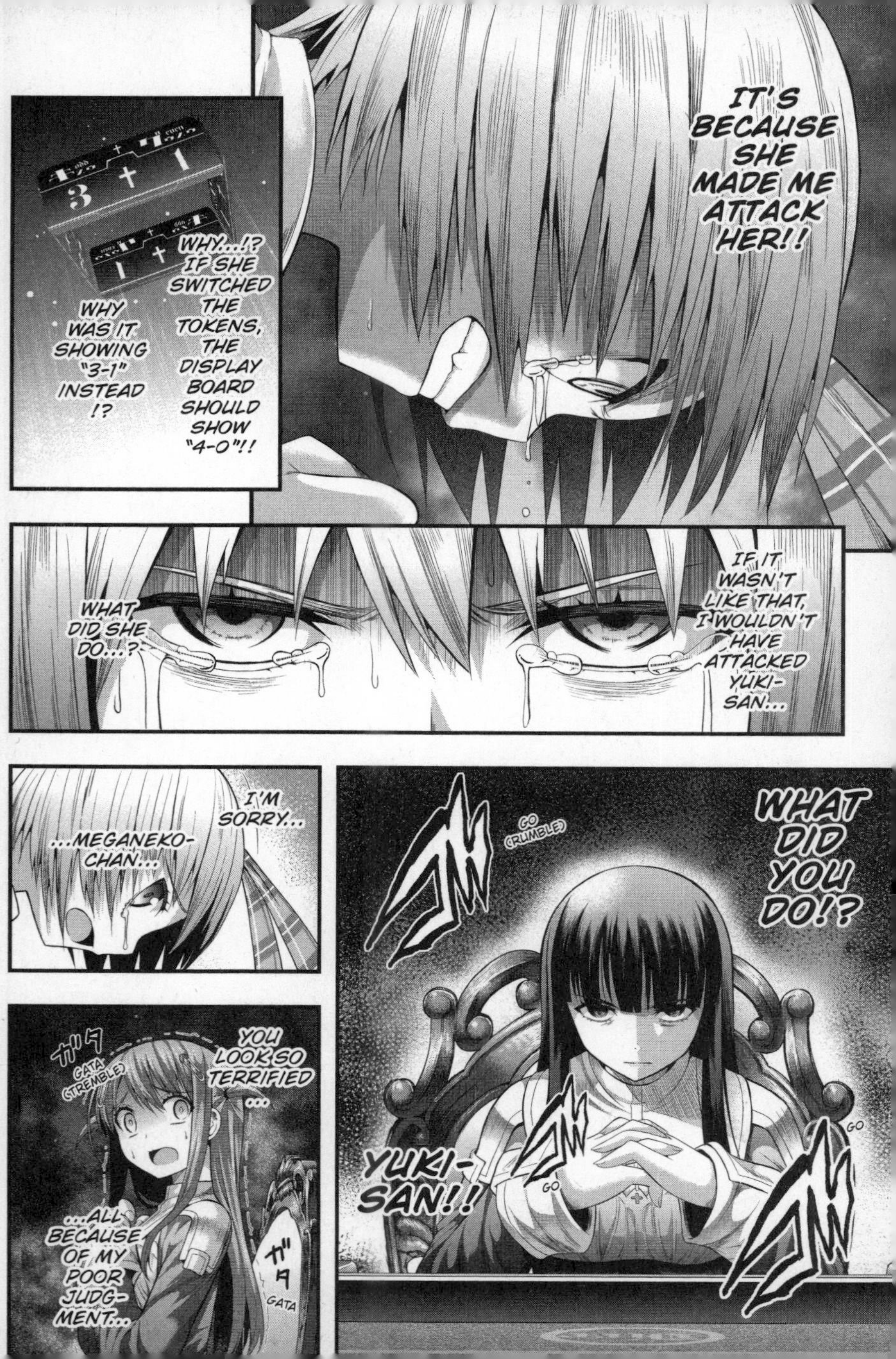
IT'S BECAUSE SHE MADE ME ATTACK HER!!
WHY...!? IF SHE SWITCHED THE TOKENS, THE DISPLAY BOARD SHOULD SHOW "4-0"!!
WHY WAS IT SHOWING "3-1" INSTEAD!?
IF IT WASN'T LIKE THAT, I WOULDN'T HAVE ATTACKED YUKI-SAN...
WHAT DID SHE DO...?
WHAT DID YOU DO!?
GO (RUMBLE)
GO
YUKI-SAN!!
GO
I'M SORRY...
...MEGANEKO-CHAN...
YOU LOOK SO TERRIFIED...
ガタ
GATA (TREMBLE)
...ALL BECAUSE OF MY POOR JUDGMENT...
ガタ
GATA

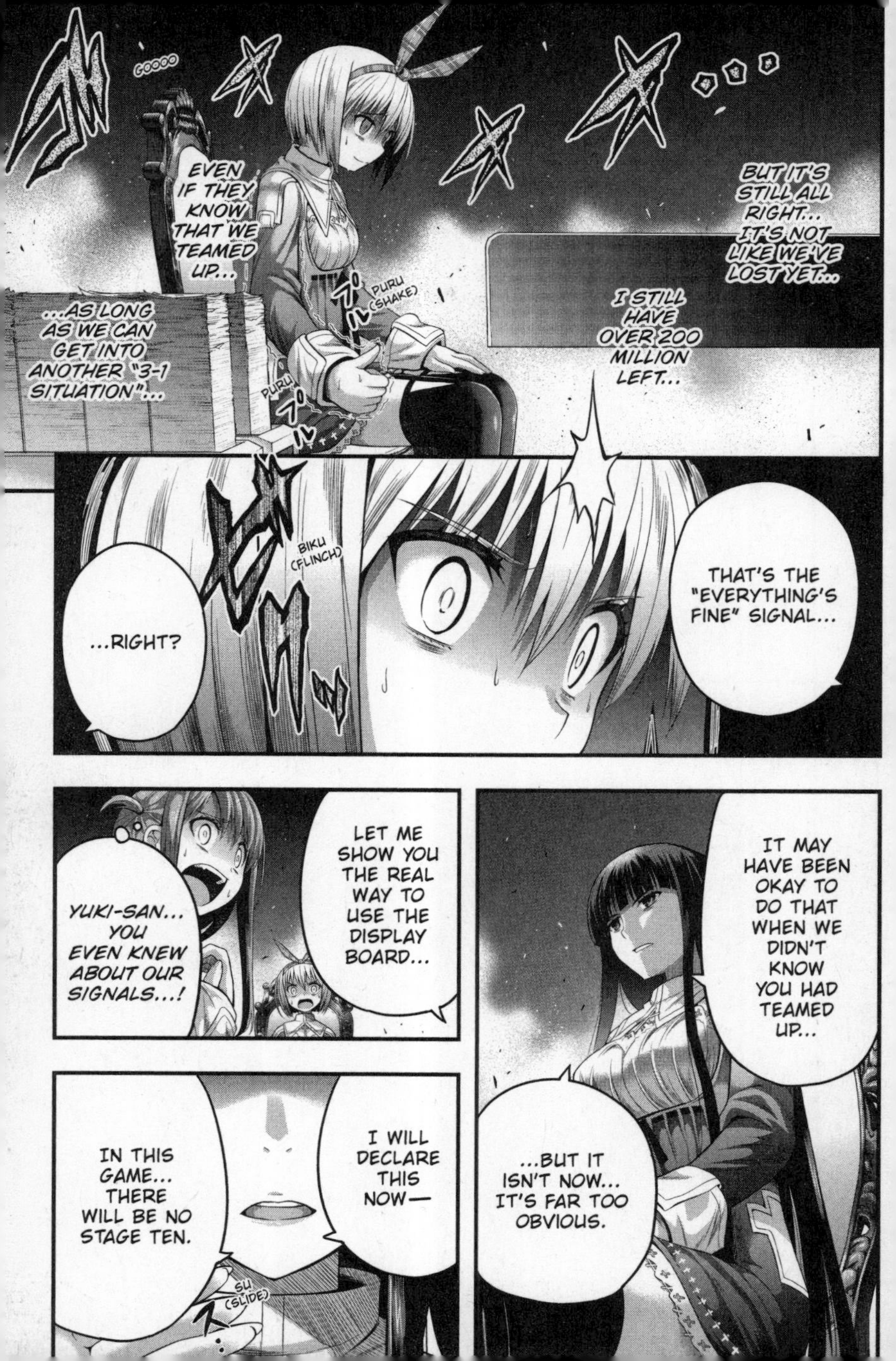
BUT IT'S STILL ALL RIGHT... IT'S NOT LIKE WE'VE LOST YET...
I STILL HAVE OVER 200 MILLION LEFT...
EVEN IF THEY KNOW THAT WE TEAMED UP...
...AS LONG AS WE CAN GET INTO ANOTHER "3-1 SITUATION"...
PURU (SHAKE)
PURU
GOOOO
THAT'S THE "EVERYTHING'S FINE" SIGNAL...
BIKU (FLINCH)
...RIGHT?
IT MAY HAVE BEEN OKAY TO DO THAT WHEN WE DIDN'T KNOW YOU HAD TEAMED UP...
...BUT IT ISN'T NOW... IT'S FAR TOO OBVIOUS.
LET ME SHOW YOU THE REAL WAY TO USE THE DISPLAY BOARD...
YUKI-SAN... YOU EVEN KNEW ABOUT OUR SIGNALS...!
I WILL DECLARE THIS NOW—
IN THIS GAME... THERE WILL BE NO STAGE TEN.
SU (SLIDE)

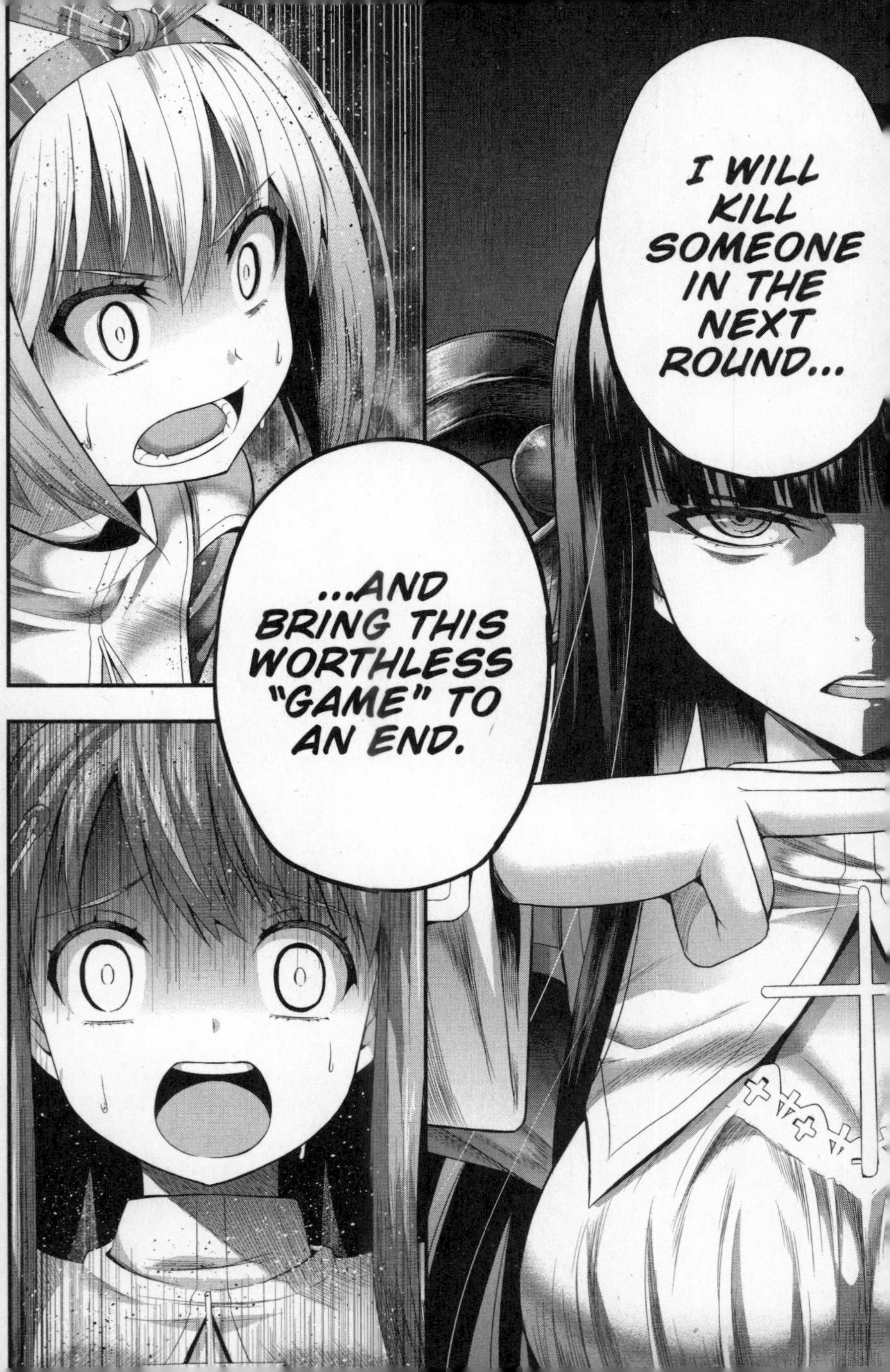
I WILL KILL SOMEONE IN THE NEXT ROUND...
...AND BRING THIS WORTHLESS "GAME" TO AN END.

Though You May Burn to ASH

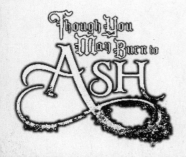

Though You May Burn to Ash

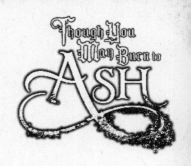

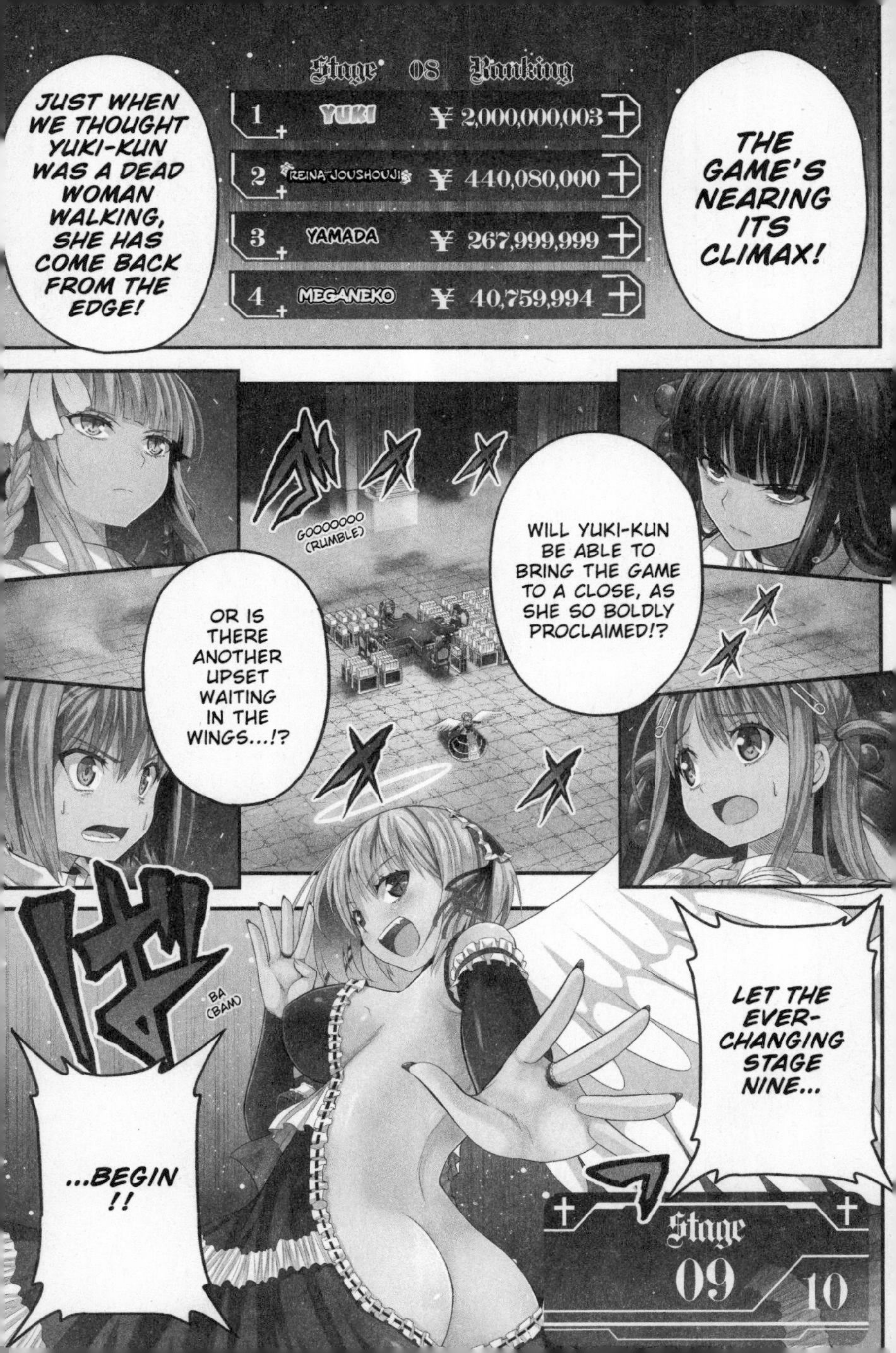
Stage 08 Ranking
1 YUKI ¥ 2,000,000,003
2 REINA JOUSHOUJI ¥ 440,080,000
3 YAMADA ¥ 267,999,999
4 MEGANEKO ¥ 40,759,994
THE GAME'S NEARING ITS CLIMAX!
JUST WHEN WE THOUGHT YUKI-KUN WAS A DEAD WOMAN WALKING, SHE HAS COME BACK FROM THE EDGE!
WILL YUKI-KUN BE ABLE TO BRING THE GAME TO A CLOSE, AS SHE SO BOLDLY PROCLAIMED!?
GOOOOOOO (RUMBLE)
OR IS THERE ANOTHER UPSET WAITING IN THE WINGS...!?
LET THE EVER-CHANGING STAGE NINE...
Stage 09 10
BA (BAN)
...BEGIN !!

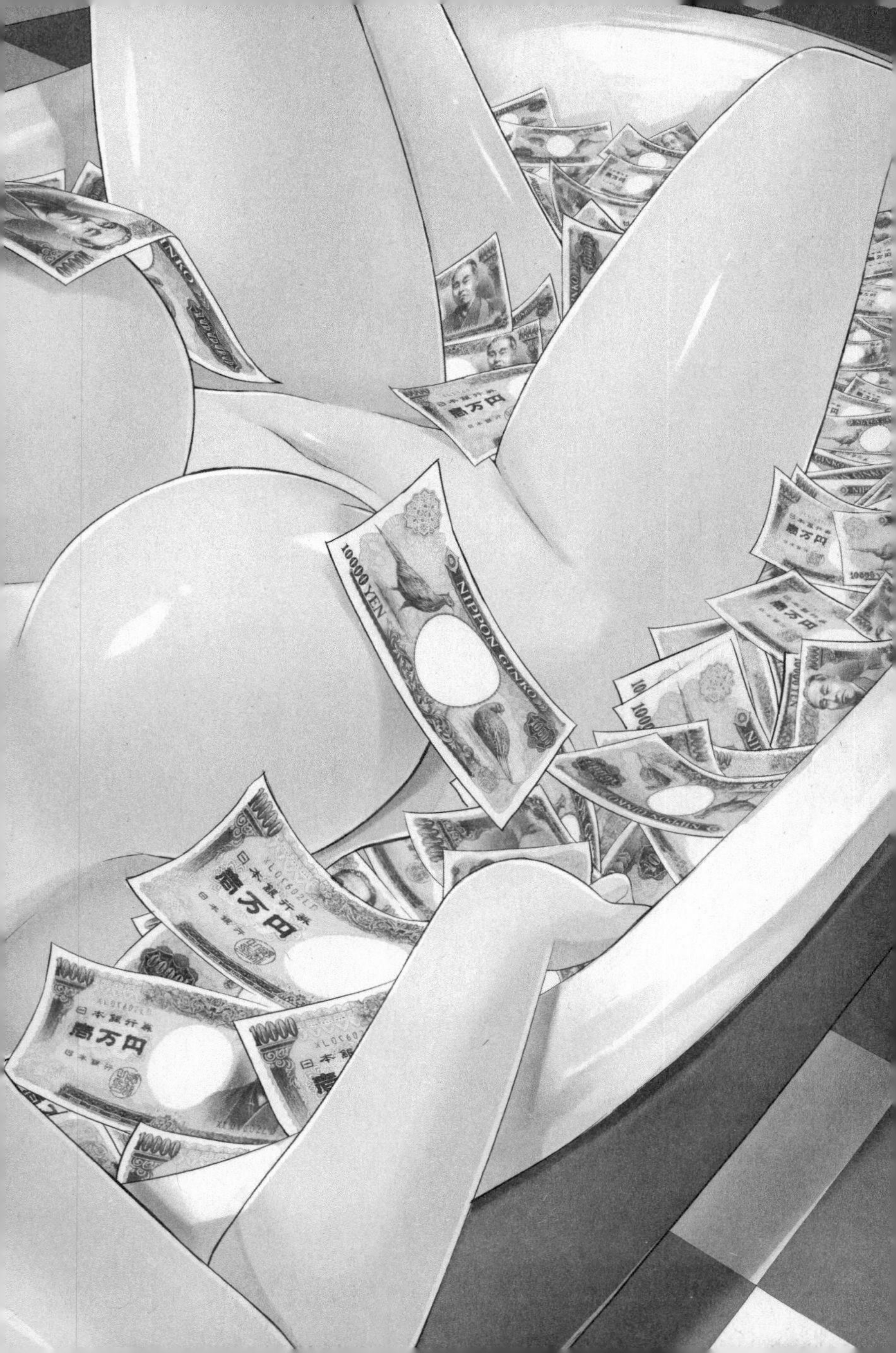
10000 YEN
NIPPON GINKO
日本銀行券
壱万円
日本銀行

CHAPTER 11: STRAY RABBIT

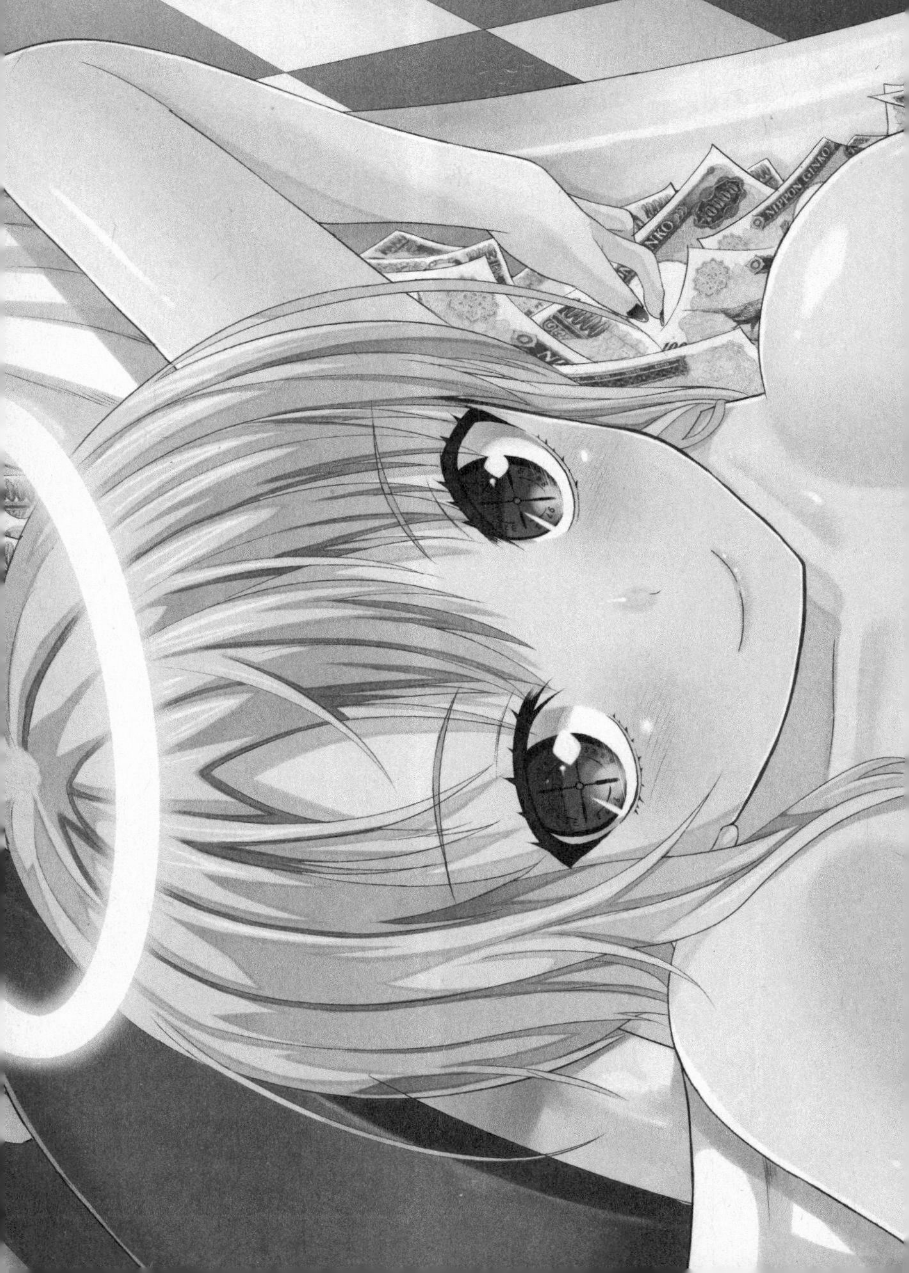

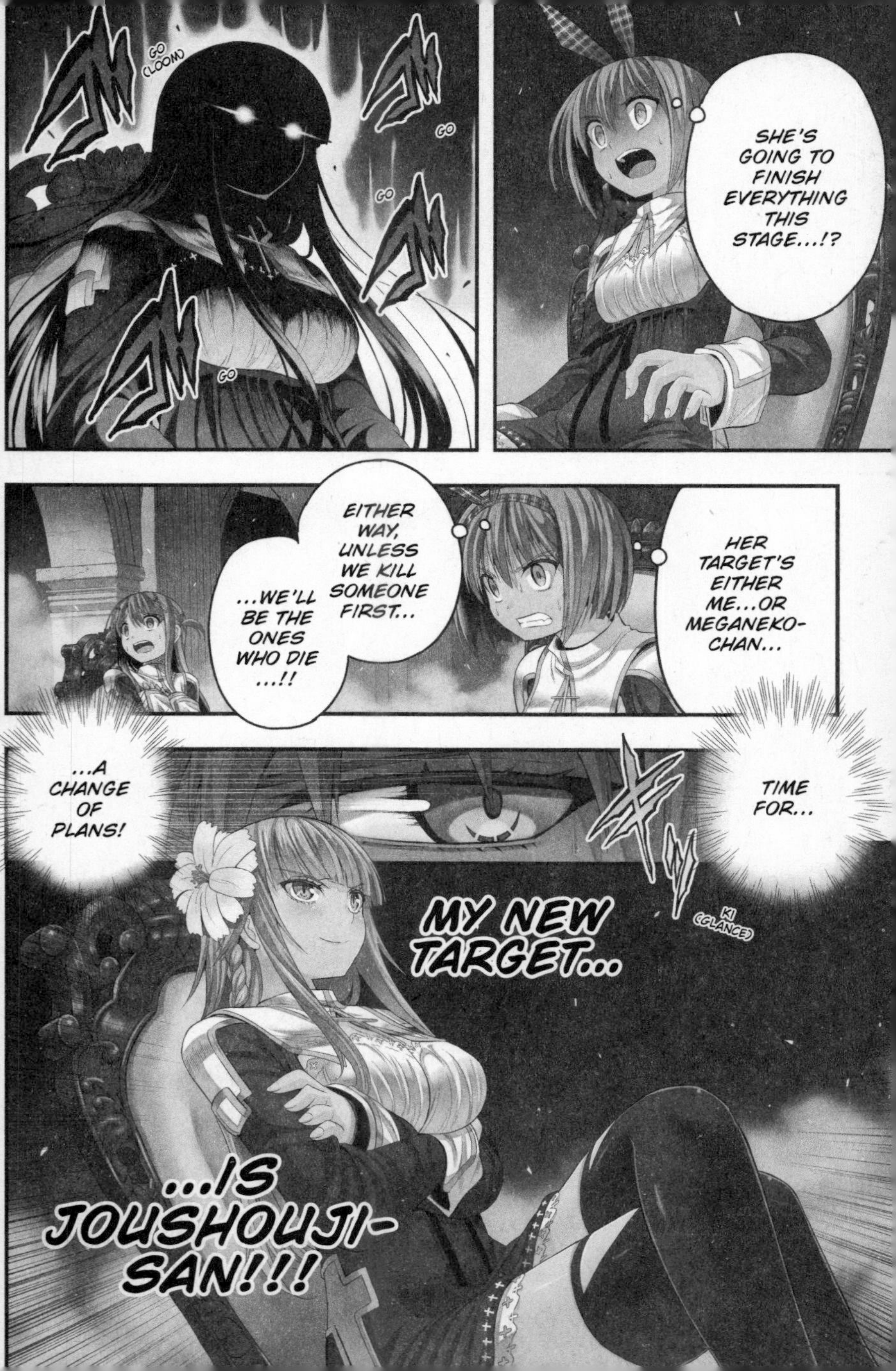
SHE'S GOING TO FINISH EVERYTHING THIS STAGE...!?
GO (LOOM)
GO
GO
GO
HER TARGET'S EITHER ME...OR MEGANEKO-CHAN...
EITHER WAY, UNLESS WE KILL SOMEONE FIRST...
...WE'LL BE THE ONES WHO DIE...!!
TIME FOR...
...A CHANGE OF PLANS!
KI (GLANCE)
MY NEW TARGET...
...IS JOUSHOUJI-SAN!!!

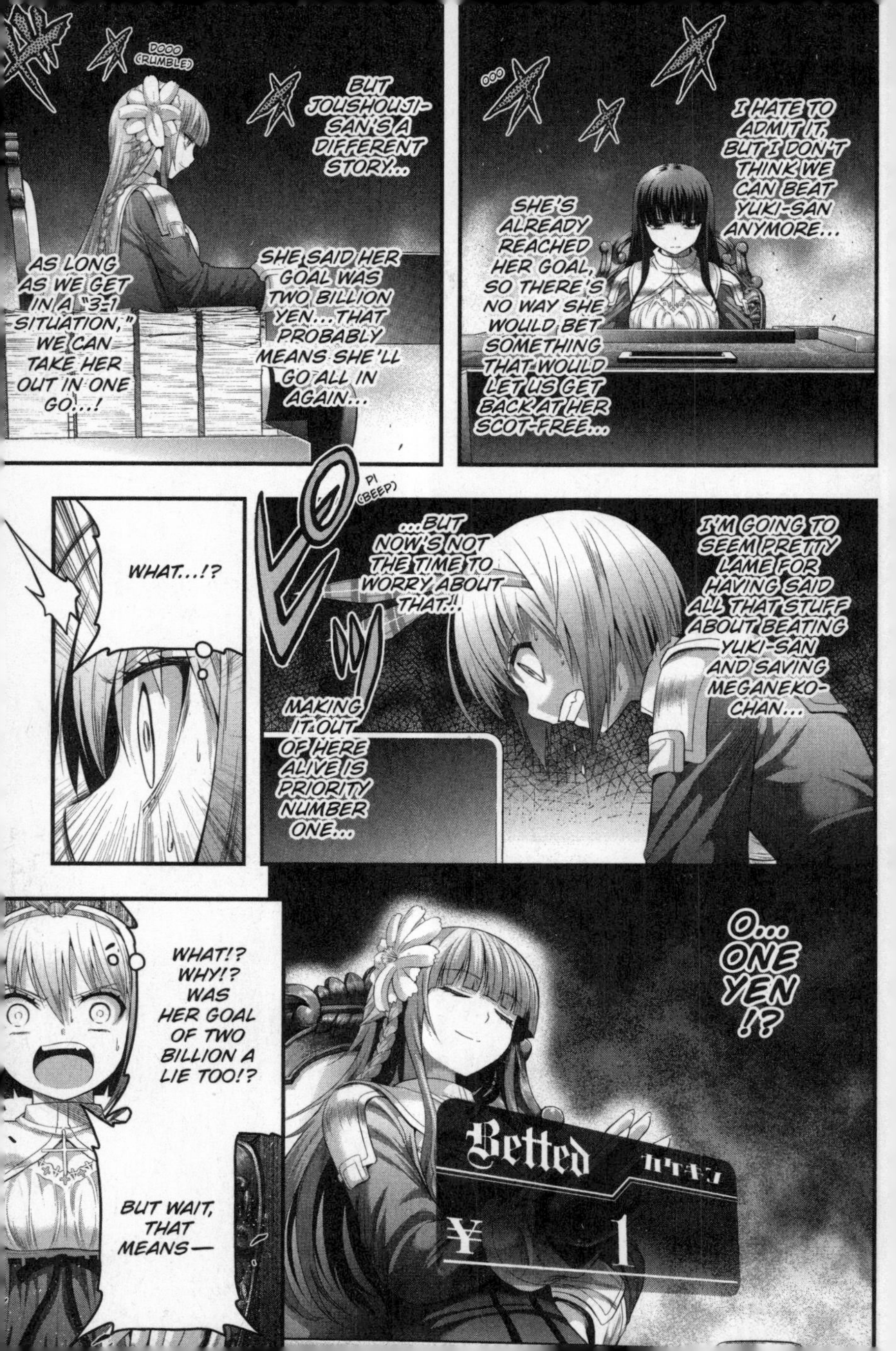
I HATE TO ADMIT IT, BUT I DON'T THINK WE CAN BEAT YUKI-SAN ANYMORE...
SHE'S ALREADY REACHED HER GOAL, SO THERE'S NO WAY SHE WOULD BET SOMETHING THAT WOULD LET US GET BACK AT HER SCOT-FREE...
DOOO (RUMBLE)
BUT JOUSHOUJI-SAN'S A DIFFERENT STORY...
SHE SAID HER GOAL WAS TWO BILLION YEN...THAT PROBABLY MEANS SHE'LL GO ALL IN AGAIN...
AS LONG AS WE GET IN A "3-1 SITUATION," WE CAN TAKE HER OUT IN ONE GO...!
I'M GOING TO SEEM PRETTY LAME FOR HAVING SAID ALL THAT STUFF ABOUT BEATING YUKI-SAN AND SAVING MEGANEKO-CHAN...
...BUT NOW'S NOT THE TIME TO WORRY ABOUT THAT!!
MAKING IT OUT OF HERE ALIVE IS PRIORITY NUMBER ONE...
PI (BEEP)
WHAT...!?
O... ONE YEN!?
Betted
¥ 1
WHAT!? WHY!? WAS HER GOAL OF TWO BILLION A LIE TOO!?
BUT WAIT, THAT MEANS—

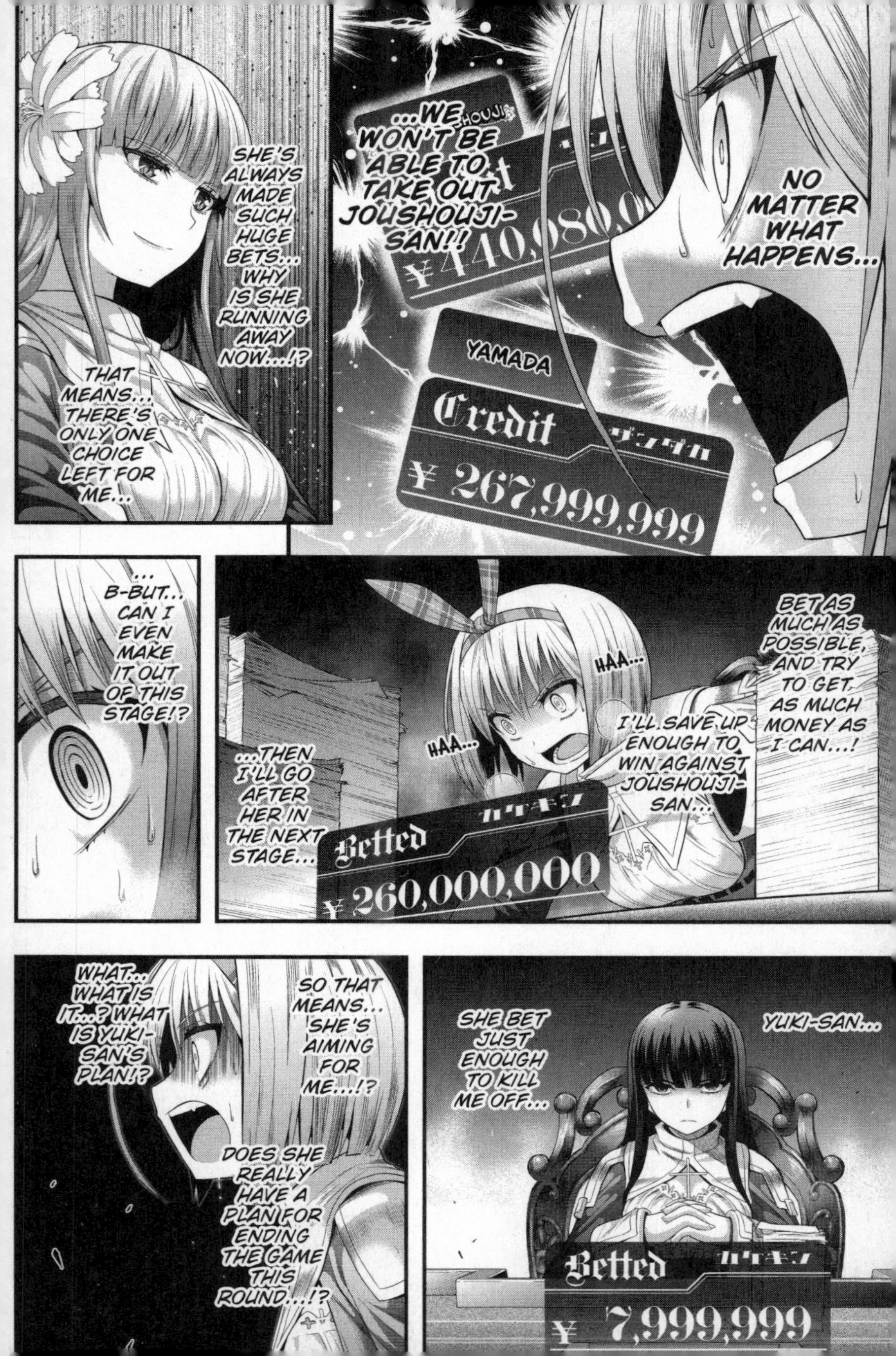
NO MATTER WHAT HAPPENS...
...WE WON'T BE ABLE TO TAKE OUT JOUSHOUJI-SAN!!
SHOUJI
YAMADA
Credit
¥ 267,999,999
SHE'S ALWAYS MADE SUCH HUGE BETS... WHY IS SHE RUNNING AWAY NOW...!?
THAT MEANS... THERE'S ONLY ONE CHOICE LEFT FOR ME...
BET AS MUCH AS POSSIBLE, AND TRY TO GET AS MUCH MONEY AS I CAN...!
HAA...
I'LL SAVE UP ENOUGH TO WIN AGAINST JOUSHOUJI-SAN...
HAA...
...THEN I'LL GO AFTER HER IN THE NEXT STAGE...
Betted
¥ 260,000,000
... B-BUT... CAN I EVEN MAKE IT OUT OF THIS STAGE!?
YUKI-SAN...
SHE BET JUST ENOUGH TO KILL ME OFF...
Betted
¥ 7,999,999
SO THAT MEANS... SHE'S AIMING FOR ME...!?
WHAT... WHAT IS IT...? WHAT IS YUKI-SAN'S PLAN!?
DOES SHE REALLY HAVE A PLAN FOR ENDING THE GAME THIS ROUND...!?

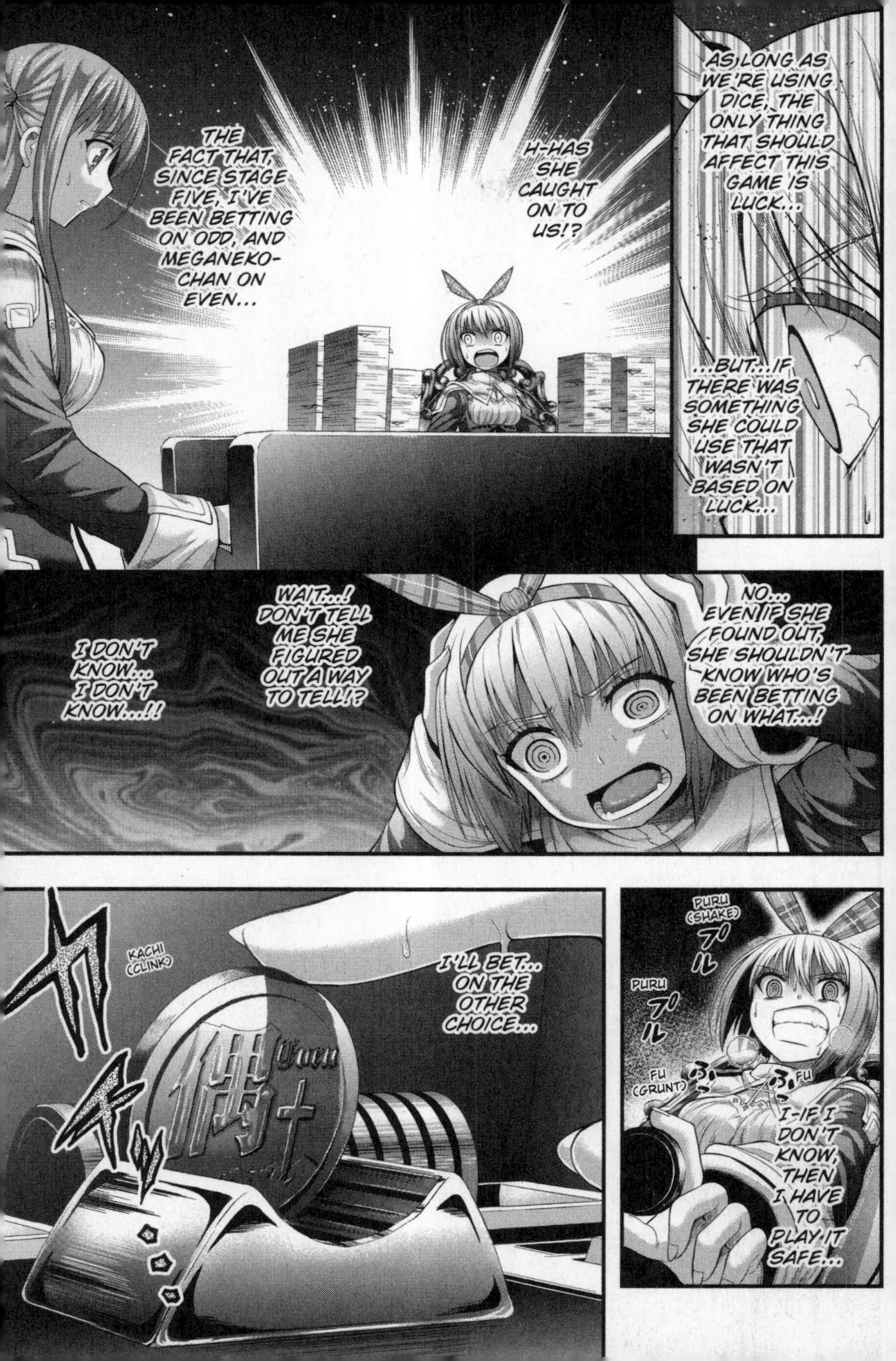
AS LONG AS WE'RE USING DICE, THE ONLY THING THAT SHOULD AFFECT THIS GAME IS LUCK...
...BUT...IF THERE WAS SOMETHING SHE COULD USE THAT WASN'T BASED ON LUCK...
H-HAS SHE CAUGHT ON TO US!?
THE FACT THAT, SINCE STAGE FIVE, I'VE BEEN BETTING ON ODD, AND MEGANEKO-CHAN ON EVEN...
NO... EVEN IF SHE FOUND OUT, SHE SHOULDN'T KNOW WHO'S BEEN BETTING ON WHAT...!
WAIT...! DON'T TELL ME SHE FIGURED OUT A WAY TO TELL!?
I DON'T KNOW... I DON'T KNOW...!!
PURU (SHAKE)
プル
PURU
プル
FU (GRUNT)
ふ
FU
ふ
I-IF I DON'T KNOW, THEN I HAVE TO PLAY IT SAFE...
I'LL BET... ON THE OTHER CHOICE...
KACHI (CLINK)

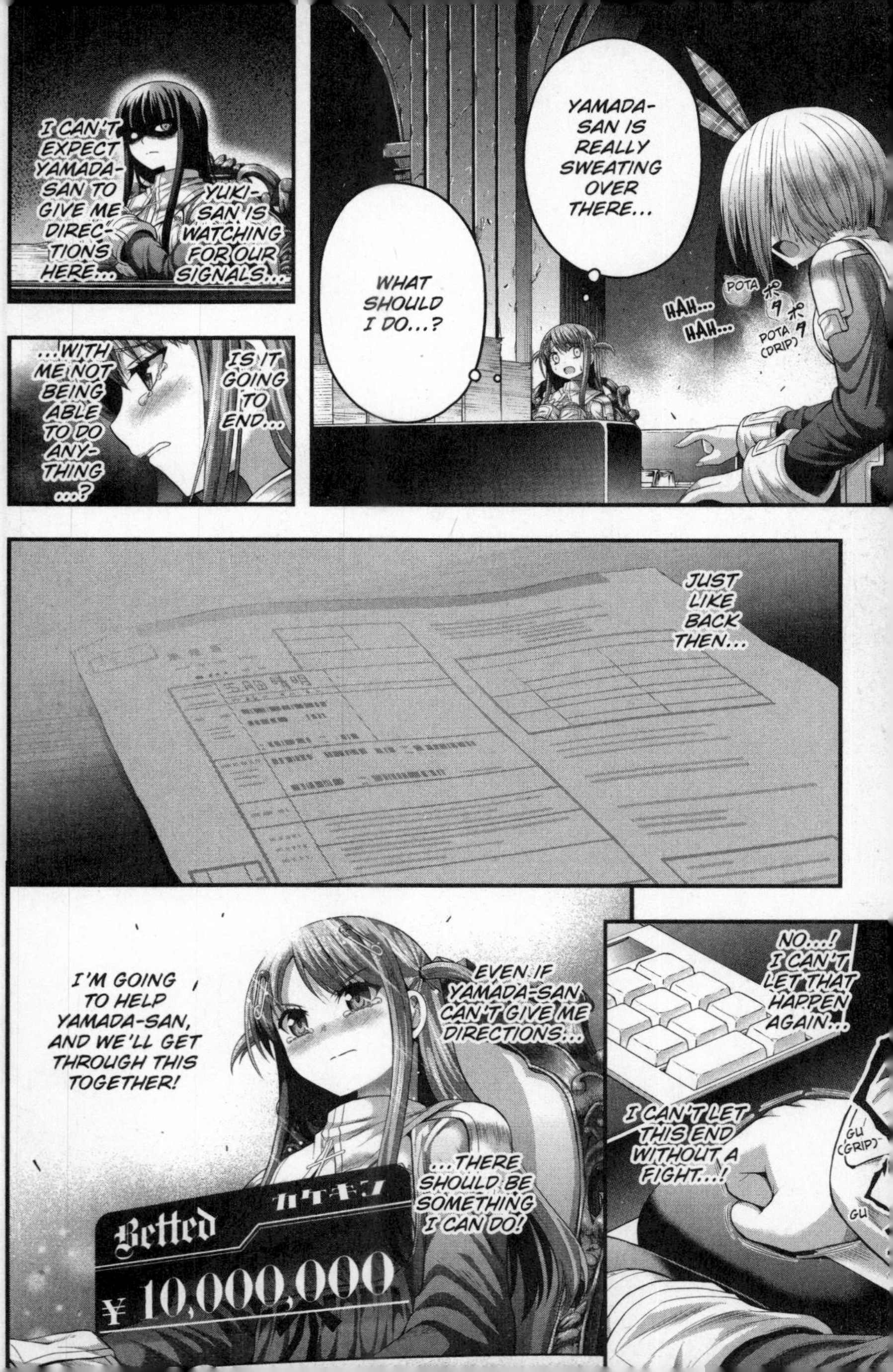
YAMADA-SAN IS REALLY SWEATING OVER THERE...
POTA ポ タ
POTA ポ タ (DRIP)
HAH... HAH...
WHAT SHOULD I DO...?
YUKI-SAN IS WATCHING FOR OUR SIGNALS...
I CAN'T EXPECT YAMADA-SAN TO GIVE ME DIRECTIONS HERE...
IS IT GOING TO END...
...WITH ME NOT BEING ABLE TO DO ANYTHING...?
JUST LIKE BACK THEN...
NO...! I CAN'T LET THAT HAPPEN AGAIN...
I CAN'T LET THIS END WITHOUT A FIGHT...!
GU (GRIP)
GU
EVEN IF YAMADA-SAN CAN'T GIVE ME DIRECTIONS...
...THERE SHOULD BE SOMETHING I CAN DO!
I'M GOING TO HELP YAMADA-SAN, AND WE'LL GET THROUGH THIS TOGETHER!
Betted
¥ 10,000,000

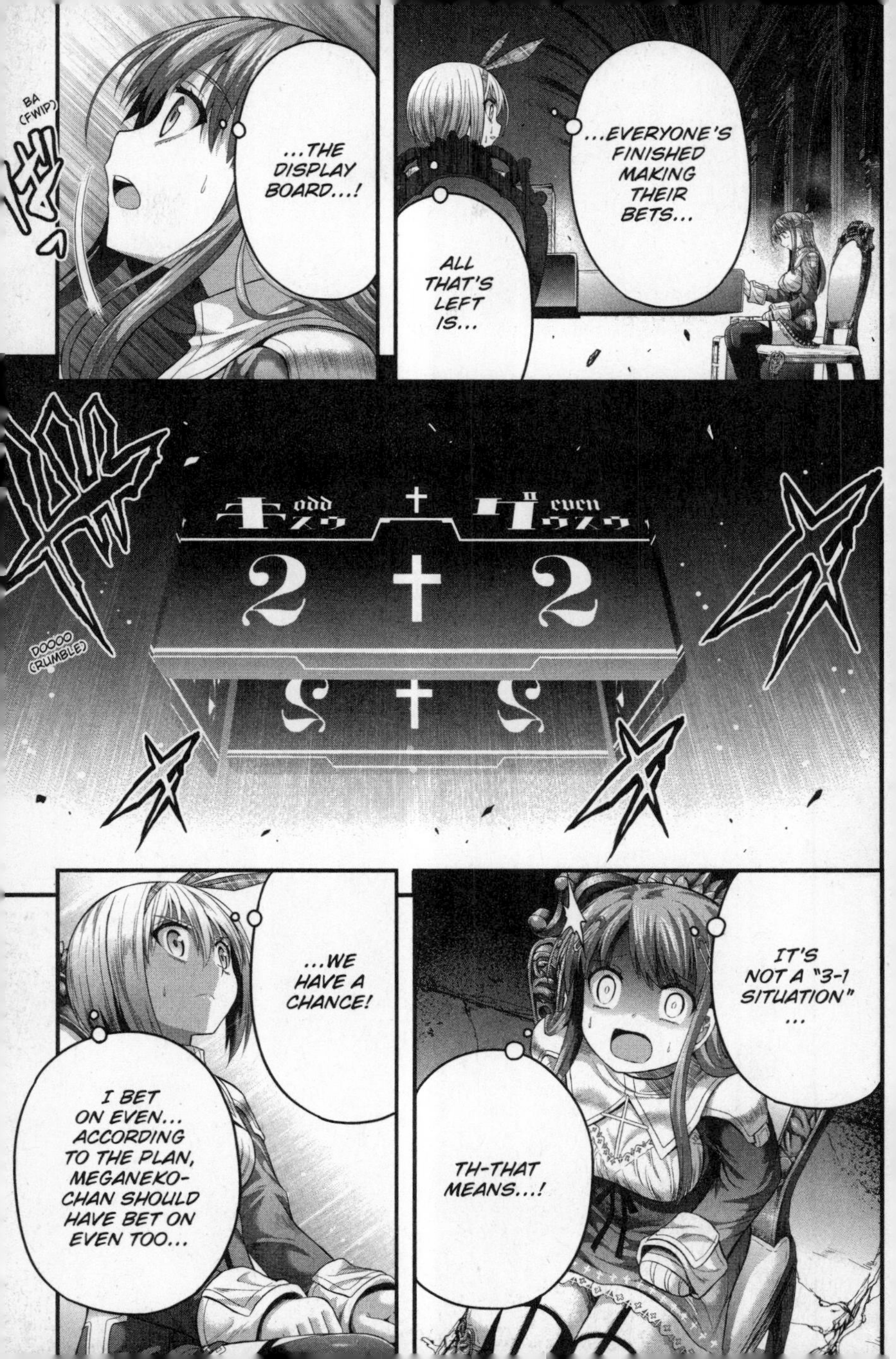
...EVERYONE'S FINISHED MAKING THEIR BETS...
ALL THAT'S LEFT IS...
BA (FWIP)
...THE DISPLAY BOARD...!
DOOOO (RUMBLE)
odd
even
2
2
IT'S NOT A "3-1 SITUATION" ...
TH-THAT MEANS...!
...WE HAVE A CHANCE!
I BET ON EVEN... ACCORDING TO THE PLAN, MEGANEKO-CHAN SHOULD HAVE BET ON EVEN TOO...

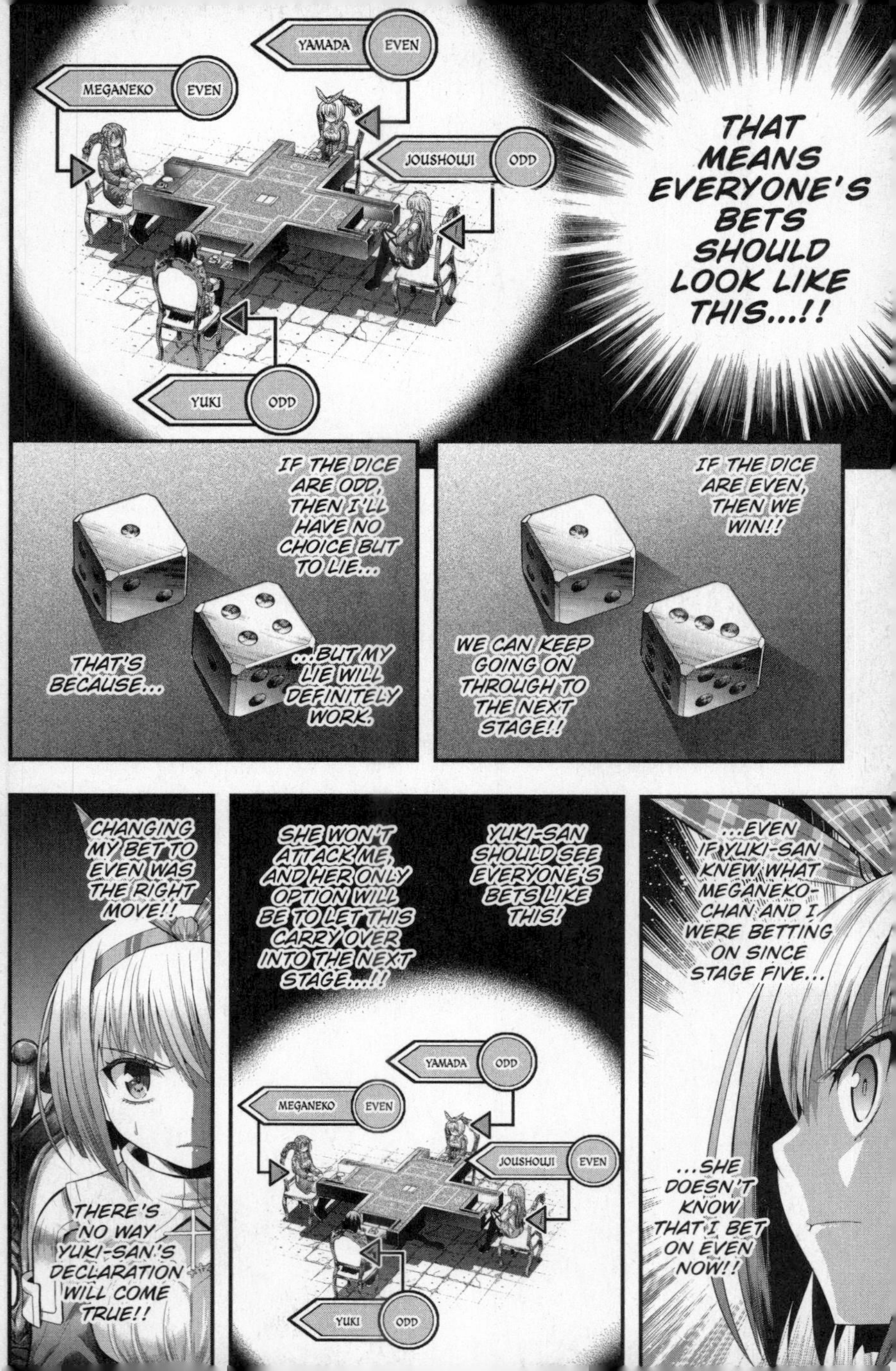

THAT MEANS EVERYONE'S BETS SHOULD LOOK LIKE THIS...!!
YAMADA EVEN
MEGANEKO EVEN
JOUSHOUJI ODD
YUKI ODD
IF THE DICE ARE EVEN, THEN WE WIN!!
WE CAN KEEP GOING ON THROUGH TO THE NEXT STAGE!!
IF THE DICE ARE ODD, THEN I'LL HAVE NO CHOICE BUT TO LIE...
...BUT MY LIE WILL DEFINITELY WORK.
THAT'S BECAUSE...
...EVEN IF YUKI-SAN KNEW WHAT MEGANEKO-CHAN AND I WERE BETTING ON SINCE STAGE FIVE...
...SHE DOESN'T KNOW THAT I BET ON EVEN NOW!!
YUKI-SAN SHOULD SEE EVERYONE'S BETS LIKE THIS!
SHE WON'T ATTACK ME, AND HER ONLY OPTION WILL BE TO LET THIS CARRY OVER INTO THE NEXT STAGE...!!
YAMADA ODD
MEGANEKO EVEN
JOUSHOUJI EVEN
YUKI ODD
CHANGING MY BET TO EVEN WAS THE RIGHT MOVE!!
THERE'S NO WAY YUKI-SAN'S DECLARATION WILL COME TRUE!!

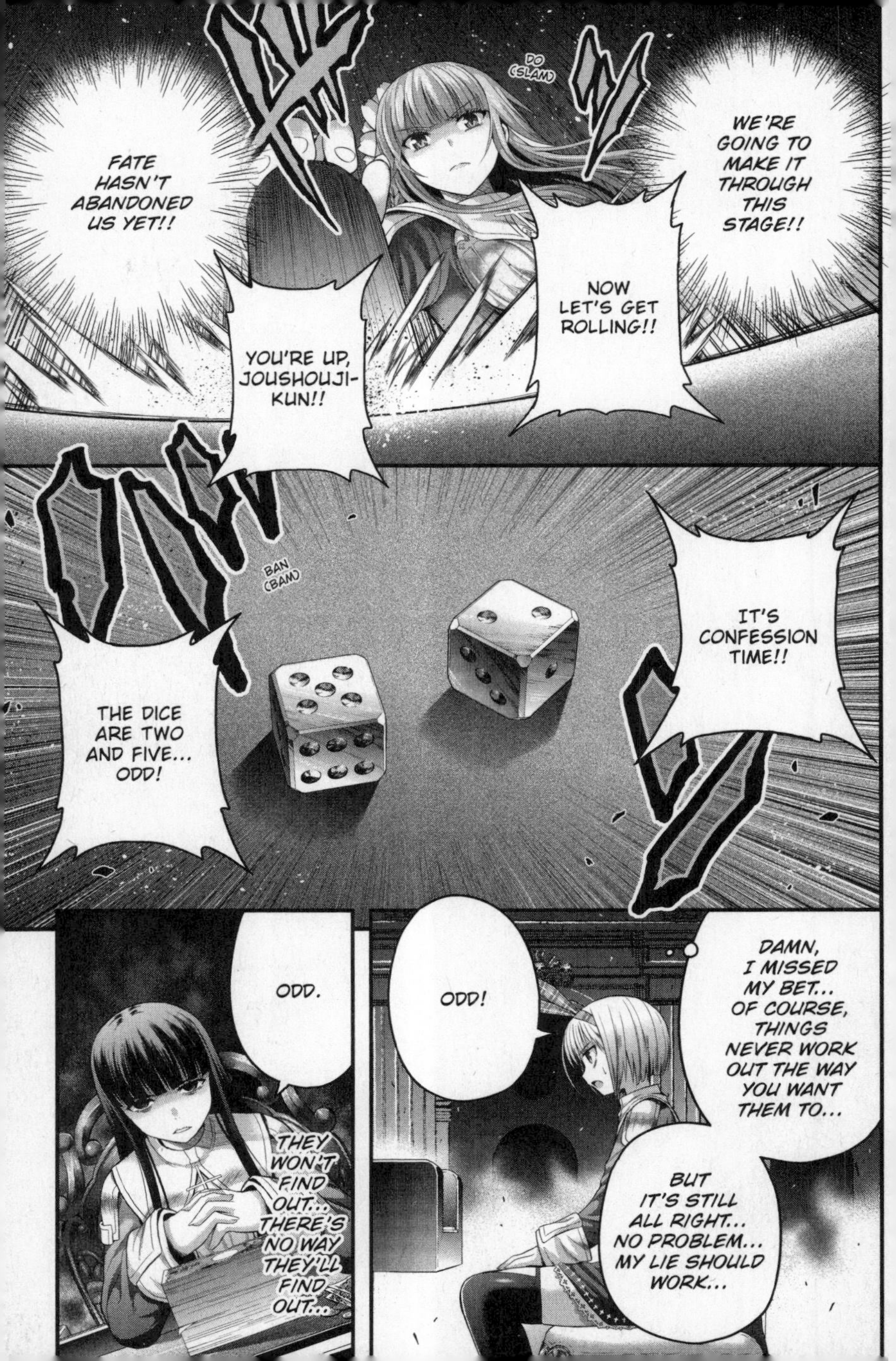
WE'RE GOING TO MAKE IT THROUGH THIS STAGE!!
DO (SLAM)
FATE HASN'T ABANDONED US YET!!
NOW LET'S GET ROLLING!!
YOU'RE UP, JOUSHOUJI-KUN!!
IT'S CONFESSION TIME!!
BAN (BAM)
THE DICE ARE TWO AND FIVE... ODD!
DAMN, I MISSED MY BET... OF COURSE, THINGS NEVER WORK OUT THE WAY YOU WANT THEM TO...
ODD!
BUT IT'S STILL ALL RIGHT... NO PROBLEM... MY LIE SHOULD WORK...
ODD.
THEY WON'T FIND OUT... THERE'S NO WAY THEY'LL FIND OUT...

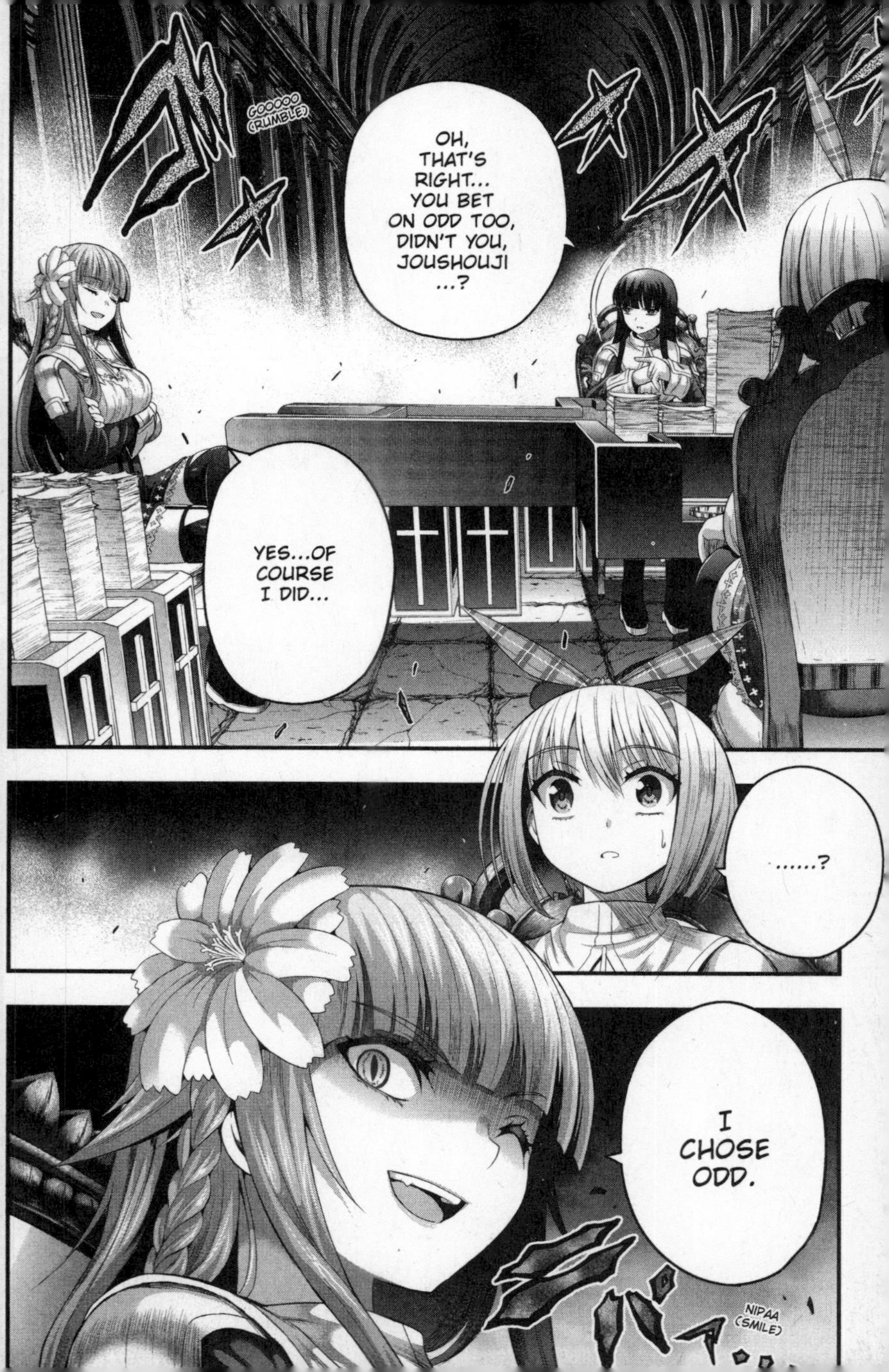
OH, THAT'S RIGHT... YOU BET ON ODD TOO, DIDN'T YOU, JOUSHOUJI ...?
GOOOOO (RUMBLE)
YES...OF COURSE I DID...
......?
I CHOSE ODD.
NIPAA (SMILE)

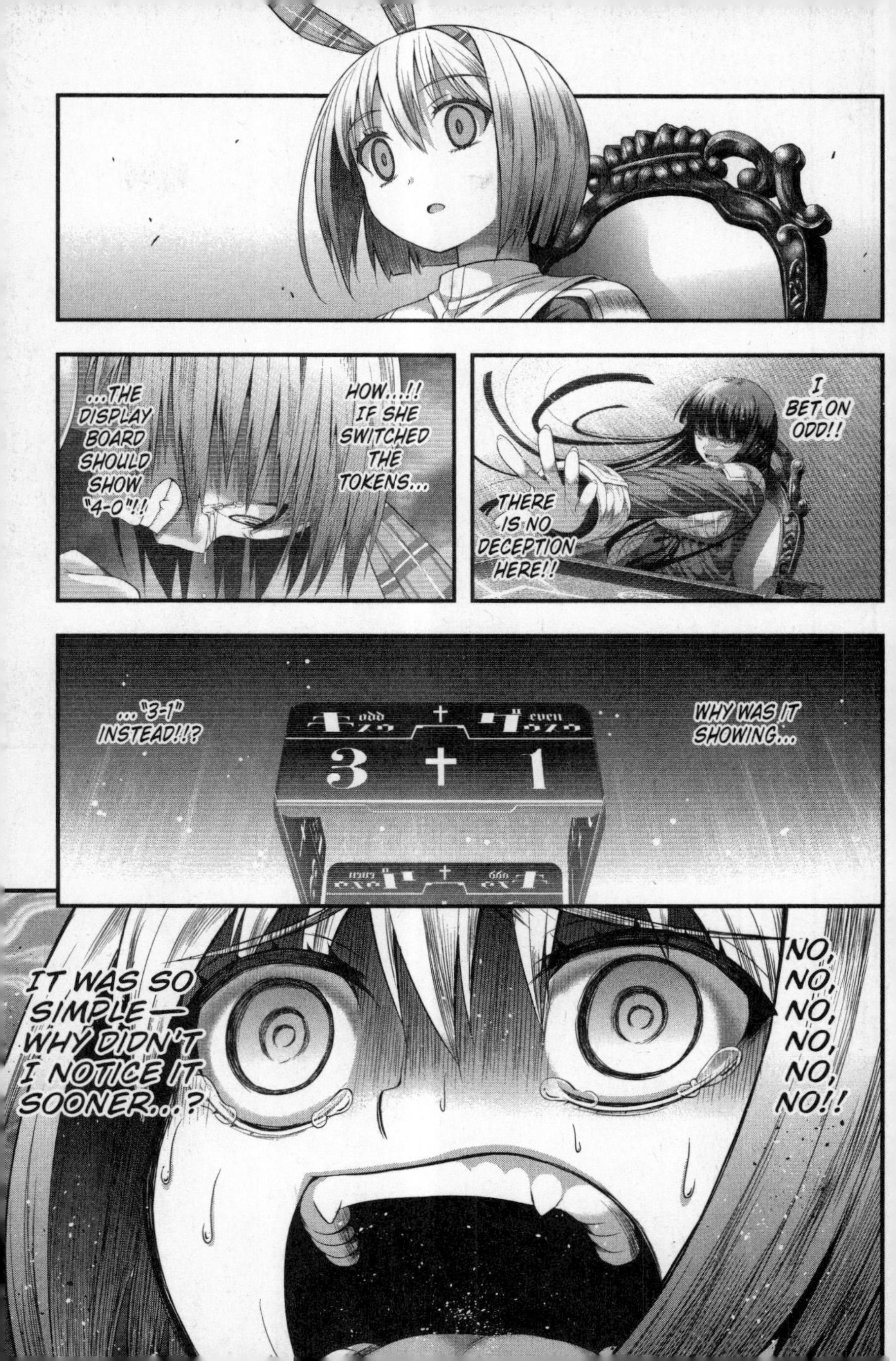

I BET ON ODD!!
THERE IS NO DECEPTION HERE!!
HOW...!! IF SHE SWITCHED THE TOKENS...
...THE DISPLAY BOARD SHOULD SHOW "4-0"!!
WHY WAS IT SHOWING...
odd † even
3 † 1
..."3-1" INSTEAD!!?
NO, NO, NO, NO, NO, NO!!
IT WAS SO SIMPLE—WHY DIDN'T I NOTICE IT SOONER...?

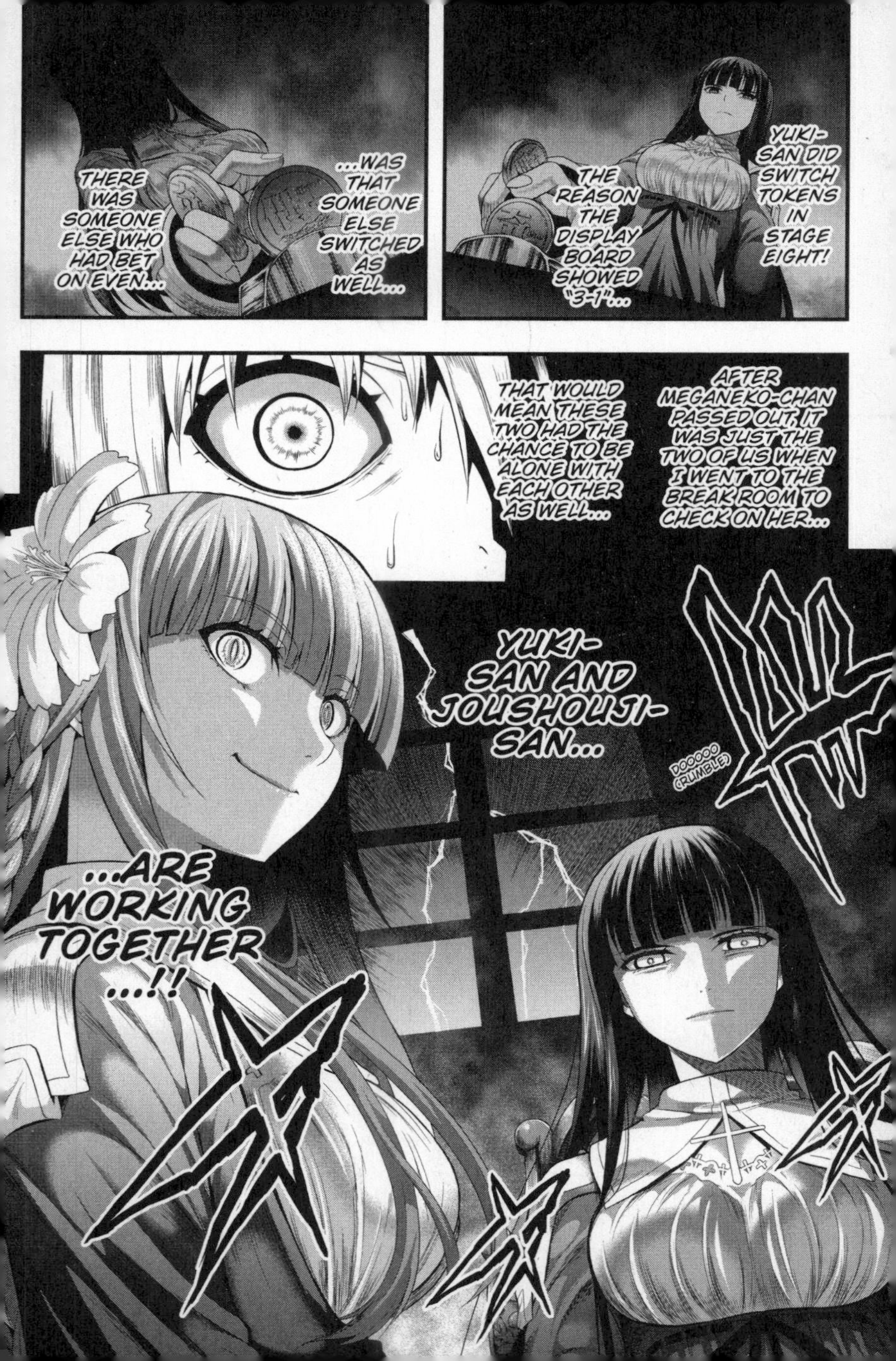
YUKI-SAN DID SWITCH TOKENS IN STAGE EIGHT!
THE REASON THE DISPLAY BOARD SHOWED "3-1"...
...WAS THAT SOMEONE ELSE SWITCHED AS WELL...
THERE WAS SOMEONE ELSE WHO HAD BET ON EVEN...
AFTER MEGANEKO-CHAN PASSED OUT, IT WAS JUST THE TWO OF US WHEN I WENT TO THE BREAK ROOM TO CHECK ON HER...
THAT WOULD MEAN THESE TWO HAD THE CHANCE TO BE ALONE WITH EACH OTHER AS WELL...
YUKI-SAN AND JOUSHOUJI-SAN...
DOOOOO (RUMBLE)
...ARE WORKING TOGETHER ...!!

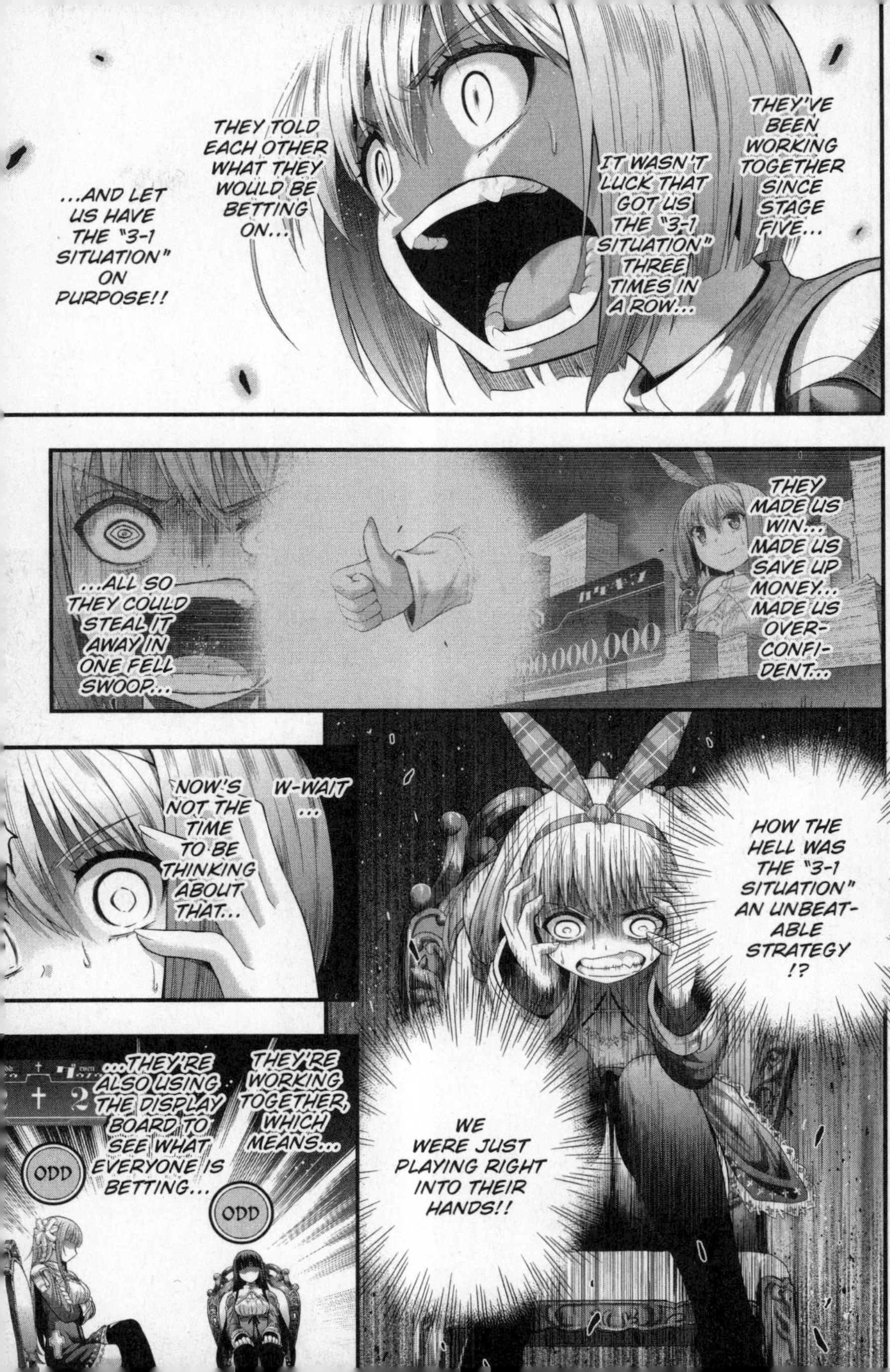

THEY'VE BEEN WORKING TOGETHER SINCE STAGE FIVE...
IT WASN'T LUCK THAT GOT US THE "3-1 SITUATION" THREE TIMES IN A ROW...
THEY TOLD EACH OTHER WHAT THEY WOULD BE BETTING ON...
...AND LET US HAVE THE "3-1 SITUATION" ON PURPOSE!!
THEY MADE US WIN... MADE US SAVE UP MONEY... MADE US OVER-CONFI-DENT...
...ALL SO THEY COULD STEAL IT AWAY IN ONE FELL SWOOP...
HOW THE HELL WAS THE "3-1 SITUATION" AN UNBEAT-ABLE STRATEGY!?
WE WERE JUST PLAYING RIGHT INTO THEIR HANDS!!
W-WAIT...
NOW'S NOT THE TIME TO BE THINKING ABOUT THAT...
THEY'RE WORKING TOGETHER, WHICH MEANS...
...THEY'RE ALSO USING THE DISPLAY BOARD TO SEE WHAT EVERYONE IS BETTING...
ODD
ODD

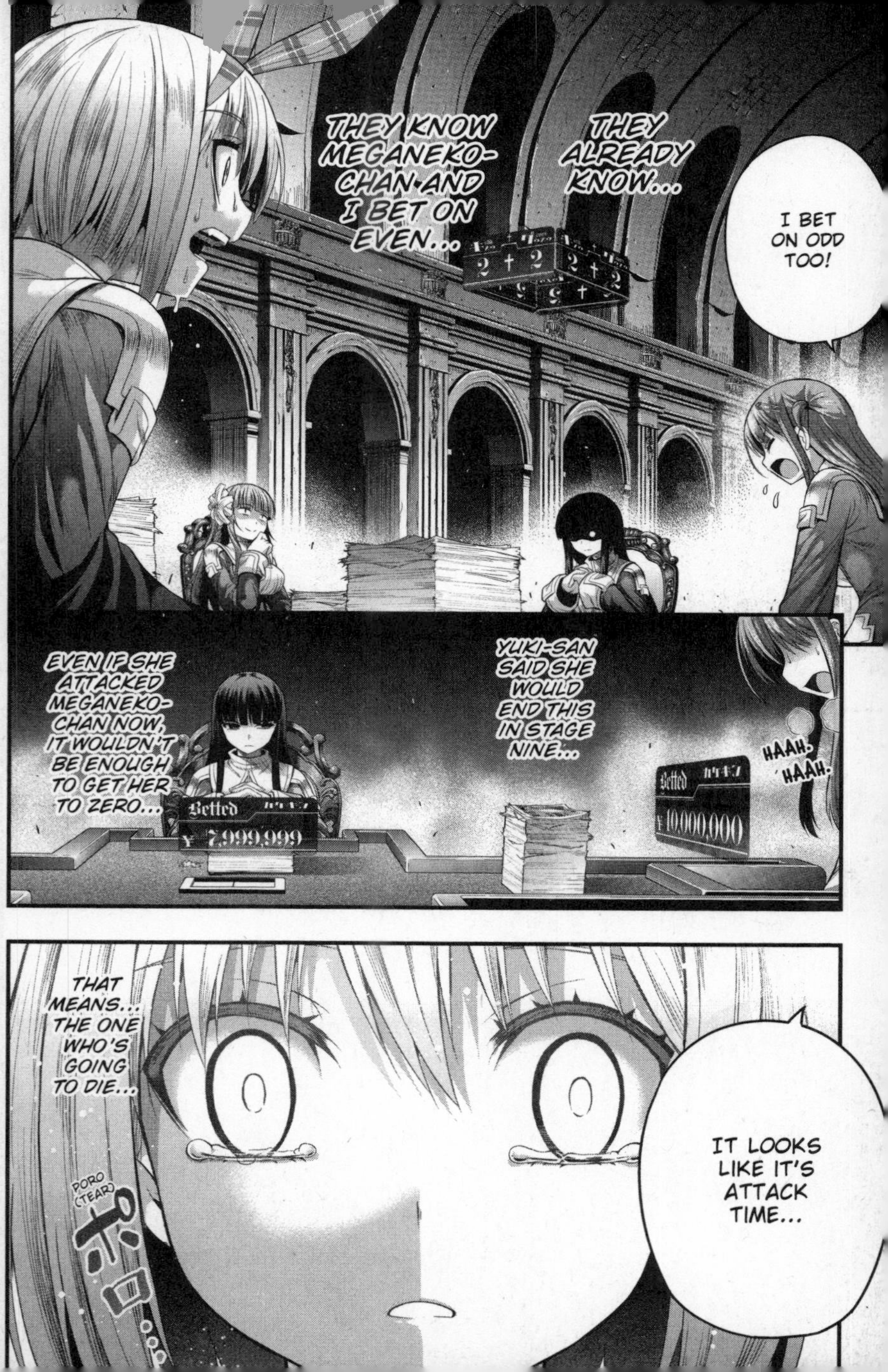
I BET ON ODD TOO!
THEY ALREADY KNOW...
THEY KNOW MEGANEKO-CHAN AND I BET ON EVEN...
HAAH. HAAH.
Betted ¥10,000,000
YUKI-SAN SAID SHE WOULD END THIS IN STAGE NINE...
EVEN IF SHE ATTACKED MEGANEKO-CHAN NOW, IT WOULDN'T BE ENOUGH TO GET HER TO ZERO...
Betted ¥7,999,999
IT LOOKS LIKE IT'S ATTACK TIME...
THAT MEANS... THE ONE WHO'S GOING TO DIE...
PORO (TEAR)

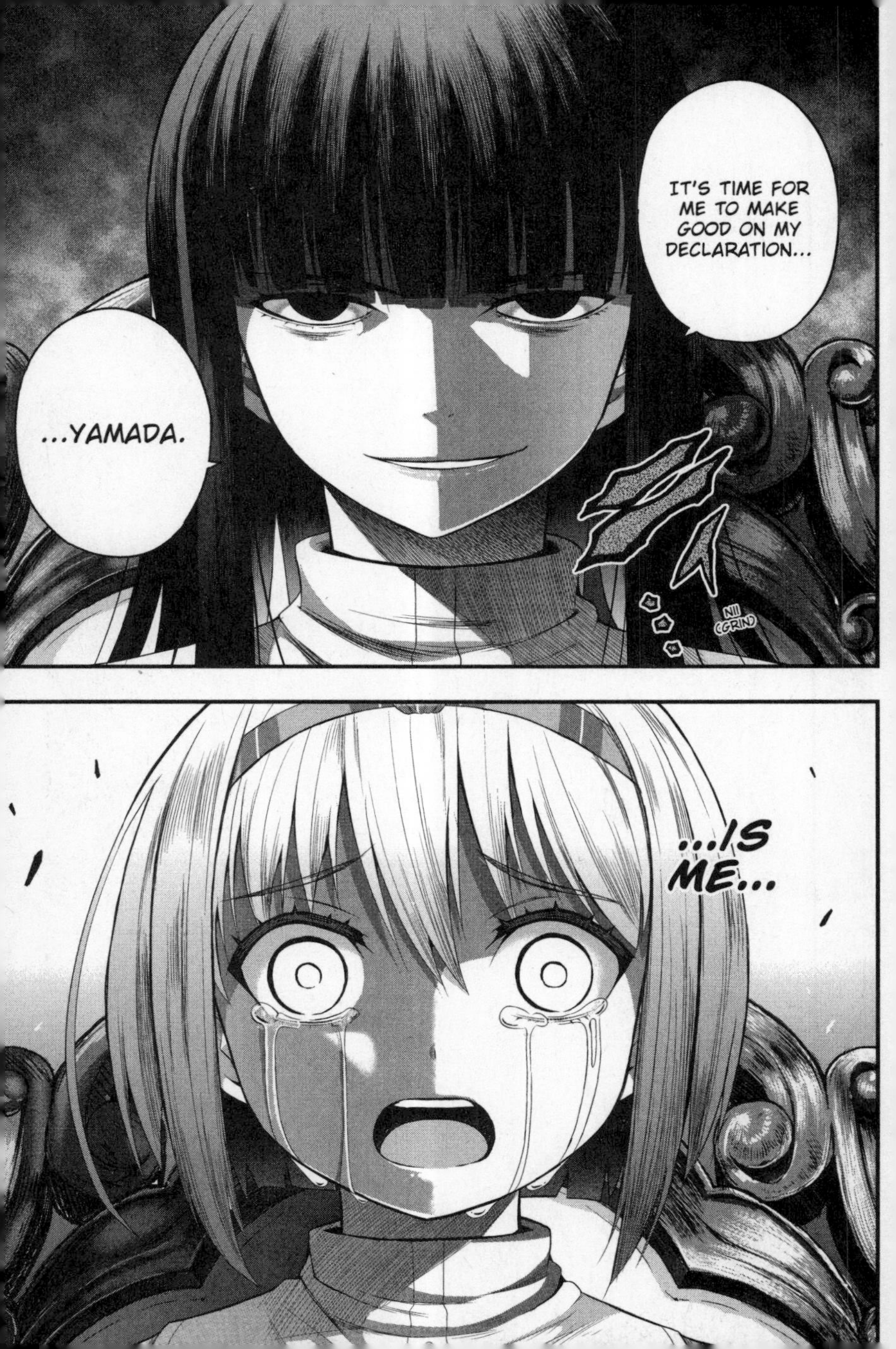
IT'S TIME FOR ME TO MAKE GOOD ON MY DECLARATION...
NII (GRIN)
...YAMADA.
...IS ME...

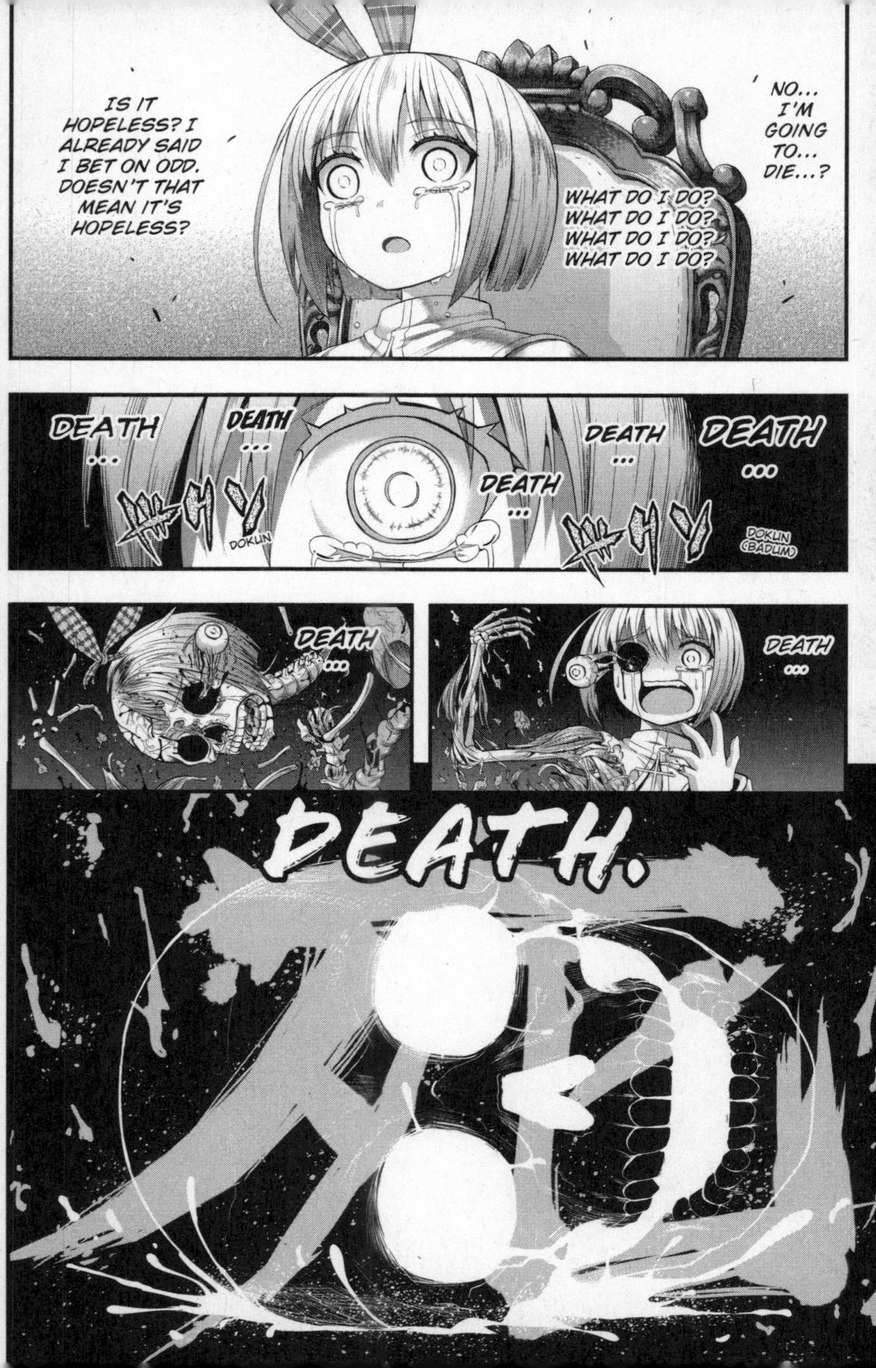
NO... I'M GOING TO... DIE...?
WHAT DO I DO? WHAT DO I DO? WHAT DO I DO? WHAT DO I DO?
IS IT HOPELESS? I ALREADY SAID I BET ON ODD. DOESN'T THAT MEAN IT'S HOPELESS?
DEATH ...
DOKUN (BADUM)
DEATH ...
DEATH ...
DEATH ...
DEATH ...
DOKUN
DEATH ...
DEATH ...
DEATH.

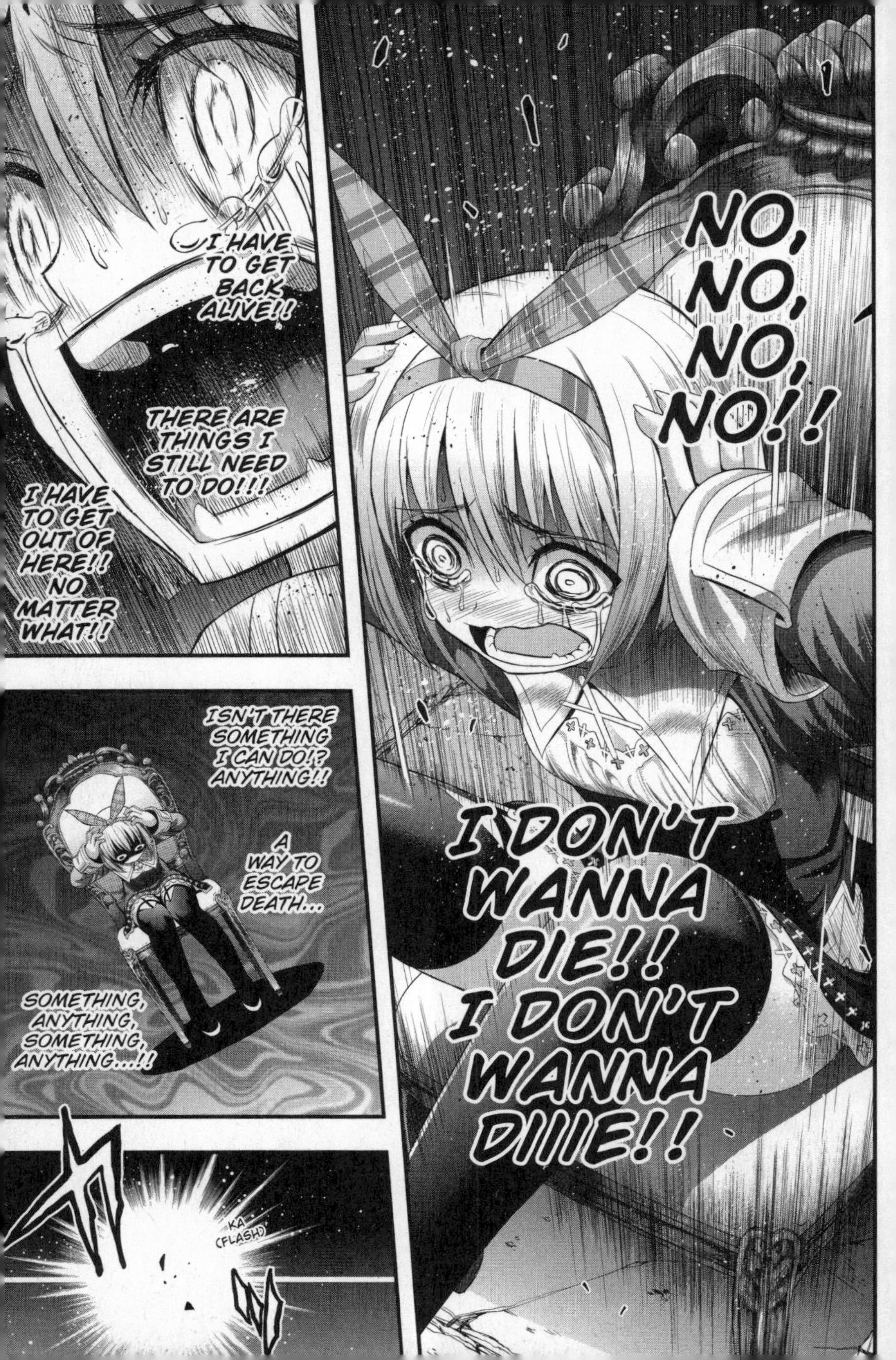
NO, NO, NO, NO!!
I DON'T WANNA DIE!! I DON'T WANNA DIIIE!!
I HAVE TO GET BACK ALIVE!!
THERE ARE THINGS I STILL NEED TO DO!!!
I HAVE TO GET OUT OF HERE!! NO MATTER WHAT!!
ISN'T THERE SOMETHING I CAN DO!? ANYTHING!!
A WAY TO ESCAPE DEATH...
SOMETHING, ANYTHING, SOMETHING, ANYTHING...!!
KA (FLASH)

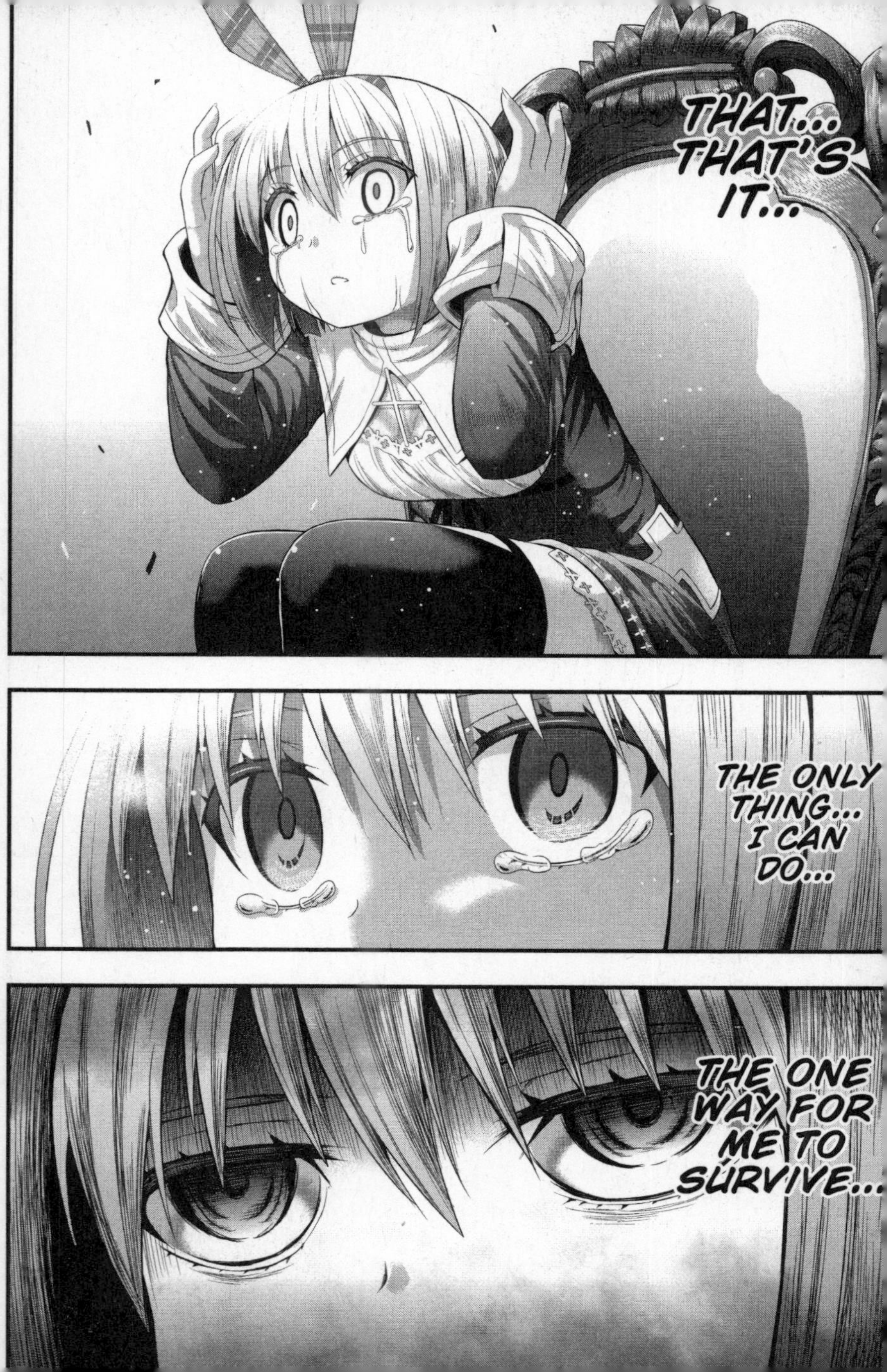
THAT... THAT'S IT...
THE ONLY THING... I CAN DO...
THE ONE WAY FOR ME TO SURVIVE...

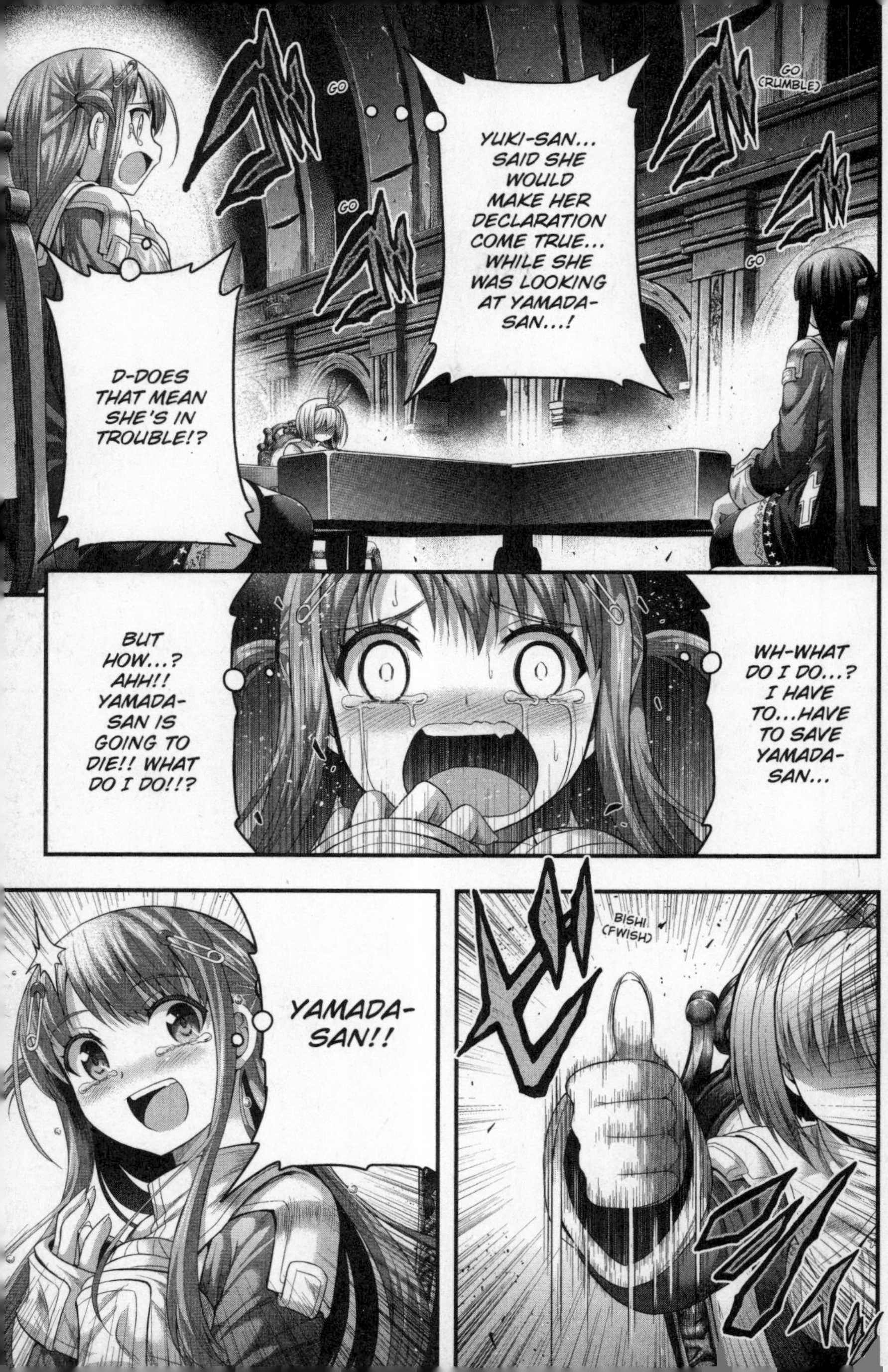
GO (RUMBLE)
GO
YUKI-SAN... SAID SHE WOULD MAKE HER DECLARATION COME TRUE... WHILE SHE WAS LOOKING AT YAMADA-SAN...!
GO
GO
D-DOES THAT MEAN SHE'S IN TROUBLE!?
WH-WHAT DO I DO...? I HAVE TO...HAVE TO SAVE YAMADA-SAN...
BUT HOW...? AHH!! YAMADA-SAN IS GOING TO DIE!! WHAT DO I DO!!?
BISHI (FWISH)
YAMADA-SAN!!

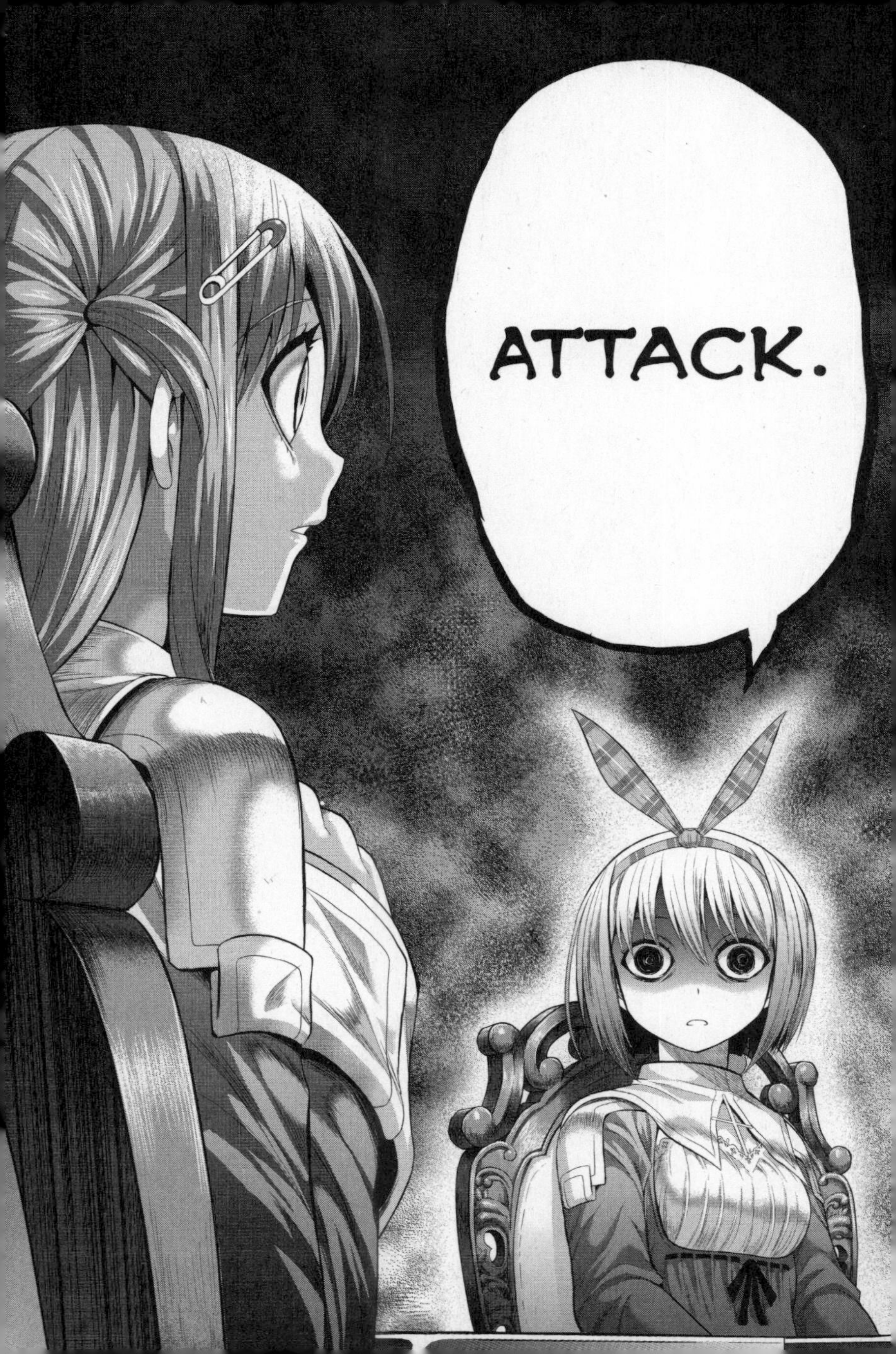
ATTACK.

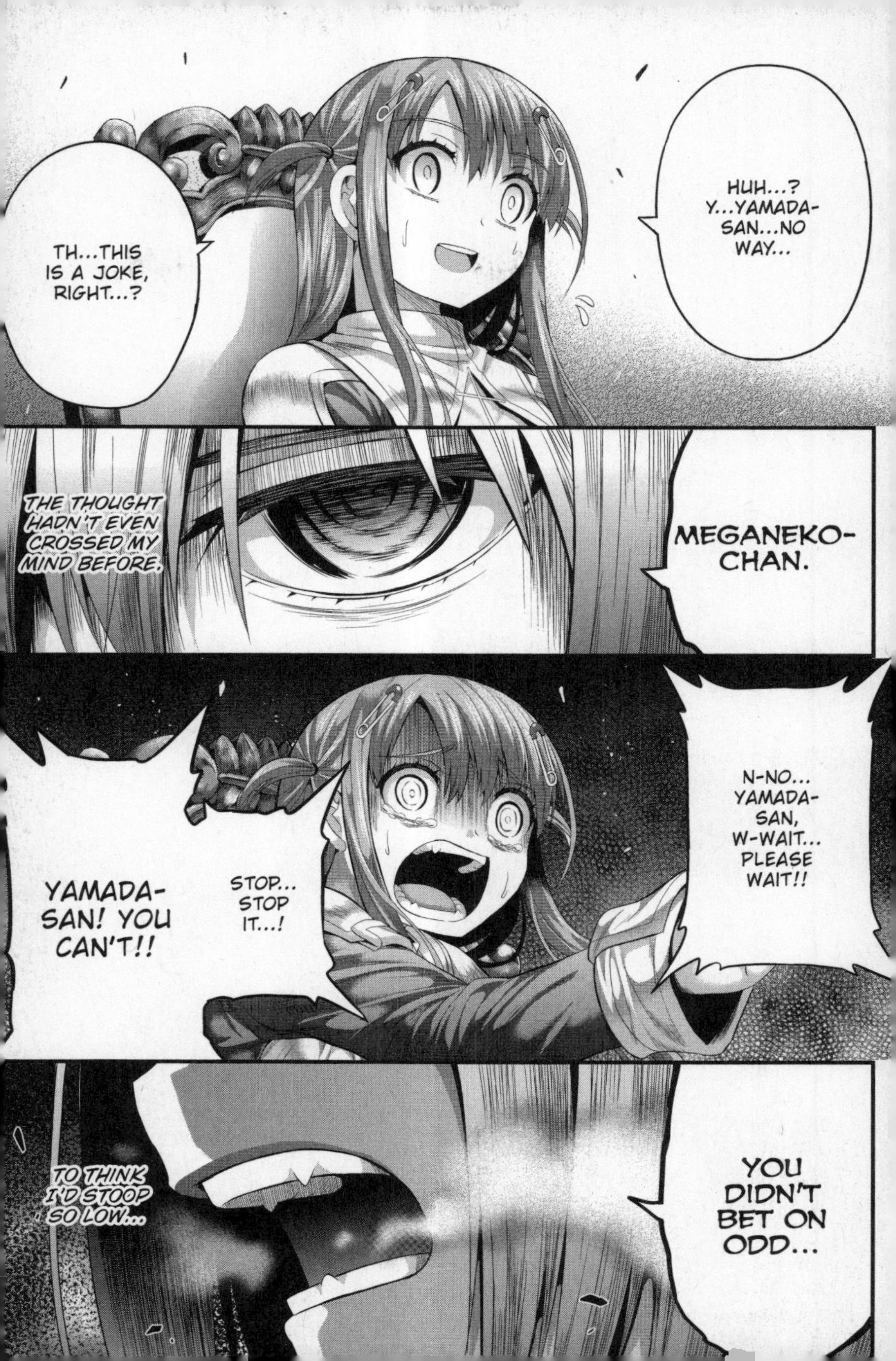

HUH...? Y...YAMADA-SAN...NO WAY...
TH...THIS IS A JOKE, RIGHT...?
MEGANEKO-CHAN.
THE THOUGHT HADN'T EVEN CROSSED MY MIND BEFORE.
N-NO... YAMADA-SAN, W-WAIT... PLEASE WAIT!!
STOP... STOP IT...!
YAMADA-SAN! YOU CAN'T!!
YOU DIDN'T BET ON ODD...
TO THINK I'D STOOP SO LOW...

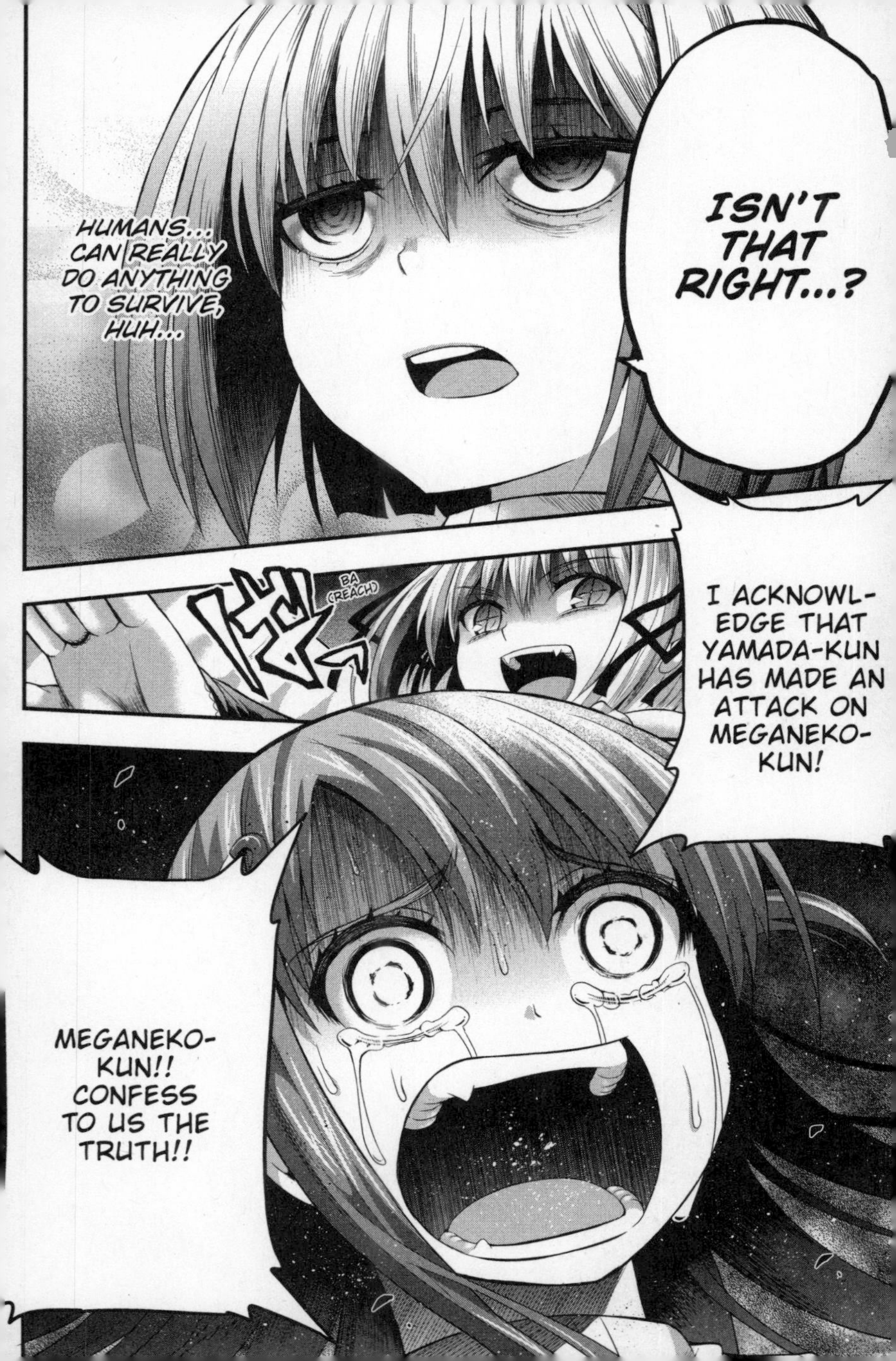
ISN'T THAT RIGHT...?
HUMANS... CAN REALLY DO ANYTHING TO SURVIVE, HUH...
I ACKNOWL-EDGE THAT YAMADA-KUN HAS MADE AN ATTACK ON MEGANEKO-KUN!
BA (REACH)
MEGANEKO-KUN!! CONFESS TO US THE TRUTH!!

Though You May Burn to Ash

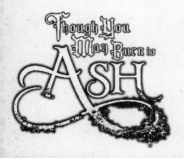

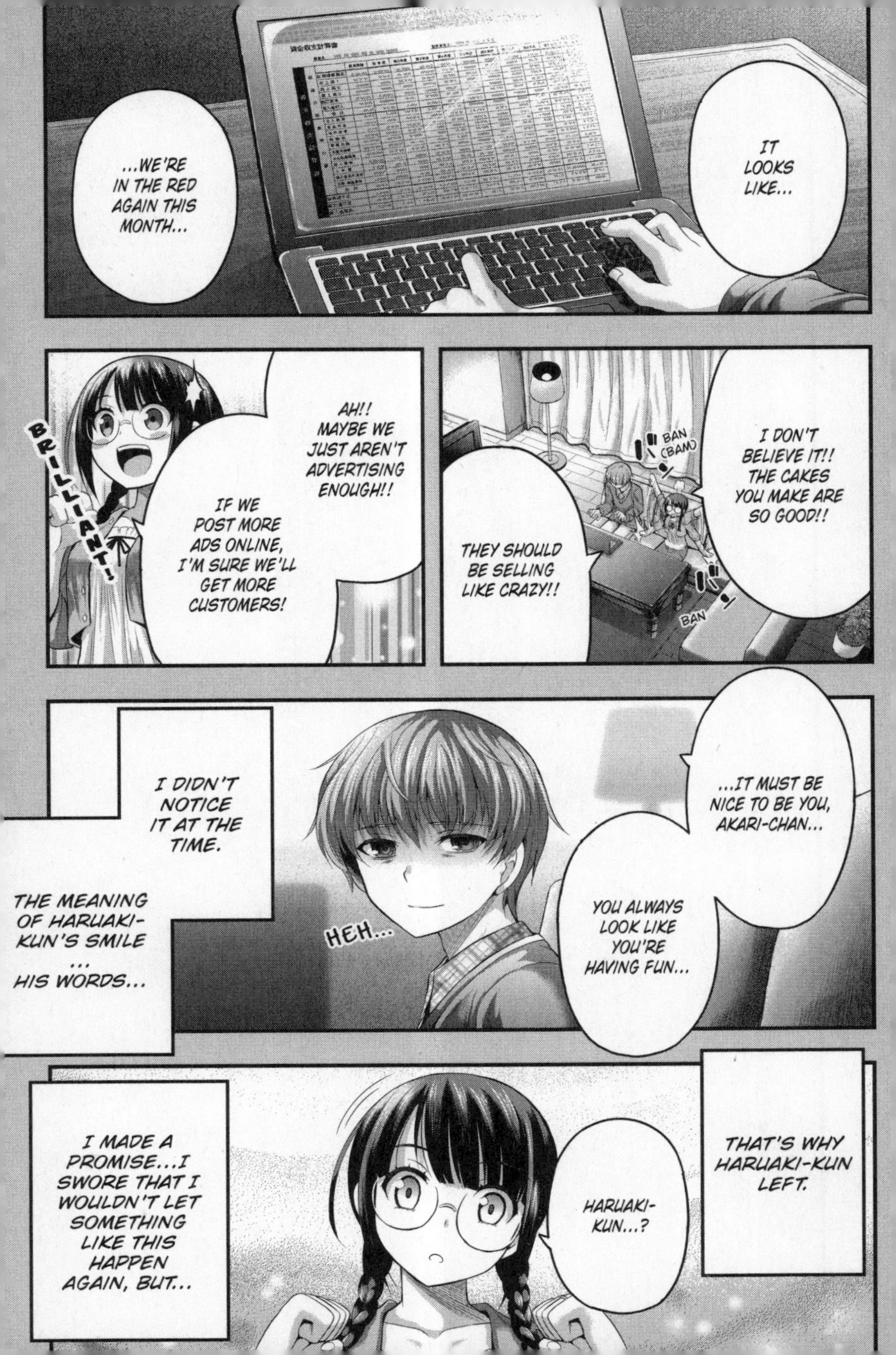
IT LOOKS LIKE...
...WE'RE IN THE RED AGAIN THIS MONTH...
BAN (BAM)
I DON'T BELIEVE IT!! THE CAKES YOU MAKE ARE SO GOOD!!
THEY SHOULD BE SELLING LIKE CRAZY!!
BAN
BRILLIANT!
AH!! MAYBE WE JUST AREN'T ADVERTISING ENOUGH!!
IF WE POST MORE ADS ONLINE, I'M SURE WE'LL GET MORE CUSTOMERS!
...IT MUST BE NICE TO BE YOU, AKARI-CHAN...
YOU ALWAYS LOOK LIKE YOU'RE HAVING FUN...
HEH...
I DIDN'T NOTICE IT AT THE TIME.
THE MEANING OF HARUAKI-KUN'S SMILE ... HIS WORDS...
THAT'S WHY HARUAKI-KUN LEFT.
HARUAKI-KUN...?
I MADE A PROMISE...I SWORE THAT I WOULDN'T LET SOMETHING LIKE THIS HAPPEN AGAIN, BUT...

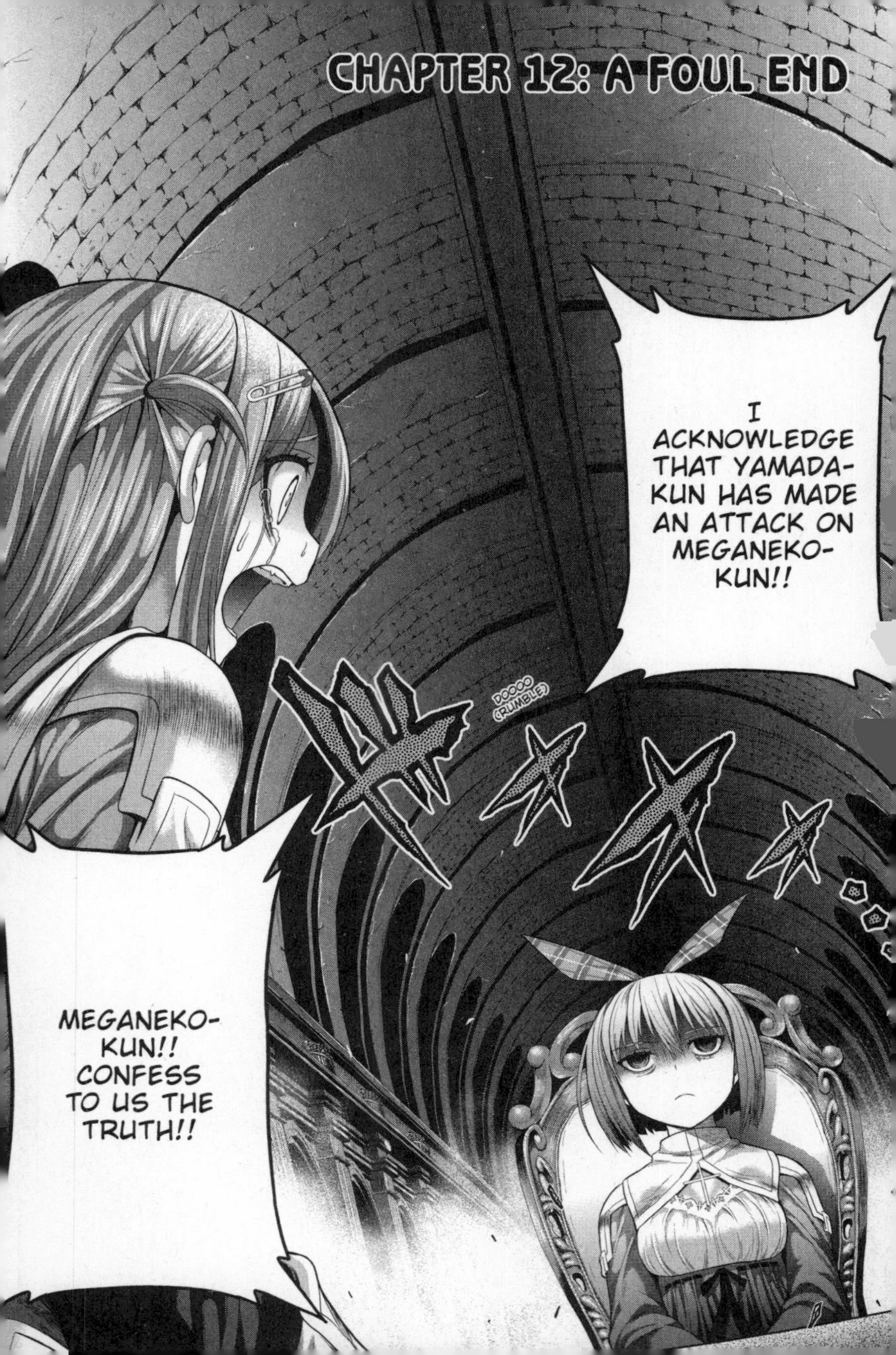
CHAPTER 12: A FOUL END
I ACKNOWLEDGE THAT YAMADA-KUN HAS MADE AN ATTACK ON MEGANEKO-KUN!!
DOOOO (RUMBLE)
MEGANEKO-KUN!! CONFESS TO US THE TRUTH!!

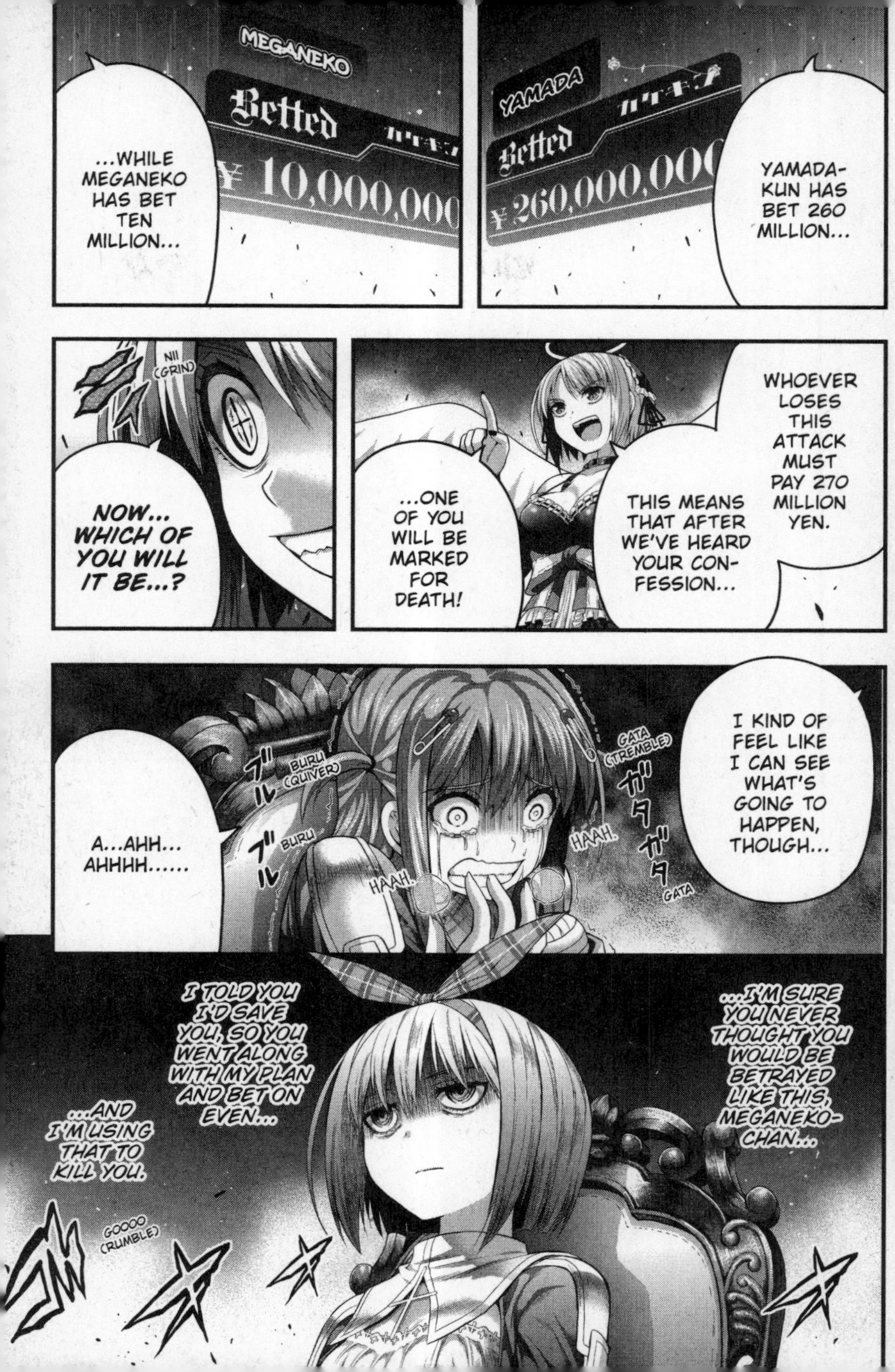
YAMADA
Betted
¥260,000,00
YAMADA-KUN HAS BET 260 MILLION...
MEGANEKO
Betted
¥10,000,00
...WHILE MEGANEKO HAS BET TEN MILLION...
WHOEVER LOSES THIS ATTACK MUST PAY 270 MILLION YEN.
THIS MEANS THAT AFTER WE'VE HEARD YOUR CONFESSION...
...ONE OF YOU WILL BE MARKED FOR DEATH!
NII (GRIN)
NOW... WHICH OF YOU WILL IT BE...?
I KIND OF FEEL LIKE I CAN SEE WHAT'S GOING TO HAPPEN, THOUGH...
GATA (TREMBLE)
GATA
HAAAH.
HAAAH.
BURU (QUIVER)
BURU
A...AHH... AHHHH......
...I'M SURE YOU NEVER THOUGHT YOU WOULD BE BETRAYED LIKE THIS, MEGANEKO-CHAN...
I TOLD YOU I'D SAVE YOU, SO YOU WENT ALONG WITH MY PLAN AND BET ON EVEN...
...AND I'M USING THAT TO KILL YOU.
GOOOO (RUMBLE)

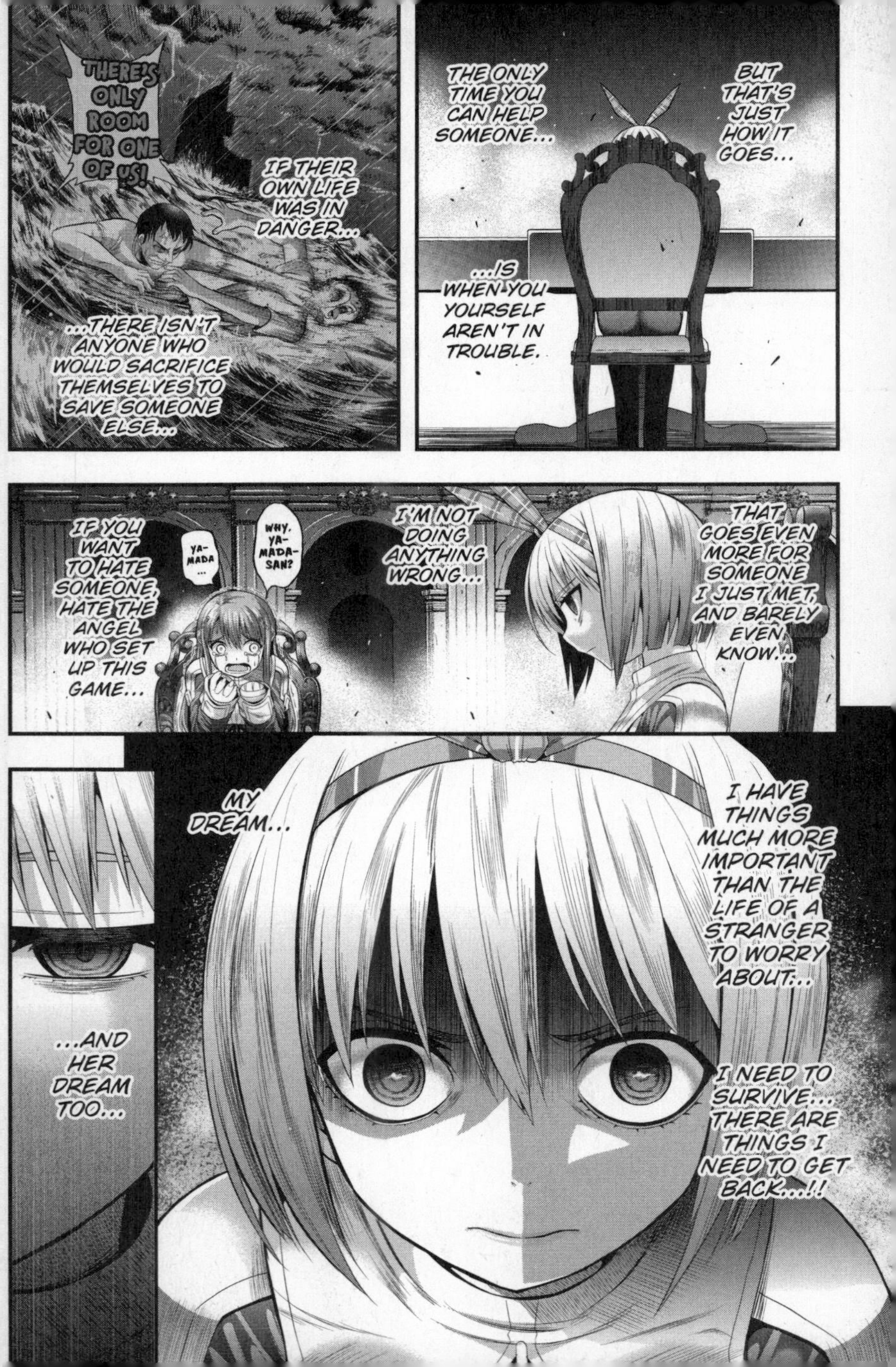
BUT THAT'S JUST HOW IT GOES...
THE ONLY TIME YOU CAN HELP SOMEONE...
...IS WHEN YOU YOURSELF AREN'T IN TROUBLE.
THERE'S ONLY ROOM FOR ONE OF US!
IF THEIR OWN LIFE WAS IN DANGER...
...THERE ISN'T ANYONE WHO WOULD SACRIFICE THEMSELVES TO SAVE SOMEONE ELSE...
THAT GOES EVEN MORE FOR SOMEONE I JUST MET, AND BARELY EVEN KNOW...
I'M NOT DOING ANYTHING WRONG...
WHY, YAMADA-SAN?
YA-MADA...
IF YOU WANT TO HATE SOMEONE, HATE THE ANGEL WHO SET UP THIS GAME...
I HAVE THINGS MUCH MORE IMPORTANT THAN THE LIFE OF A STRANGER TO WORRY ABOUT...
MY DREAM...
I NEED TO SURVIVE... THERE ARE THINGS I NEED TO GET BACK...!!
...AND HER DREAM TOO...

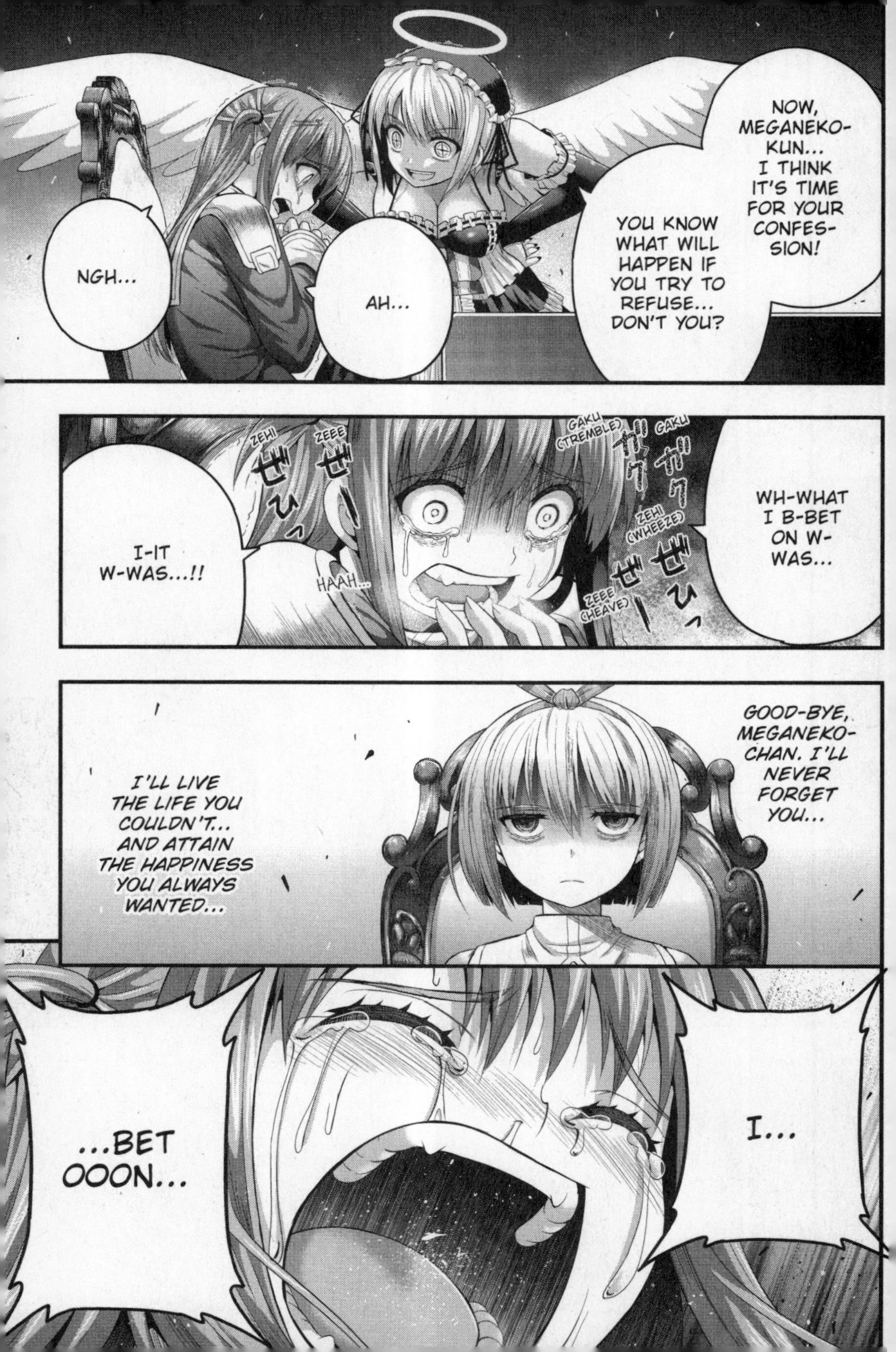
NOW, MEGANEKO-KUN... I THINK IT'S TIME FOR YOUR CONFESSION!
YOU KNOW WHAT WILL HAPPEN IF YOU TRY TO REFUSE... DON'T YOU?
AH...
NGH...
WH-WHAT I B-BET ON W-WAS...
GAKU GAKU (TREMBLE)
ZEHI (WHEEZE)
ZEEE (HEAVE)
HAAH...
ZEEE
ZEHI
I-IT W-WAS...!!
GOOD-BYE, MEGANEKO-CHAN. I'LL NEVER FORGET YOU...
I'LL LIVE THE LIFE YOU COULDN'T... AND ATTAIN THE HAPPINESS YOU ALWAYS WANTED...
I...
...BET OOON...

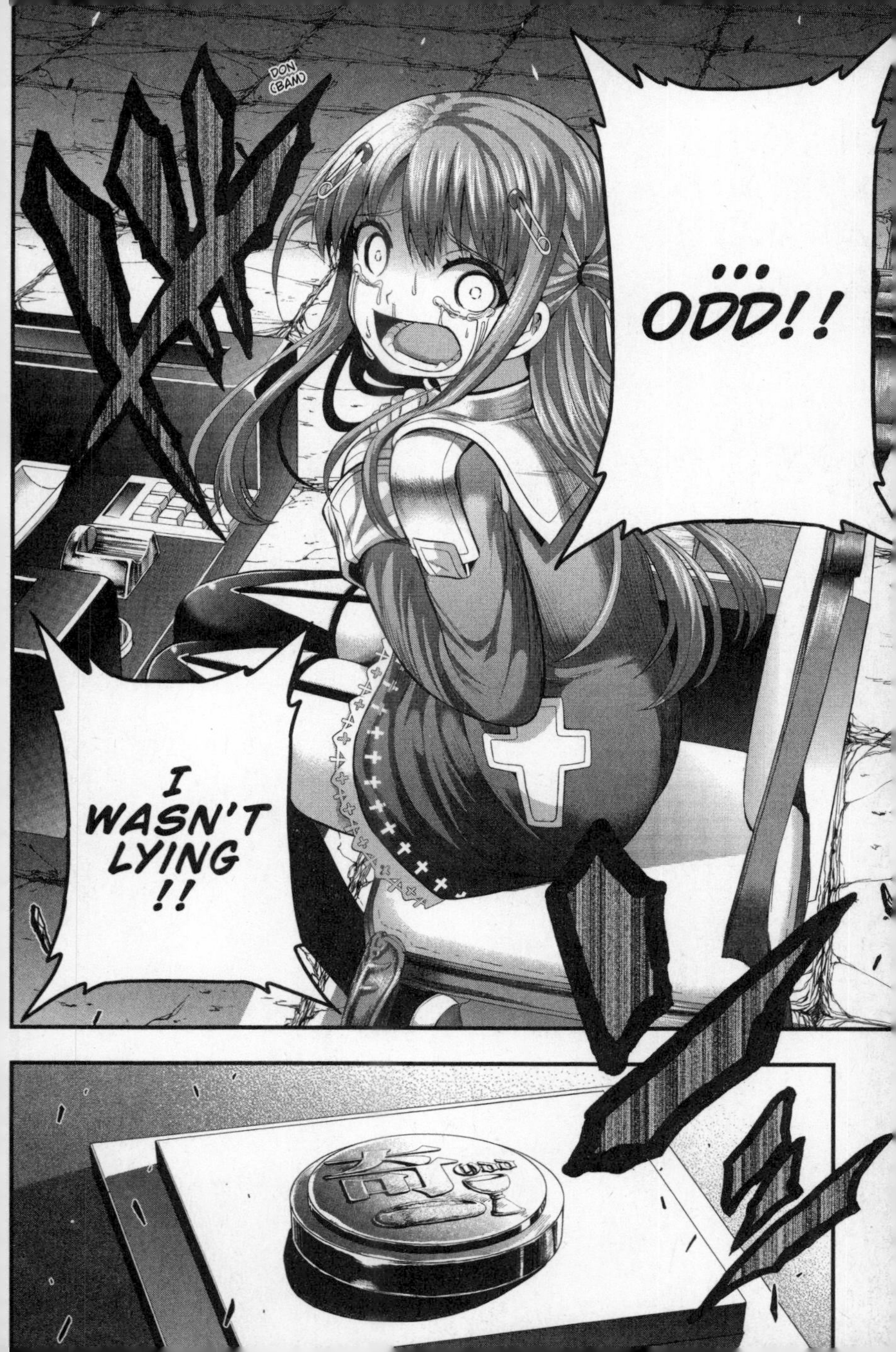
...ODD!!
DON (BAM)
I WASN'T LYING!!

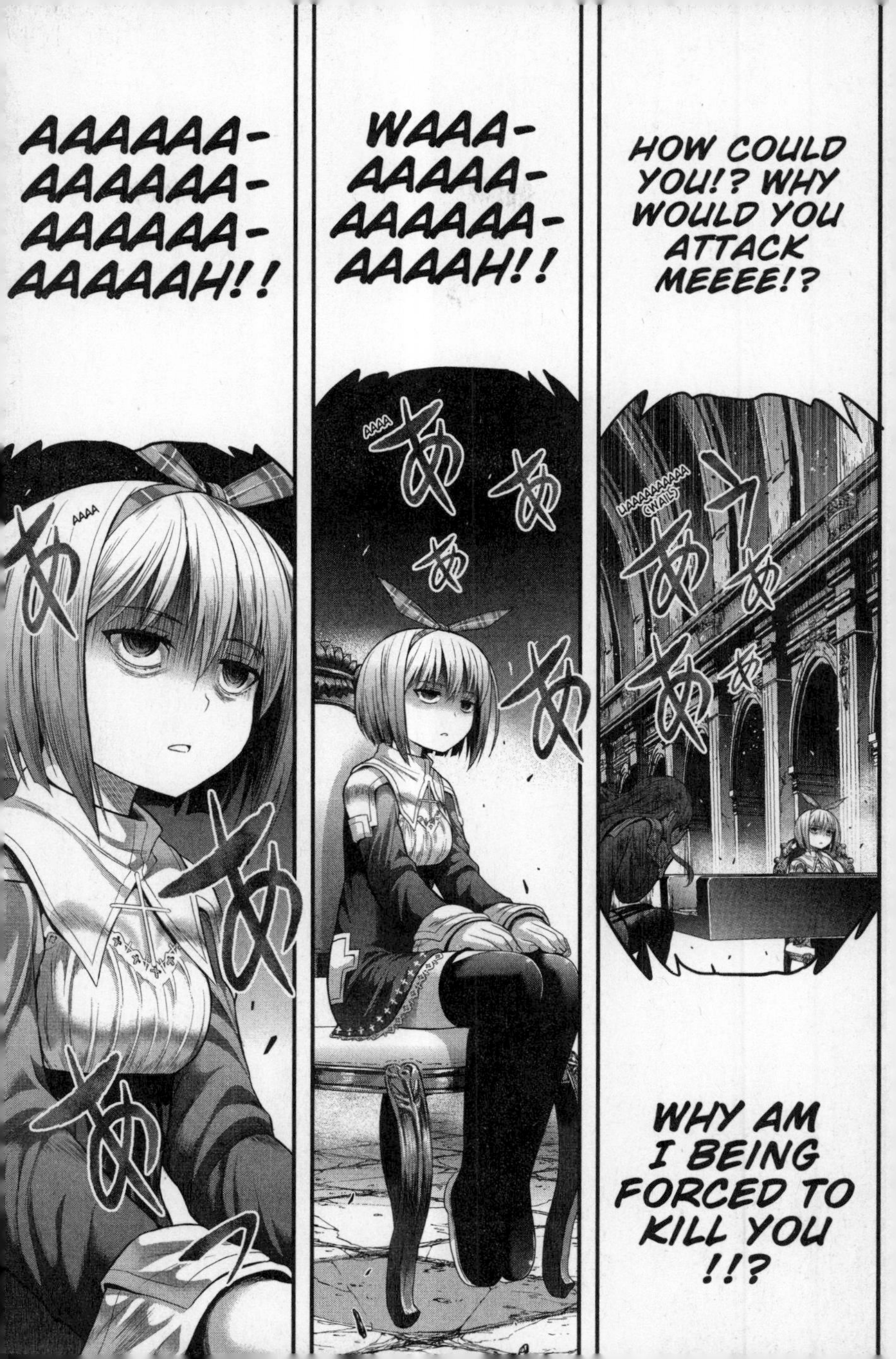
HOW COULD YOU!? WHY WOULD YOU ATTACK MEEEE!?
UAAAAAAAAAA (WAILS)
WHY AM I BEING FORCED TO KILL YOU !!?
WAAA-AAAAAA-AAAAAAA-AAAAAH!!
AAAA
AAAAAA-AAAAAAA-AAAAAAA-AAAAAAH!!
AAAA

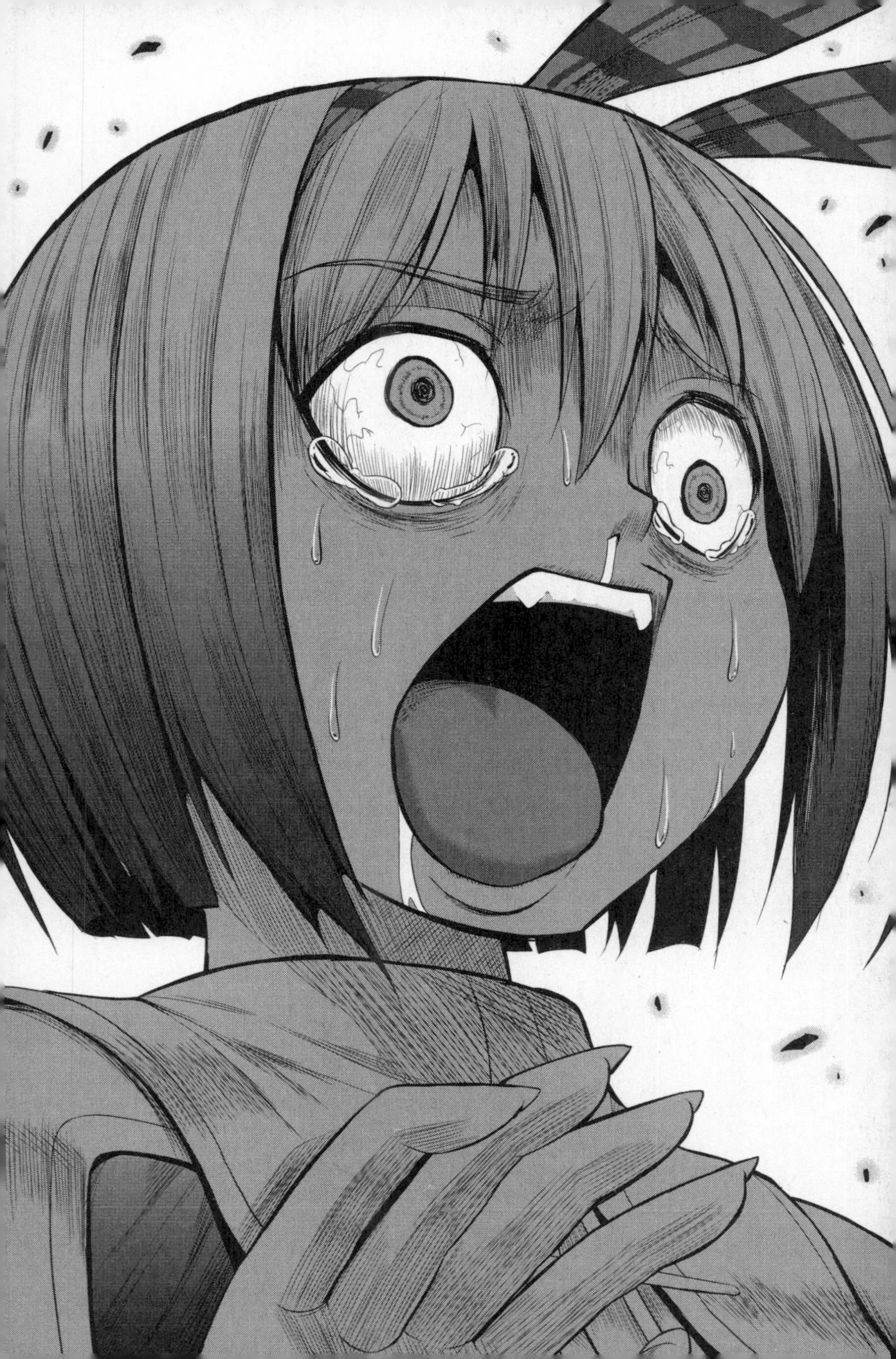

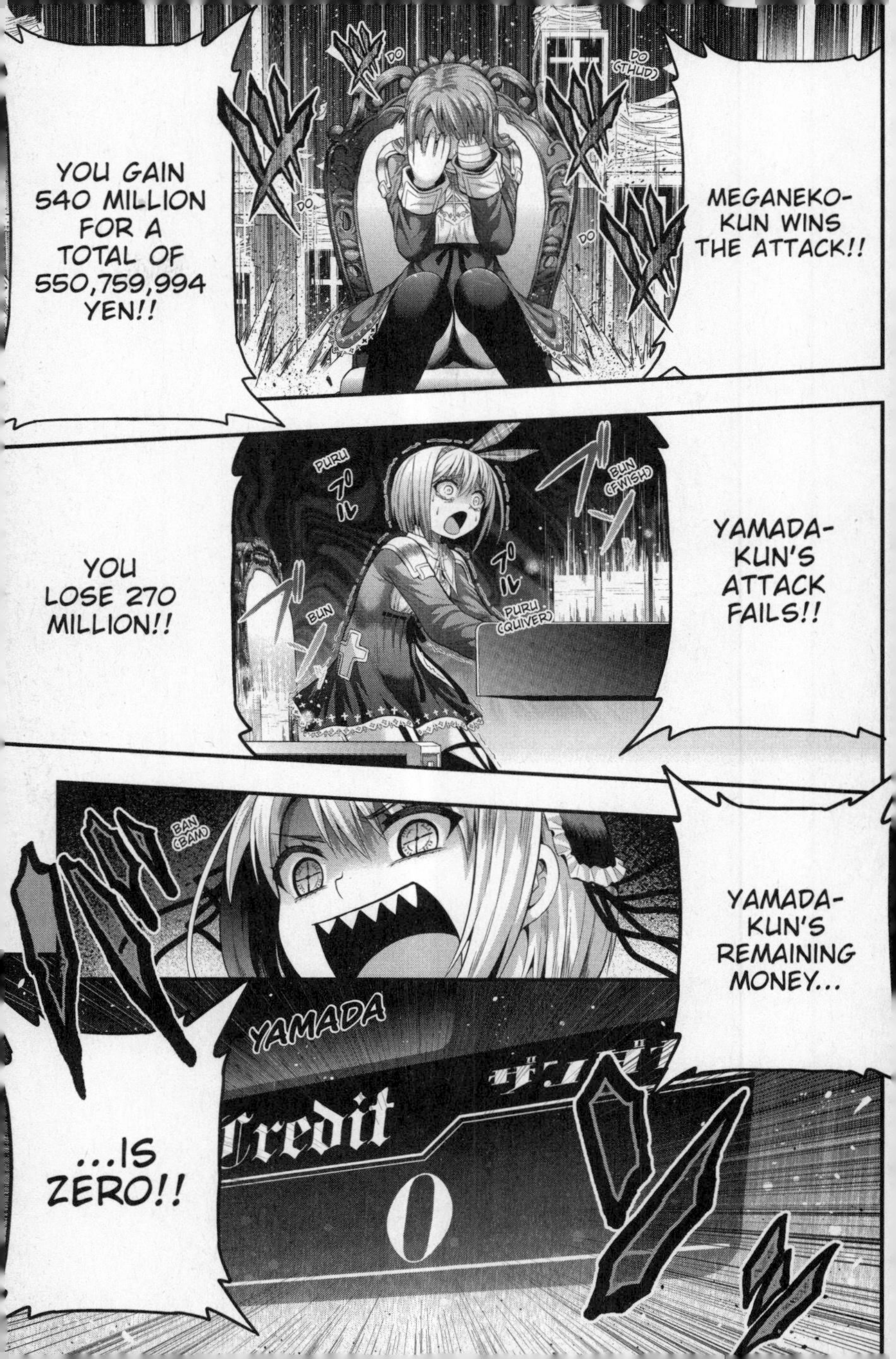
DO (THUD)
DO
DO
DO
MEGANEKO-KUN WINS THE ATTACK!!
YOU GAIN 540 MILLION FOR A TOTAL OF 550,759,994 YEN!!
BUN (FWISH)
PURU
PURU (QUIVER)
BUN
YAMADA-KUN'S ATTACK FAILS!!
YOU LOSE 270 MILLION!!
BAN (BAM)
YAMADA-KUN'S REMAINING MONEY...
YAMADA
Credit
0
...IS ZERO!!

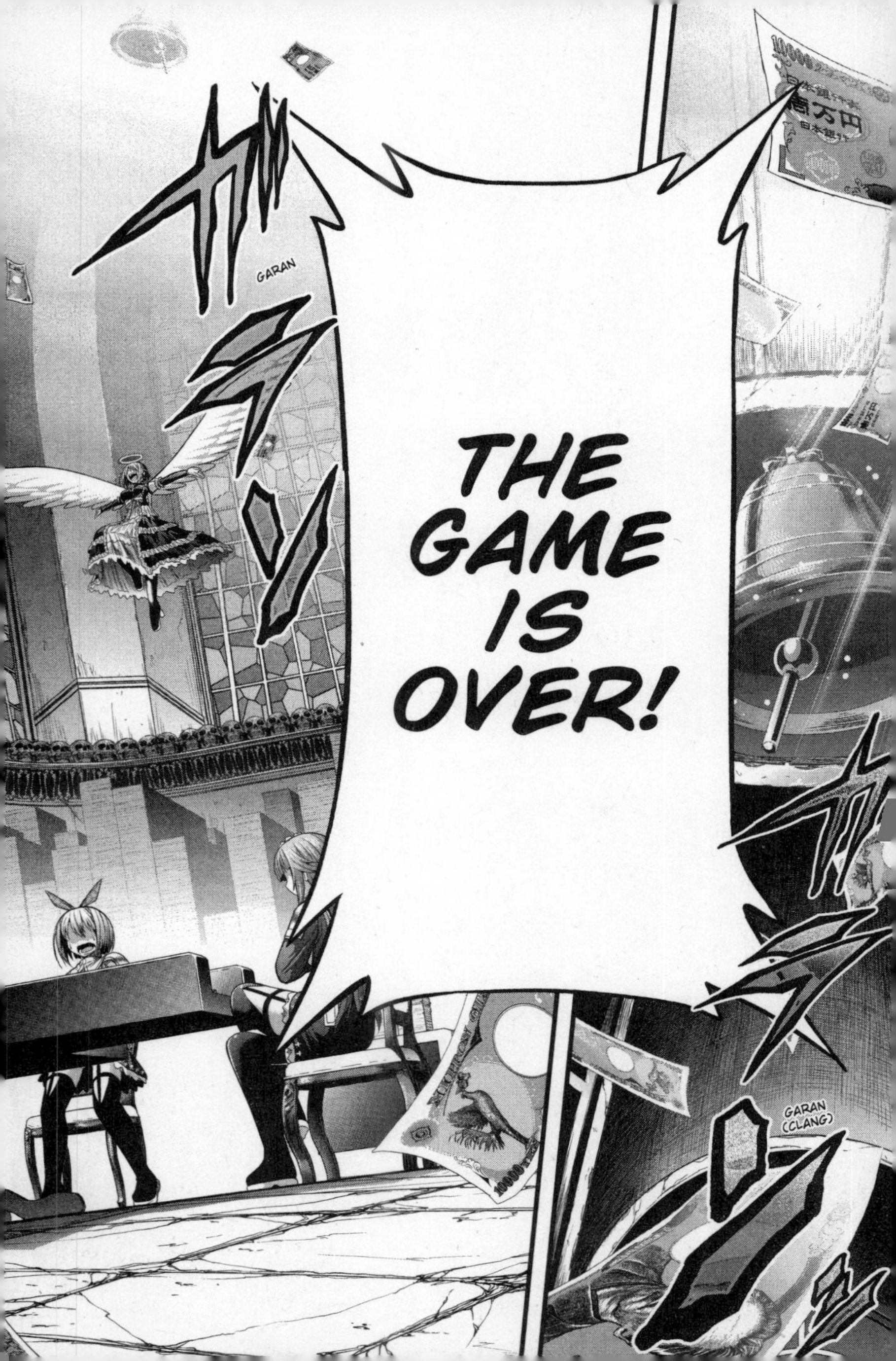
THE GAME IS OVER!
GARAN (CLANG)
GARAN

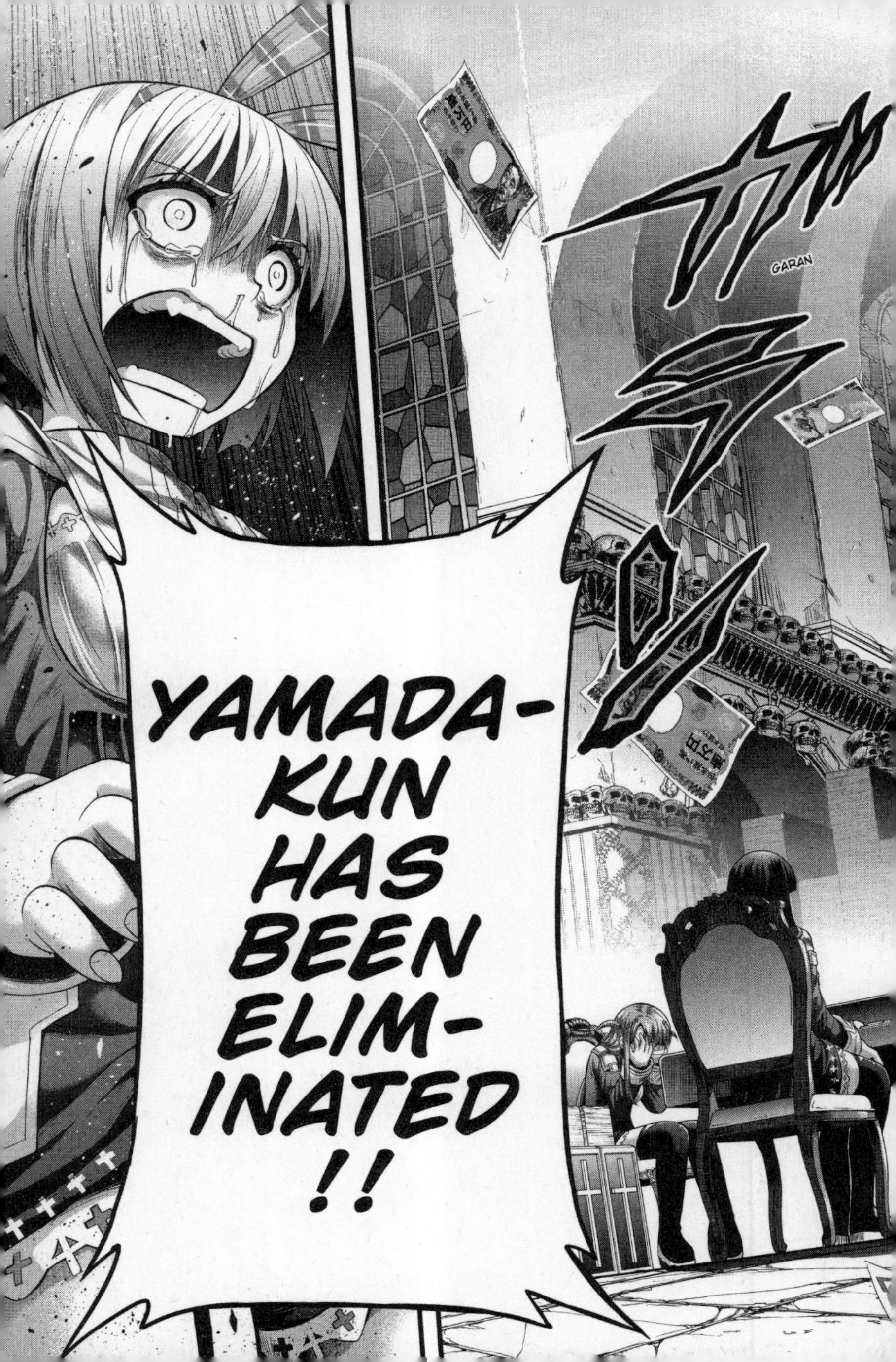
YAMADA-KUN HAS BEEN ELIMINATED!!
GARAN

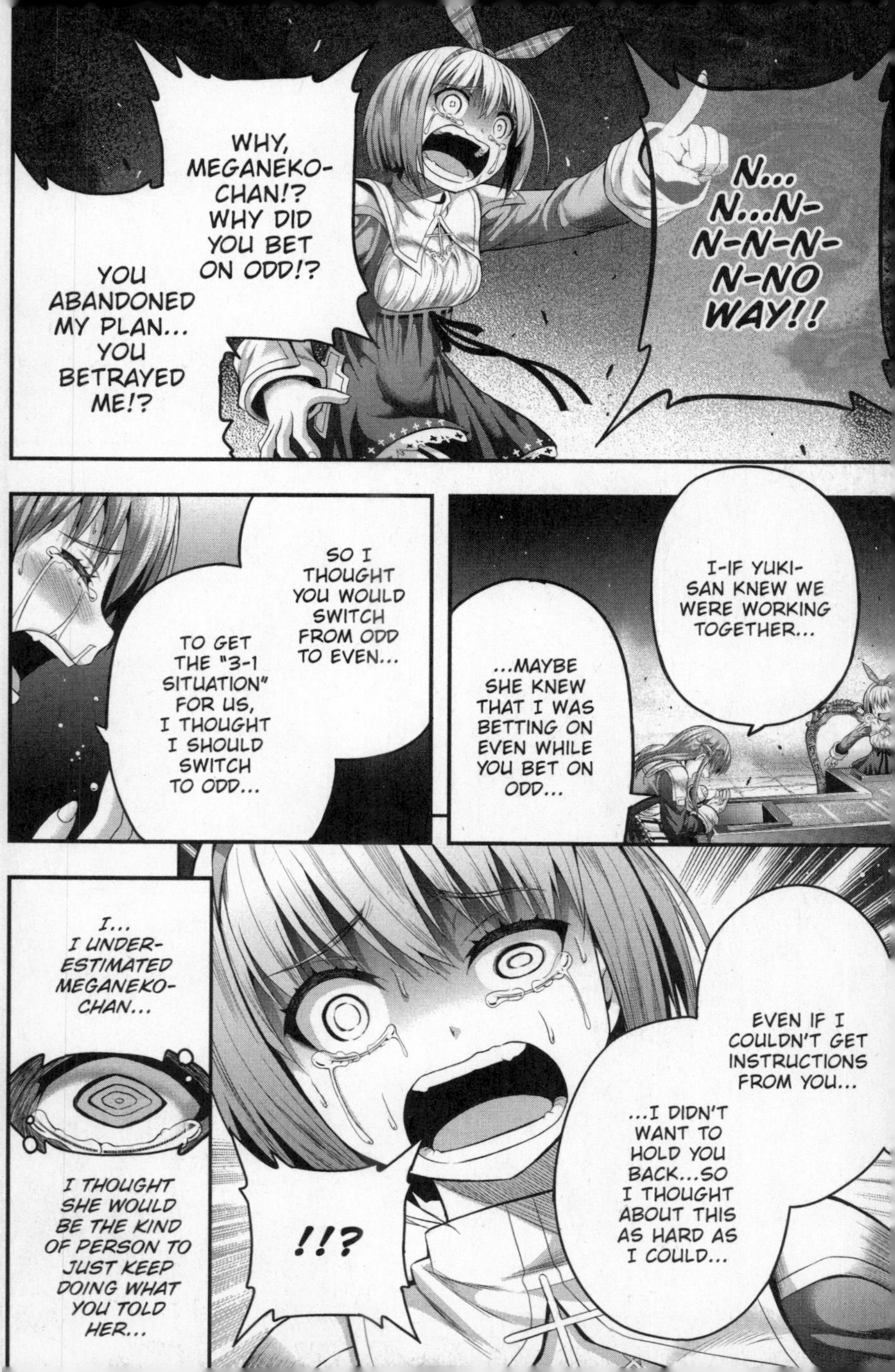
N... N...N- N-N-N- N-NO WAY!!
WHY, MEGANEKO-CHAN!? WHY DID YOU BET ON ODD!?
YOU ABANDONED MY PLAN... YOU BETRAYED ME!?
I-IF YUKI-SAN KNEW WE WERE WORKING TOGETHER...
...MAYBE SHE KNEW THAT I WAS BETTING ON EVEN WHILE YOU BET ON ODD...
SO I THOUGHT YOU WOULD SWITCH FROM ODD TO EVEN...
TO GET THE "3-1 SITUATION" FOR US, I THOUGHT I SHOULD SWITCH TO ODD...
EVEN IF I COULDN'T GET INSTRUCTIONS FROM YOU...
...I DIDN'T WANT TO HOLD YOU BACK...SO I THOUGHT ABOUT THIS AS HARD AS I COULD...
!!?
I... I UNDER-ESTIMATED MEGANEKO-CHAN...
I THOUGHT SHE WOULD BE THE KIND OF PERSON TO JUST KEEP DOING WHAT YOU TOLD HER...

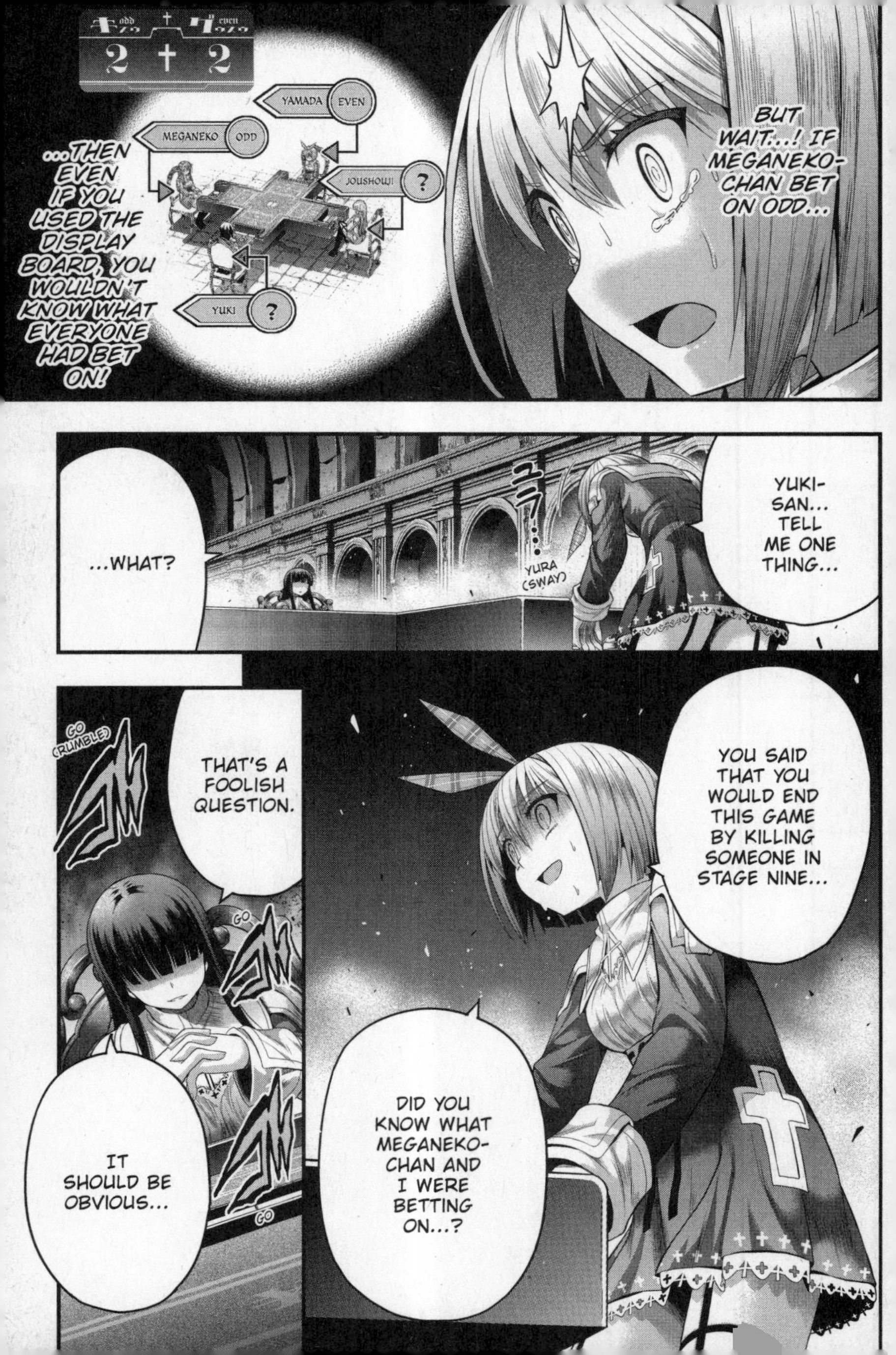
BUT WAIT...! IF MEGANEKO-CHAN BET ON ODD...
odd 2 + 2 even
YAMADA EVEN
MEGANEKO ODD
JOUSHOWJI ?
YUKI ?
...THEN EVEN IF YOU USED THE DISPLAY BOARD, YOU WOULDN'T KNOW WHAT EVERYONE HAD BET ON!
YUKI-SAN... TELL ME ONE THING...
YURA (SWAY)
...WHAT?
YOU SAID THAT YOU WOULD END THIS GAME BY KILLING SOMEONE IN STAGE NINE...
DID YOU KNOW WHAT MEGANEKO-CHAN AND I WERE BETTING ON...?
GO (RUMBLE)
THAT'S A FOOLISH QUESTION.
GO
IT SHOULD BE OBVIOUS...
GO

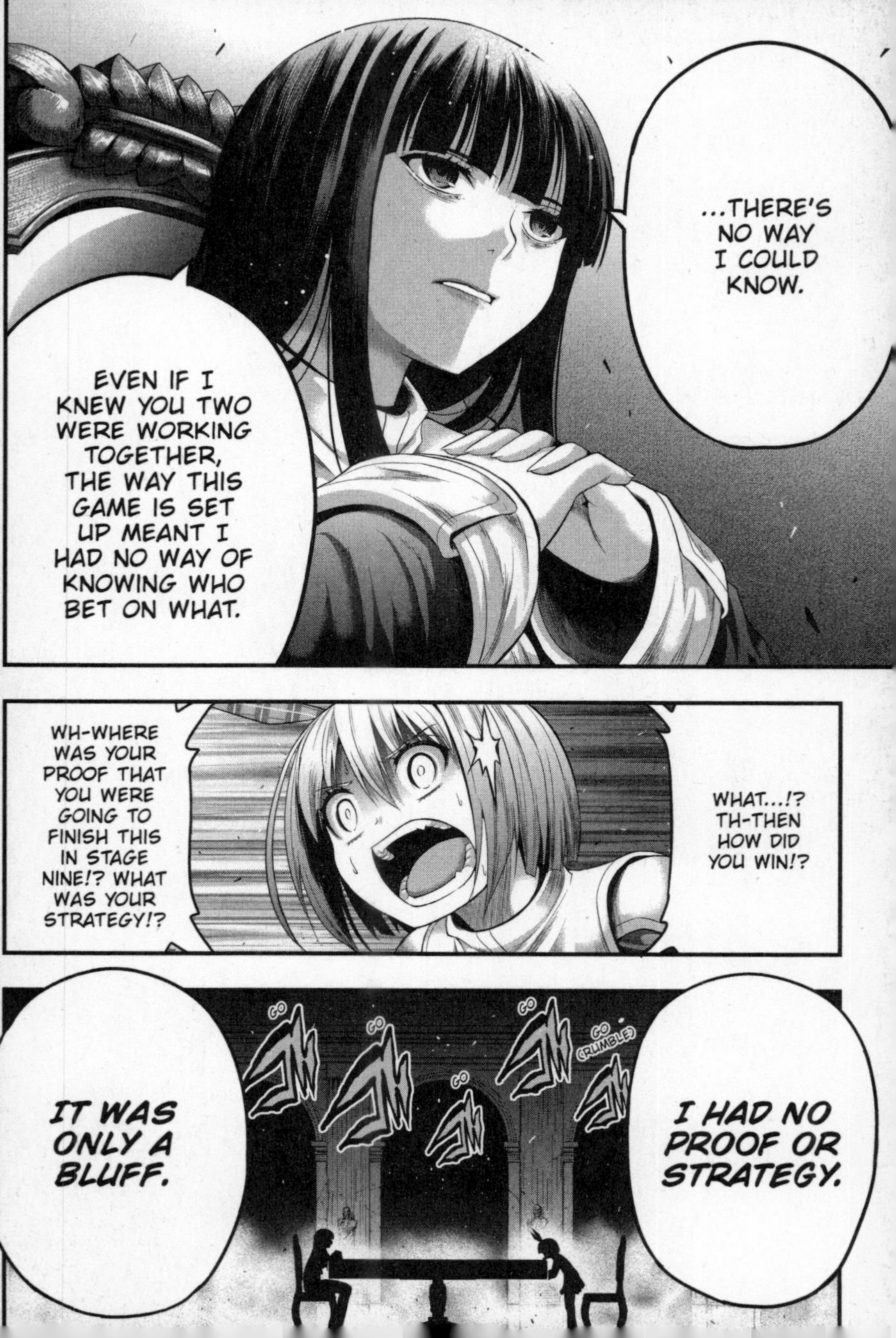
...THERE'S NO WAY I COULD KNOW.
EVEN IF I KNEW YOU TWO WERE WORKING TOGETHER, THE WAY THIS GAME IS SET UP MEANT I HAD NO WAY OF KNOWING WHO BET ON WHAT.
WHAT...!? TH-THEN HOW DID YOU WIN!?
WH-WHERE WAS YOUR PROOF THAT YOU WERE GOING TO FINISH THIS IN STAGE NINE!? WHAT WAS YOUR STRATEGY!?
I HAD NO PROOF OR STRATEGY.
GO (RUMBLE)
GO
GO
GO
GO
IT WAS ONLY A BLUFF.

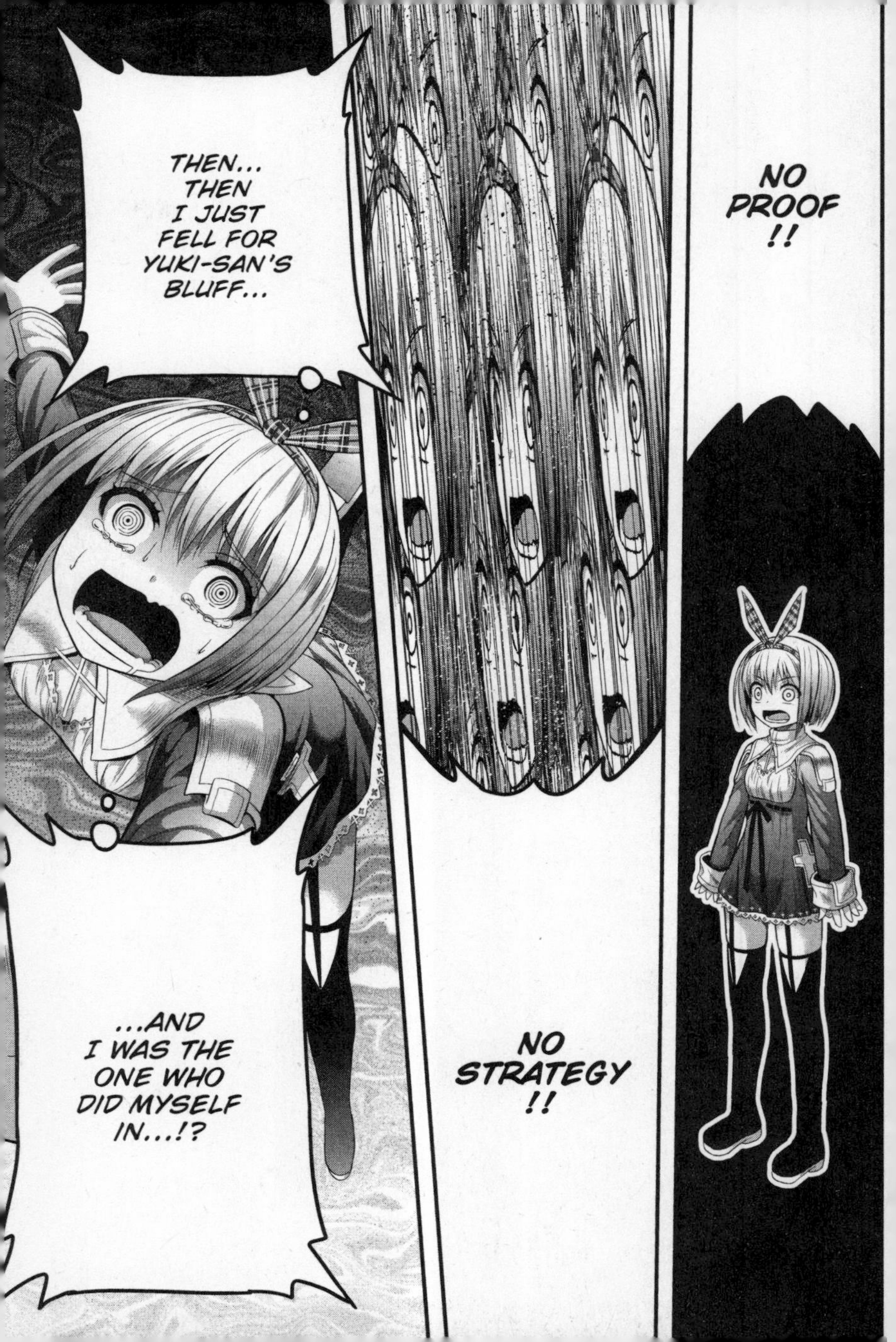
NO PROOF !!
NO STRATEGY !!
THEN... THEN I JUST FELL FOR YUKI-SAN'S BLUFF...
...AND I WAS THE ONE WHO DID MYSELF IN...!?

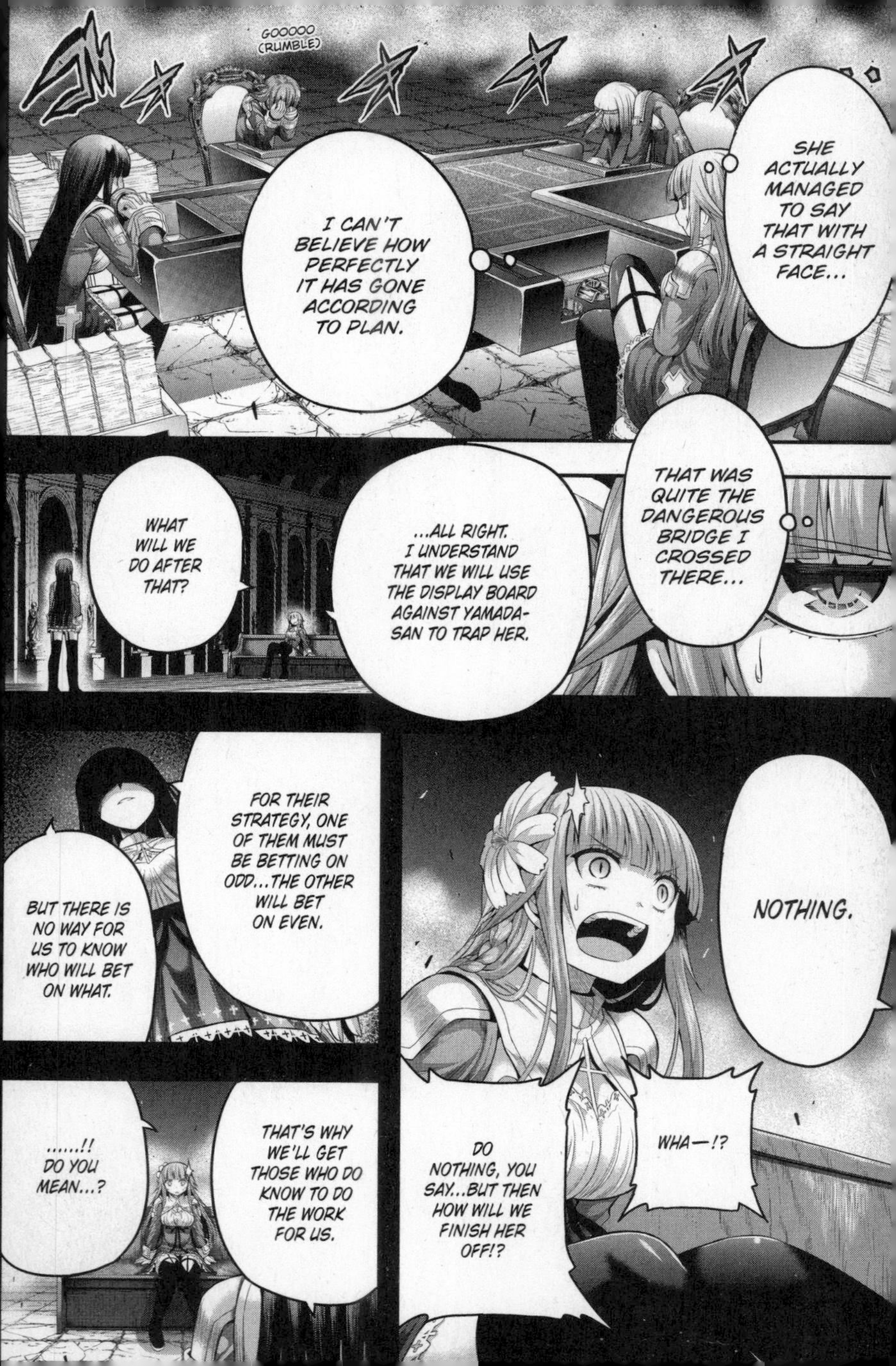
SHE ACTUALLY MANAGED TO SAY THAT WITH A STRAIGHT FACE...
GOOOOO (RUMBLE)
I CAN'T BELIEVE HOW PERFECTLY IT HAS GONE ACCORDING TO PLAN.
THAT WAS QUITE THE DANGEROUS BRIDGE I CROSSED THERE...
...ALL RIGHT. I UNDERSTAND THAT WE WILL USE THE DISPLAY BOARD AGAINST YAMADA-SAN TO TRAP HER.
WHAT WILL WE DO AFTER THAT?
NOTHING.
WHA—!?
DO NOTHING, YOU SAY...BUT THEN HOW WILL WE FINISH HER OFF!?
FOR THEIR STRATEGY, ONE OF THEM MUST BE BETTING ON ODD...THE OTHER WILL BET ON EVEN.
BUT THERE IS NO WAY FOR US TO KNOW WHO WILL BET ON WHAT.
THAT'S WHY WE'LL GET THOSE WHO DO KNOW TO DO THE WORK FOR US.
......!! DO YOU MEAN...?

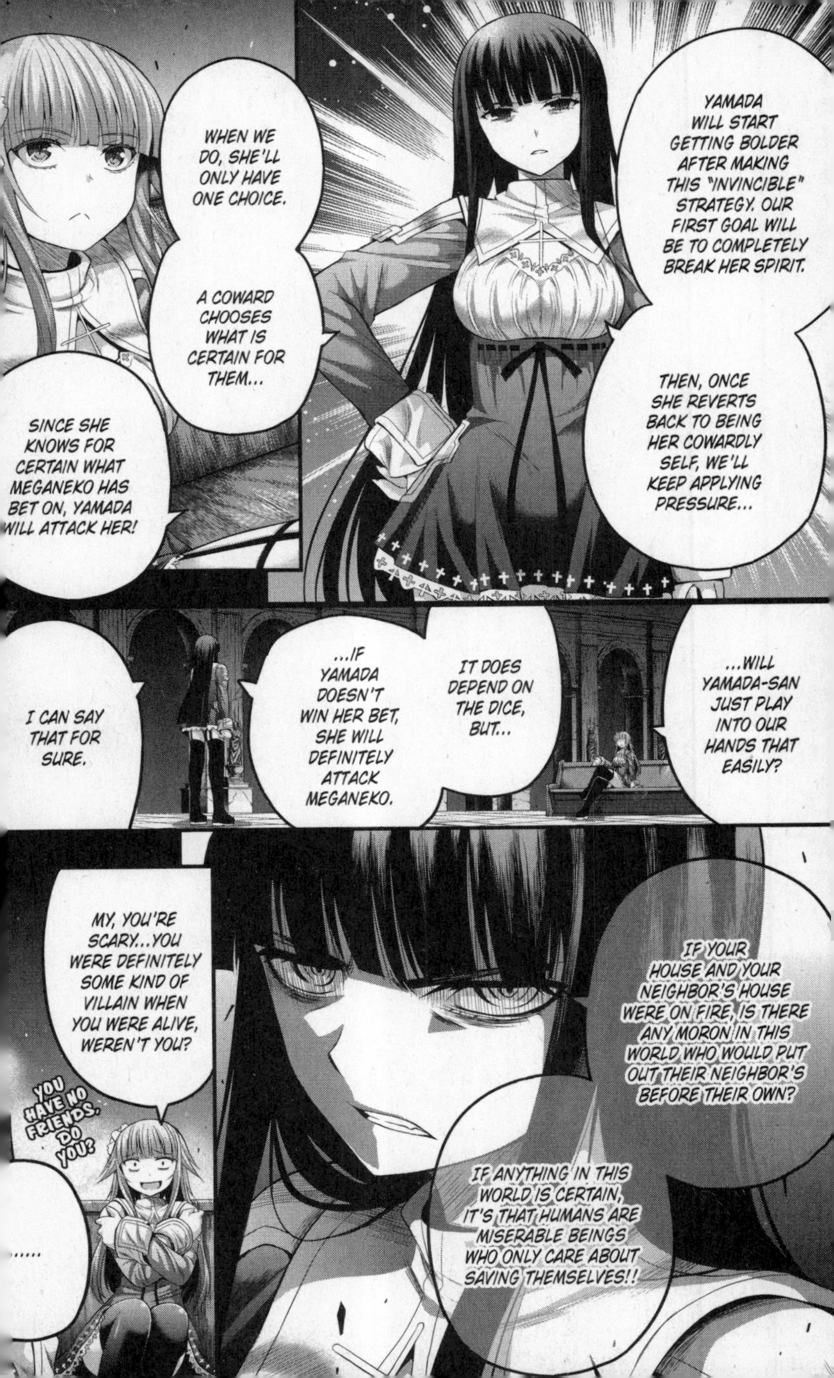
YAMADA WILL START GETTING BOLDER AFTER MAKING THIS "INVINCIBLE" STRATEGY. OUR FIRST GOAL WILL BE TO COMPLETELY BREAK HER SPIRIT.
THEN, ONCE SHE REVERTS BACK TO BEING HER COWARDLY SELF, WE'LL KEEP APPLYING PRESSURE...
WHEN WE DO, SHE'LL ONLY HAVE ONE CHOICE.
A COWARD CHOOSES WHAT IS CERTAIN FOR THEM...
SINCE SHE KNOWS FOR CERTAIN WHAT MEGANEKO HAS BET ON, YAMADA WILL ATTACK HER!
...WILL YAMADA-SAN JUST PLAY INTO OUR HANDS THAT EASILY?
IT DOES DEPEND ON THE DICE, BUT...
...IF YAMADA DOESN'T WIN HER BET, SHE WILL DEFINITELY ATTACK MEGANEKO.
I CAN SAY THAT FOR SURE.
IF YOUR HOUSE AND YOUR NEIGHBOR'S HOUSE WERE ON FIRE, IS THERE ANY MORON IN THIS WORLD WHO WOULD PUT OUT THEIR NEIGHBOR'S BEFORE THEIR OWN?
IF ANYTHING IN THIS WORLD IS CERTAIN, IT'S THAT HUMANS ARE MISERABLE BEINGS WHO ONLY CARE ABOUT SAVING THEMSELVES!!
MY, YOU'RE SCARY...YOU WERE DEFINITELY SOME KIND OF VILLAIN WHEN YOU WERE ALIVE, WEREN'T YOU?
YOU HAVE NO FRIENDS, DO YOU?
......

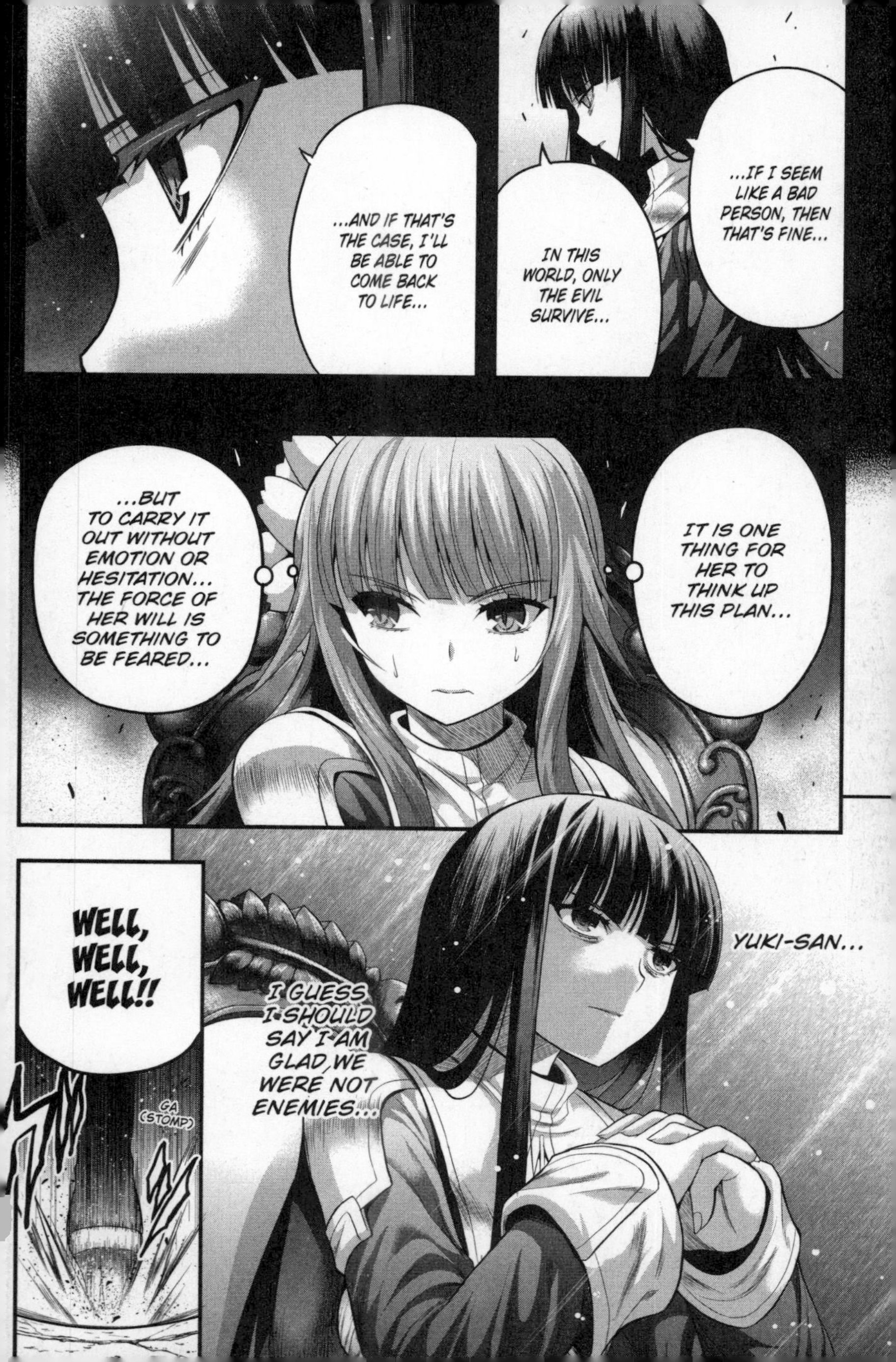
...IF I SEEM LIKE A BAD PERSON, THEN THAT'S FINE...
IN THIS WORLD, ONLY THE EVIL SURVIVE...
...AND IF THAT'S THE CASE, I'LL BE ABLE TO COME BACK TO LIFE...
IT IS ONE THING FOR HER TO THINK UP THIS PLAN...
...BUT TO CARRY IT OUT WITHOUT EMOTION OR HESITATION... THE FORCE OF HER WILL IS SOMETHING TO BE FEARED...
YUKI-SAN...
I GUESS I SHOULD SAY I AM GLAD WE WERE NOT ENEMIES...
WELL, WELL, WELL!!
GA (STOMP)

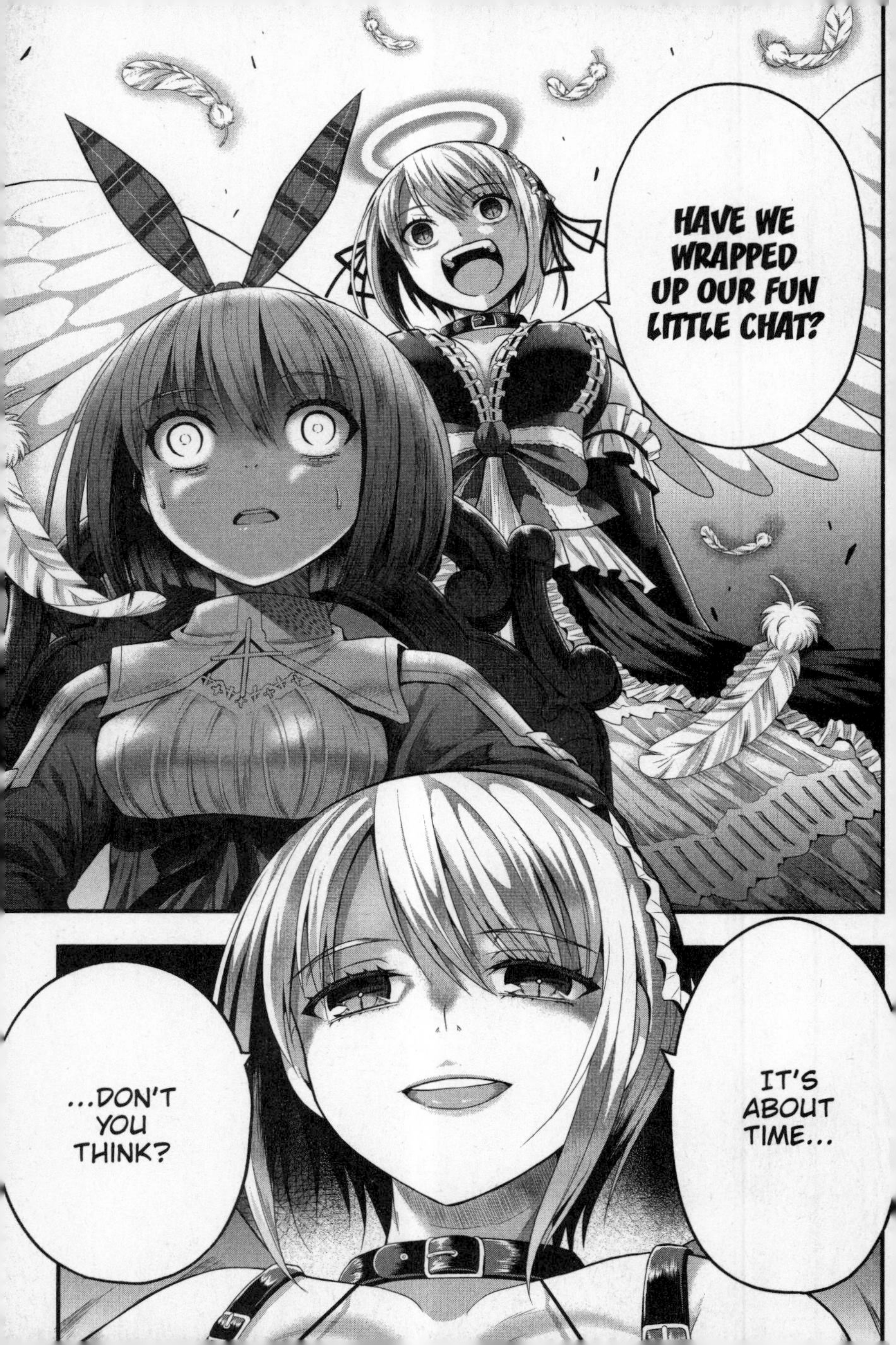
HAVE WE WRAPPED UP OUR FUN LITTLE CHAT?
IT'S ABOUT TIME...
...DON'T YOU THINK?

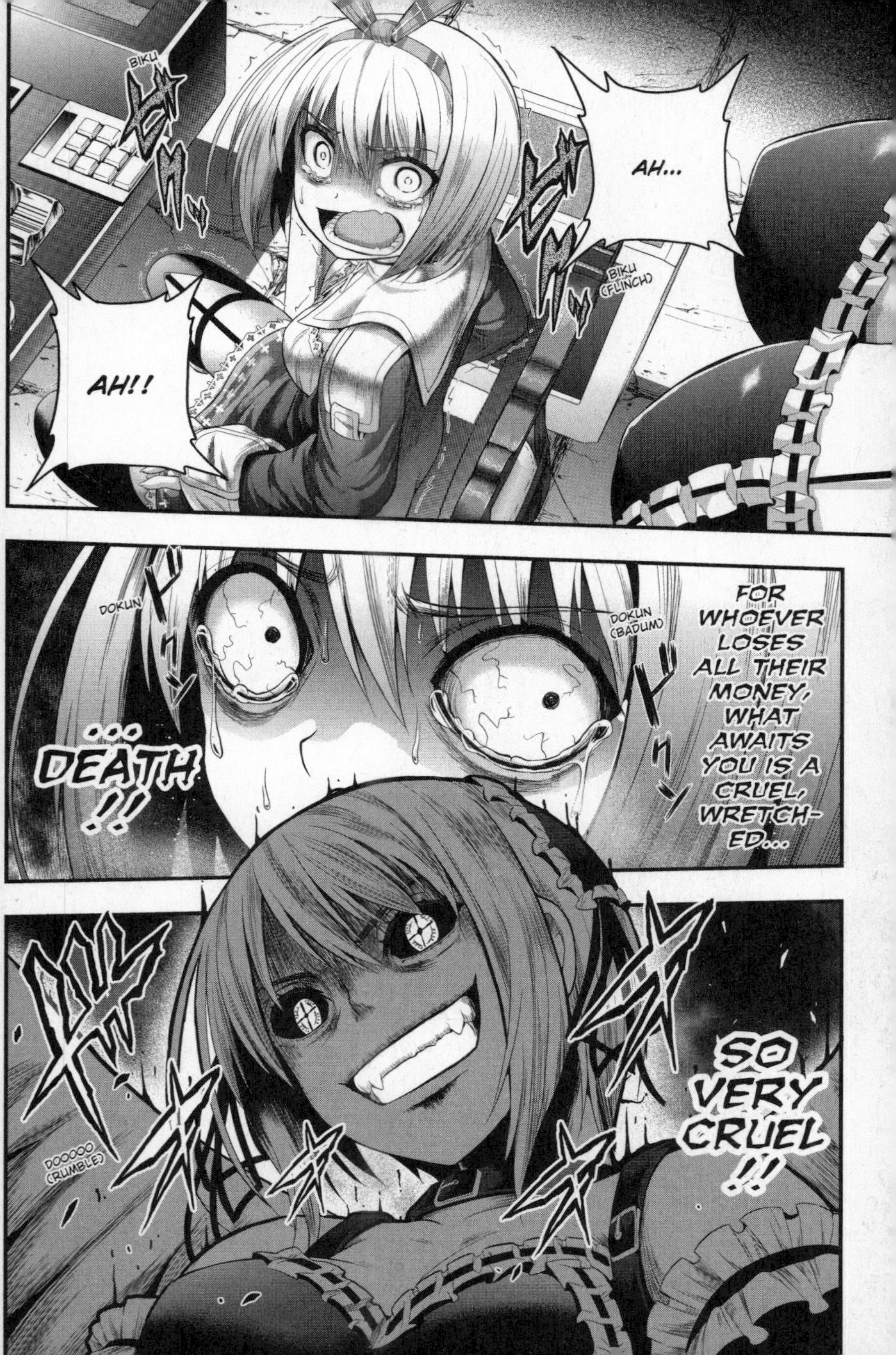

AH...
BIKU (FLINCH)
BIKU
AH!!
FOR WHOEVER LOSES ALL THEIR MONEY, WHAT AWAITS YOU IS A CRUEL, WRETCH-ED...
DOKUN (BADUM)
DOKUN
...DEATH!!
SO VERY CRUEL!!
DOOOOO (RUMBLE)

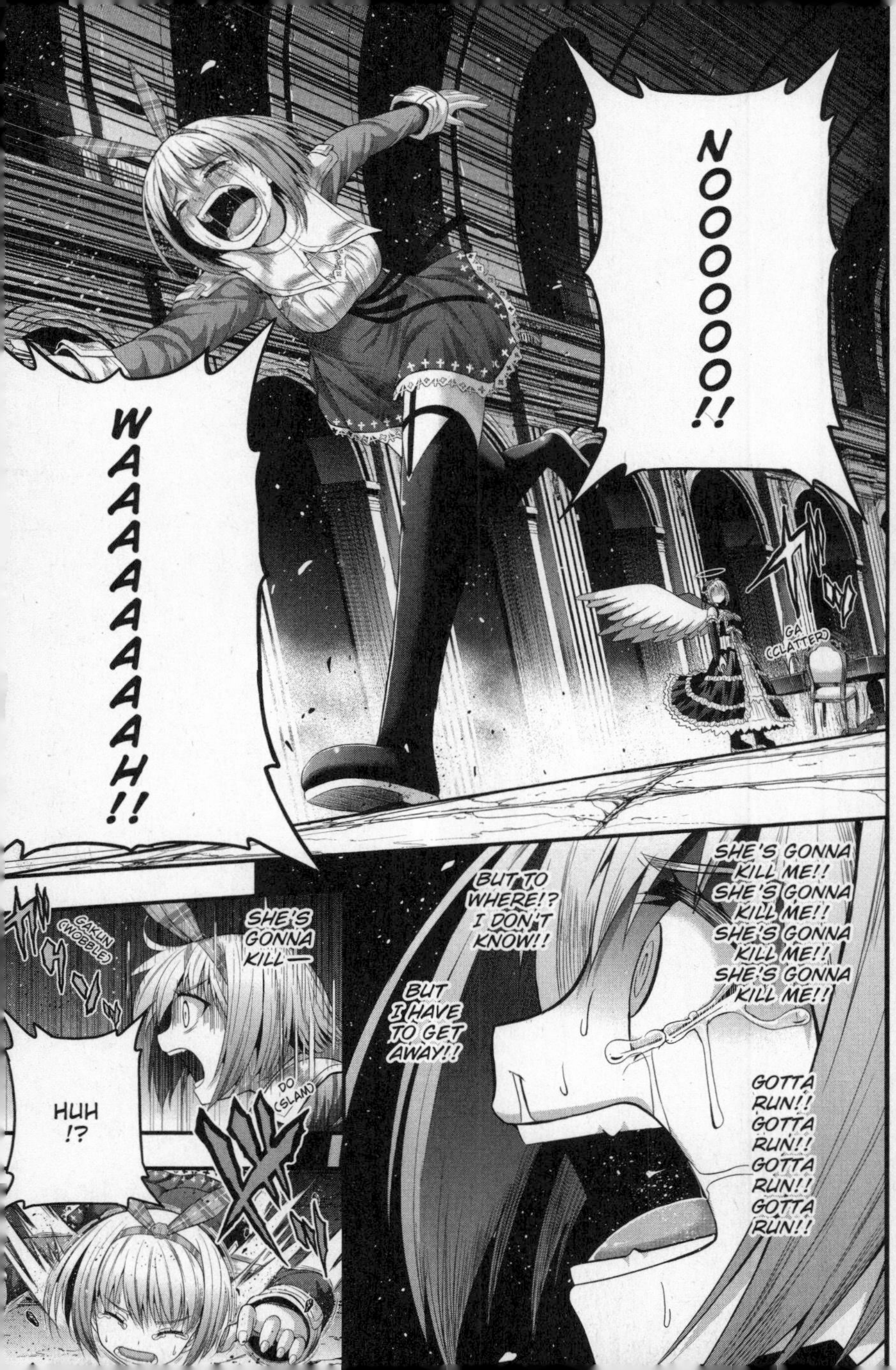
NOOOOOOO!!
GA (CLATTER)
WAAAAAAAAH!!
SHE'S GONNA KILL ME!! SHE'S GONNA KILL ME!! SHE'S GONNA KILL ME!! SHE'S GONNA KILL ME!!
BUT TO WHERE!? I DON'T KNOW!!
BUT I HAVE TO GET AWAY!!
GOTTA RUN!! GOTTA RUN!! GOTTA RUN!! GOTTA RUN!!
SHE'S GONNA KILL—
GAKUN (WOBBLE)
HUH!?
DO (SLAM)

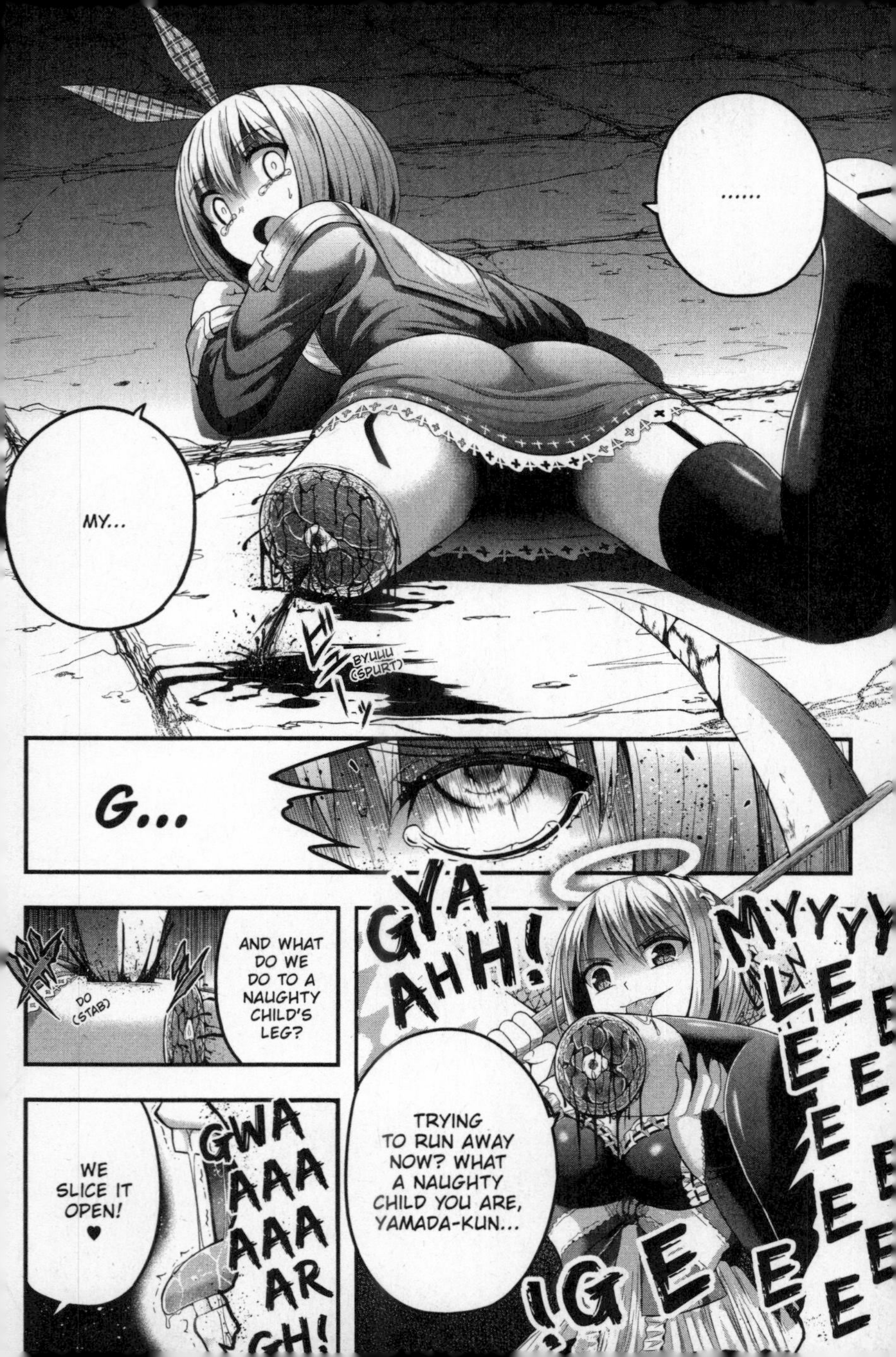

......
MY...
BYUUU (SPURT)
G...
GYA AHH!
MYYYY LEEEE GEEEE
TRYING TO RUN AWAY NOW? WHAT A NAUGHTY CHILD YOU ARE, YAMADA-KUN...
DO (STAB)
AND WHAT DO WE DO TO A NAUGHTY CHILD'S LEG?
WE SLICE IT OPEN! ♥
GWAAAAAAAAARGH!

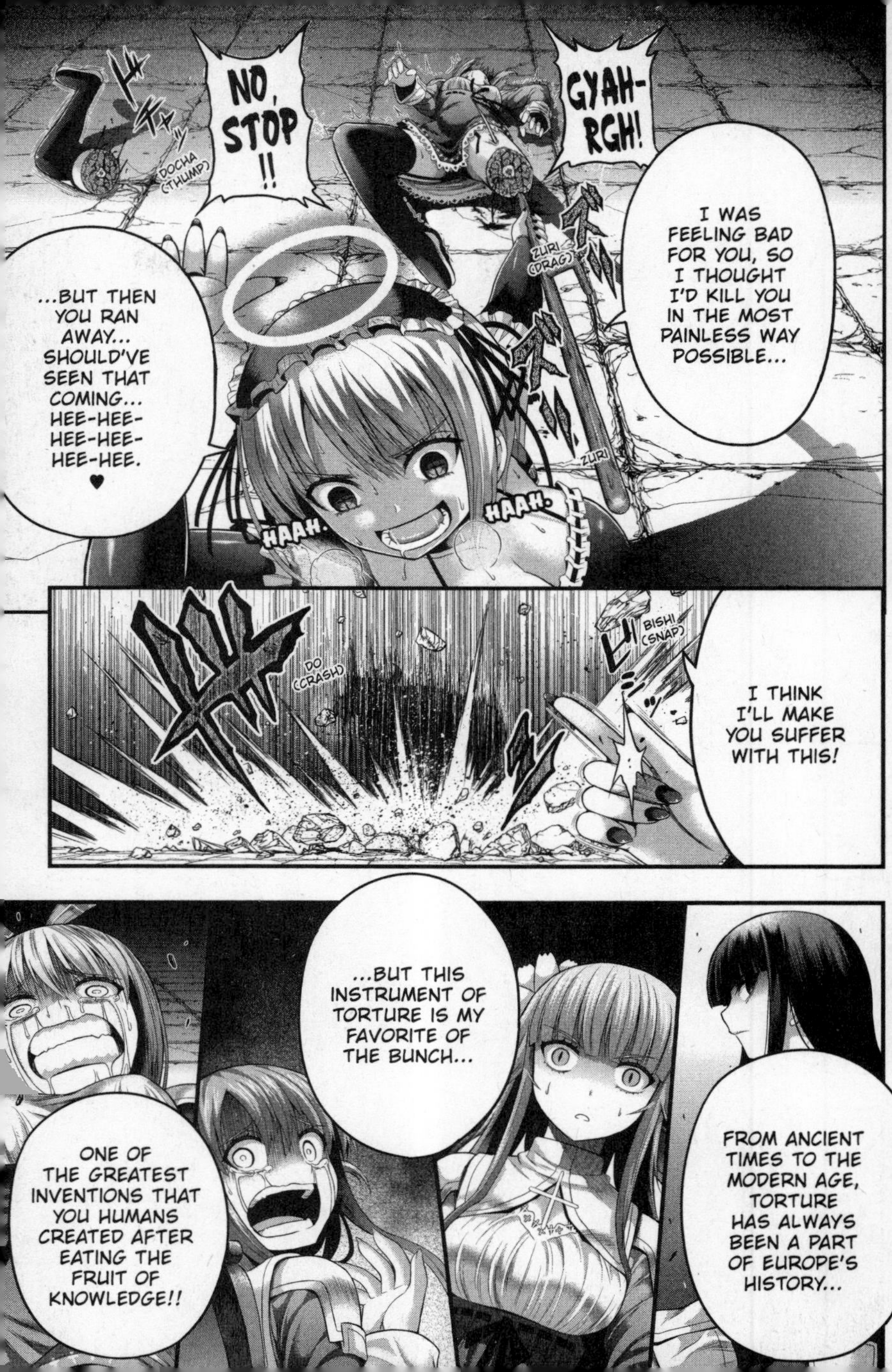
GYAH-RGH!
NO, STOP!!
DOCHA (THUMP)
I WAS FEELING BAD FOR YOU, SO I THOUGHT I'D KILL YOU IN THE MOST PAINLESS WAY POSSIBLE...
ZURI (DRAG)
...BUT THEN YOU RAN AWAY... SHOULD'VE SEEN THAT COMING... HEE-HEE-HEE-HEE-HEE-HEE. ♥
ZURI
HAAH.
HAAH.
I THINK I'LL MAKE YOU SUFFER WITH THIS!
BISHI (SNAP)
DO (CRASH)
FROM ANCIENT TIMES TO THE MODERN AGE, TORTURE HAS ALWAYS BEEN A PART OF EUROPE'S HISTORY...
...BUT THIS INSTRUMENT OF TORTURE IS MY FAVORITE OF THE BUNCH...
ONE OF THE GREATEST INVENTIONS THAT YOU HUMANS CREATED AFTER EATING THE FRUIT OF KNOWLEDGE!!

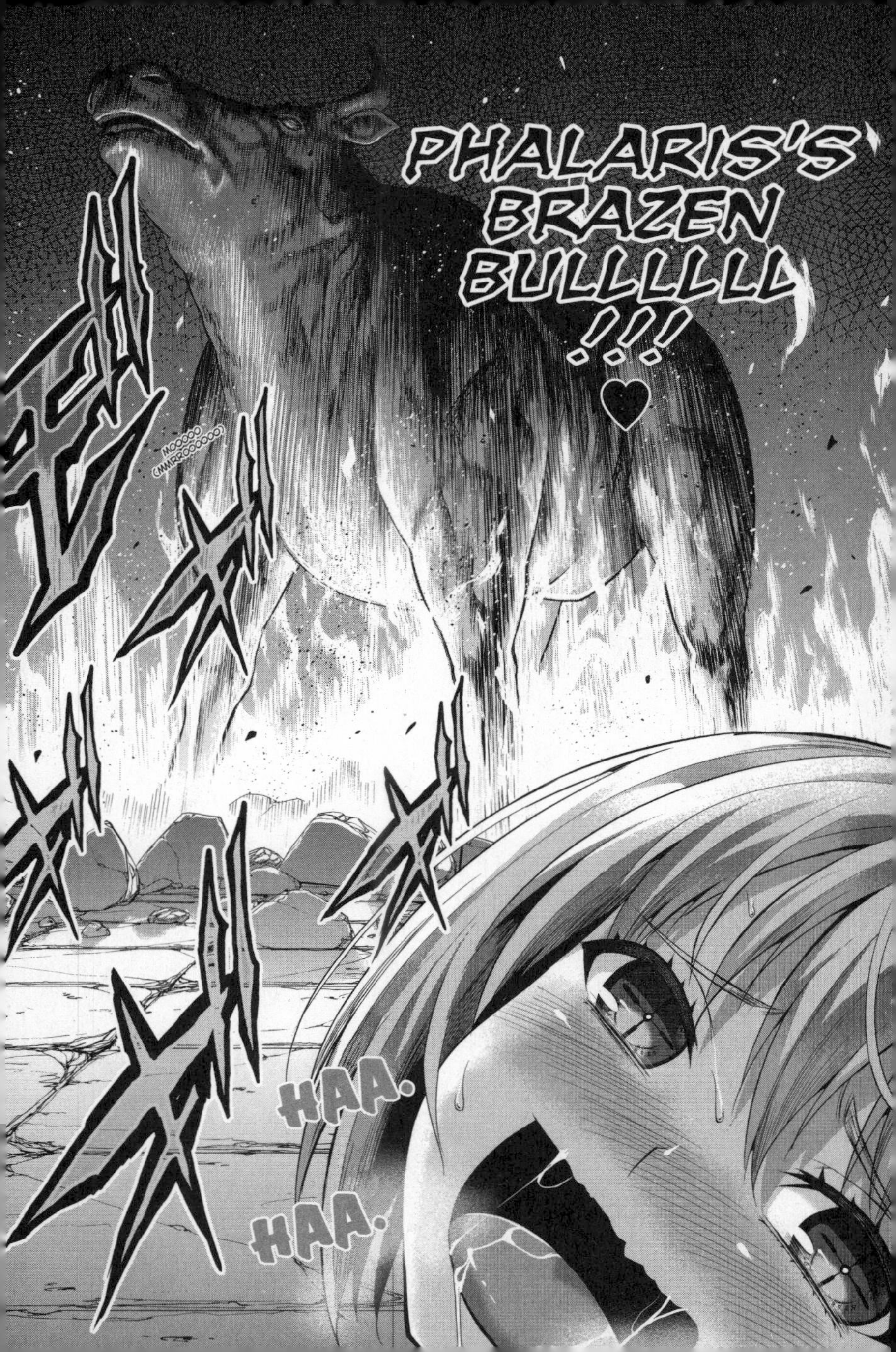
PHALARIS'S BRAZEN BULLLLLL!!! ♥
MOOOOO (MMRROOOOOO)
HAA.
HAA.

Though You May Burn to Ash

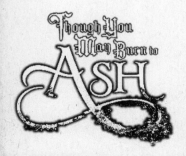

Though You May Burn to Ash

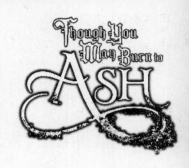

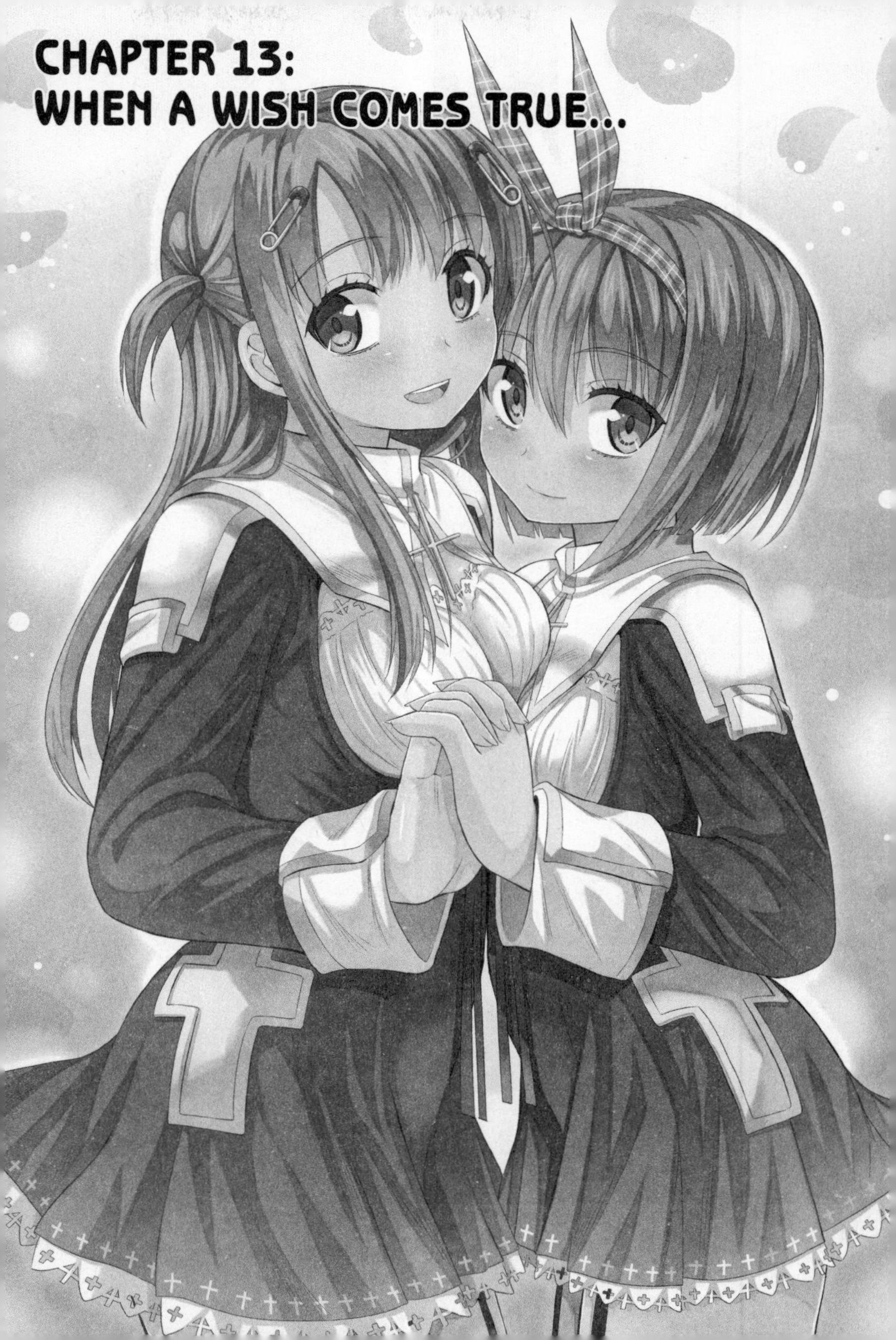
CHAPTER 13:
WHEN A WISH COMES TRUE...

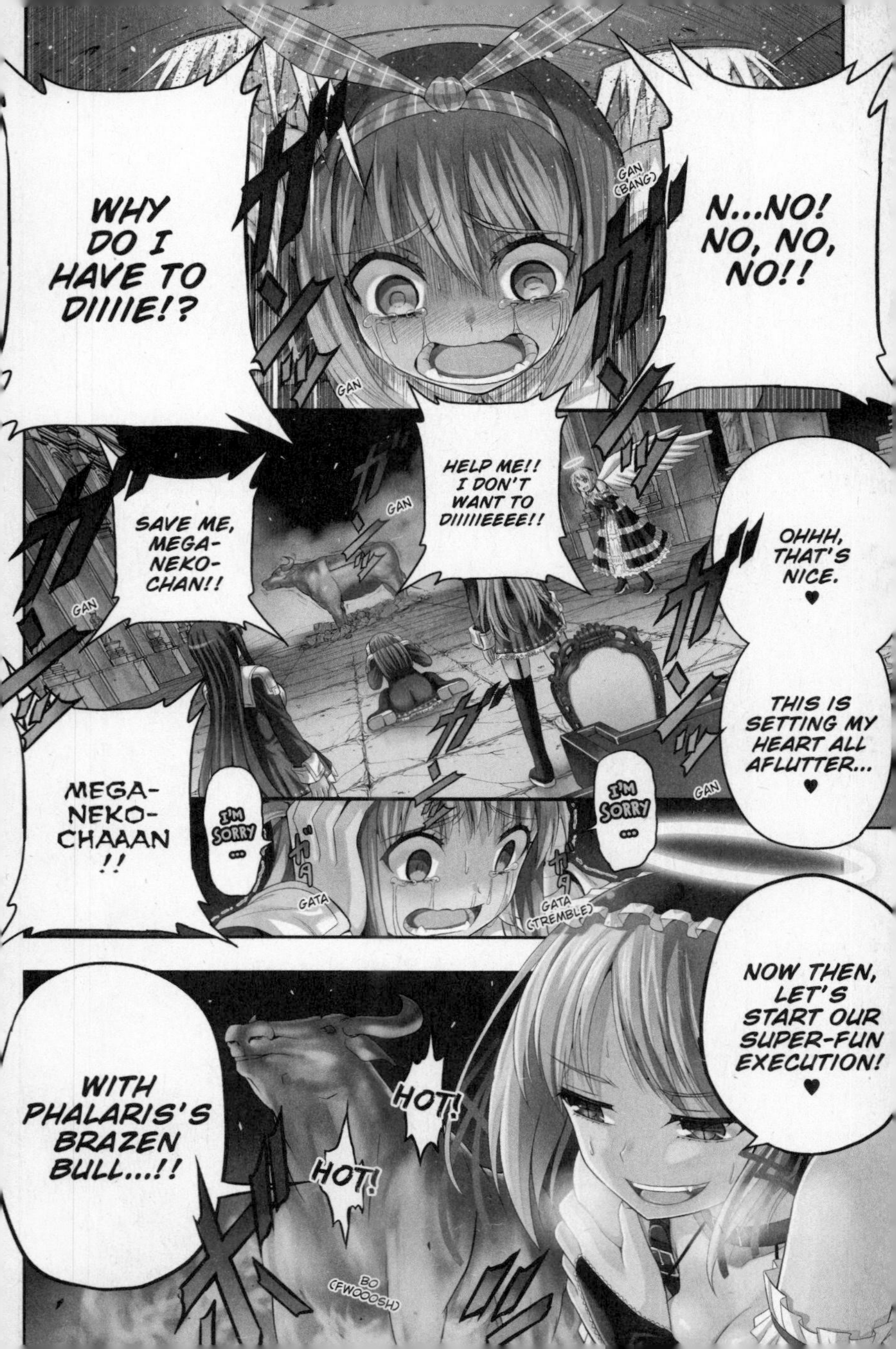
N...NO! NO, NO, NO!!
GAN (BANG)
WHY DO I HAVE TO DIIIIE!?
GAN
OHHH, THAT'S NICE. ♥
THIS IS SETTING MY HEART ALL AFLUTTER... ♥
HELP ME!! I DON'T WANT TO DIIIIEEEE!!
GAN
SAVE ME, MEGA-NEKO-CHAN!!
GAN
GAN
I'M SORRY...
GATA (TREMBLE)
I'M SORRY...
GATA
MEGA-NEKO-CHAAAN!!
NOW THEN, LET'S START OUR SUPER-FUN EXECUTION! ♥
HOT!
HOT!
BO (FWOOOSH)
WITH PHALARIS'S BRAZEN BULL...!!

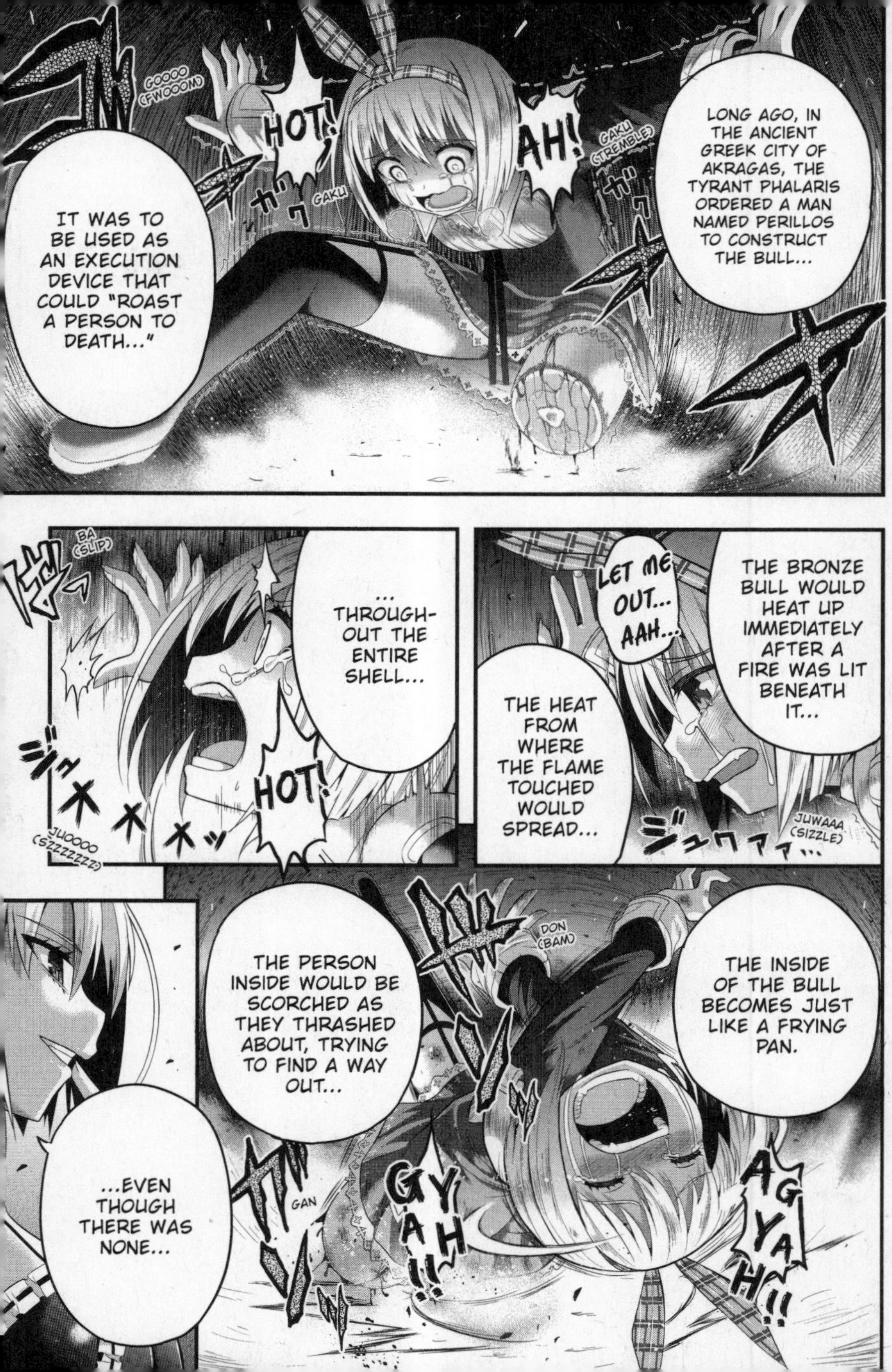
LONG AGO, IN THE ANCIENT GREEK CITY OF AKRAGAS, THE TYRANT PHALARIS ORDERED A MAN NAMED PERILLOS TO CONSTRUCT THE BULL...
GAKU (TREMBLE)
AH!
GAKU
HOT!
GOOOO (FWOOOM)
IT WAS TO BE USED AS AN EXECUTION DEVICE THAT COULD "ROAST A PERSON TO DEATH..."
THE BRONZE BULL WOULD HEAT UP IMMEDIATELY AFTER A FIRE WAS LIT BENEATH IT...
LET ME OUT... AAH...
THE HEAT FROM WHERE THE FLAME TOUCHED WOULD SPREAD...
JUWAAA (SIZZLE)
... THROUGH-OUT THE ENTIRE SHELL...
BA (SLIP)
HOT!
JUOOOO (SZZZZZZZ)
THE INSIDE OF THE BULL BECOMES JUST LIKE A FRYING PAN.
DON (BAM)
THE PERSON INSIDE WOULD BE SCORCHED AS THEY THRASHED ABOUT, TRYING TO FIND A WAY OUT...
AGYAH!!
GYAH!!
GAN
...EVEN THOUGH THERE WAS NONE...

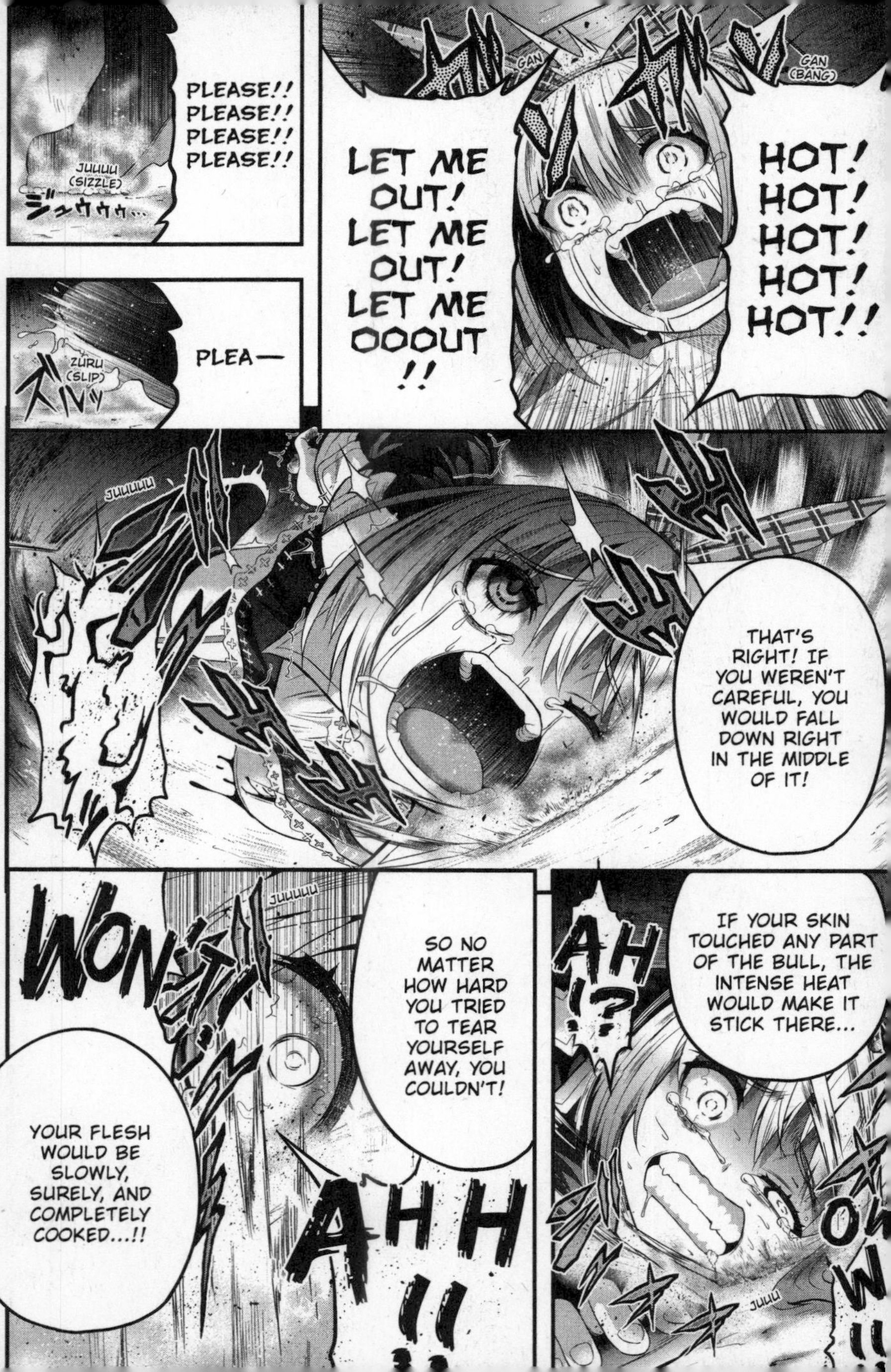

GAN
GAN (BANG)
HOT! HOT! HOT! HOT! HOT!!
LET ME OUT! LET ME OUT! LET ME OOOUT!!
PLEASE!! PLEASE!! PLEASE!! PLEASE!!
JUUUU (SIZZLE)
ジュウウウ…
PLEA—
ZURU (SLIP)
ズルッ
JUUUUU
ズルッ
THAT'S RIGHT! IF YOU WEREN'T CAREFUL, YOU WOULD FALL DOWN RIGHT IN THE MIDDLE OF IT!
IF YOUR SKIN TOUCHED ANY PART OF THE BULL, THE INTENSE HEAT WOULD MAKE IT STICK THERE…
AH!?
OWW!!
JUUU
SO NO MATTER HOW HARD YOU TRIED TO TEAR YOURSELF AWAY, YOU COULDN'T!
JUUUUU
WON'T!!
AHH!!
YOUR FLESH WOULD BE SLOWLY, SURELY, AND COMPLETELY COOKED…!!

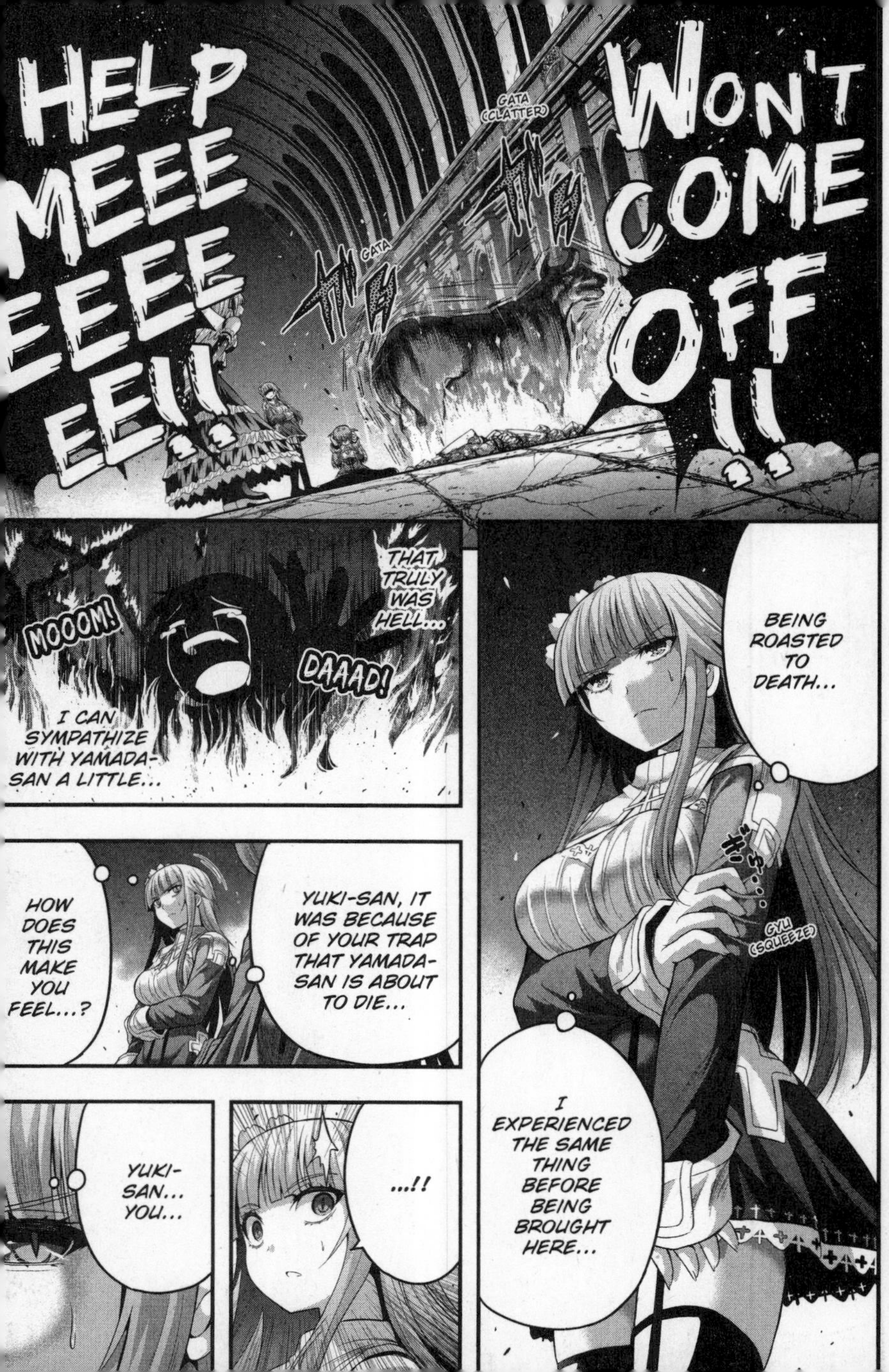
WON'T COME OFF!!
GATA (CLATTER)
GATA
HELP MEEEEEEEEEEEEE!!
BEING ROASTED TO DEATH...
GYU (SQUEEZE)
I EXPERIENCED THE SAME THING BEFORE BEING BROUGHT HERE...
THAT TRULY WAS HELL...
DAAAD!
MOOOM!
I CAN SYMPATHIZE WITH YAMADA-SAN A LITTLE...
YUKI-SAN, IT WAS BECAUSE OF YOUR TRAP THAT YAMADA-SAN IS ABOUT TO DIE...
HOW DOES THIS MAKE YOU FEEL...?
...!!
YUKI-SAN... YOU...

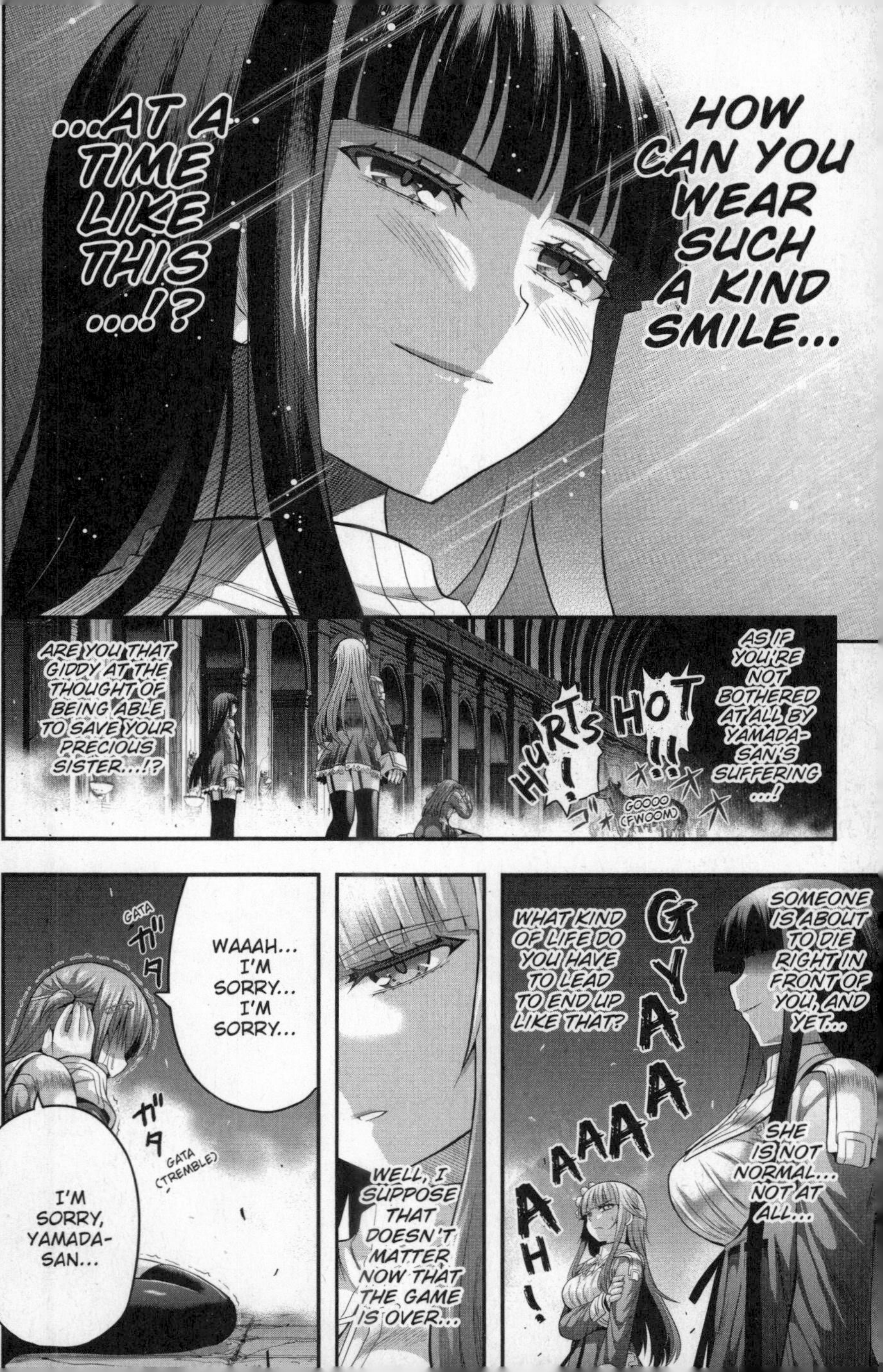
HOW CAN YOU WEAR SUCH A KIND SMILE...
...AT A TIME LIKE THIS...!?
AS IF YOU'RE NOT BOTHERED AT ALL BY YAMADA-SAN'S SUFFERING...!
HURTS HOT!!!
GOOOO (FWOOM)
ARE YOU THAT GIDDY AT THE THOUGHT OF BEING ABLE TO SAVE YOUR PRECIOUS SISTER...!?
SOMEONE IS ABOUT TO DIE RIGHT IN FRONT OF YOU, AND YET...
GYAAAAAAAH!
WHAT KIND OF LIFE DO YOU HAVE TO LEAD TO END UP LIKE THAT?
SHE IS NOT NORMAL... NOT AT ALL...
WELL, I SUPPOSE THAT DOESN'T MATTER NOW THAT THE GAME IS OVER...
GATA
WAAAH... I'M SORRY... I'M SORRY...
GATA (TREMBLE)
I'M SORRY, YAMADA-SAN...

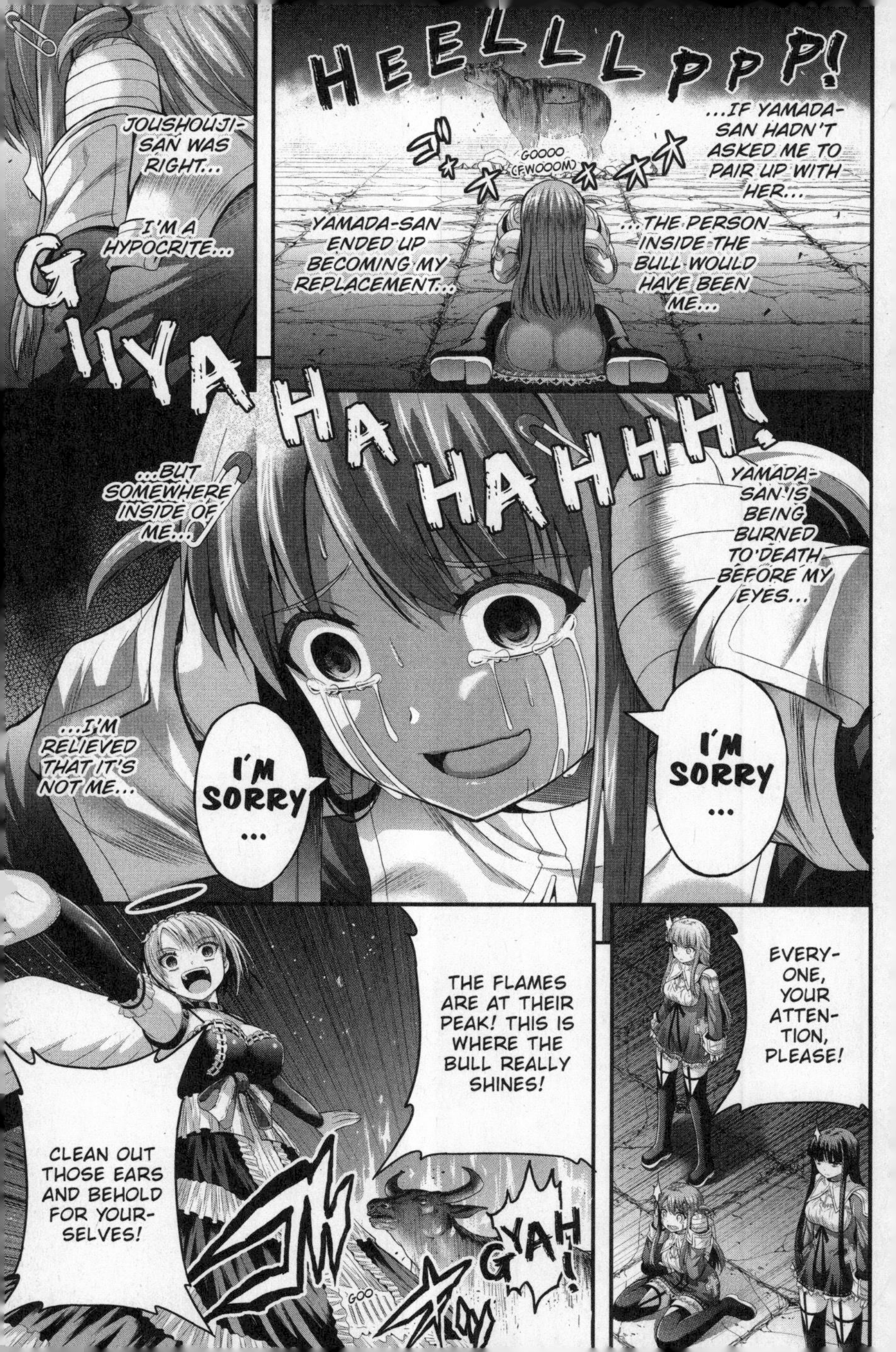
HEELLLPPPP!
GOOOO (FWOOOM)
...IF YAMADA-SAN HADN'T ASKED ME TO PAIR UP WITH HER...
...THE PERSON INSIDE THE BULL WOULD HAVE BEEN ME...
YAMADA-SAN ENDED UP BECOMING MY REPLACEMENT...
JOUSHOUJI-SAN WAS RIGHT...
I'M A HYPOCRITE...
GIIYAHAHAHHH!
YAMADA-SAN IS BEING BURNED TO DEATH BEFORE MY EYES...
...BUT SOMEWHERE INSIDE OF ME...
I'M SORRY...
I'M SORRY...
...I'M RELIEVED THAT IT'S NOT ME...
EVERYONE, YOUR ATTENTION, PLEASE!
THE FLAMES ARE AT THEIR PEAK! THIS IS WHERE THE BULL REALLY SHINES!
CLEAN OUT THOSE EARS AND BEHOLD FOR YOURSELVES!
GYAH!
GOO

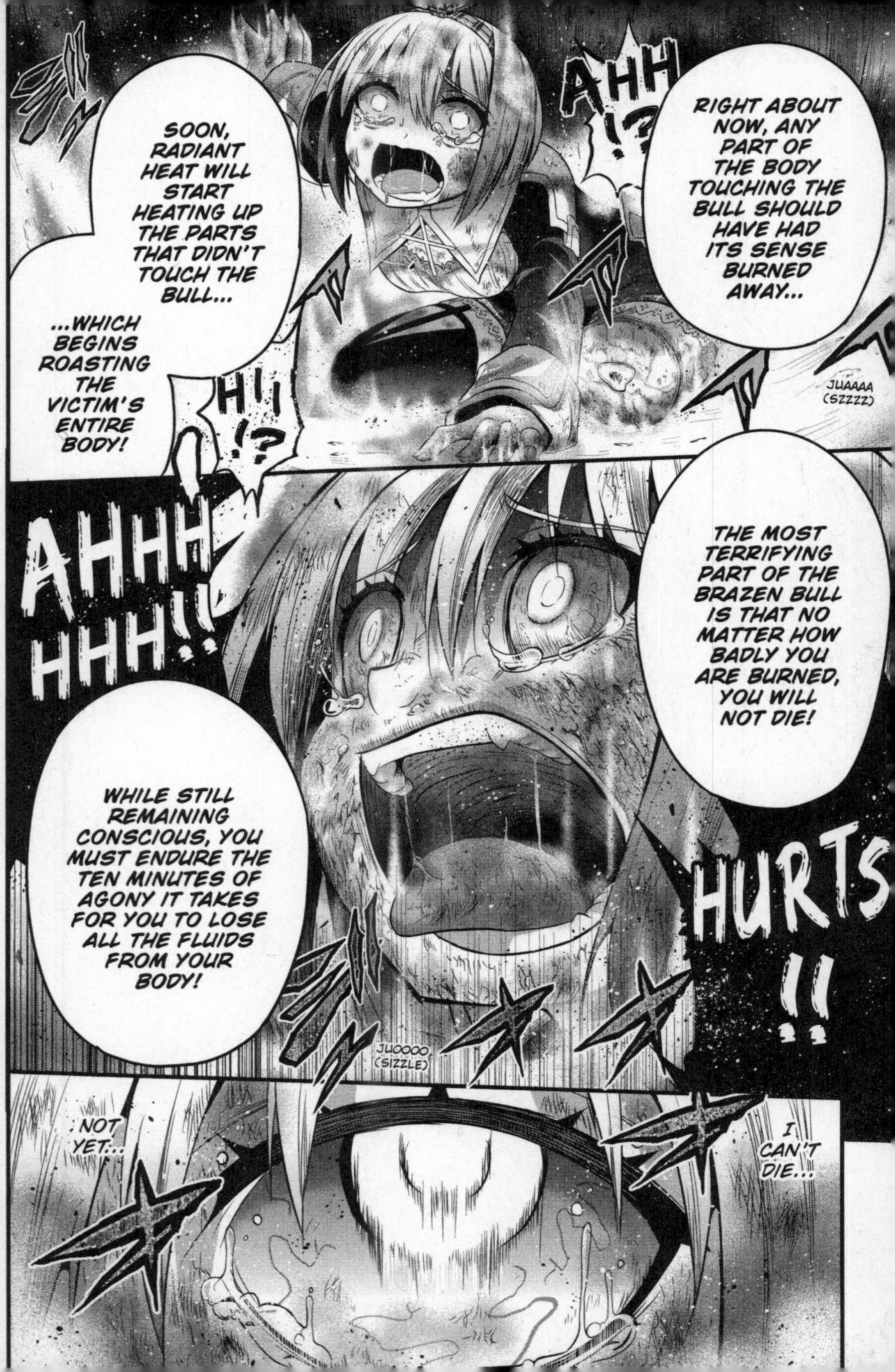
RIGHT ABOUT NOW, ANY PART OF THE BODY TOUCHING THE BULL SHOULD HAVE HAD ITS SENSE BURNED AWAY...
AHH!?
SOON, RADIANT HEAT WILL START HEATING UP THE PARTS THAT DIDN'T TOUCH THE BULL...
...WHICH BEGINS ROASTING THE VICTIM'S ENTIRE BODY!
JUAAAA (SZZZZ)
HII!?
THE MOST TERRIFYING PART OF THE BRAZEN BULL IS THAT NO MATTER HOW BADLY YOU ARE BURNED, YOU WILL NOT DIE!
AHHHHH!!
HURTS!!
WHILE STILL REMAINING CONSCIOUS, YOU MUST ENDURE THE TEN MINUTES OF AGONY IT TAKES FOR YOU TO LOSE ALL THE FLUIDS FROM YOUR BODY!
JUOOOO (SIZZLE)
I CAN'T DIE...
NOT YET...

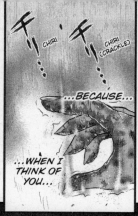

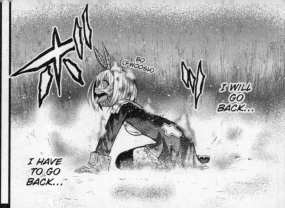

BO (FWOOSH)
I WILL GO BACK...
I HAVE TO GO BACK...
CHIRI (CRACKLE)
CHIRI
...BECAUSE...
...WHEN I THINK OF YOU...
...EVEN NOW...
...YOU'RE STILL CRYING...
IT WAS ME...I MADE YOU CRY...
THAT'S WHY I'M THE ONLY ONE WHO CAN MAKE YOU SMILE AGAIN!!
AS WE REACH THE END, THE VICTIM STARTS HAVING TROUBLE BREATHING DUE TO THE SMOKE FROM THEIR COOKED FLESH AND THE HEAT INSIDE...
ZEHI (HEAVE)
ZEHI
I WILL COME BACK... TO LIFE!!
GOOOOO (FWOOOM)
THAT'S WHEN THE PERSON INSIDE WILL REACH OUT TO A CERTAIN "SOMETHING" IN THE BULL...

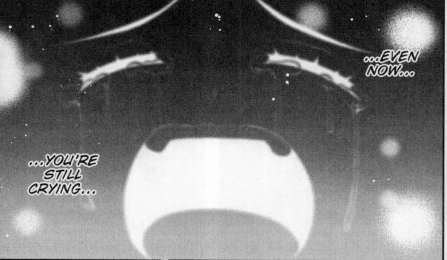

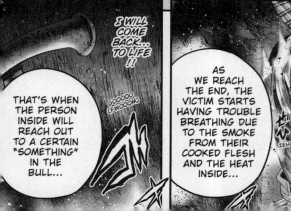

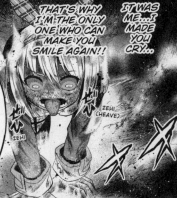

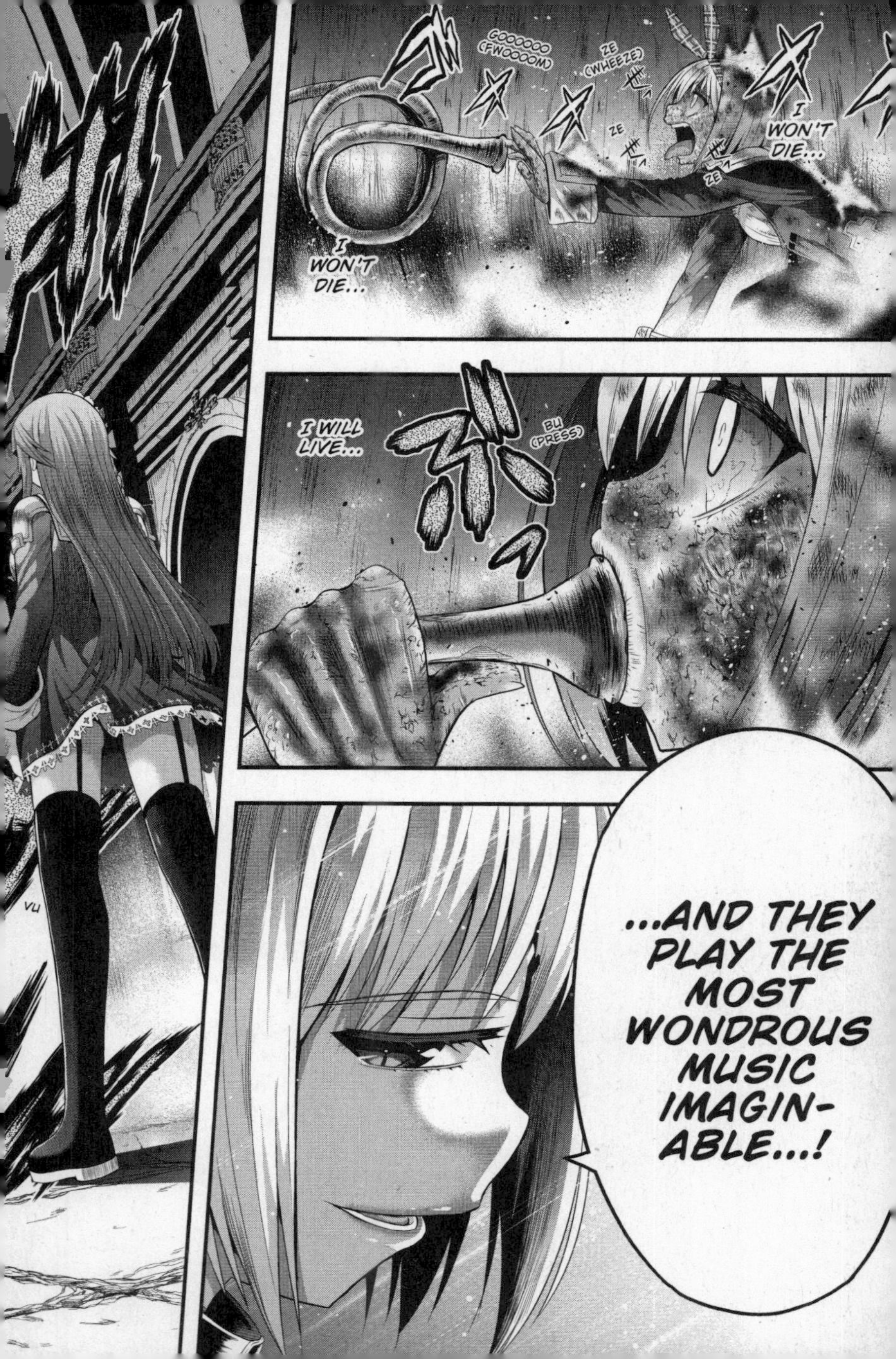
I WON'T DIE...
ZE (WHEEZE)
GOOOOOO (FWOOOOOM)
ZE
ZE
I WON'T DIE...
BU (PRESS)
I WILL LIVE...
...AND THEY PLAY THE MOST WONDROUS MUSIC IMAGINABLE...!
VU

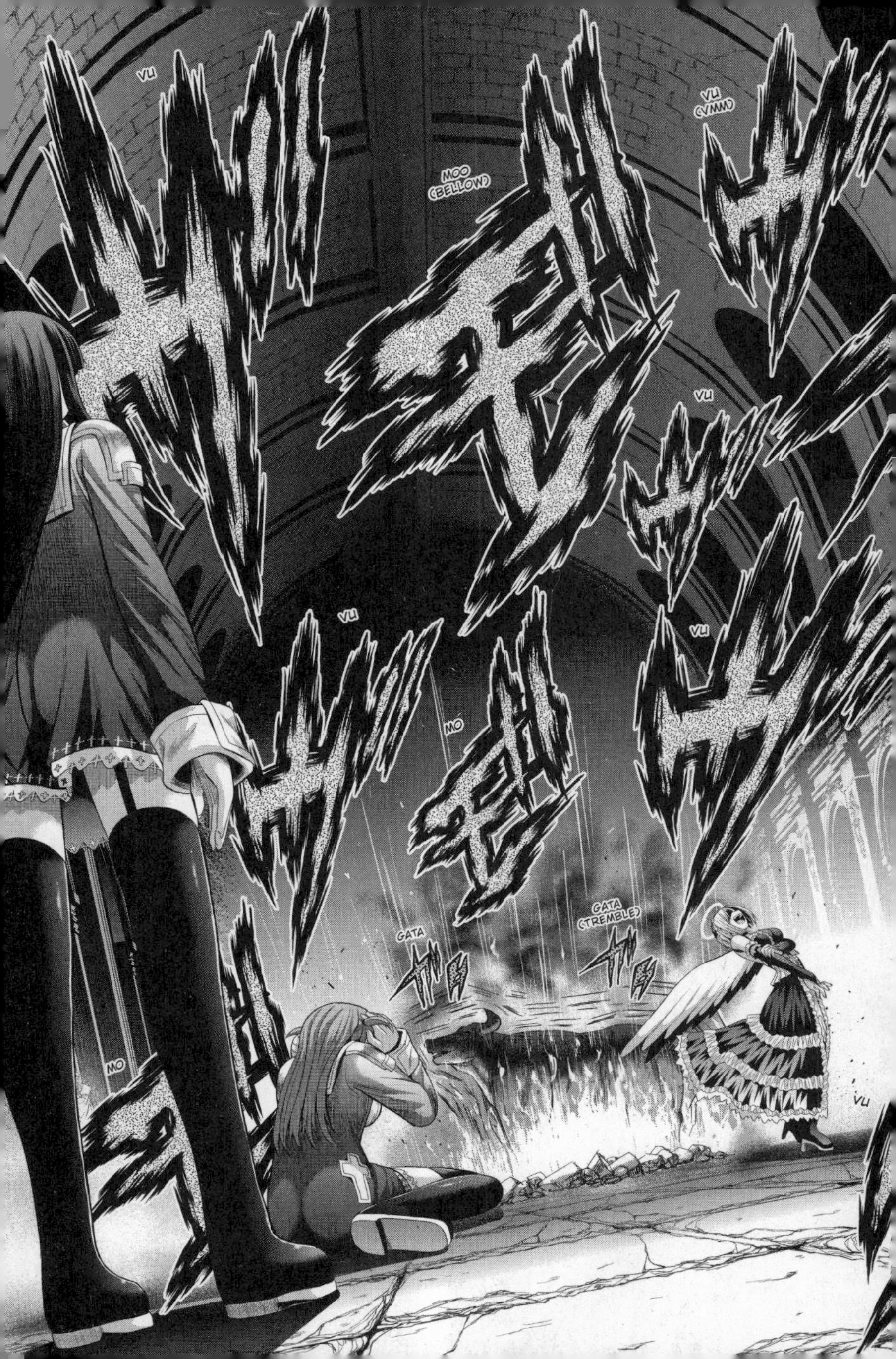
VU
(VMM)
MOO
(BELLOW)
VU
VU
VU
VU
MO
GATA
(TREMBLE)
GATA
VU
MO

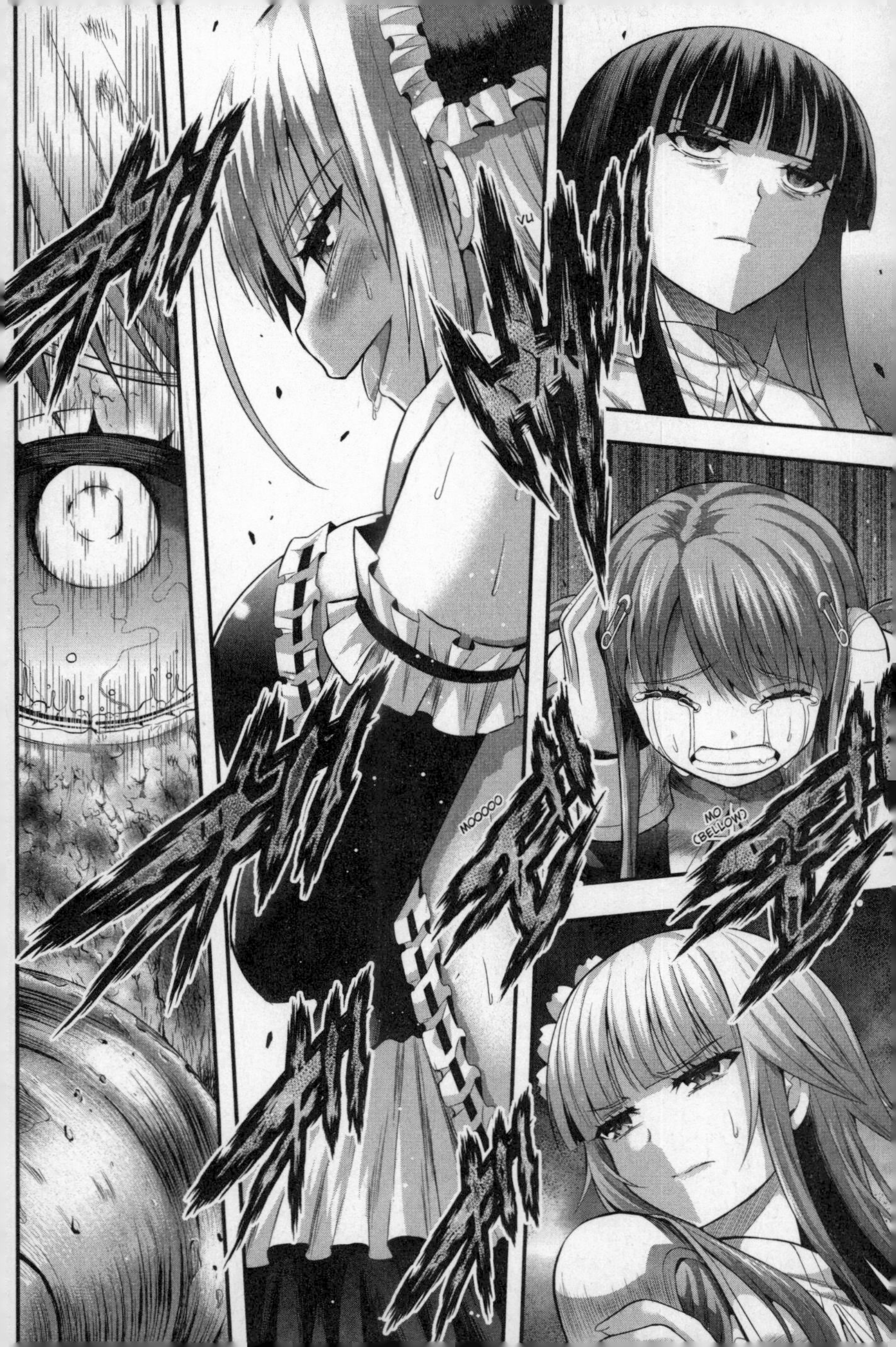
VU
MO (BELLOW)
MOOOOO

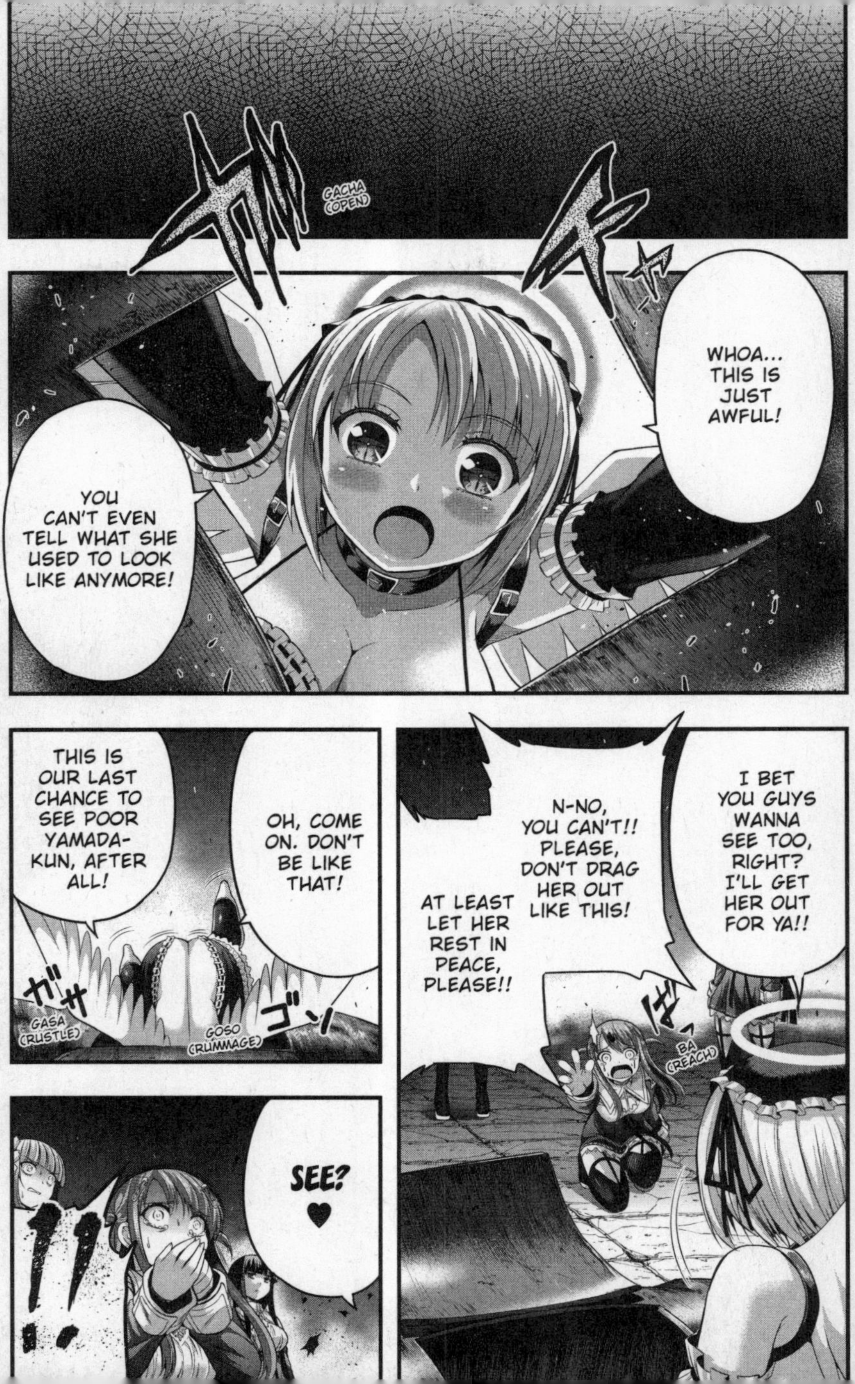
GACHA (OPEN)
WHOA... THIS IS JUST AWFUL!
YOU CAN'T EVEN TELL WHAT SHE USED TO LOOK LIKE ANYMORE!
I BET YOU GUYS WANNA SEE TOO, RIGHT? I'LL GET HER OUT FOR YA!!
N-NO, YOU CAN'T!! PLEASE, DON'T DRAG HER OUT LIKE THIS!
AT LEAST LET HER REST IN PEACE, PLEASE!!
BA (REACH)
OH, COME ON. DON'T BE LIKE THAT!
THIS IS OUR LAST CHANCE TO SEE POOR YAMADA-KUN, AFTER ALL!
GOSO (RUMMAGE)
GASA (RUSTLE)
SEE? ♥

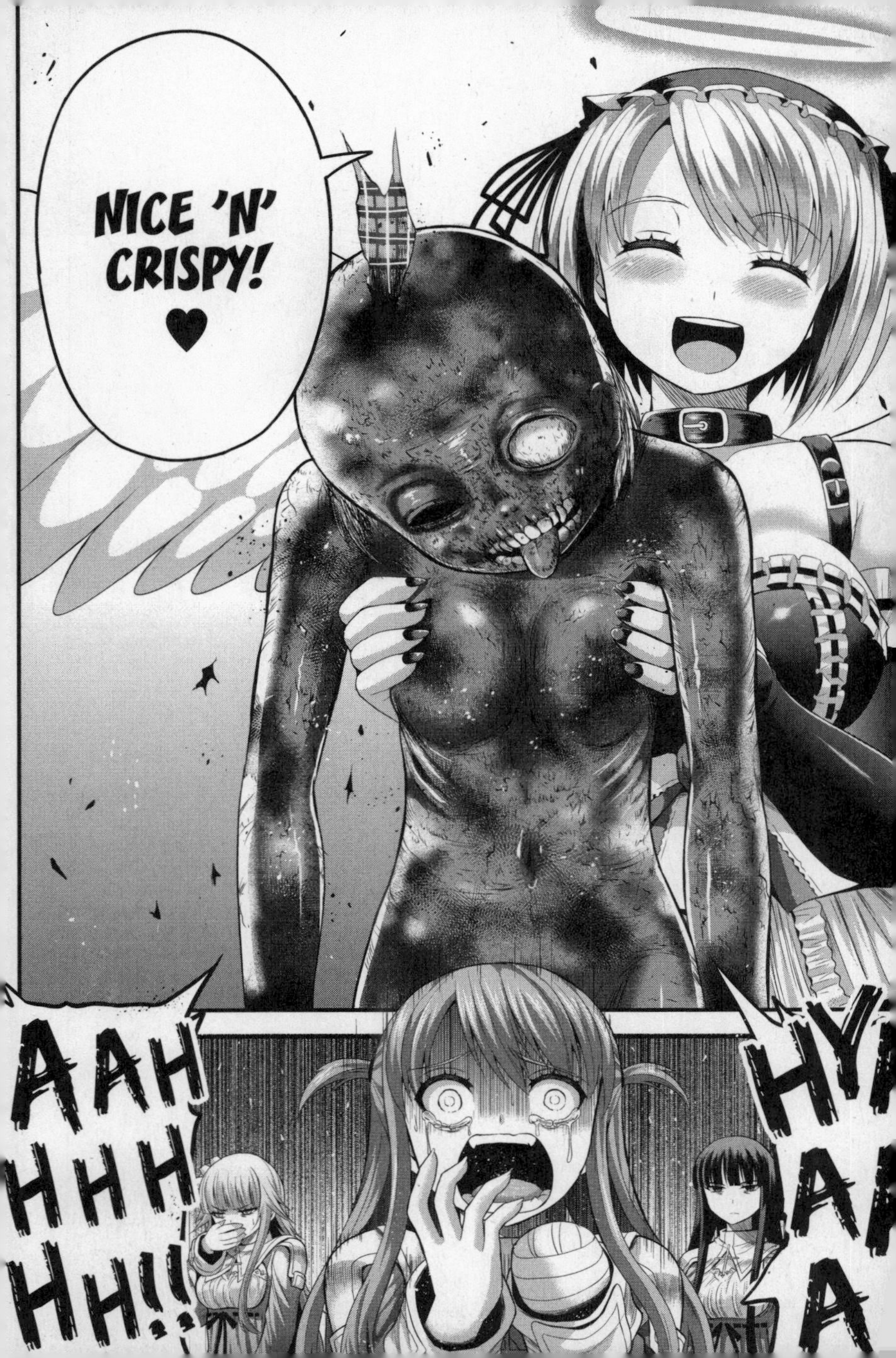
NICE 'N' CRISPY! ♥
HYAAA
AAHHHHHH!!

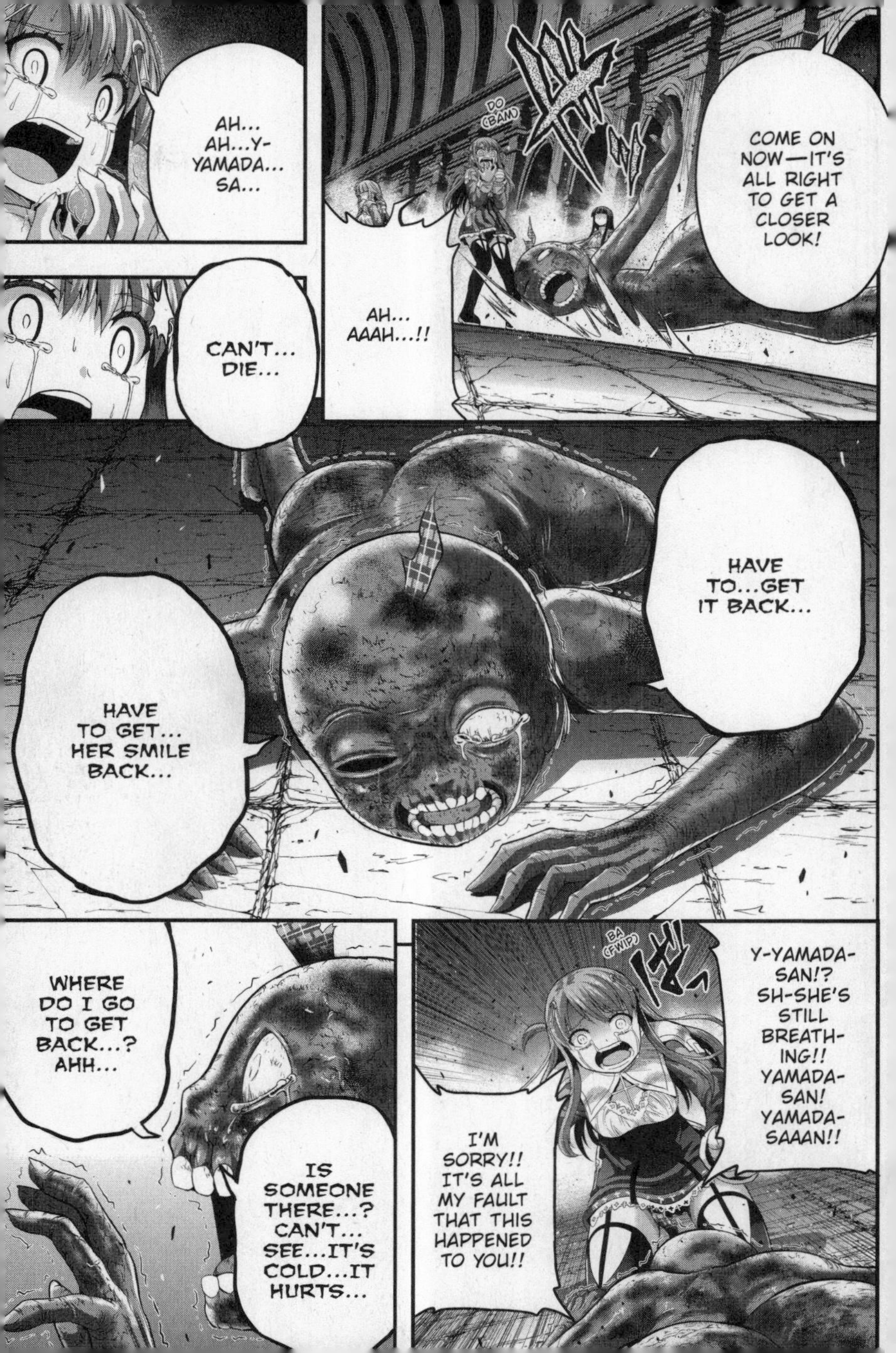
COME ON NOW—IT'S ALL RIGHT TO GET A CLOSER LOOK!
DO (BAM)
AH... AAAH...!!
AH... AH...Y-YAMADA... SA...
CAN'T... DIE...
HAVE TO...GET IT BACK...
HAVE TO GET... HER SMILE BACK...
BA (FWIP)
Y-YAMADA-SAN!? SH-SHE'S STILL BREATHING!! YAMADA-SAN! YAMADA-SAAAN!!
I'M SORRY!! IT'S ALL MY FAULT THAT THIS HAPPENED TO YOU!!
WHERE DO I GO TO GET BACK...? AHH...
IS SOMEONE THERE...? CAN'T... SEE...IT'S COLD...IT HURTS...

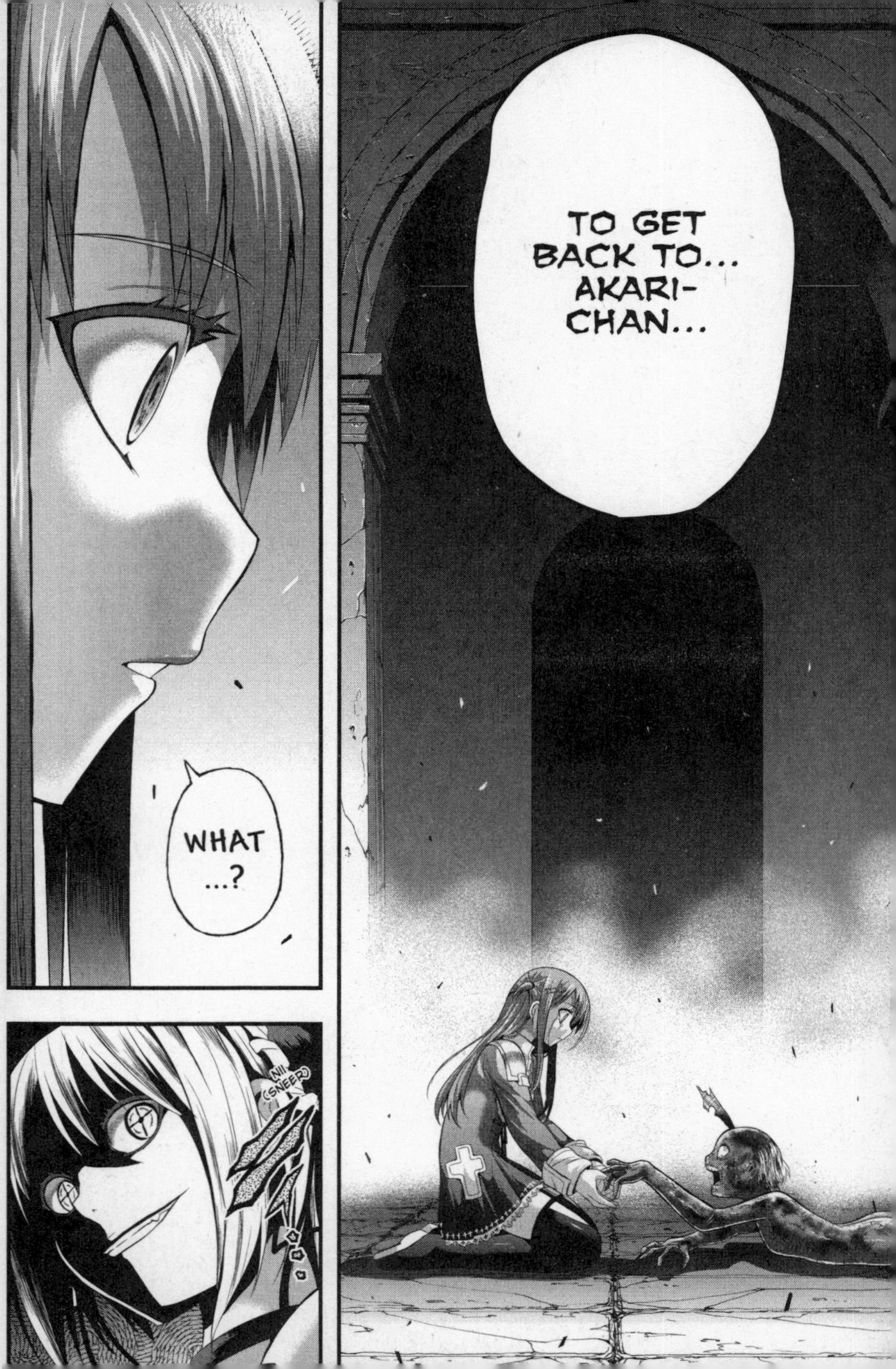
TO GET BACK TO... AKARI-CHAN...
WHAT ...?
NII (SNEER)

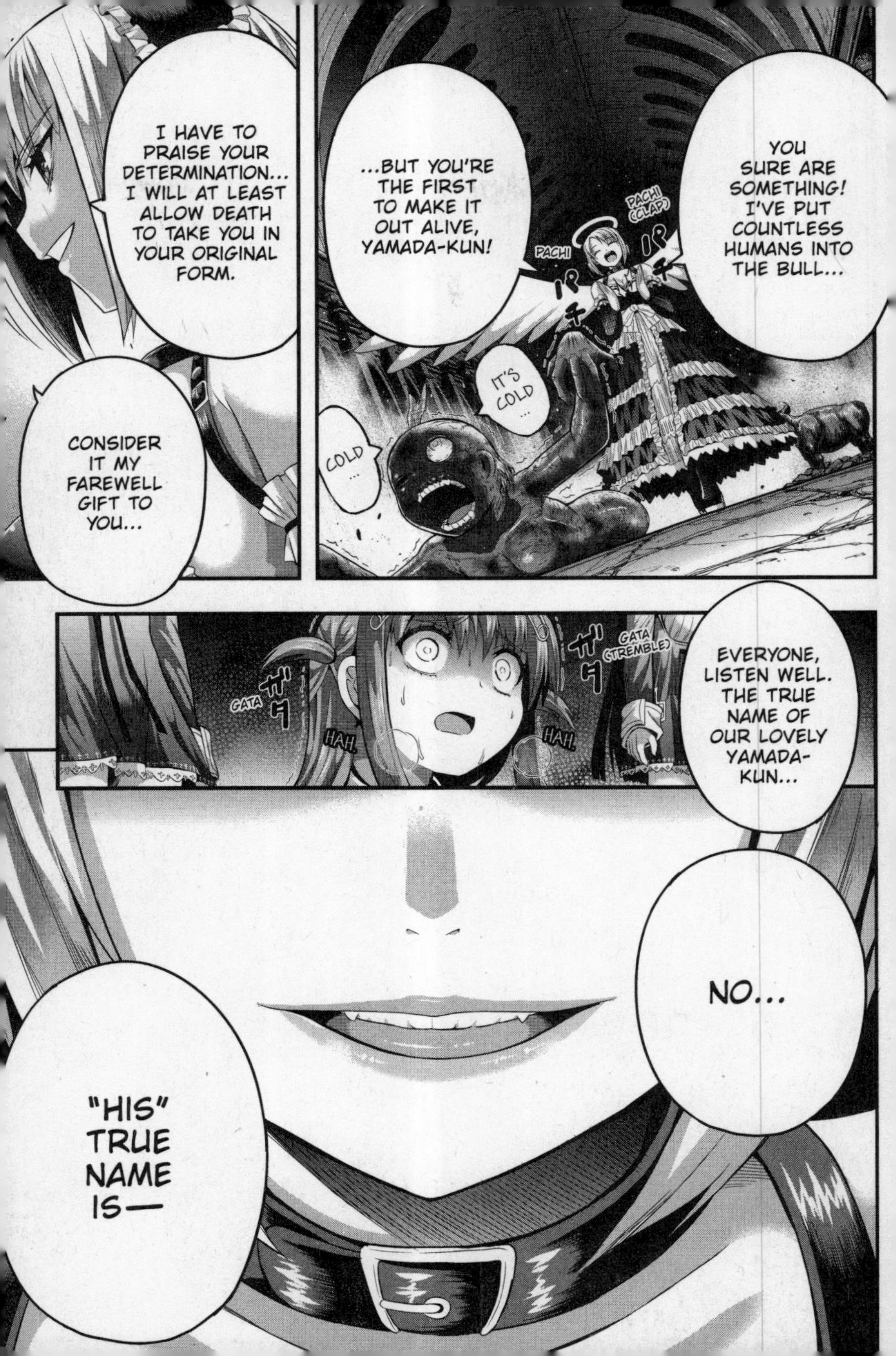

YOU SURE ARE SOMETHING! I'VE PUT COUNTLESS HUMANS INTO THE BULL...
PACHI (CLAP)
PACHI
...BUT YOU'RE THE FIRST TO MAKE IT OUT ALIVE, YAMADA-KUN!
IT'S COLD...
COLD...
I HAVE TO PRAISE YOUR DETERMINATION... I WILL AT LEAST ALLOW DEATH TO TAKE YOU IN YOUR ORIGINAL FORM.
CONSIDER IT MY FAREWELL GIFT TO YOU...
EVERYONE, LISTEN WELL. THE TRUE NAME OF OUR LOVELY YAMADA-KUN...
GATA (TREMBLE)
HAH.
HAH.
GATA
NO...
"HIS" TRUE NAME IS—

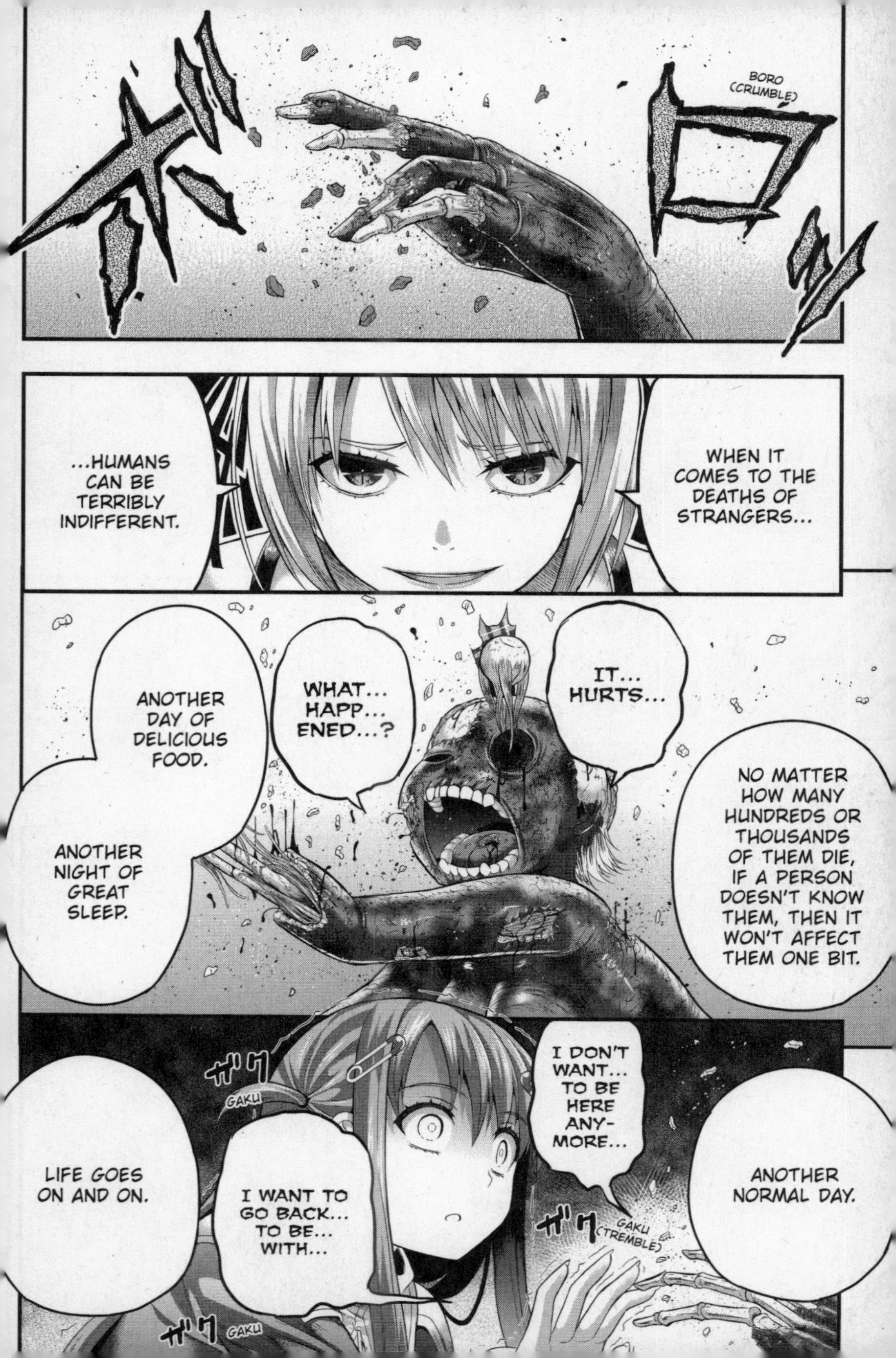
BORO (CRUMBLE)
WHEN IT COMES TO THE DEATHS OF STRANGERS...
...HUMANS CAN BE TERRIBLY INDIFFERENT.
IT... HURTS...
NO MATTER HOW MANY HUNDREDS OR THOUSANDS OF THEM DIE, IF A PERSON DOESN'T KNOW THEM, THEN IT WON'T AFFECT THEM ONE BIT.
WHAT... HAPP... ENED...?
ANOTHER DAY OF DELICIOUS FOOD.
ANOTHER NIGHT OF GREAT SLEEP.
ANOTHER NORMAL DAY.
I DON'T WANT... TO BE HERE ANY-MORE...
GAKU
GAKU (TREMBLE)
I WANT TO GO BACK... TO BE... WITH...
LIFE GOES ON AND ON.
GAKU

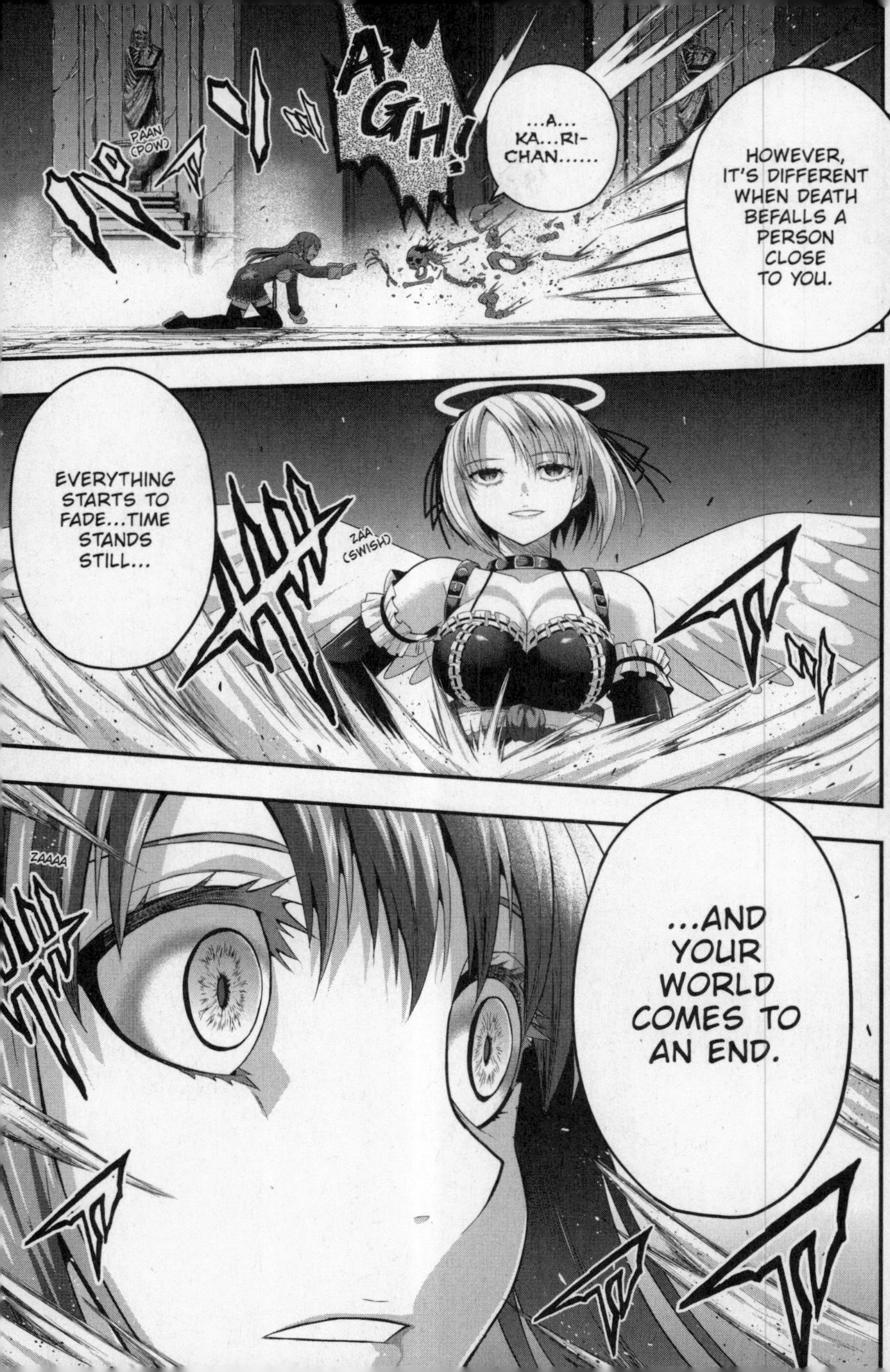
HOWEVER, IT'S DIFFERENT WHEN DEATH BEFALLS A PERSON CLOSE TO YOU.
...A... KA...RI-CHAN......
AGH!
PAAN (POW)
ZAA (SWISH)
EVERYTHING STARTS TO FADE...TIME STANDS STILL...
...AND YOUR WORLD COMES TO AN END.
ZAAAA

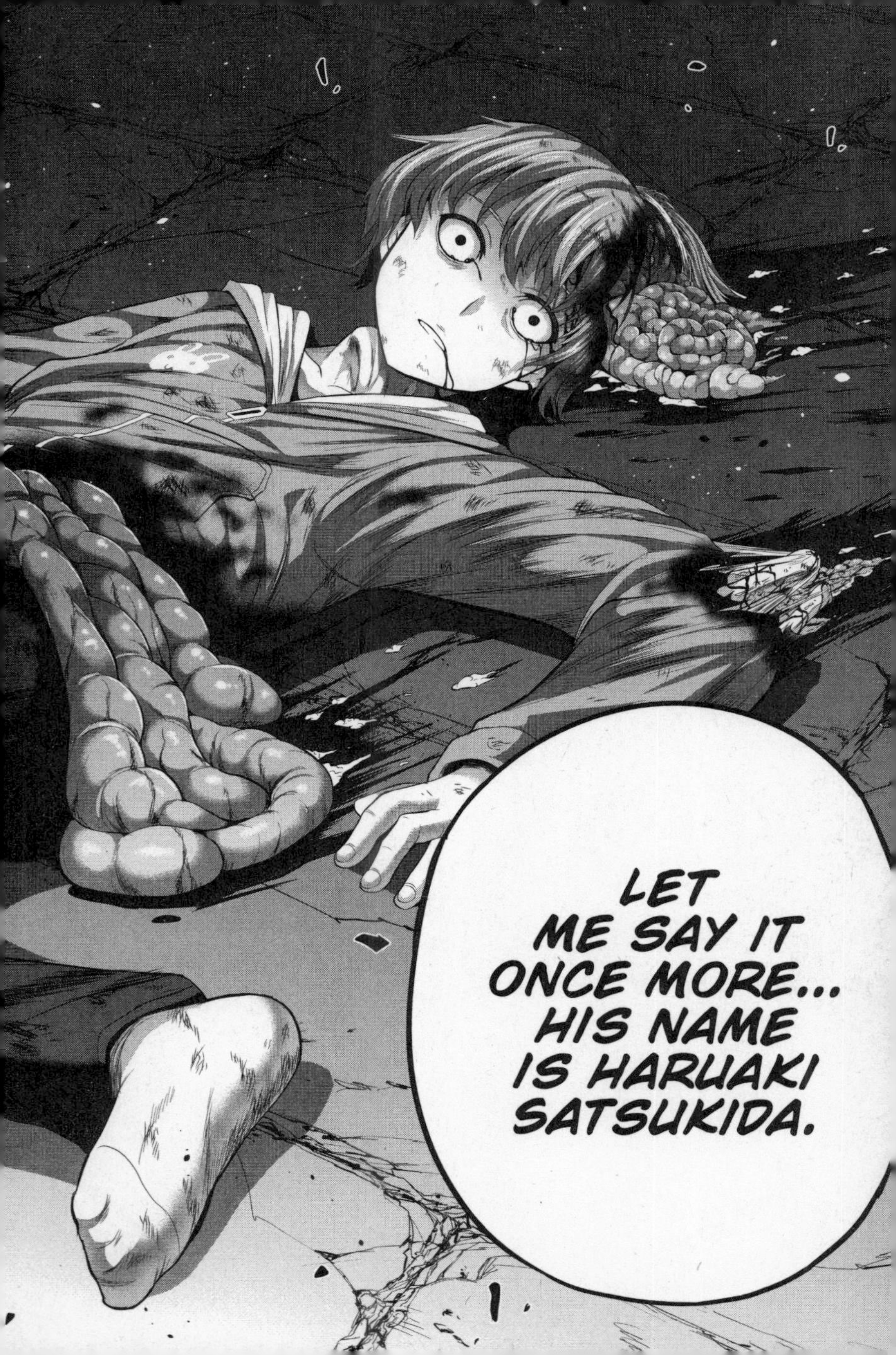
LET ME SAY IT ONCE MORE... HIS NAME IS HARUAKI SATSUKIDA.

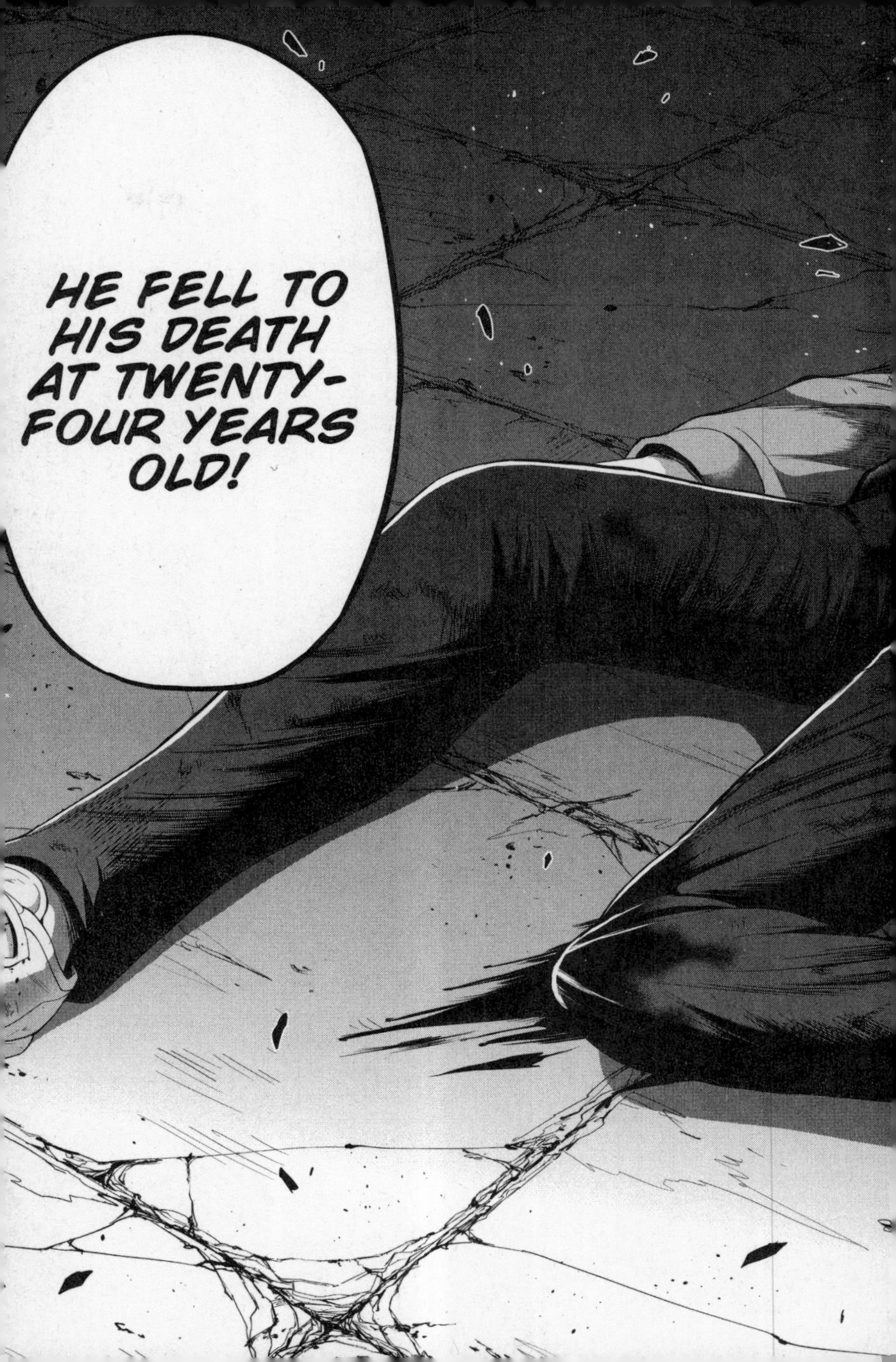
HE FELL TO HIS DEATH AT TWENTY-FOUR YEARS OLD!

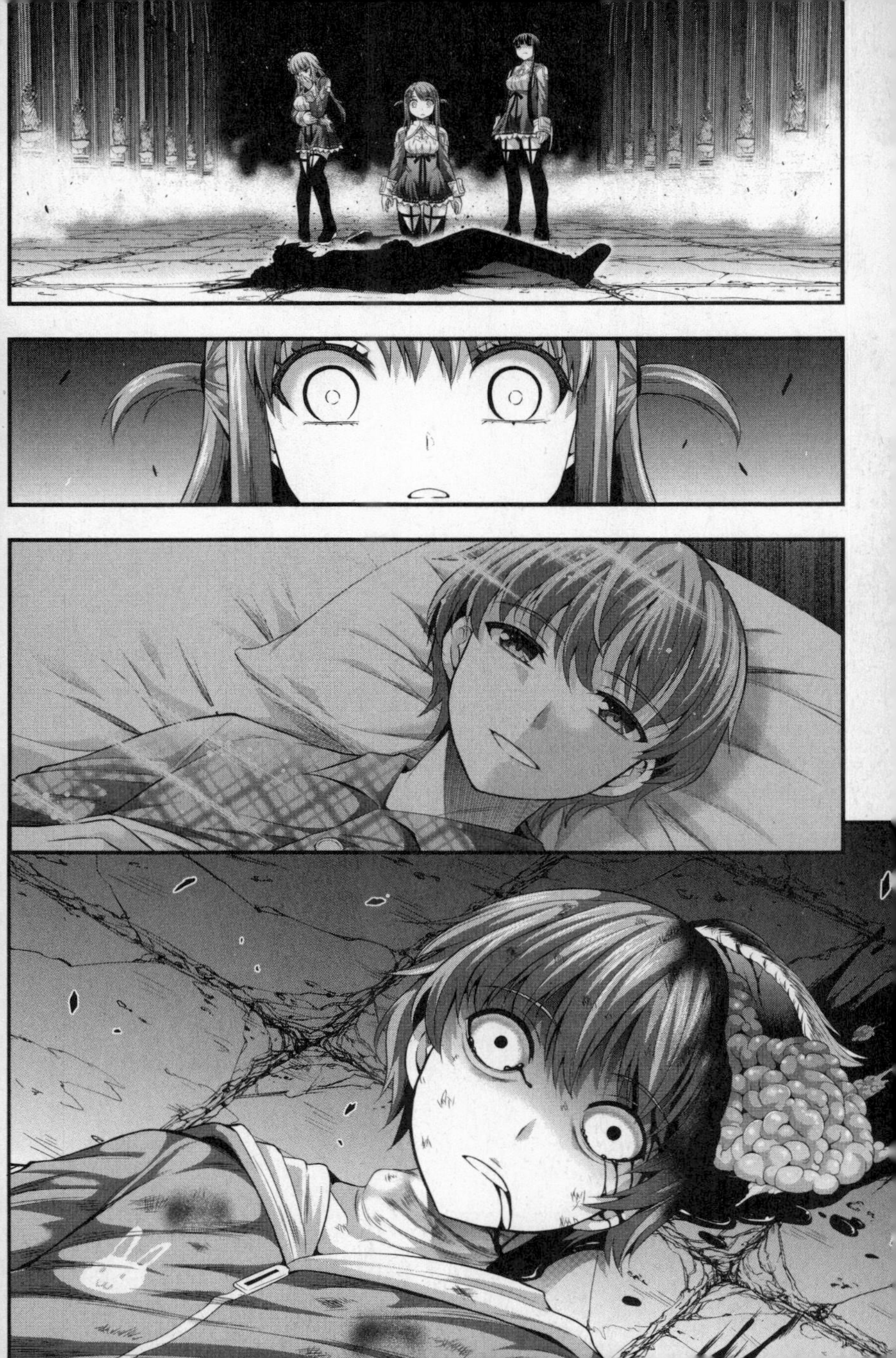

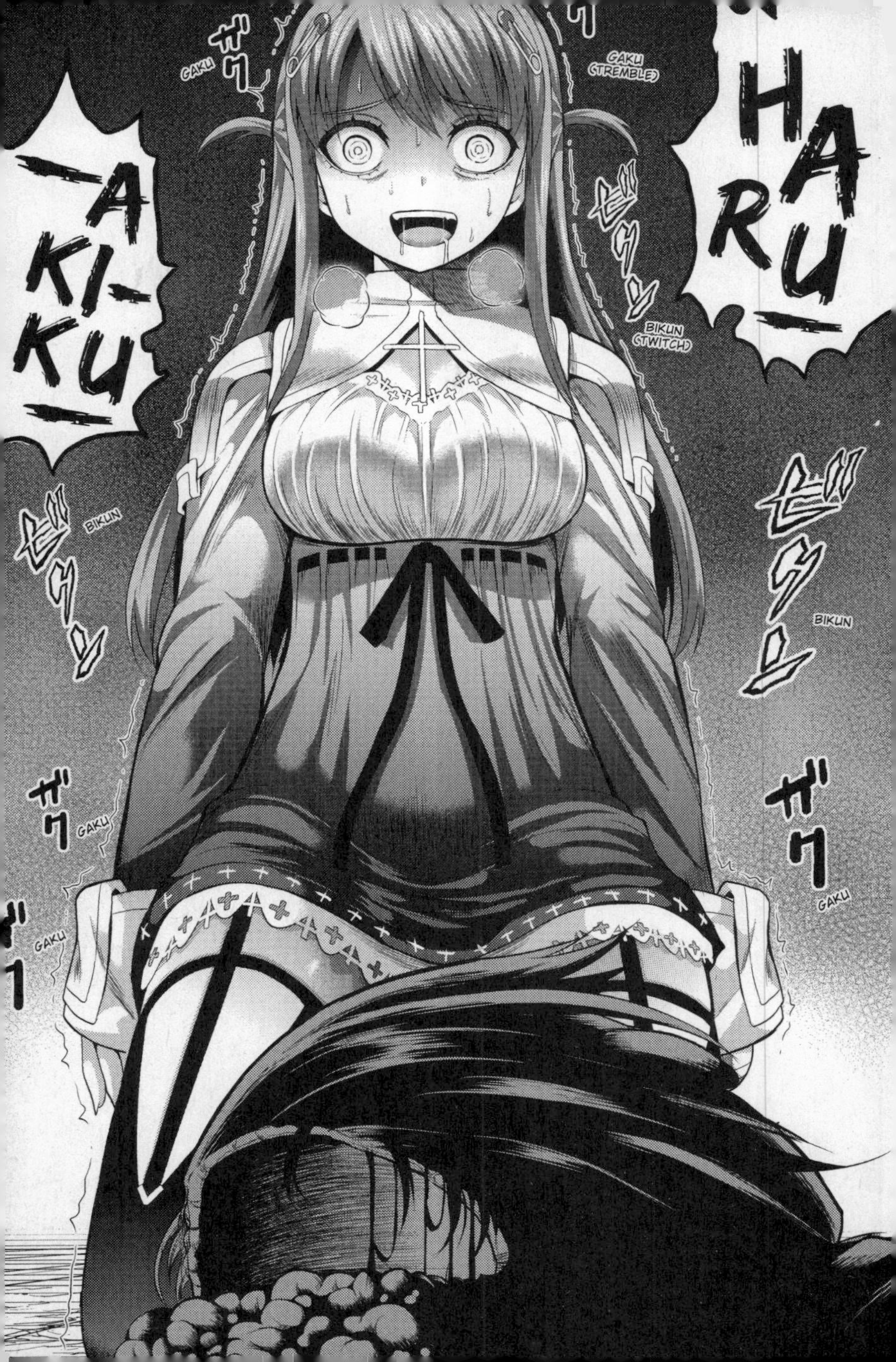
HARU—
—AKI-KU—
ガク
GAKU (TREMBLE)
ガク
GAKU
ビクン
BIKUN (TWITCH)
ビクン
BIKUN
ビクン
BIKUN
ガク
GAKU
ガク
GAKU
ガク
GAKU

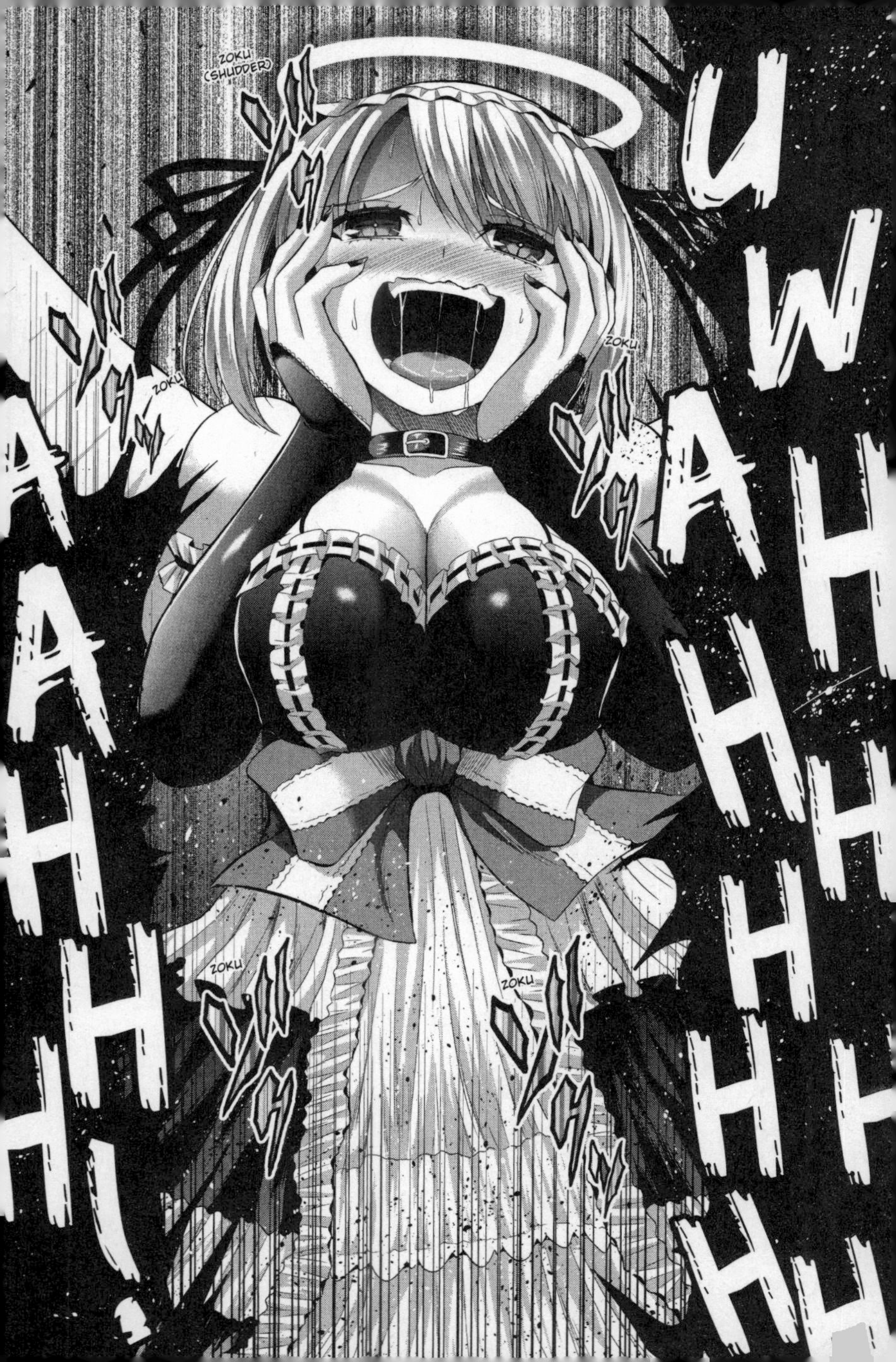
UWAHHHHHHHHHH
ZOKU (SHUDDER)
ZOKU
ZOKU
ZOKU
ZOKU
AAHHHH!

Though You May Burn to ASH

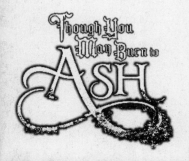

Though You May Burn to Ash

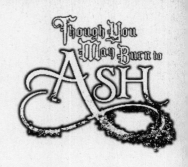

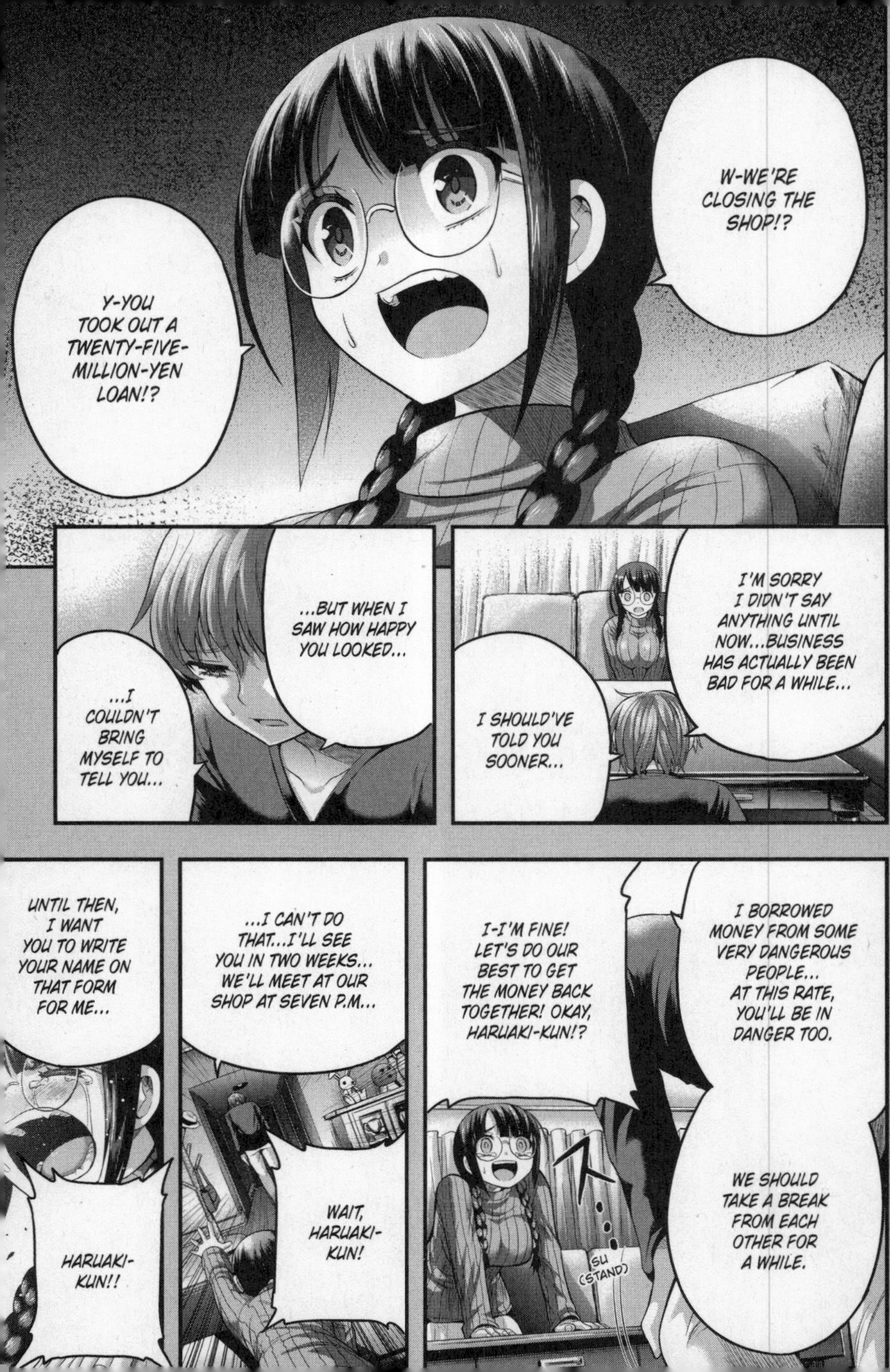
W-WE'RE CLOSING THE SHOP!?
Y-YOU TOOK OUT A TWENTY-FIVE-MILLION-YEN LOAN!?
I'M SORRY I DIDN'T SAY ANYTHING UNTIL NOW...BUSINESS HAS ACTUALLY BEEN BAD FOR A WHILE...
I SHOULD'VE TOLD YOU SOONER...
...BUT WHEN I SAW HOW HAPPY YOU LOOKED...
...I COULDN'T BRING MYSELF TO TELL YOU...
I BORROWED MONEY FROM SOME VERY DANGEROUS PEOPLE... AT THIS RATE, YOU'LL BE IN DANGER TOO.
WE SHOULD TAKE A BREAK FROM EACH OTHER FOR A WHILE.
SU (STAND)
I-I'M FINE! LET'S DO OUR BEST TO GET THE MONEY BACK TOGETHER! OKAY, HARUAKI-KUN!?
...I CAN'T DO THAT...I'LL SEE YOU IN TWO WEEKS... WE'LL MEET AT OUR SHOP AT SEVEN P.M...
WAIT, HARUAKI-KUN!
UNTIL THEN, I WANT YOU TO WRITE YOUR NAME ON THAT FORM FOR ME...
HARUAKI-KUN!!

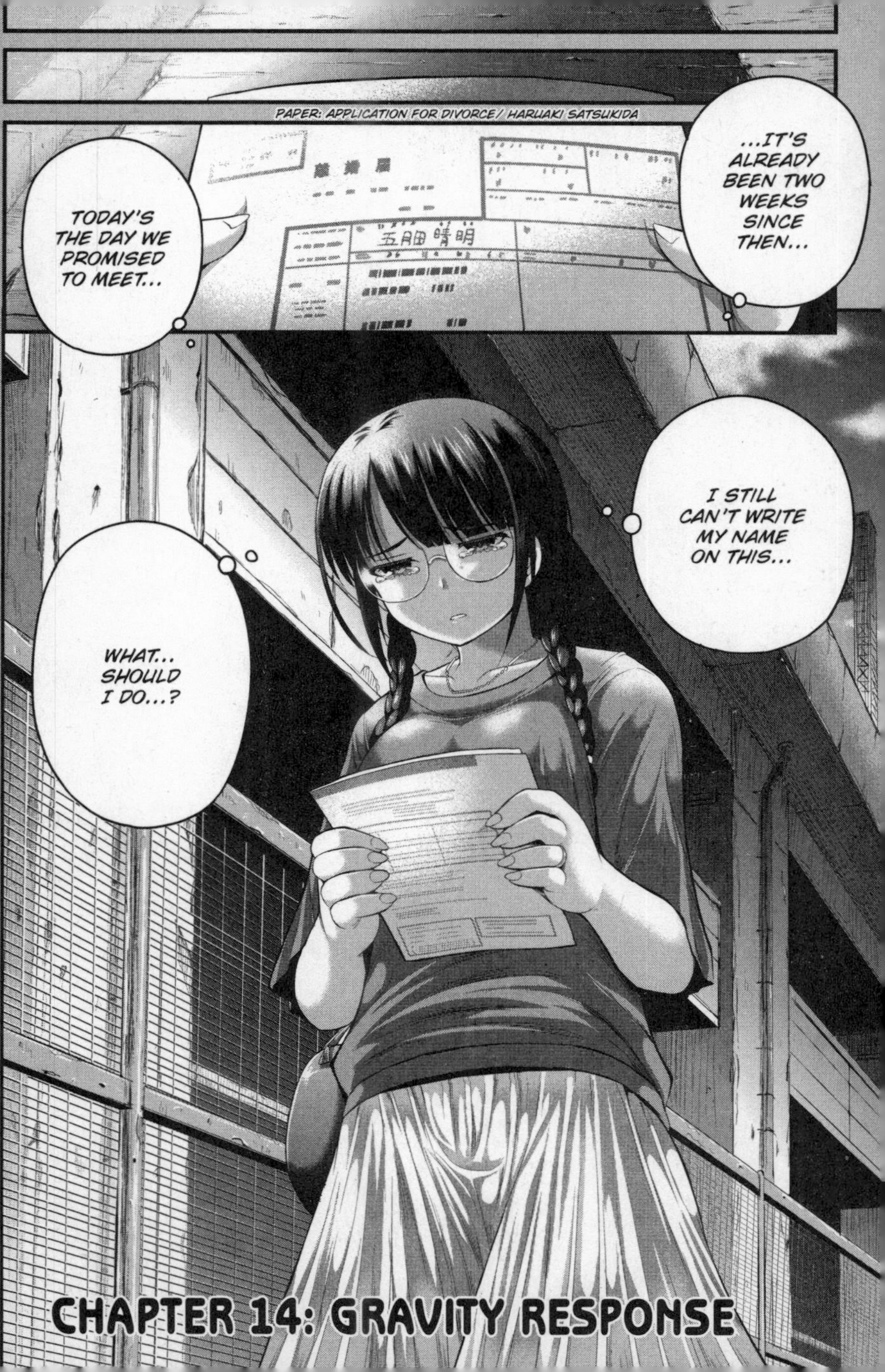
PAPER: APPLICATION FOR DIVORCE/ HARUAKI SATSUKIDA
...IT'S ALREADY BEEN TWO WEEKS SINCE THEN...
TODAY'S THE DAY WE PROMISED TO MEET...
I STILL CAN'T WRITE MY NAME ON THIS...
WHAT... SHOULD I DO...?

CHAPTER 14: GRAVITY RESPONSE

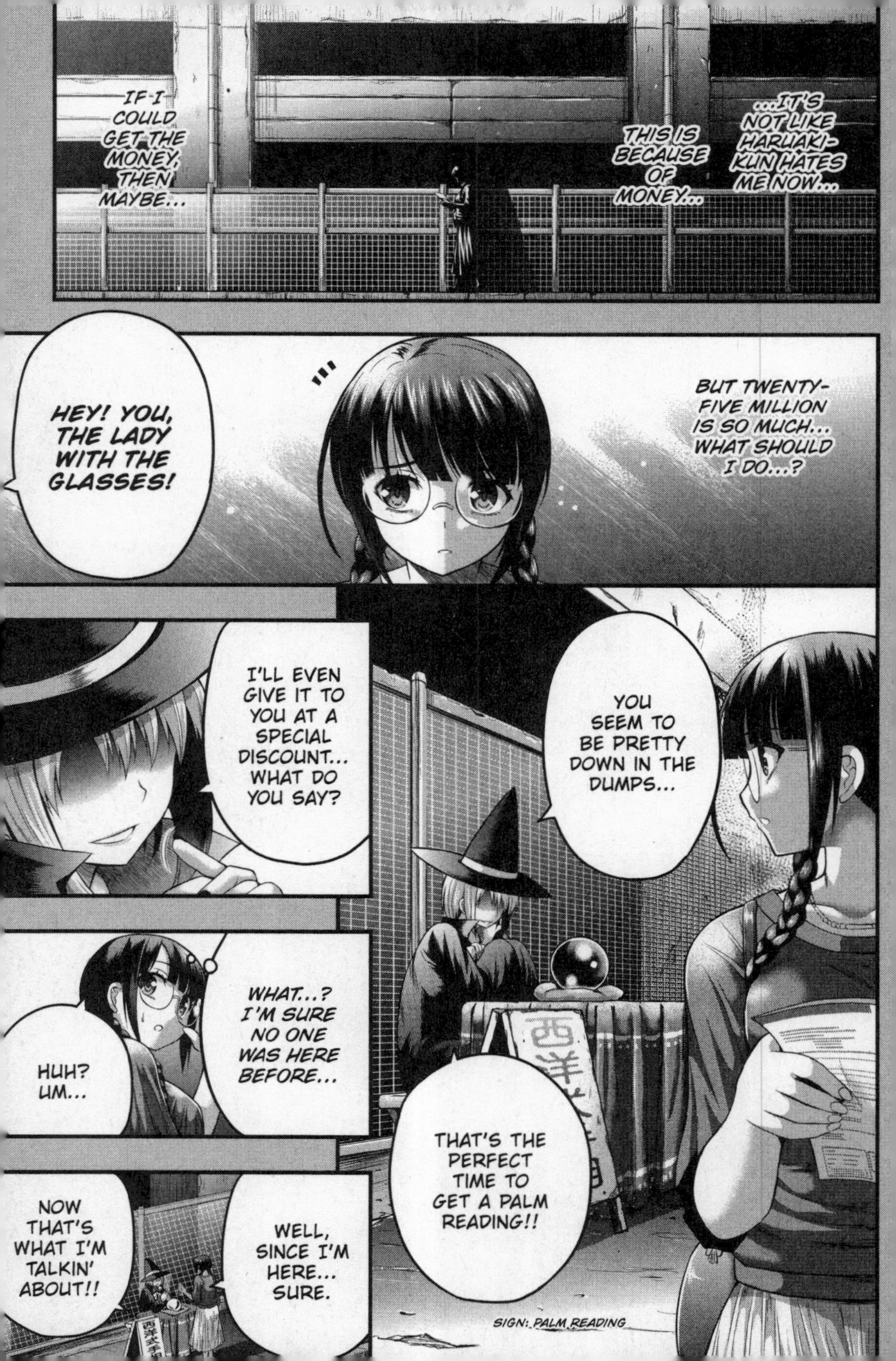
...IT'S NOT LIKE HARUAKI-KUN HATES ME NOW...
THIS IS BECAUSE OF MONEY...
IF I COULD GET THE MONEY, THEN MAYBE...
BUT TWENTY-FIVE MILLION IS SO MUCH... WHAT SHOULD I DO...?
HEY! YOU, THE LADY WITH THE GLASSES!
YOU SEEM TO BE PRETTY DOWN IN THE DUMPS...
THAT'S THE PERFECT TIME TO GET A PALM READING!!
SIGN: PALM READING
I'LL EVEN GIVE IT TO YOU AT A SPECIAL DISCOUNT... WHAT DO YOU SAY?
WHAT...? I'M SURE NO ONE WAS HERE BEFORE...
HUH? UM...
WELL, SINCE I'M HERE... SURE.
NOW THAT'S WHAT I'M TALKIN' ABOUT!!

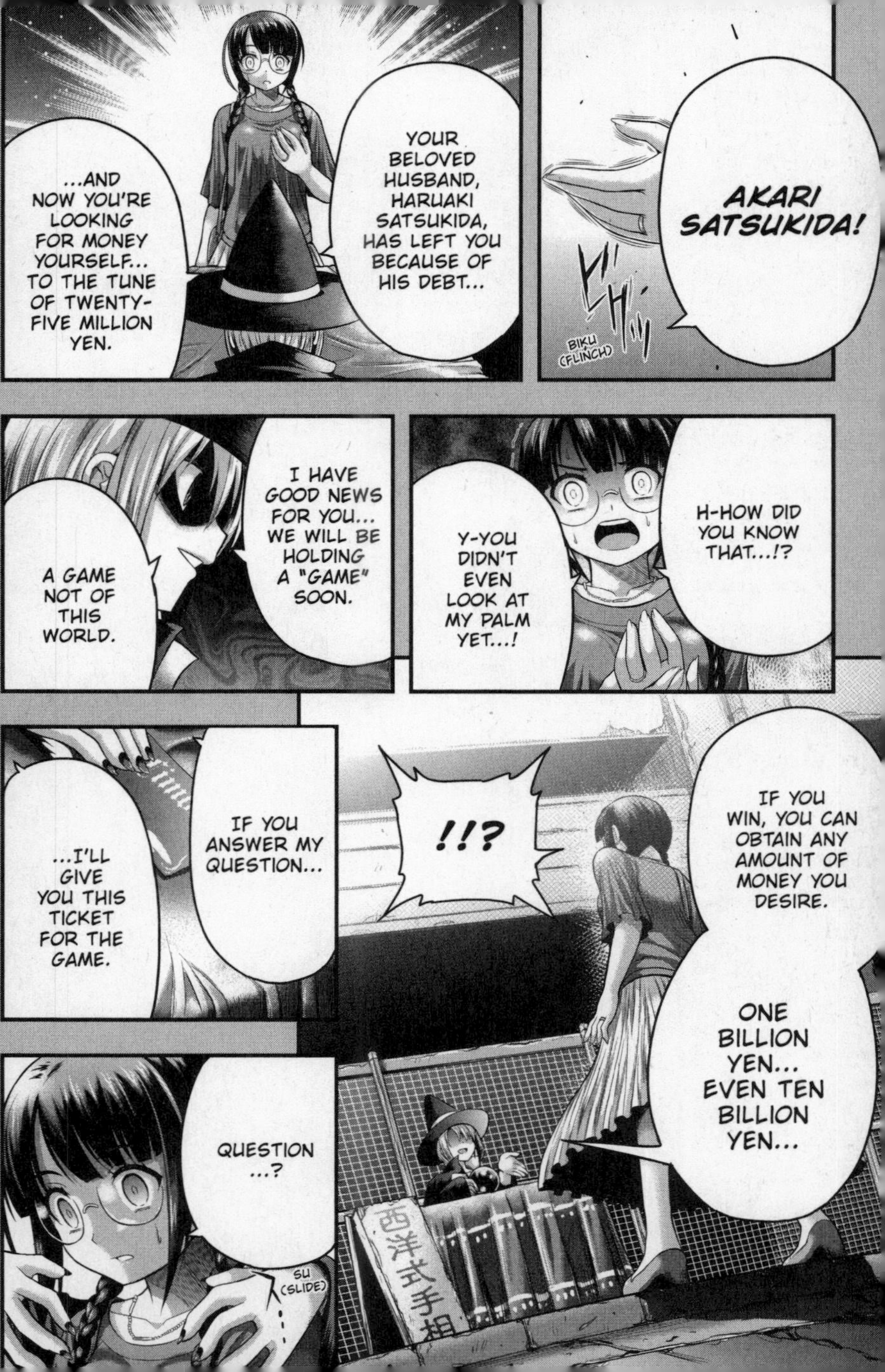
AKARI SATSUKIDA!
BIKU (FLINCH)
YOUR BELOVED HUSBAND, HARUAKI SATSUKIDA, HAS LEFT YOU BECAUSE OF HIS DEBT...
...AND NOW YOU'RE LOOKING FOR MONEY YOURSELF... TO THE TUNE OF TWENTY-FIVE MILLION YEN.
H-HOW DID YOU KNOW THAT...!?
Y-YOU DIDN'T EVEN LOOK AT MY PALM YET...!
I HAVE GOOD NEWS FOR YOU... WE WILL BE HOLDING A "GAME" SOON.
A GAME NOT OF THIS WORLD.
IF YOU WIN, YOU CAN OBTAIN ANY AMOUNT OF MONEY YOU DESIRE.
!!?
ONE BILLION YEN... EVEN TEN BILLION YEN...
西洋式手相
IF YOU ANSWER MY QUESTION...
...I'LL GIVE YOU THIS TICKET FOR THE GAME.
QUESTION ...?
SU (SLIDE)
...

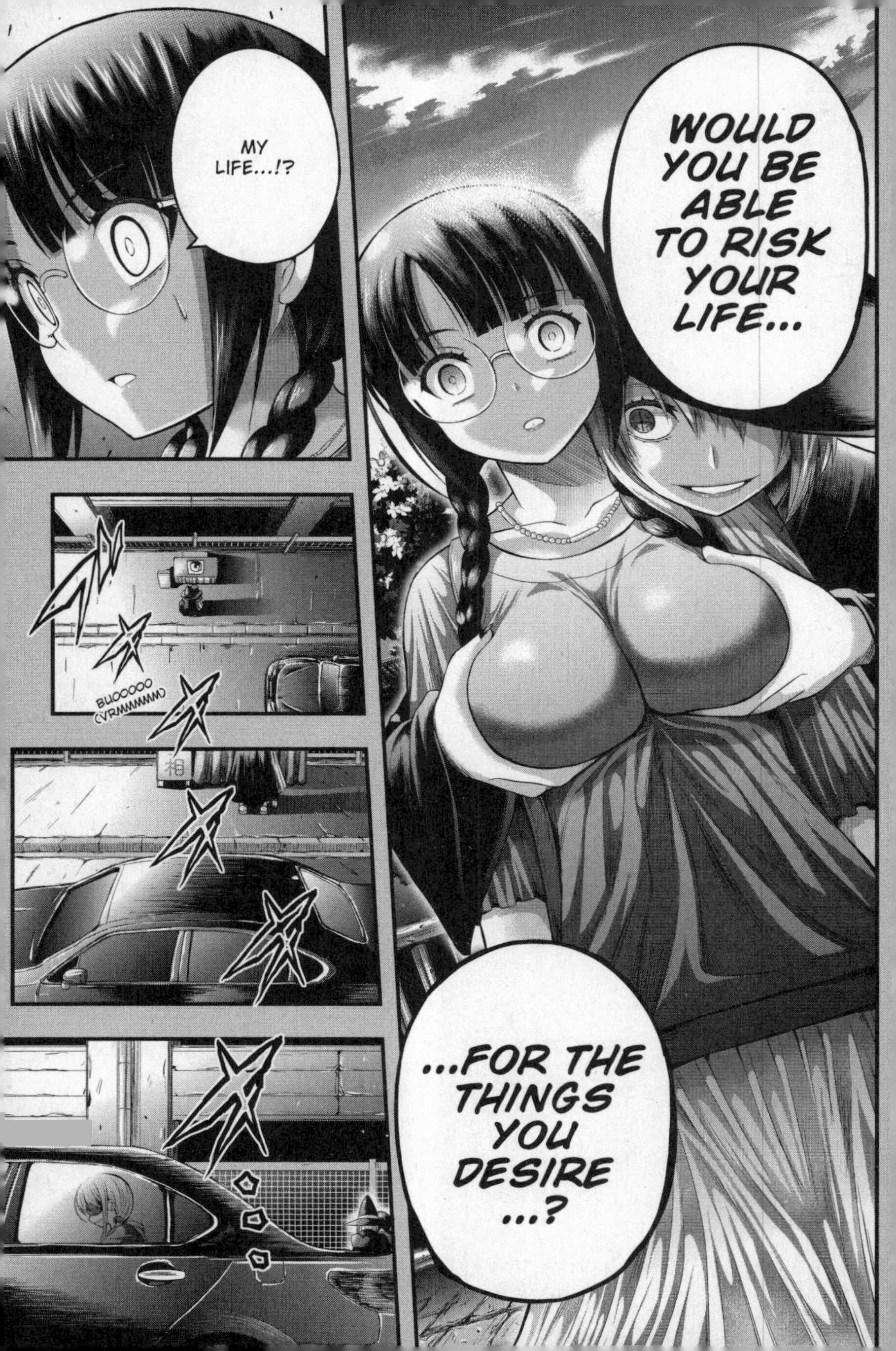
WOULD YOU BE ABLE TO RISK YOUR LIFE...
...FOR THE THINGS YOU DESIRE ...?
MY LIFE...!?
BUOOOOO (VRMMMMM)
相

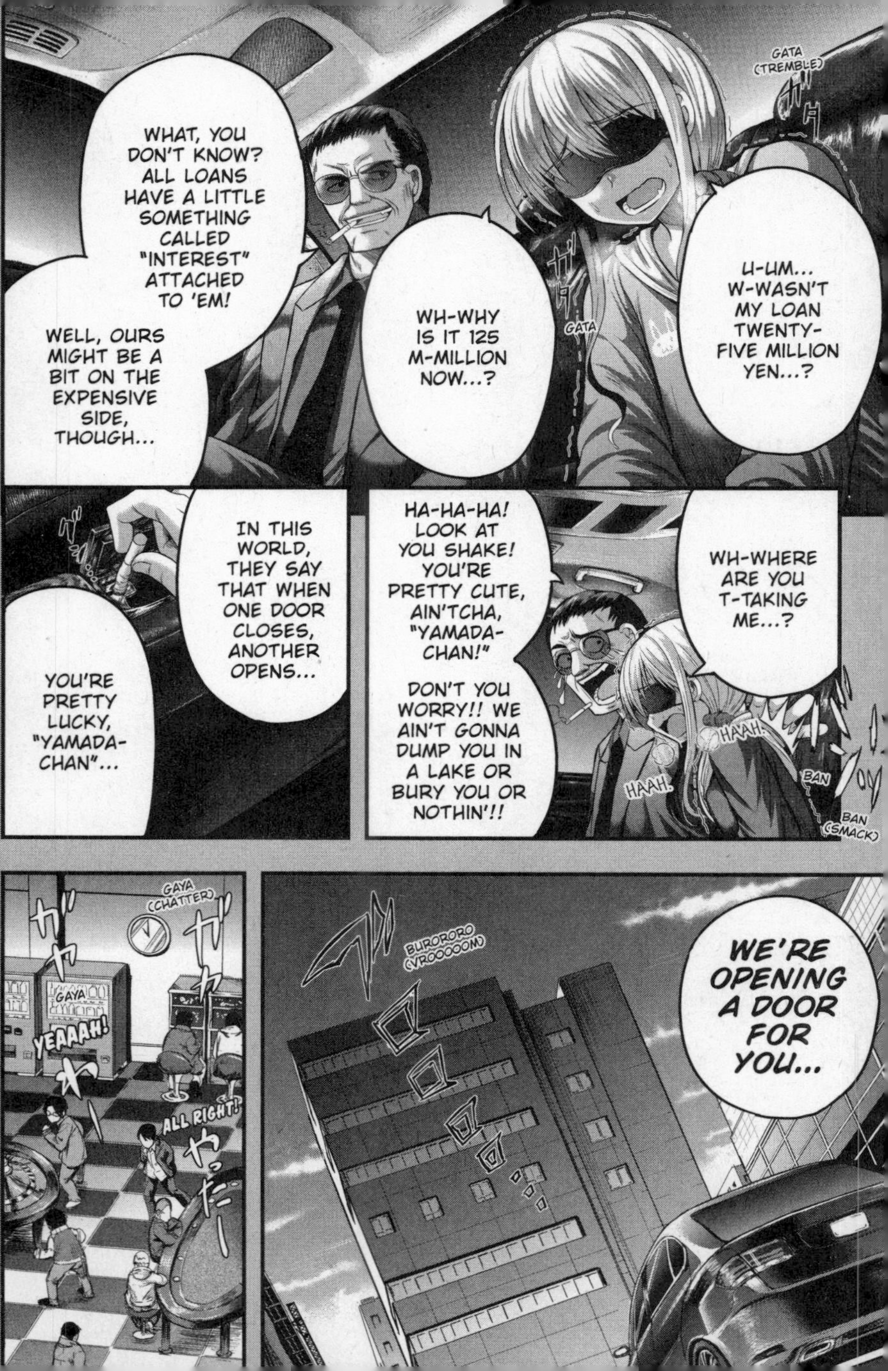
GATA (TREMBLE)
U-UM... W-WASN'T MY LOAN TWENTY-FIVE MILLION YEN...?
GATA
WH-WHY IS IT 125 M-MILLION NOW...?
WHAT, YOU DON'T KNOW? ALL LOANS HAVE A LITTLE SOMETHING CALLED "INTEREST" ATTACHED TO 'EM!
WELL, OURS MIGHT BE A BIT ON THE EXPENSIVE SIDE, THOUGH...
WH-WHERE ARE YOU T-TAKING ME...?
HA-HA-HA! LOOK AT YOU SHAKE! YOU'RE PRETTY CUTE, AIN'TCHA, "YAMADA-CHAN!"
DON'T YOU WORRY!! WE AIN'T GONNA DUMP YOU IN A LAKE OR BURY YOU OR NOTHIN'!!
HAAH.
HAAH.
BAN
BAN (SMACK)
IN THIS WORLD, THEY SAY THAT WHEN ONE DOOR CLOSES, ANOTHER OPENS...
YOU'RE PRETTY LUCKY, "YAMADA-CHAN"...
BURORORO (VROOOOOM)
WE'RE OPENING A DOOR FOR YOU...
GAYA (CHATTER)
GAYA
YEAAAH!
ALL RIGHT!

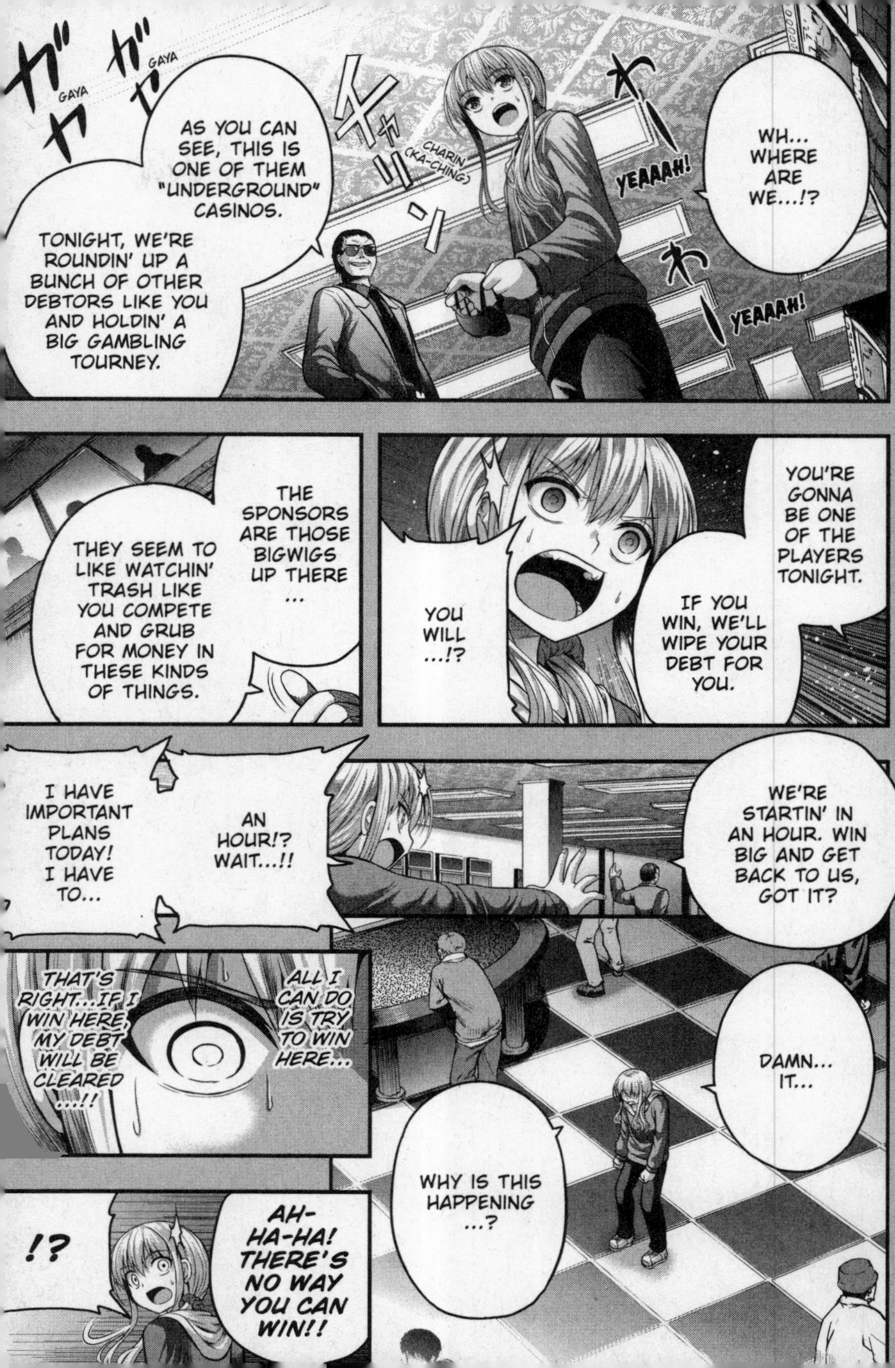
WH... WHERE ARE WE...!?
YEAAAH!
YEAAAH!
CHARIN (KA-CHING)
AS YOU CAN SEE, THIS IS ONE OF THEM "UNDERGROUND" CASINOS.
TONIGHT, WE'RE ROUNDIN' UP A BUNCH OF OTHER DEBTORS LIKE YOU AND HOLDIN' A BIG GAMBLING TOURNEY.
GAYA
GAYA
YOU'RE GONNA BE ONE OF THE PLAYERS TONIGHT.
IF YOU WIN, WE'LL WIPE YOUR DEBT FOR YOU.
YOU WILL ...!?
THE SPONSORS ARE THOSE BIGWIGS UP THERE ...
THEY SEEM TO LIKE WATCHIN' TRASH LIKE YOU COMPETE AND GRUB FOR MONEY IN THESE KINDS OF THINGS.
WE'RE STARTIN' IN AN HOUR. WIN BIG AND GET BACK TO US, GOT IT?
AN HOUR!? WAIT...!!
I HAVE IMPORTANT PLANS TODAY! I HAVE TO...
DAMN... IT...
WHY IS THIS HAPPENING ...?
ALL I CAN DO IS TRY TO WIN HERE...
THAT'S RIGHT...IF I WIN HERE, MY DEBT WILL BE CLEARED ...!!
AH-HA-HA! THERE'S NO WAY YOU CAN WIN!!
!?

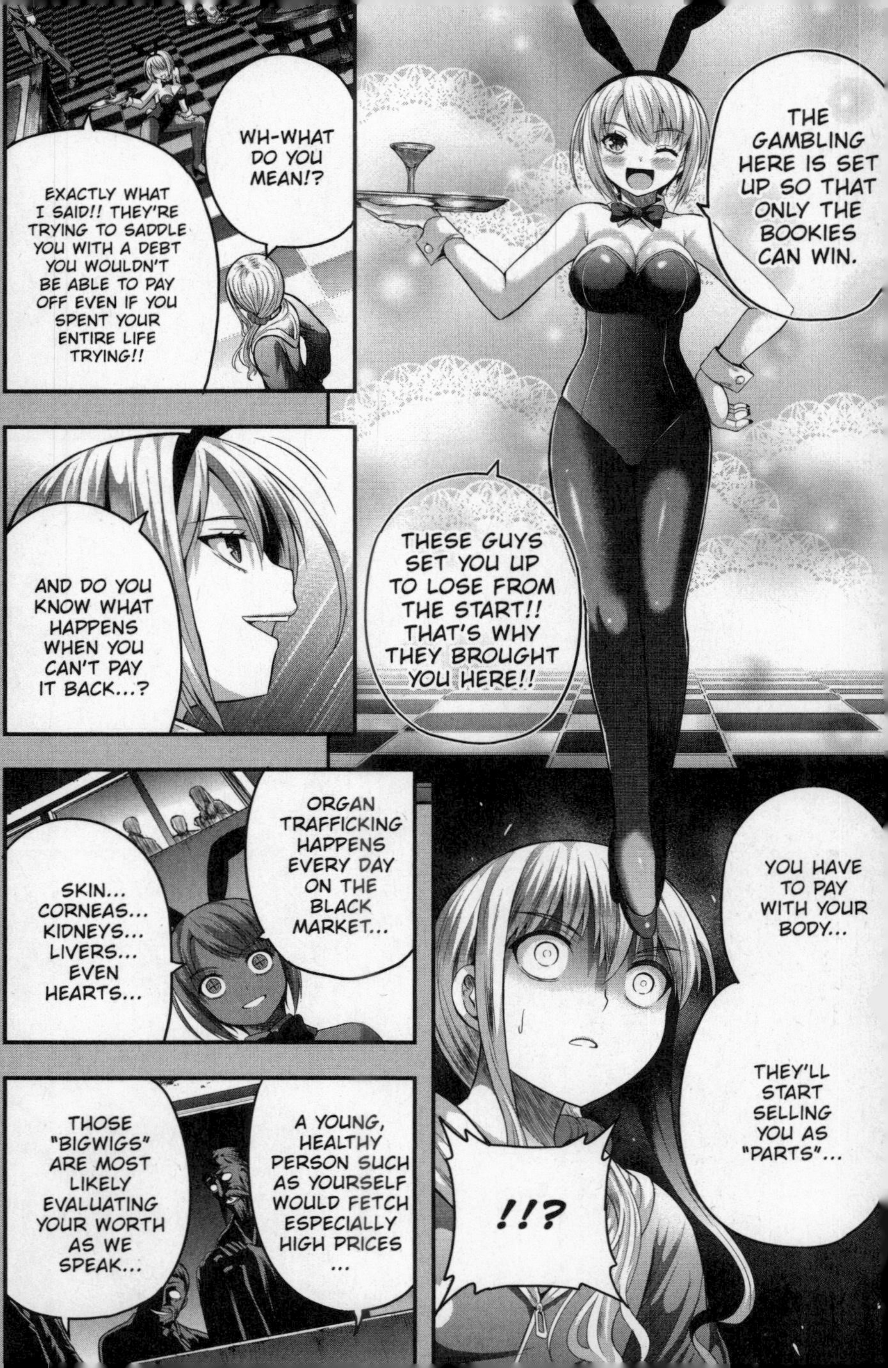
THE GAMBLING HERE IS SET UP SO THAT ONLY THE BOOKIES CAN WIN.
THESE GUYS SET YOU UP TO LOSE FROM THE START!! THAT'S WHY THEY BROUGHT YOU HERE!!
WH-WHAT DO YOU MEAN!?
EXACTLY WHAT I SAID!! THEY'RE TRYING TO SADDLE YOU WITH A DEBT YOU WOULDN'T BE ABLE TO PAY OFF EVEN IF YOU SPENT YOUR ENTIRE LIFE TRYING!!
AND DO YOU KNOW WHAT HAPPENS WHEN YOU CAN'T PAY IT BACK...?
YOU HAVE TO PAY WITH YOUR BODY...
THEY'LL START SELLING YOU AS "PARTS"...
!!?
ORGAN TRAFFICKING HAPPENS EVERY DAY ON THE BLACK MARKET...
SKIN... CORNEAS... KIDNEYS... LIVERS... EVEN HEARTS...
A YOUNG, HEALTHY PERSON SUCH AS YOURSELF WOULD FETCH ESPECIALLY HIGH PRICES ...
THOSE "BIGWIGS" ARE MOST LIKELY EVALUATING YOUR WORTH AS WE SPEAK...

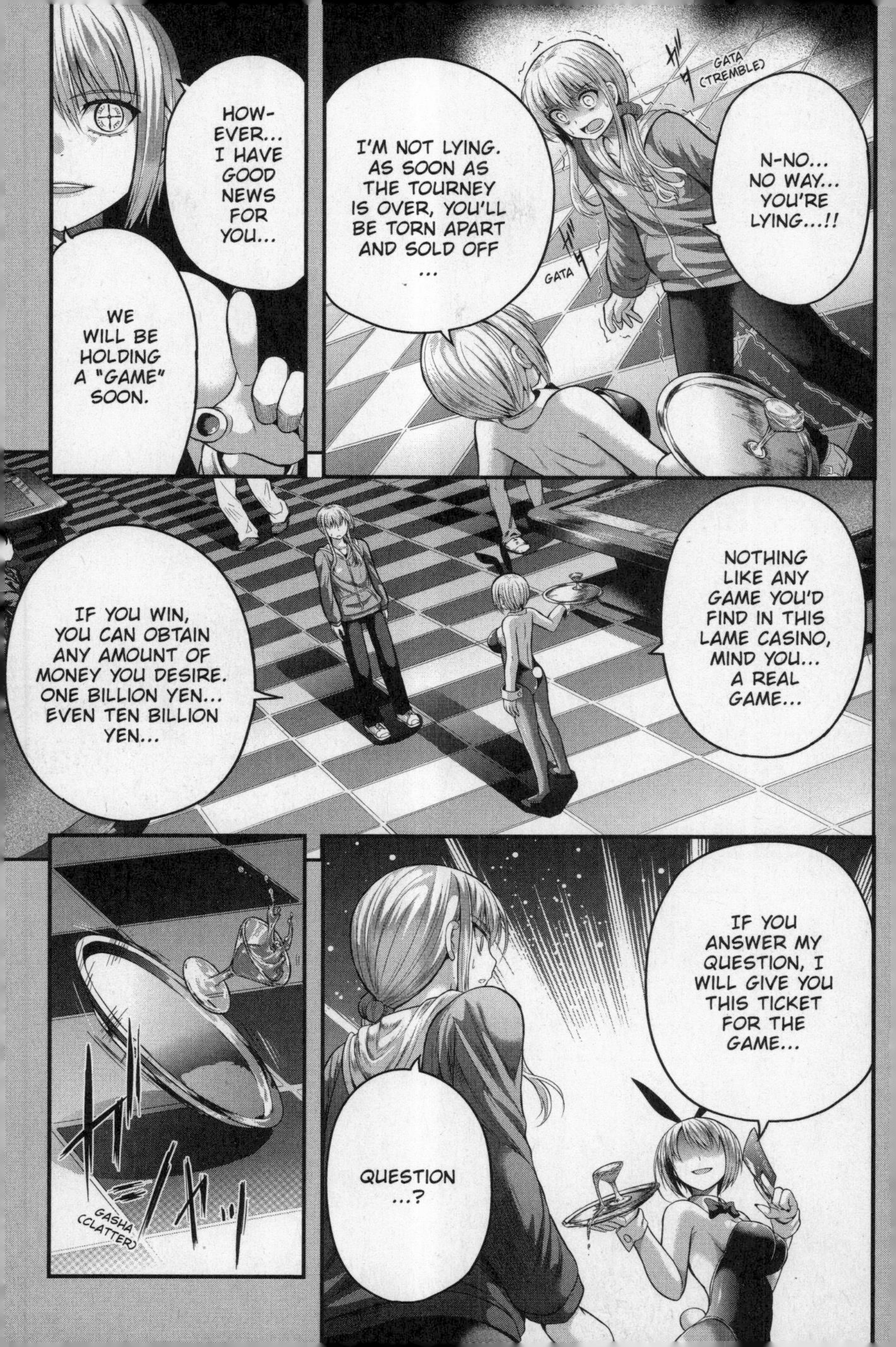
GATA (TREMBLE)
N-NO... NO WAY... YOU'RE LYING...!!
I'M NOT LYING. AS SOON AS THE TOURNEY IS OVER, YOU'LL BE TORN APART AND SOLD OFF ...
GATA
HOW-EVER... I HAVE GOOD NEWS FOR YOU...
WE WILL BE HOLDING A "GAME" SOON.
NOTHING LIKE ANY GAME YOU'D FIND IN THIS LAME CASINO, MIND YOU... A REAL GAME...
IF YOU WIN, YOU CAN OBTAIN ANY AMOUNT OF MONEY YOU DESIRE. ONE BILLION YEN... EVEN TEN BILLION YEN...
IF YOU ANSWER MY QUESTION, I WILL GIVE YOU THIS TICKET FOR THE GAME...
QUESTION ...?
GASHA (CLATTER)

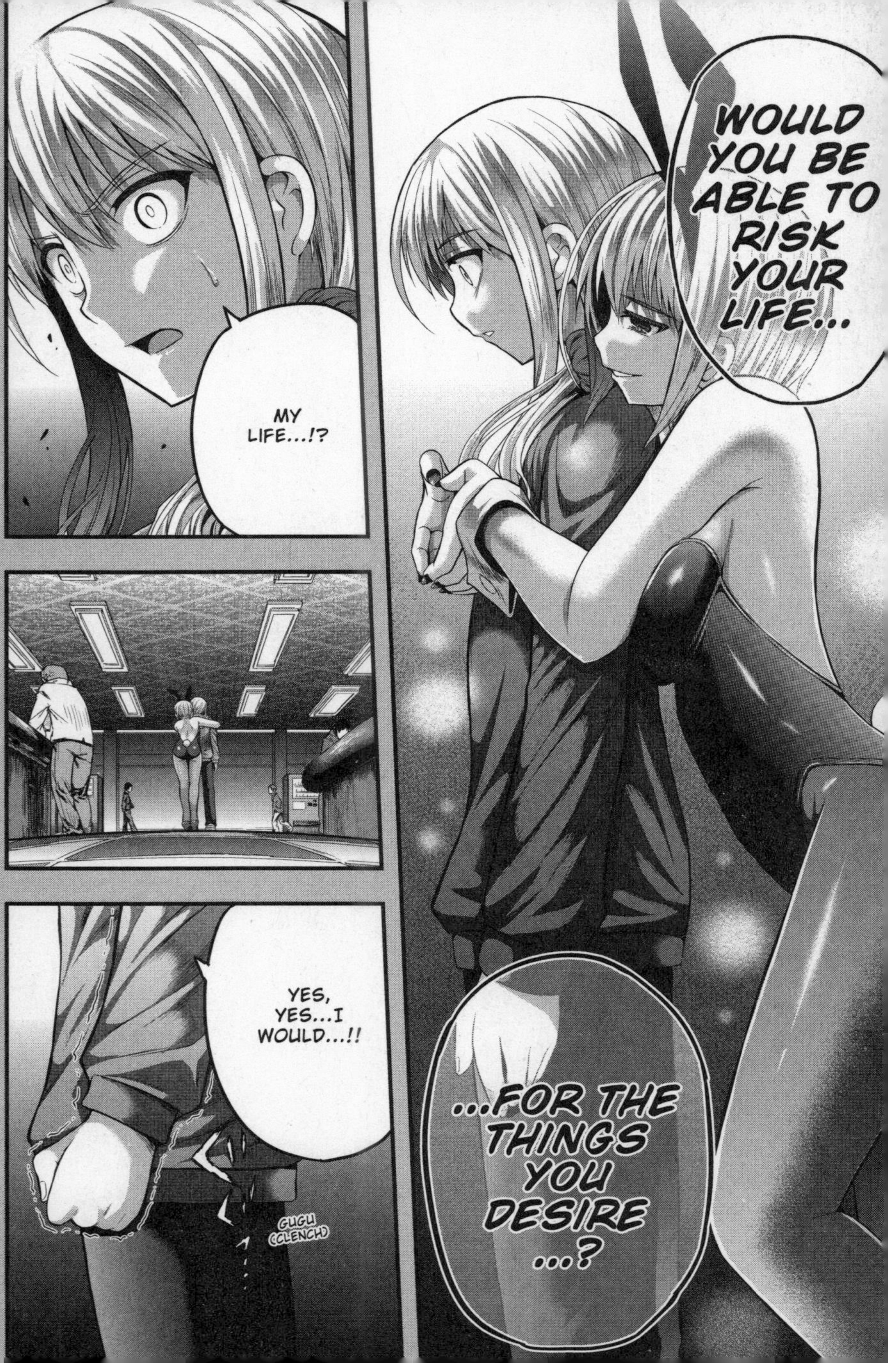
WOULD YOU BE ABLE TO RISK YOUR LIFE...
...FOR THE THINGS YOU DESIRE ...?
MY LIFE...!?
YES, YES...I WOULD...!!
GUGU (CLENCH)

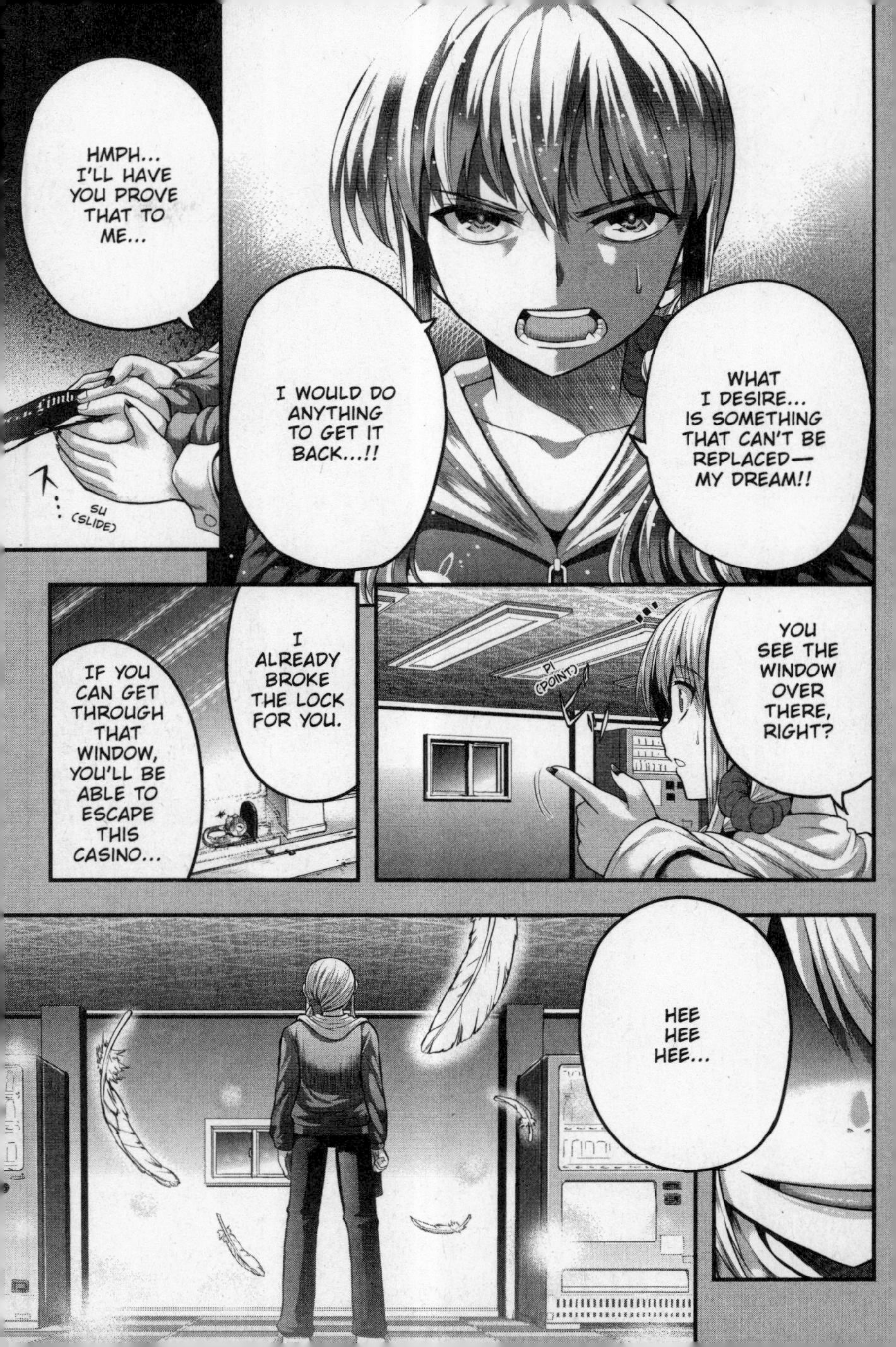
WHAT I DESIRE... IS SOMETHING THAT CAN'T BE REPLACED— MY DREAM!!
I WOULD DO ANYTHING TO GET IT BACK...!!
HMPH... I'LL HAVE YOU PROVE THAT TO ME...
SU (SLIDE)
YOU SEE THE WINDOW OVER THERE, RIGHT?
PI (POINT)
I ALREADY BROKE THE LOCK FOR YOU.
IF YOU CAN GET THROUGH THAT WINDOW, YOU'LL BE ABLE TO ESCAPE THIS CASINO...
HEE HEE HEE...

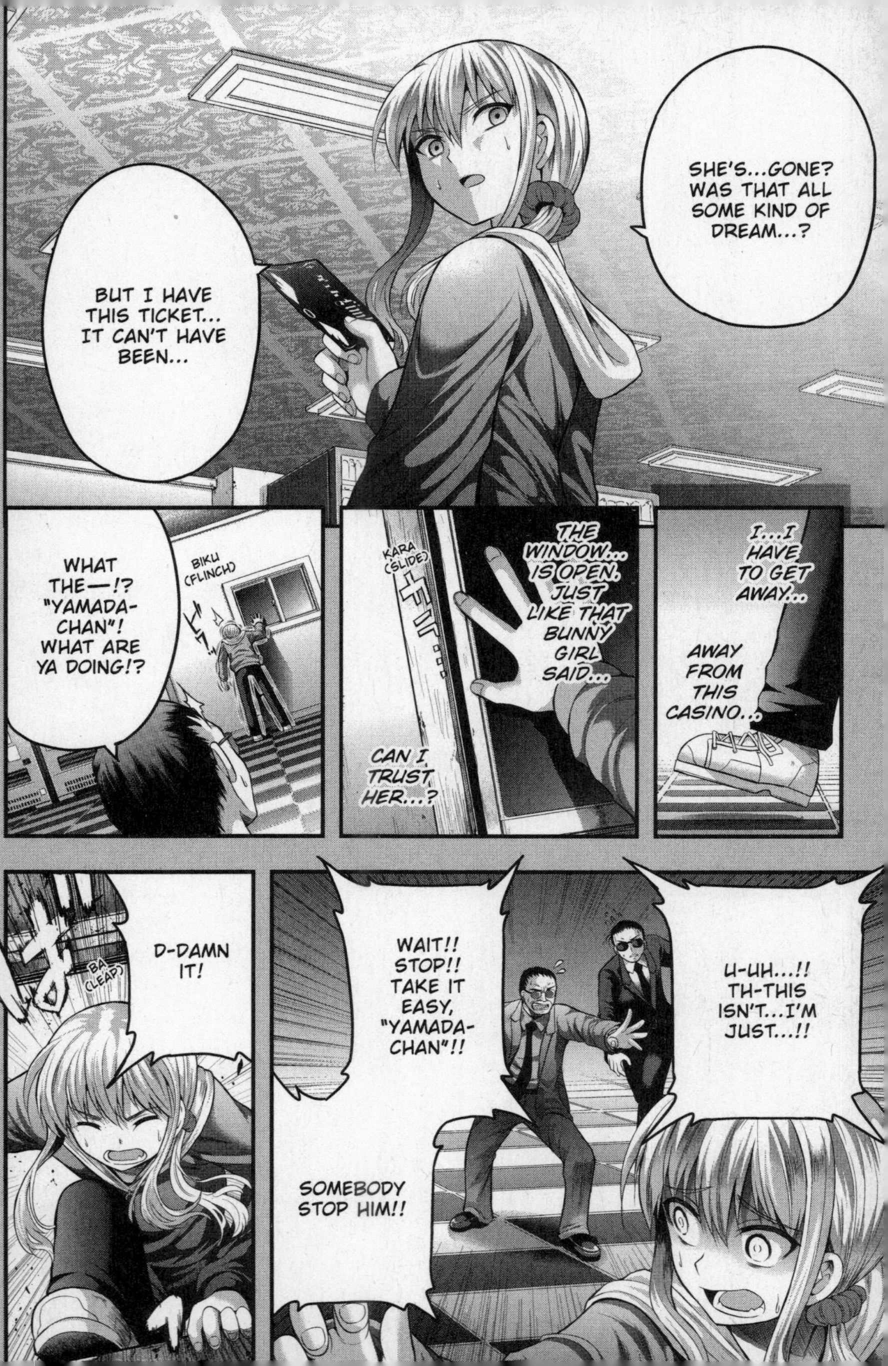
SHE'S...GONE? WAS THAT ALL SOME KIND OF DREAM...?
BUT I HAVE THIS TICKET... IT CAN'T HAVE BEEN...
I...I HAVE TO GET AWAY...
AWAY FROM THIS CASINO...
THE WINDOW... IS OPEN. JUST LIKE THAT BUNNY GIRL SAID...
KARA (SLIDE)
CAN I TRUST HER...?
WHAT THE—!? "YAMADA-CHAN"! WHAT ARE YA DOING!?
BIKU (FLINCH)
U-UH...!! TH-THIS ISN'T...I'M JUST...!!
WAIT!! STOP!! TAKE IT EASY, "YAMADA-CHAN"!!
SOMEBODY STOP HIM!!
D-DAMN IT!
BA (LEAP)

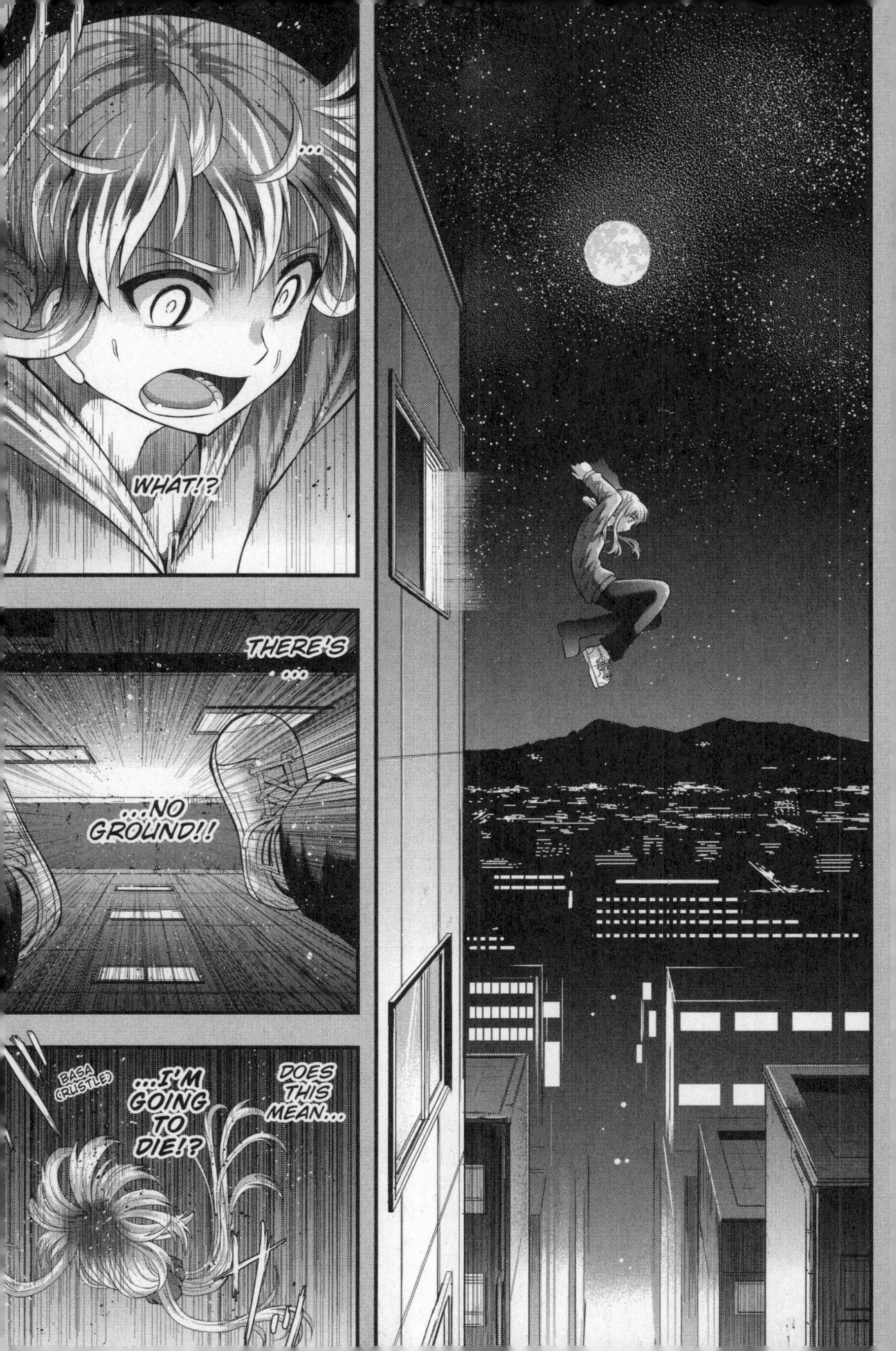
...
WHAT!?
THERE'S ...
...NO GROUND!!
DOES THIS MEAN...
...I'M GOING TO DIE!?
BASA (RUSTLE)

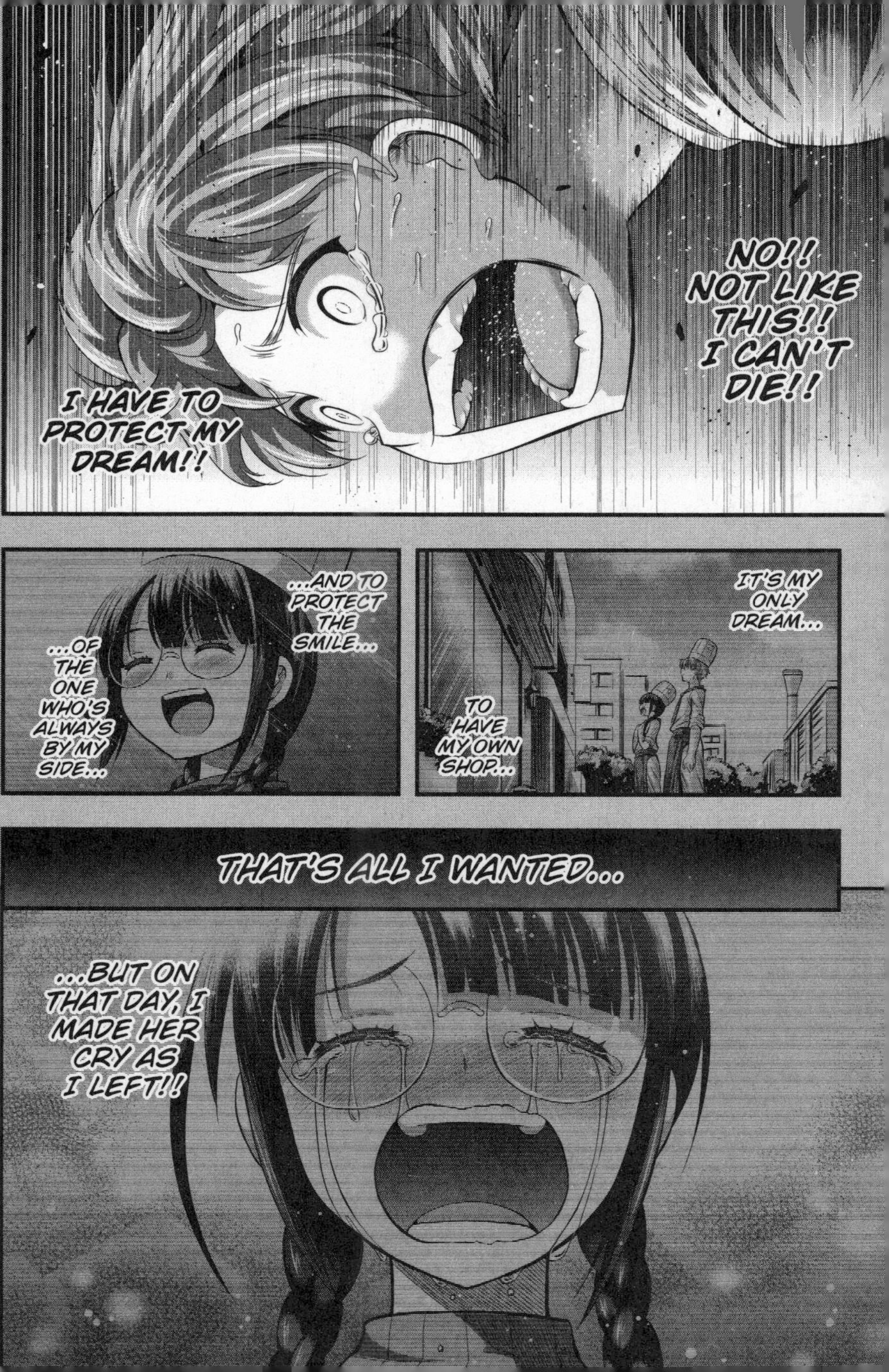
NO!! NOT LIKE THIS!! I CAN'T DIE!!
I HAVE TO PROTECT MY DREAM!!
IT'S MY ONLY DREAM...
TO HAVE MY OWN SHOP...
...AND TO PROTECT THE SMILE...
...OF THE ONE WHO'S ALWAYS BY MY SIDE...
THAT'S ALL I WANTED...
...BUT ON THAT DAY, I MADE HER CRY AS I LEFT!!

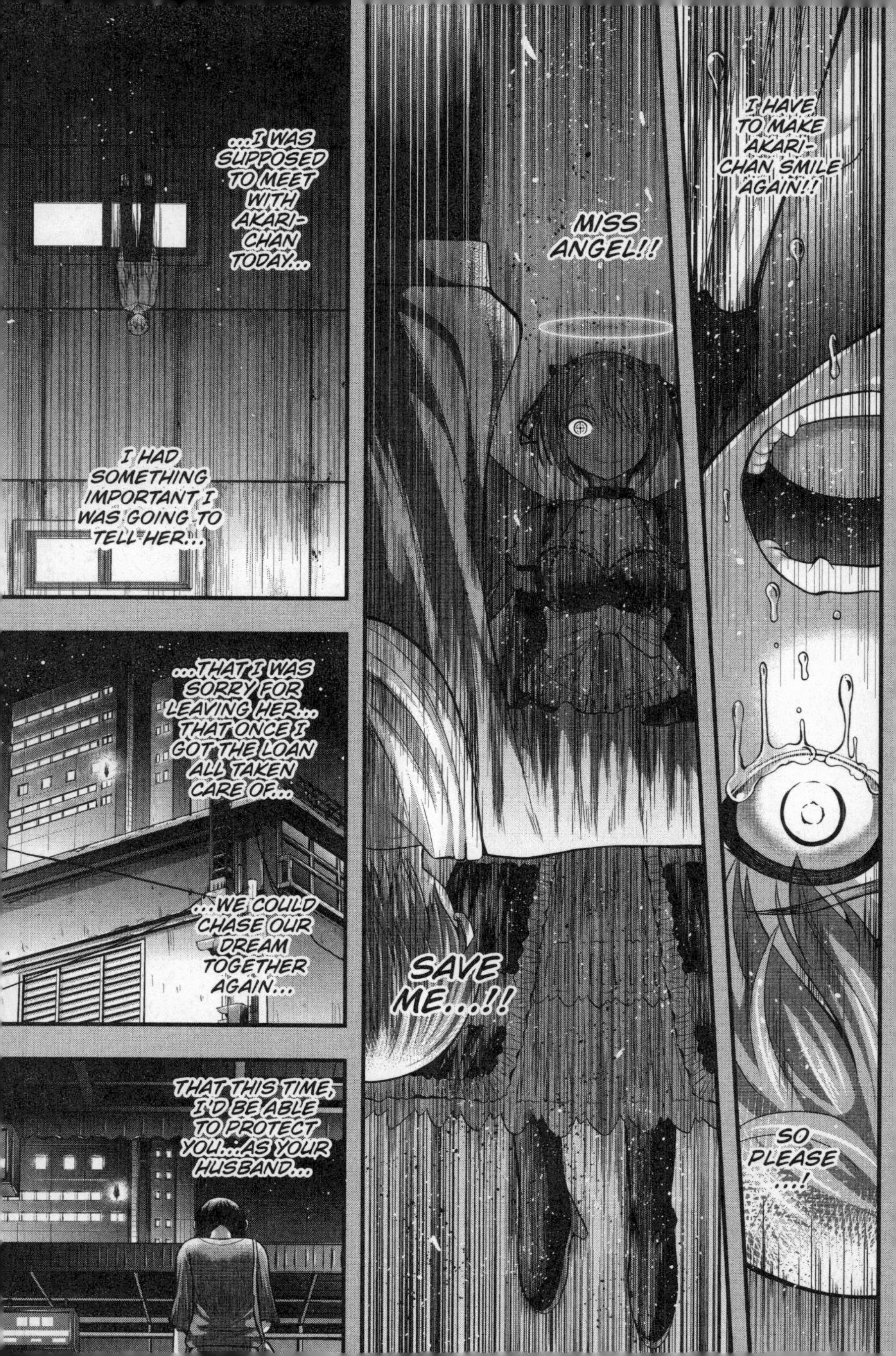
I HAVE TO MAKE AKARI-CHAN SMILE AGAIN!!
SO PLEASE...!
MISS ANGEL!!
SAVE ME...!!
...I WAS SUPPOSED TO MEET WITH AKARI-CHAN TODAY...
I HAD SOMETHING IMPORTANT I WAS GOING TO TELL HER...
...THAT I WAS SORRY FOR LEAVING HER... THAT ONCE I GOT THE LOAN ALL TAKEN CARE OF...
...WE COULD CHASE OUR DREAM TOGETHER AGAIN...
THAT THIS TIME, I'D BE ABLE TO PROTECT YOU...AS YOUR HUSBAND...

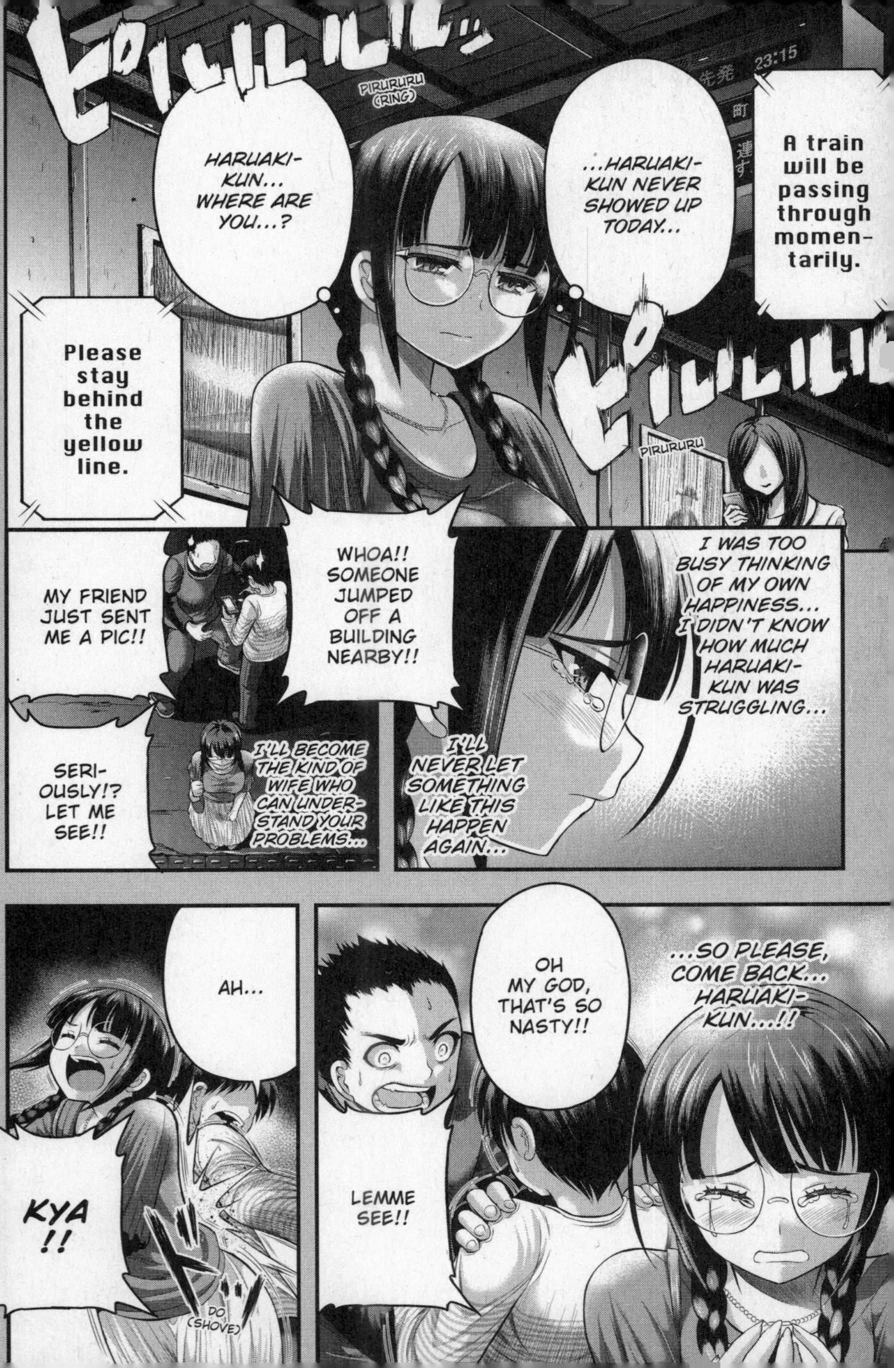

23:15
A train will be passing through momentarily.
...HARUAKI-KUN NEVER SHOWED UP TODAY...
PIRURURU (RING)
HARUAKI-KUN... WHERE ARE YOU...?
PIRURURU
Please stay behind the yellow line.
I WAS TOO BUSY THINKING OF MY OWN HAPPINESS... I DIDN'T KNOW HOW MUCH HARUAKI-KUN WAS STRUGGLING...
I'LL NEVER LET SOMETHING LIKE THIS HAPPEN AGAIN...
WHOA!! SOMEONE JUMPED OFF A BUILDING NEARBY!!
MY FRIEND JUST SENT ME A PIC!!
I'LL BECOME THE KIND OF WIFE WHO CAN UNDERSTAND YOUR PROBLEMS...
SERIOUSLY!? LET ME SEE!!
...SO PLEASE, COME BACK... HARUAKI-KUN...!!
OH MY GOD, THAT'S SO NASTY!!
LEMME SEE!!
AH...
KYA!!
DO (SHOVE)

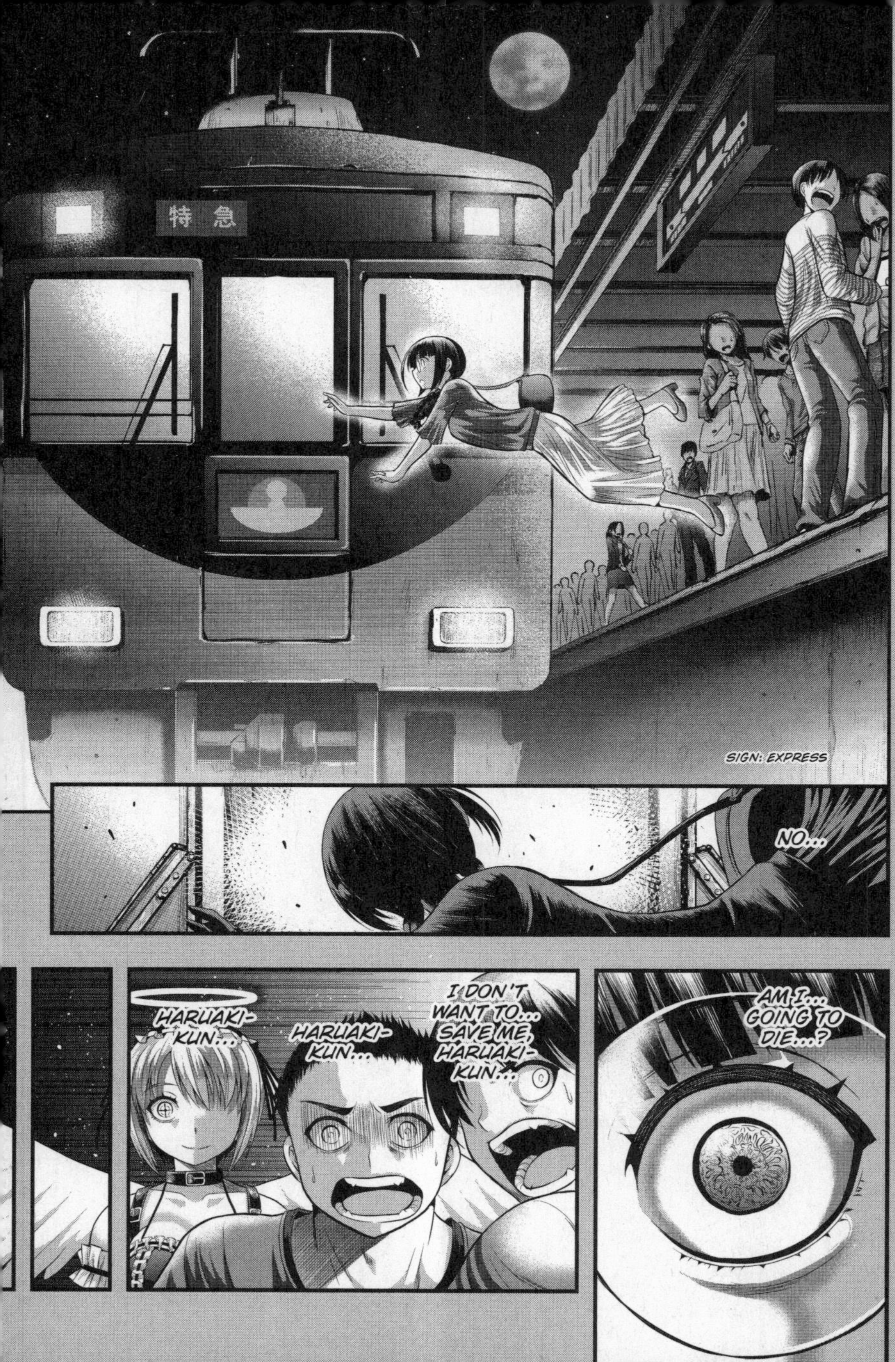
特急
SIGN: EXPRESS
NO...
AM I... GOING TO DIE...?
I DON'T WANT TO... SAVE ME, HARUAKI-KUN...
HARUAKI-KUN...
HARUAKI-KUN...

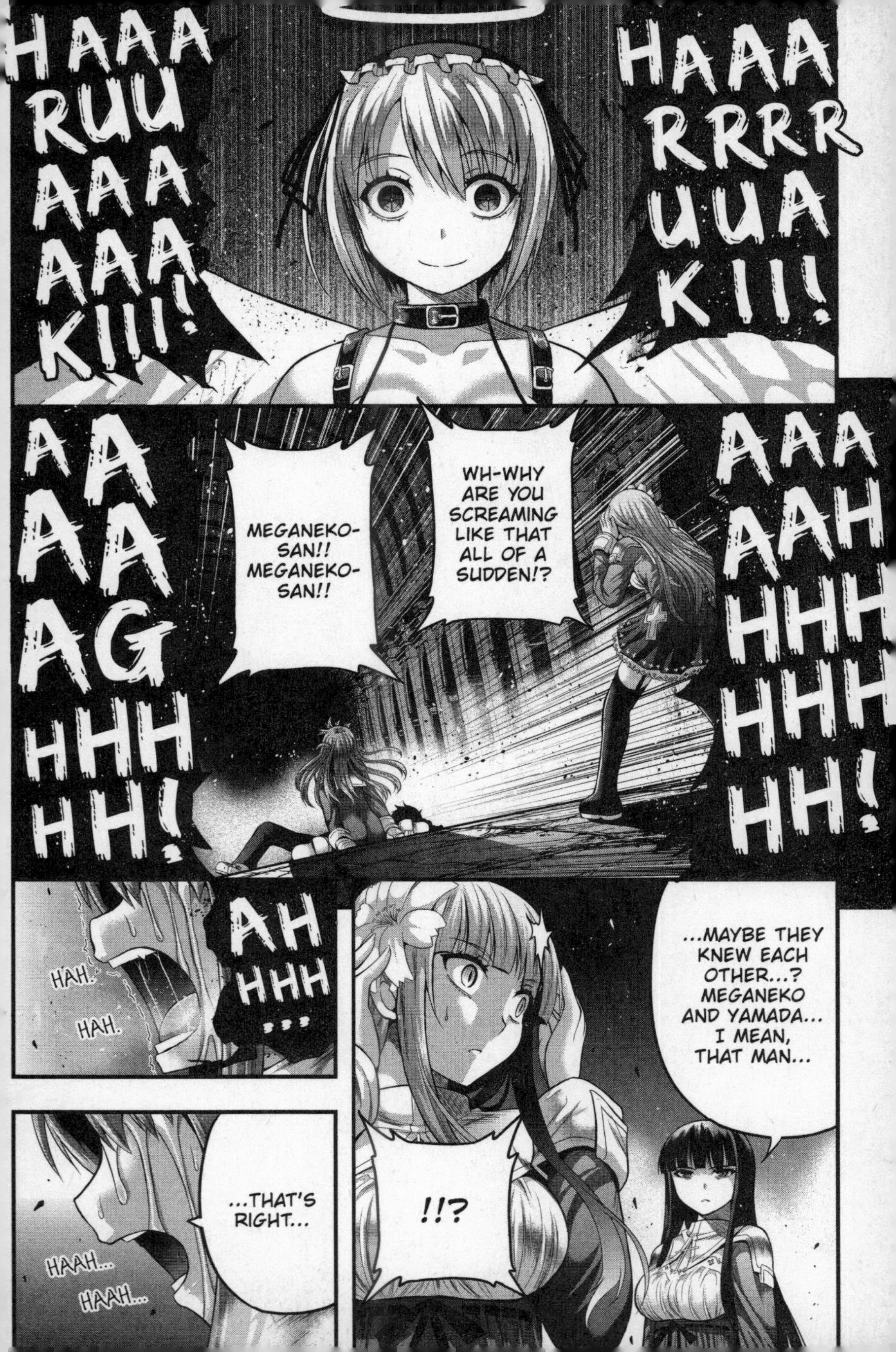
HAAARRRRUUAKII!
HAAARUUAAAAAAKI!!!
AAAAAHHHHHHHHHHH!
WH-WHY ARE YOU SCREAMING LIKE THAT ALL OF A SUDDEN!?
MEGANEKO-SAN!! MEGANEKO-SAN!!
AAAAAAAGHHHHH!
...MAYBE THEY KNEW EACH OTHER...? MEGANEKO AND YAMADA... I MEAN, THAT MAN...
!!?
AHHHH...
HAH. HAH.
...THAT'S RIGHT...
HAAH... HAAH...

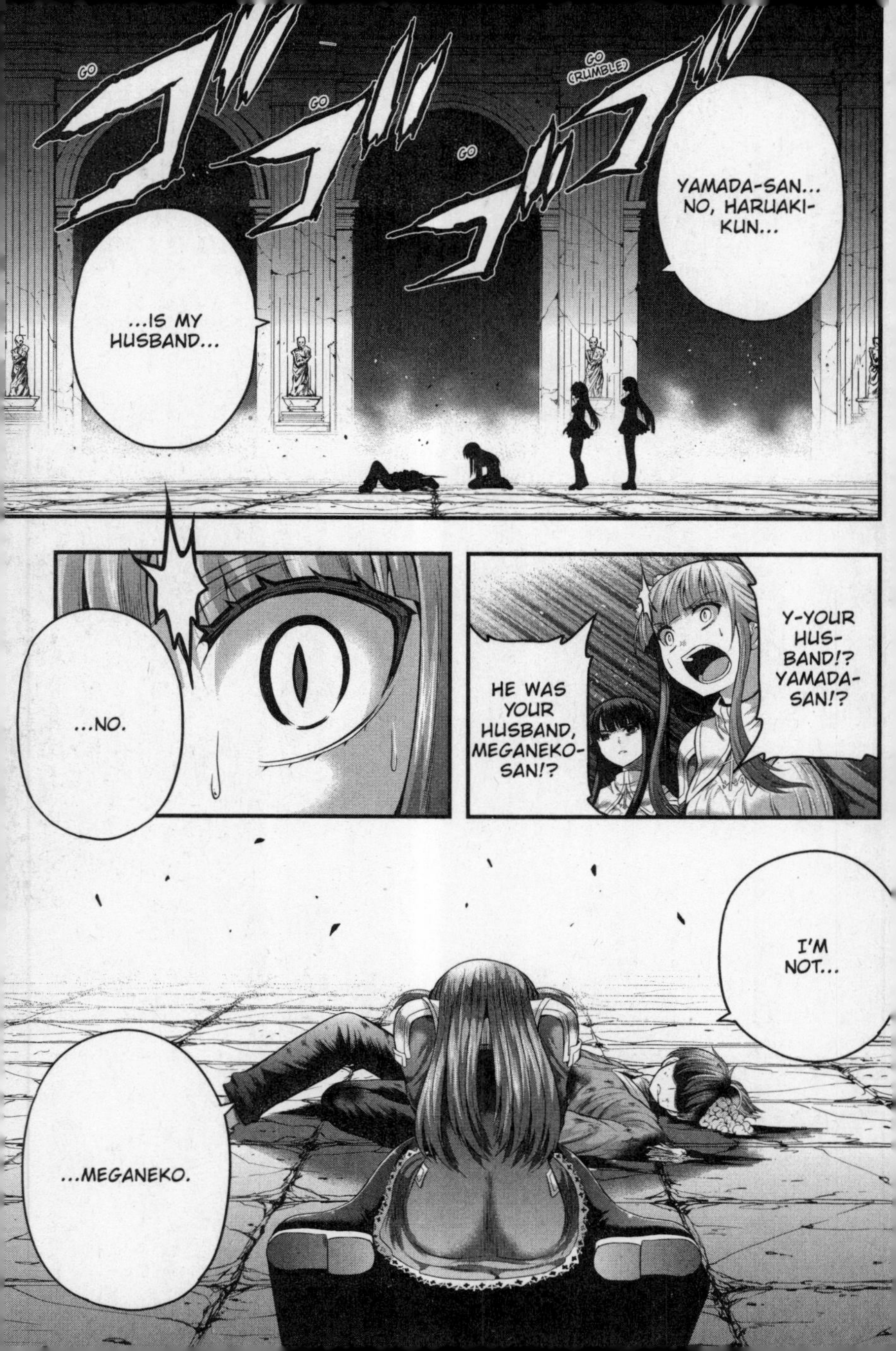
GO (RUMBLE)
GO
GO
GO
YAMADA-SAN... NO, HARUAKI-KUN...
...IS MY HUSBAND...
Y-YOUR HUSBAND!? YAMADA-SAN!?
HE WAS YOUR HUSBAND, MEGANEKO-SAN!?
...NO.
I'M NOT...
...MEGANEKO.

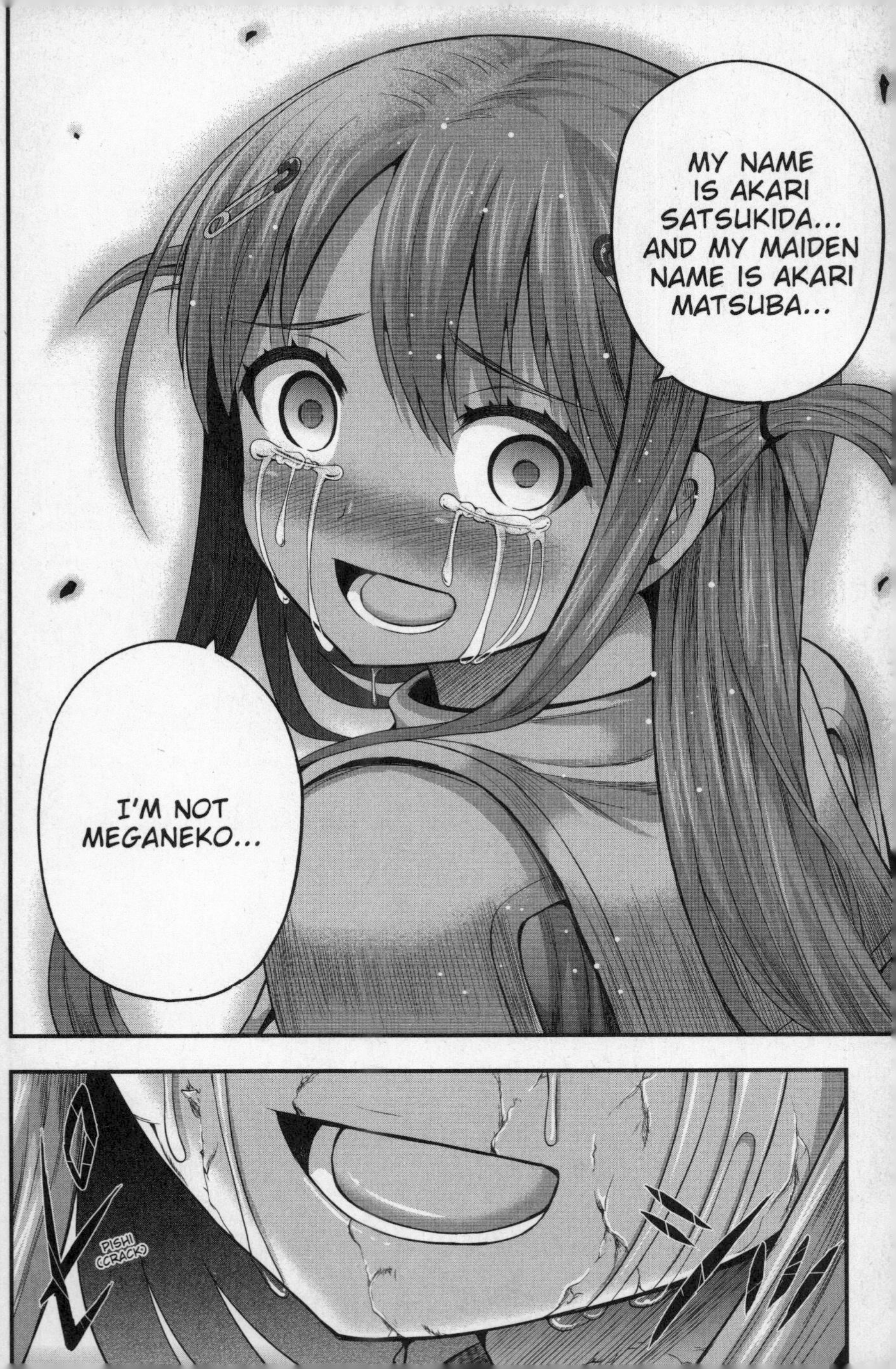
MY NAME IS AKARI SATSUKIDA... AND MY MAIDEN NAME IS AKARI MATSUBA...
I'M NOT MEGANEKO...
PISHI (CRACK)

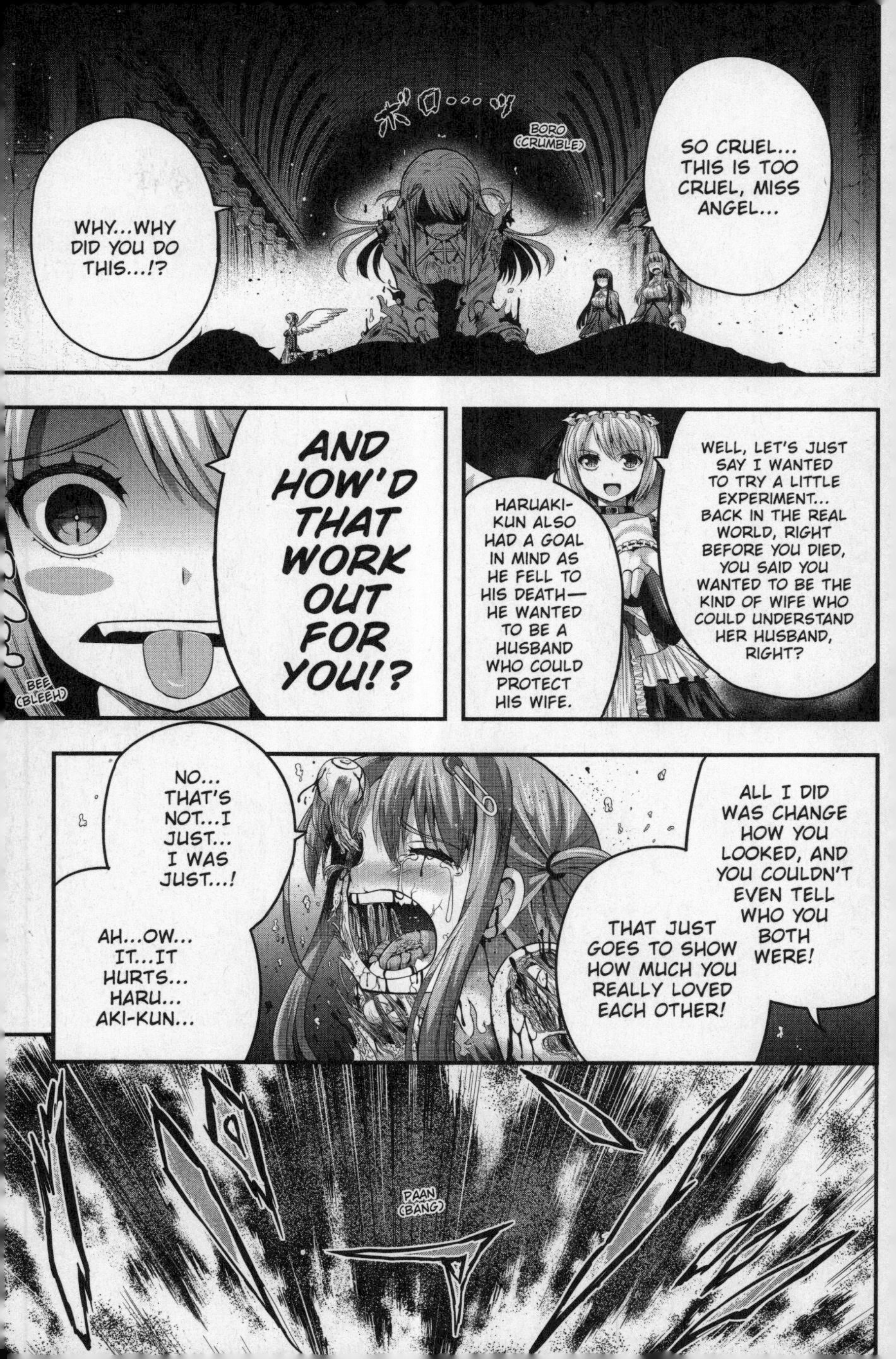
SO CRUEL... THIS IS TOO CRUEL, MISS ANGEL...
BORO (CRUMBLE)
WHY...WHY DID YOU DO THIS...!?
WELL, LET'S JUST SAY I WANTED TO TRY A LITTLE EXPERIMENT... BACK IN THE REAL WORLD, RIGHT BEFORE YOU DIED, YOU SAID YOU WANTED TO BE THE KIND OF WIFE WHO COULD UNDERSTAND HER HUSBAND, RIGHT?
HARUAKI-KUN ALSO HAD A GOAL IN MIND AS HE FELL TO HIS DEATH—HE WANTED TO BE A HUSBAND WHO COULD PROTECT HIS WIFE.
AND HOW'D THAT WORK OUT FOR YOU!?
BEE (BLEEH)
ALL I DID WAS CHANGE HOW YOU LOOKED, AND YOU COULDN'T EVEN TELL WHO YOU BOTH WERE!
THAT JUST GOES TO SHOW HOW MUCH YOU REALLY LOVED EACH OTHER!
NO... THAT'S NOT...I JUST... I WAS JUST...!
AH...OW... IT...IT HURTS... HARU... AKI-KUN...
PAAN (BANG)

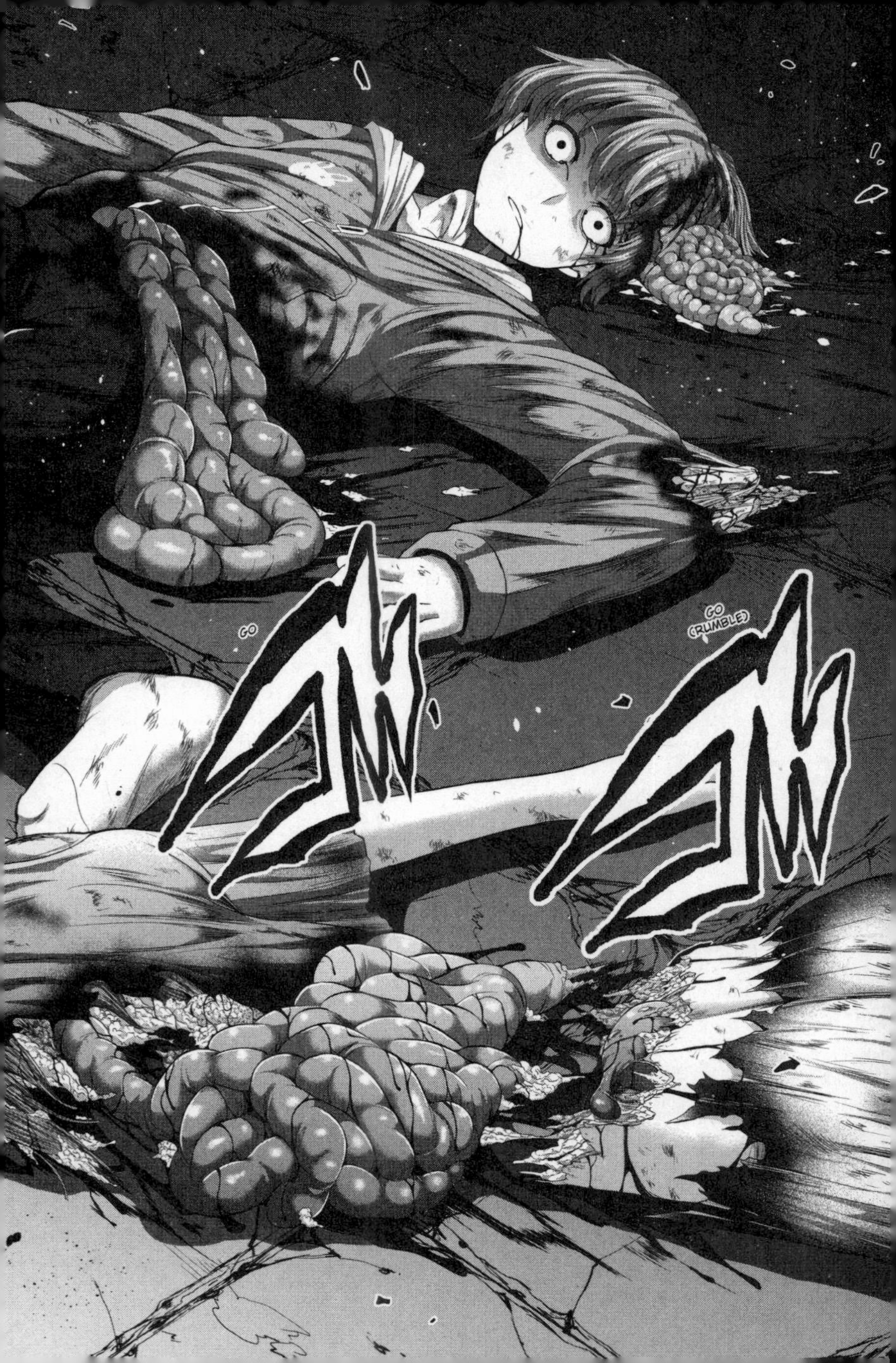
GO
GO
(RUMBLE)

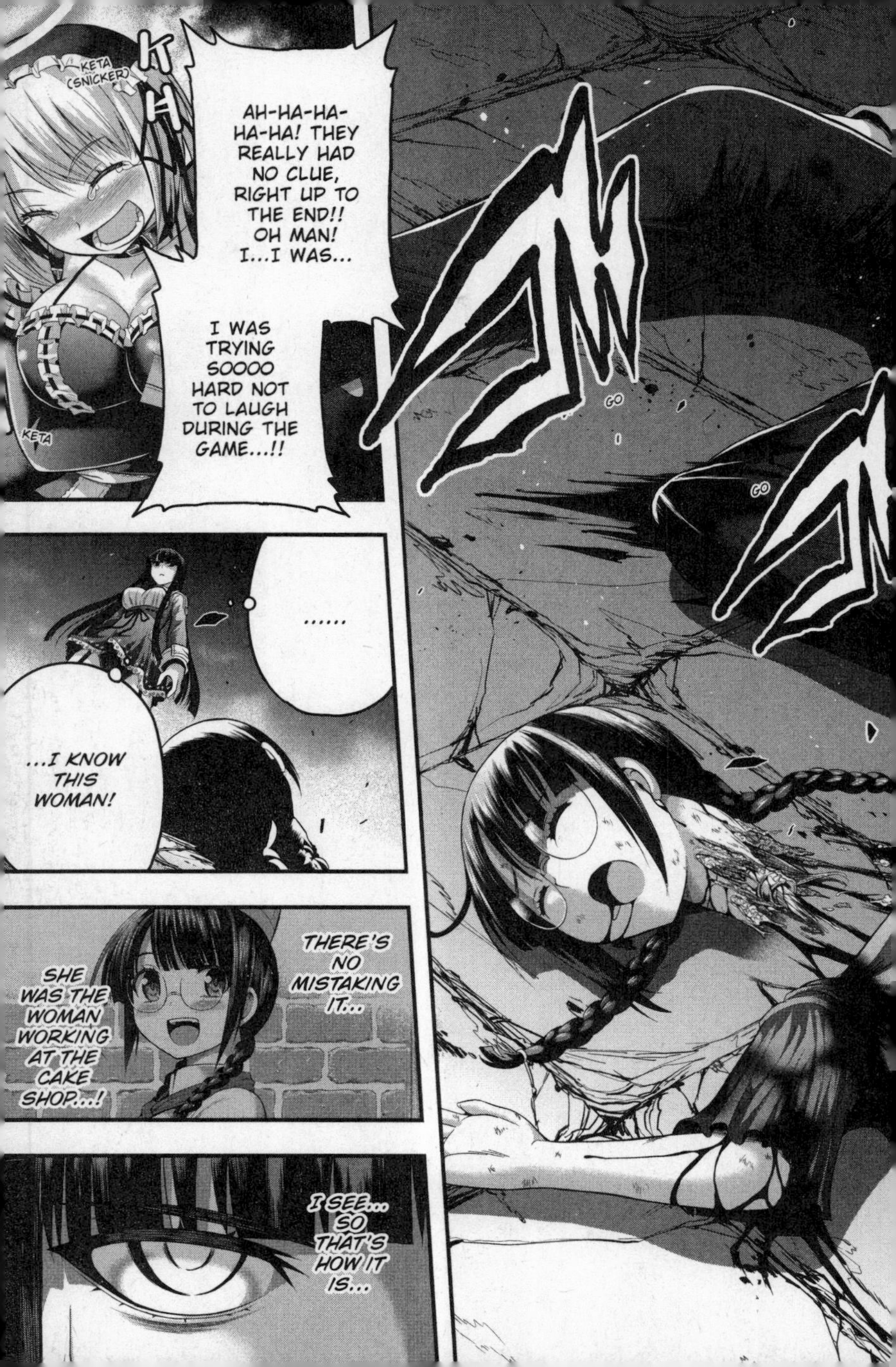
GO
GO
KH
KETA (SNICKER)
AH-HA-HA-HA-HA! THEY REALLY HAD NO CLUE, RIGHT UP TO THE END!! OH MAN! I...I WAS...
I WAS TRYING SOOOO HARD NOT TO LAUGH DURING THE GAME...!!
KETA
......
...I KNOW THIS WOMAN!
THERE'S NO MISTAKING IT...
SHE WAS THE WOMAN WORKING AT THE CAKE SHOP...!
I SEE... SO THAT'S HOW IT IS...

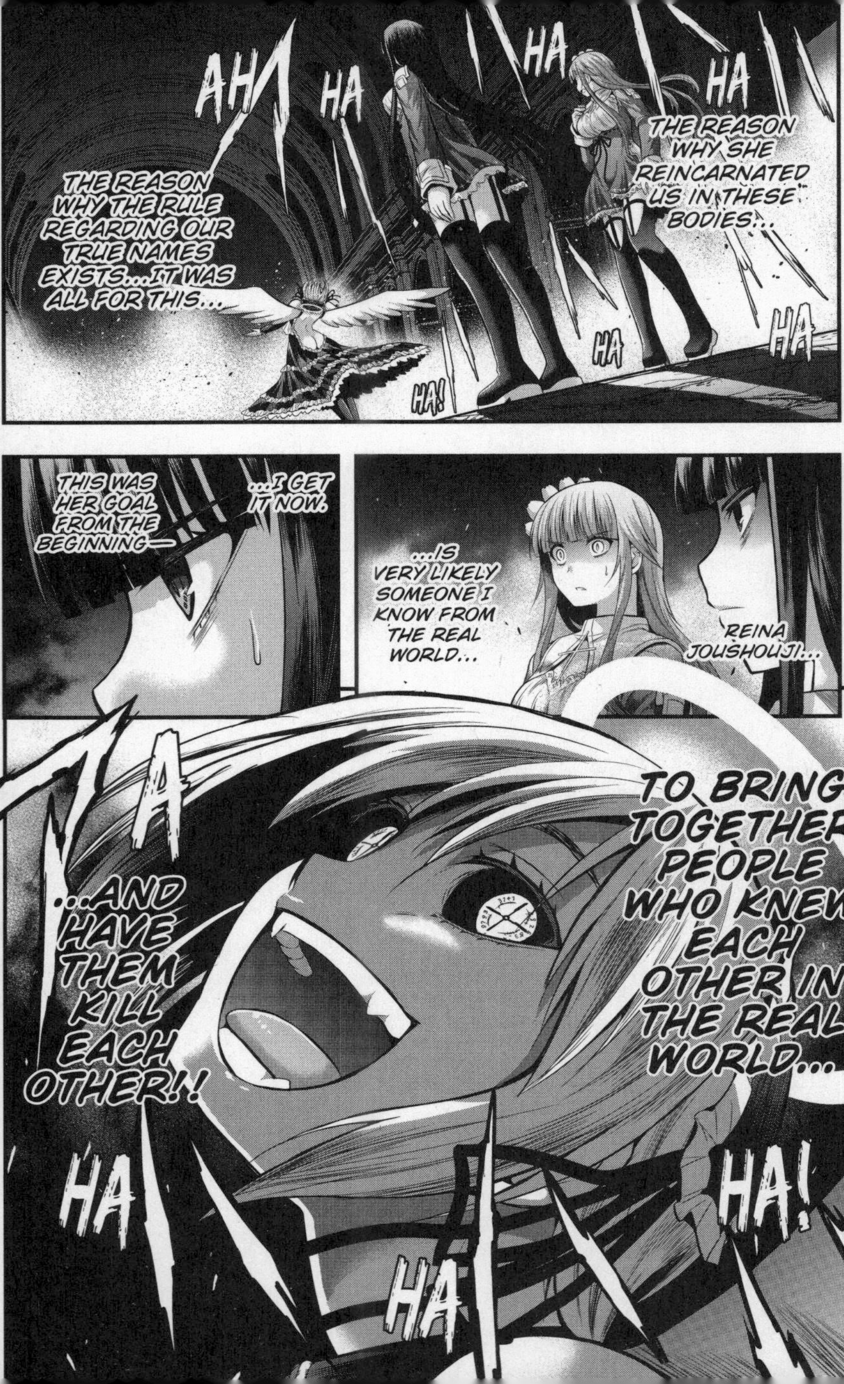
HA
HA
THE REASON WHY SHE REINCARNATED US IN THESE BODIES...
HA
AHA
HA
THE REASON WHY THE RULE REGARDING OUR TRUE NAMES EXISTS...IT WAS ALL FOR THIS...
HA
HA
HA!
REINA JOUSHOUJI...
...IS VERY LIKELY SOMEONE I KNOW FROM THE REAL WORLD...
...I GET IT NOW.
THIS WAS HER GOAL FROM THE BEGINNING—
HA
TO BRING TOGETHER PEOPLE WHO KNEW EACH OTHER IN THE REAL WORLD...
...AND HAVE THEM KILL EACH OTHER!!
HA!
HA
HA

Though You May Burn to ASH

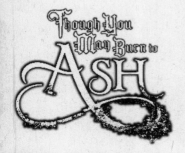

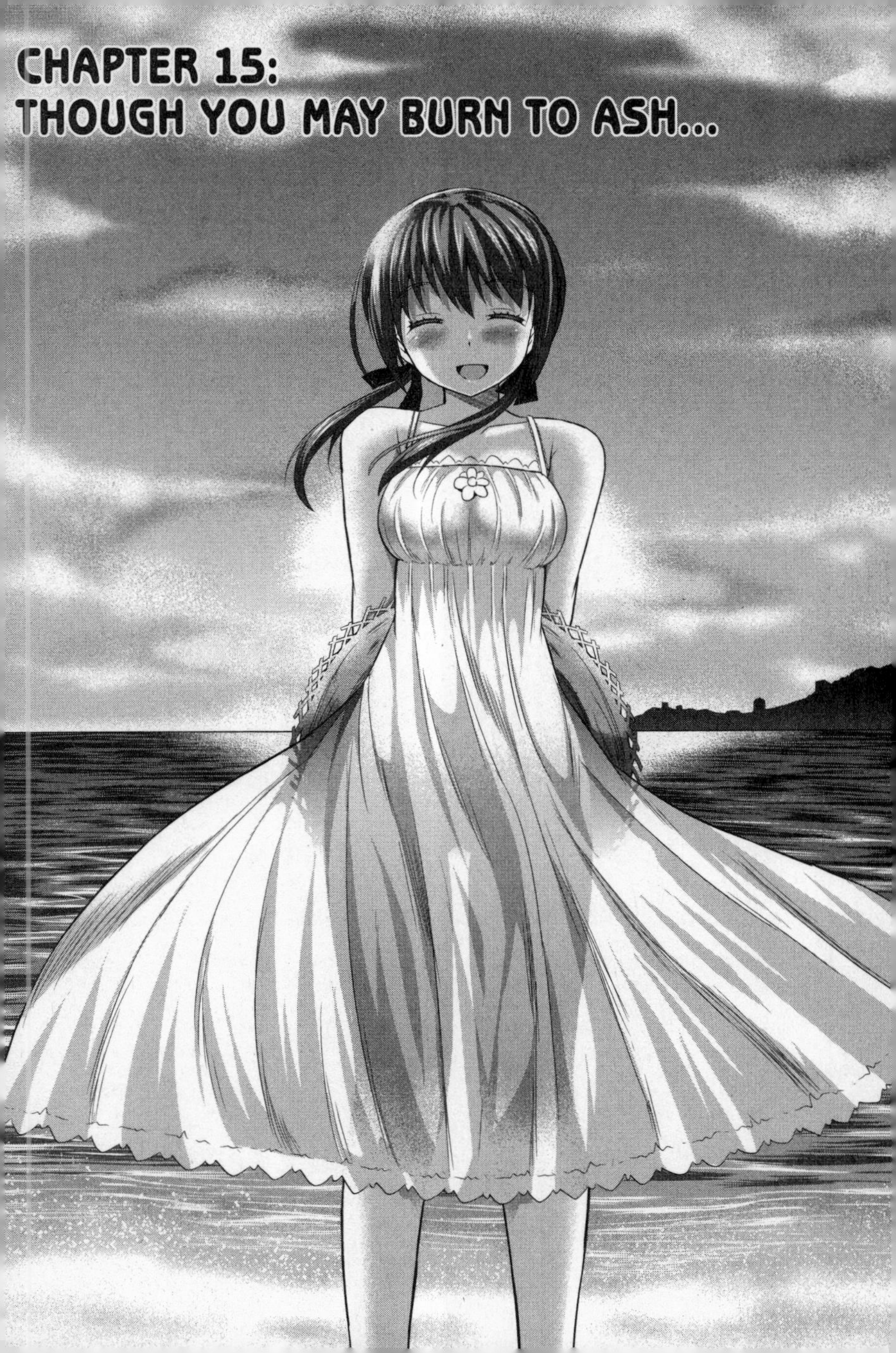
CHAPTER 15:
THOUGH YOU MAY BURN TO ASH...

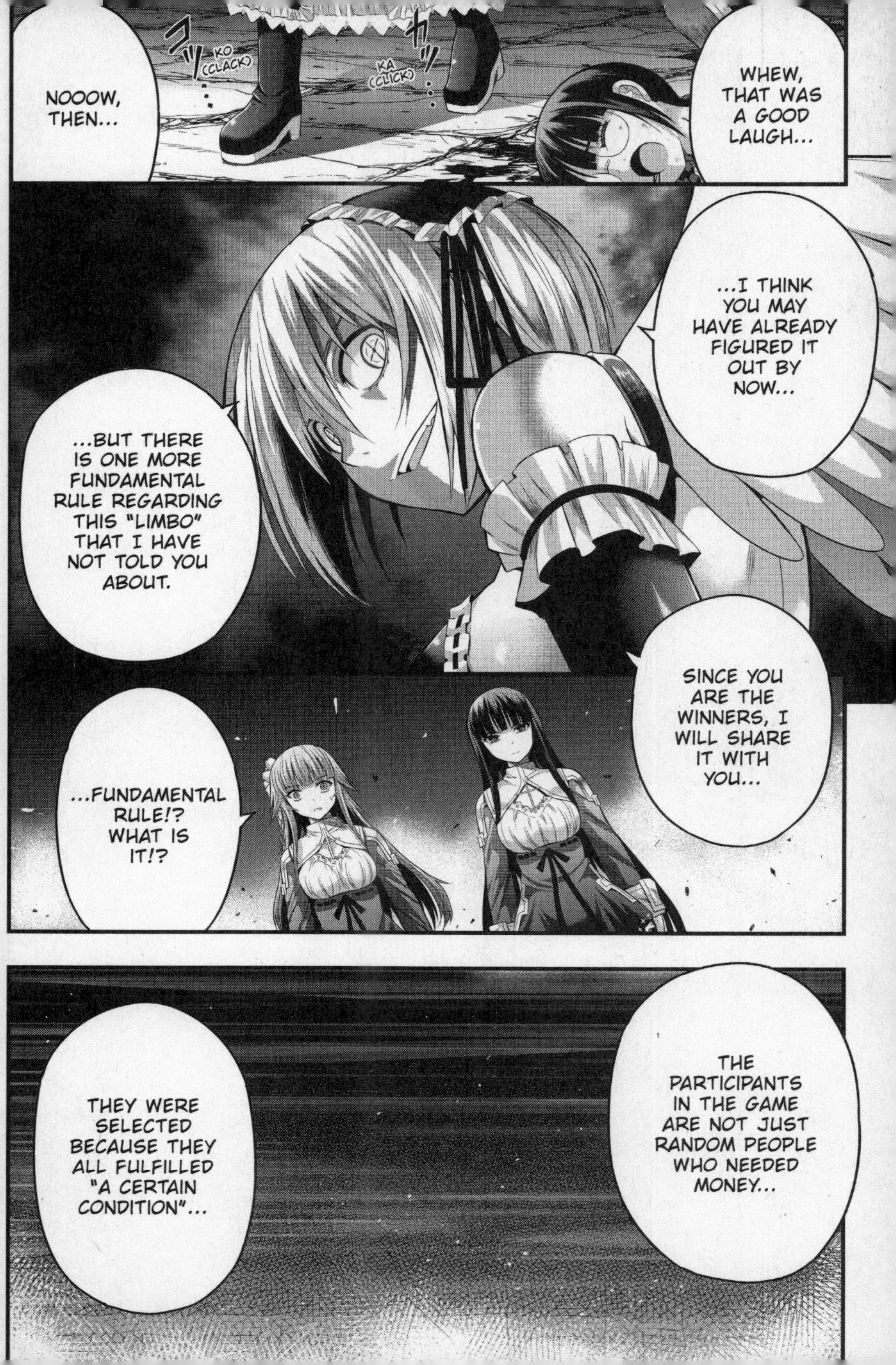
WHEW, THAT WAS A GOOD LAUGH...
KA (CLICK)
KO (CLACK)
NOOOW, THEN...
...I THINK YOU MAY HAVE ALREADY FIGURED IT OUT BY NOW...
...BUT THERE IS ONE MORE FUNDAMENTAL RULE REGARDING THIS "LIMBO" THAT I HAVE NOT TOLD YOU ABOUT.
SINCE YOU ARE THE WINNERS, I WILL SHARE IT WITH YOU...
...FUNDAMENTAL RULE!? WHAT IS IT!?
THE PARTICIPANTS IN THE GAME ARE NOT JUST RANDOM PEOPLE WHO NEEDED MONEY...
THEY WERE SELECTED BECAUSE THEY ALL FULFILLED "A CERTAIN CONDITION"...

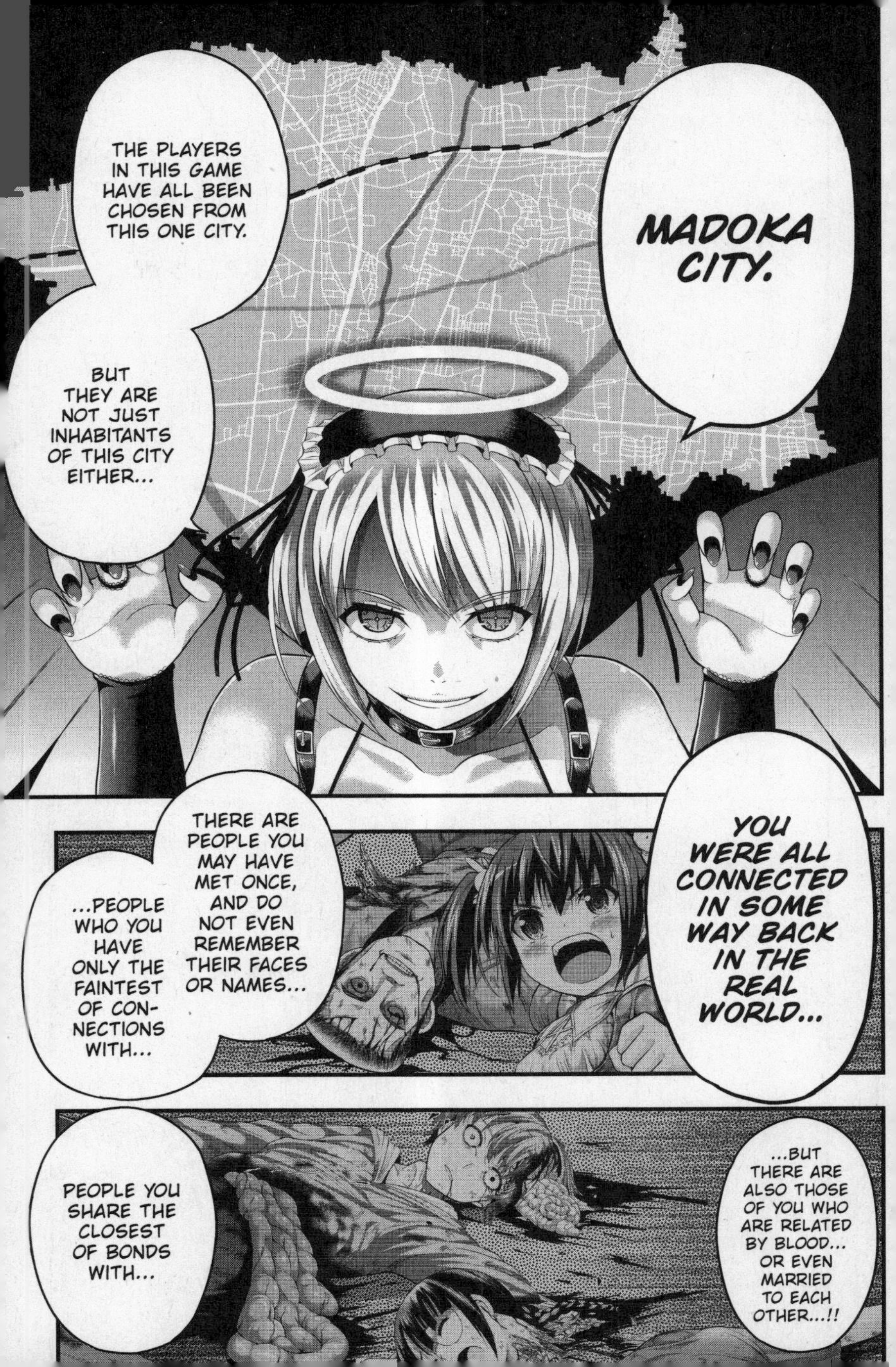
MADOKA CITY.
THE PLAYERS IN THIS GAME HAVE ALL BEEN CHOSEN FROM THIS ONE CITY.
BUT THEY ARE NOT JUST INHABITANTS OF THIS CITY EITHER...
YOU WERE ALL CONNECTED IN SOME WAY BACK IN THE REAL WORLD...
THERE ARE PEOPLE YOU MAY HAVE MET ONCE, AND DO NOT EVEN REMEMBER THEIR FACES OR NAMES...
...PEOPLE WHO YOU HAVE ONLY THE FAINTEST OF CON-NECTIONS WITH...
...BUT THERE ARE ALSO THOSE OF YOU WHO ARE RELATED BY BLOOD... OR EVEN MARRIED TO EACH OTHER...!!
PEOPLE YOU SHARE THE CLOSEST OF BONDS WITH...

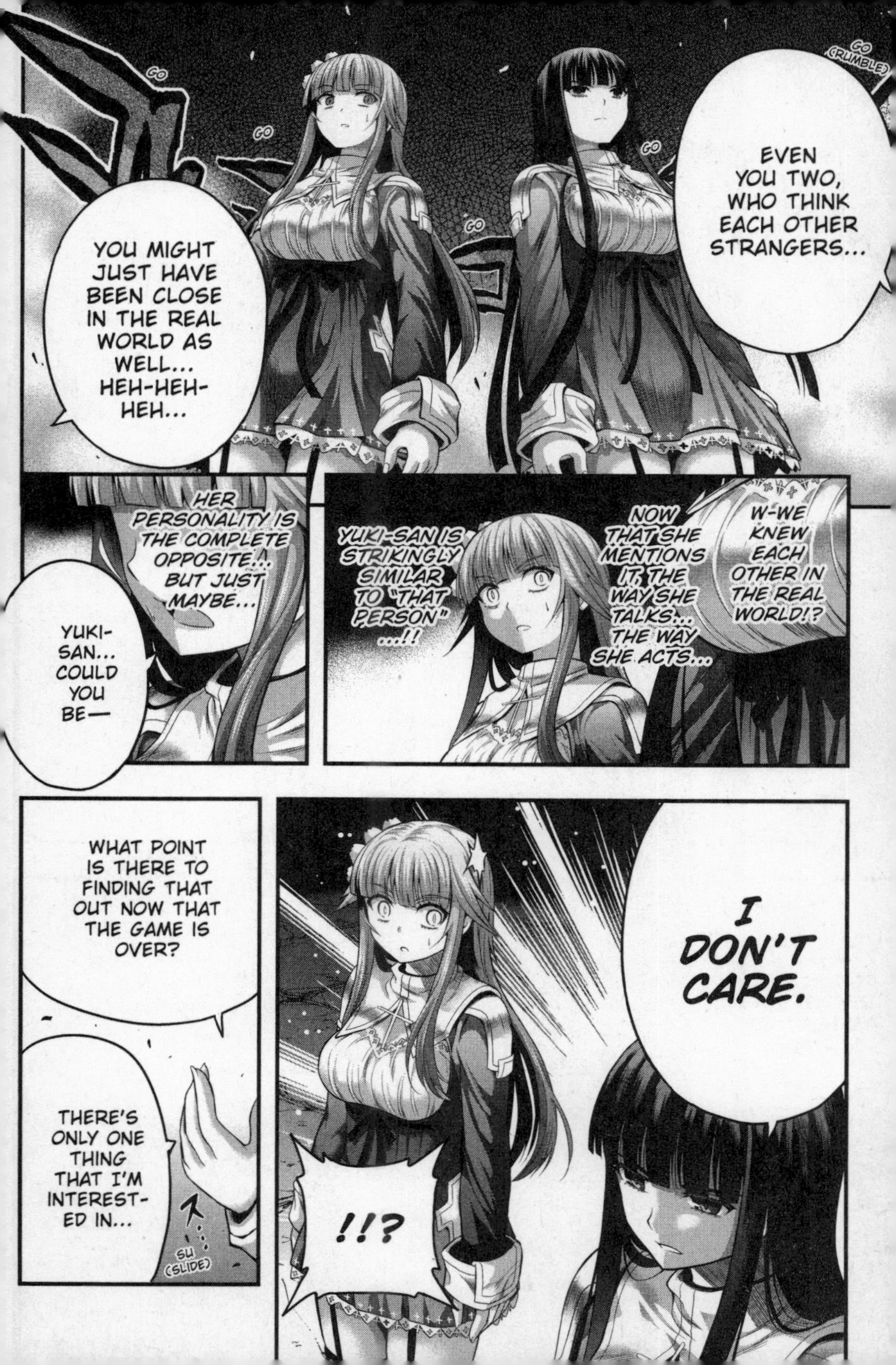
GO (RUMBLE)
EVEN YOU TWO, WHO THINK EACH OTHER STRANGERS...
GO
GO
GO
GO
YOU MIGHT JUST HAVE BEEN CLOSE IN THE REAL WORLD AS WELL... HEH-HEH-HEH...
W-WE KNEW EACH OTHER IN THE REAL WORLD!?
NOW THAT SHE MENTIONS IT, THE WAY SHE TALKS... THE WAY SHE ACTS...
YUKI-SAN IS STRIKINGLY SIMILAR TO "THAT PERSON"...!!
HER PERSONALITY IS THE COMPLETE OPPOSITE... BUT JUST MAYBE...
YUKI-SAN... COULD YOU BE—
I DON'T CARE.
!!?
WHAT POINT IS THERE TO FINDING THAT OUT NOW THAT THE GAME IS OVER?
THERE'S ONLY ONE THING THAT I'M INTEREST-ED IN...
SU (SLIDE)

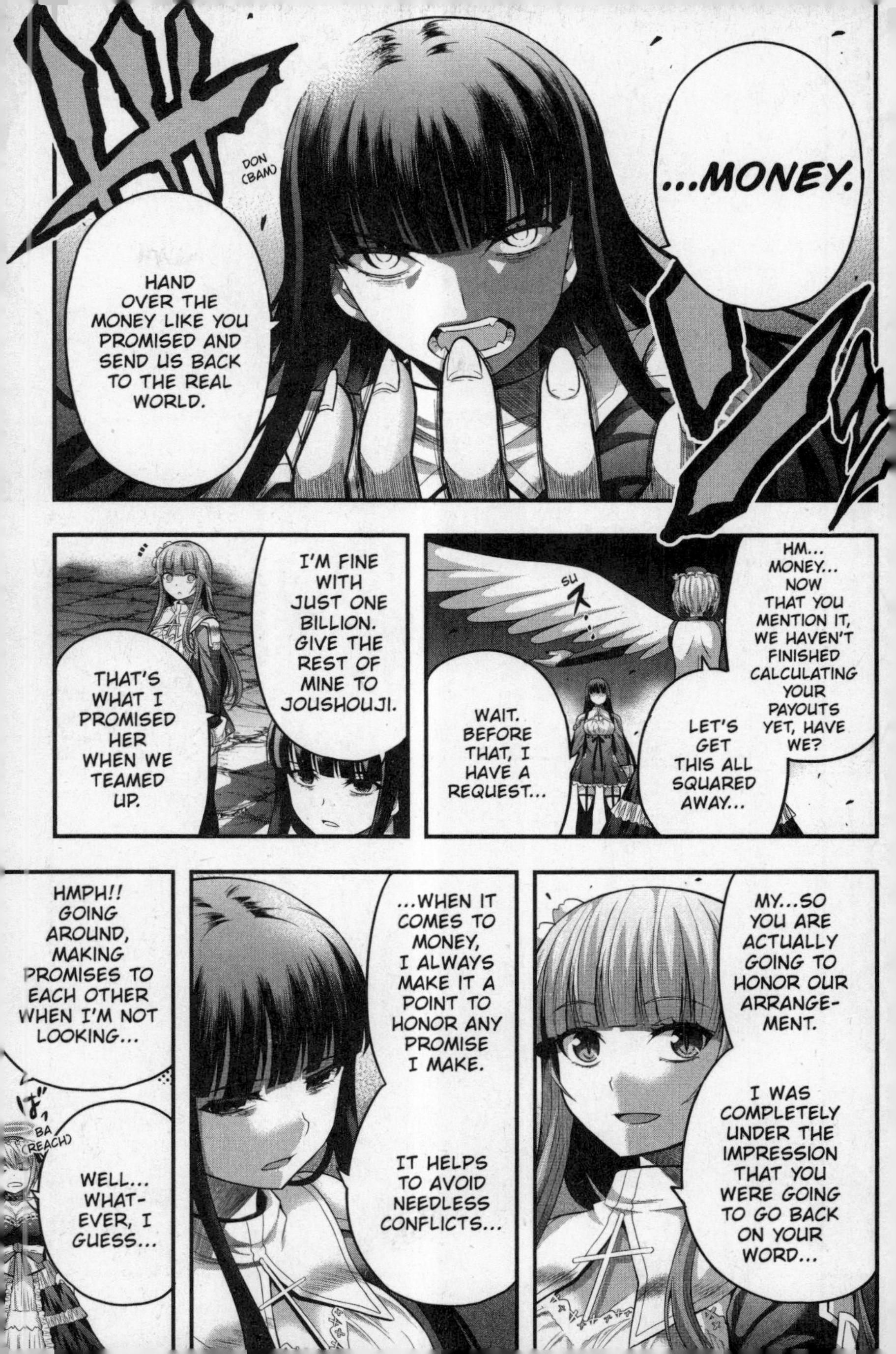
...MONEY.
DON (BAM)
HAND OVER THE MONEY LIKE YOU PROMISED AND SEND US BACK TO THE REAL WORLD.
HM... MONEY... NOW THAT YOU MENTION IT, WE HAVEN'T FINISHED CALCULATING YOUR PAYOUTS YET, HAVE WE?
SU
LET'S GET THIS ALL SQUARED AWAY...
WAIT. BEFORE THAT, I HAVE A REQUEST...
I'M FINE WITH JUST ONE BILLION. GIVE THE REST OF MINE TO JOUSHOUJI.
THAT'S WHAT I PROMISED HER WHEN WE TEAMED UP.
MY...SO YOU ARE ACTUALLY GOING TO HONOR OUR ARRANGEMENT.
I WAS COMPLETELY UNDER THE IMPRESSION THAT YOU WERE GOING TO GO BACK ON YOUR WORD...
...WHEN IT COMES TO MONEY, I ALWAYS MAKE IT A POINT TO HONOR ANY PROMISE I MAKE.
IT HELPS TO AVOID NEEDLESS CONFLICTS...
HMPH!! GOING AROUND, MAKING PROMISES TO EACH OTHER WHEN I'M NOT LOOKING...
BA (REACH)
WELL... WHATEVER, I GUESS...

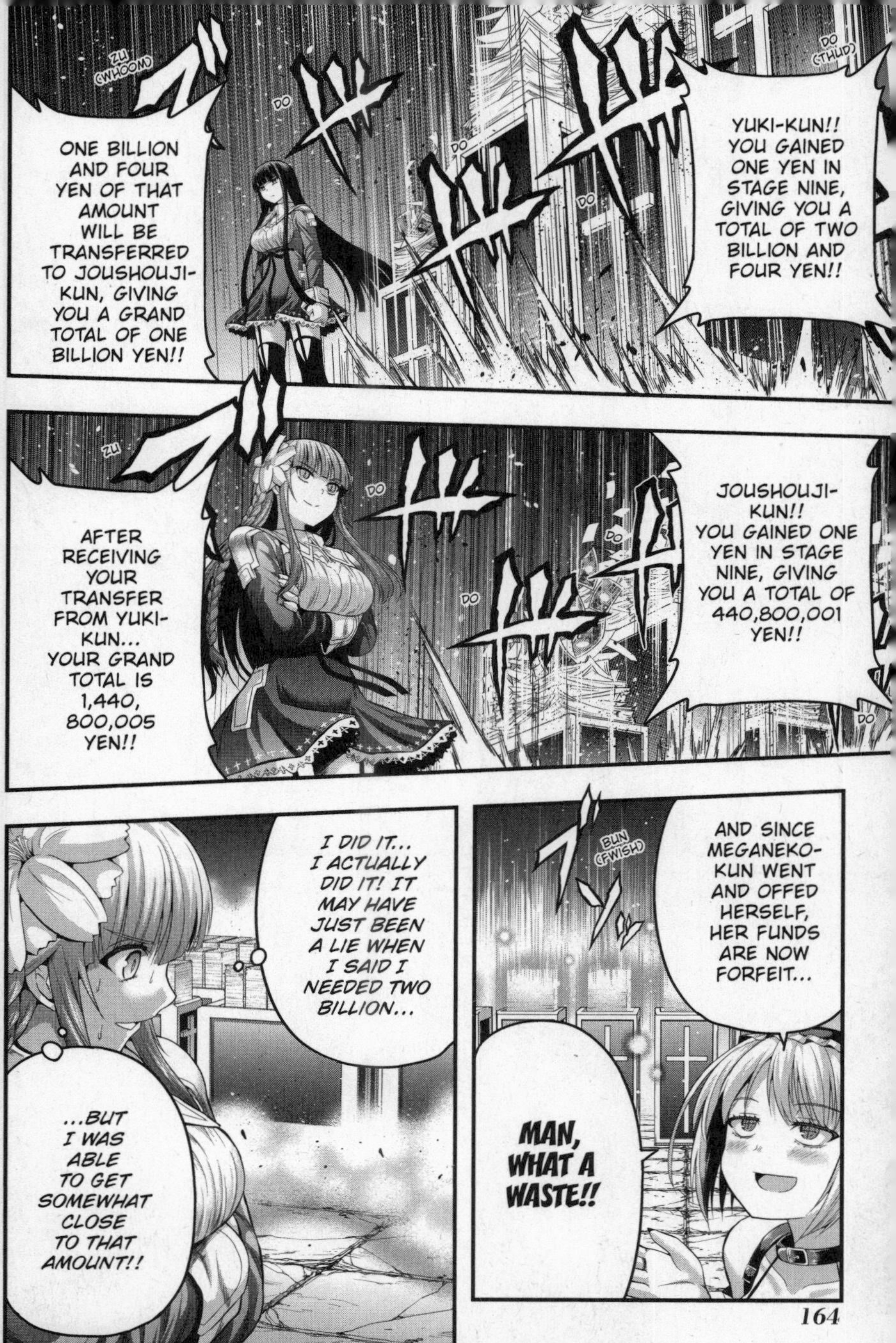
DO (THUD)
YUKI-KUN!! YOU GAINED ONE YEN IN STAGE NINE, GIVING YOU A TOTAL OF TWO BILLION AND FOUR YEN!!
DO
DO
DO
ZU (WHOOM)
ONE BILLION AND FOUR YEN OF THAT AMOUNT WILL BE TRANSFERRED TO JOUSHOUJI-KUN, GIVING YOU A GRAND TOTAL OF ONE BILLION YEN!!
JOUSHOUJI-KUN!! YOU GAINED ONE YEN IN STAGE NINE, GIVING YOU A TOTAL OF 440,800,001 YEN!!
DO
DO
DO
DO
ZU
AFTER RECEIVING YOUR TRANSFER FROM YUKI-KUN... YOUR GRAND TOTAL IS 1,440, 800,005 YEN!!
BUN (FWISH)
AND SINCE MEGANEKO-KUN WENT AND OFFED HERSELF, HER FUNDS ARE NOW FORFEIT...
MAN, WHAT A WASTE!!
I DID IT... I ACTUALLY DID IT! IT MAY HAVE JUST BEEN A LIE WHEN I SAID I NEEDED TWO BILLION...
...BUT I WAS ABLE TO GET SOMEWHAT CLOSE TO THAT AMOUNT!!

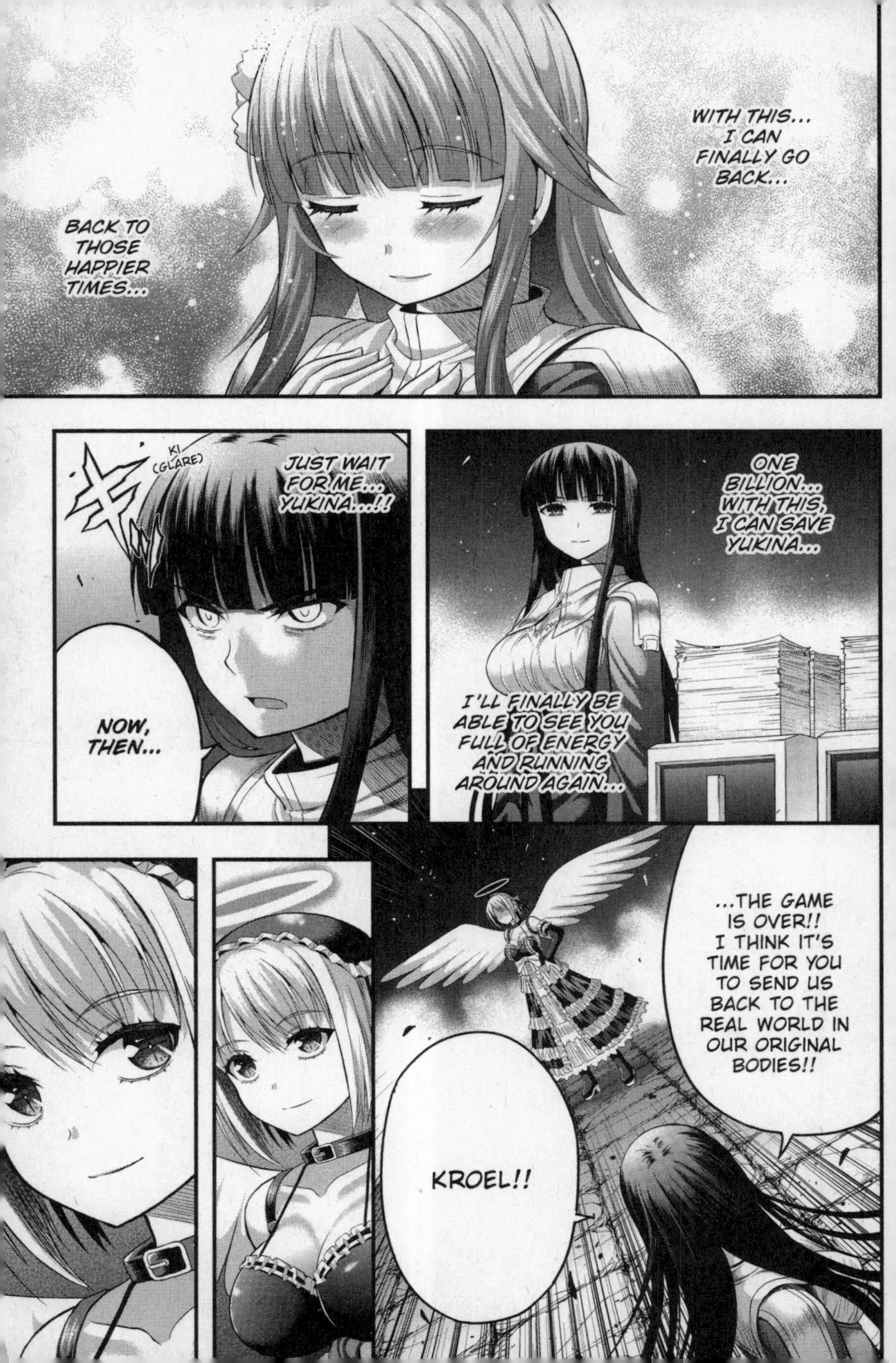
WITH THIS... I CAN FINALLY GO BACK...
BACK TO THOSE HAPPIER TIMES...
ONE BILLION... WITH THIS, I CAN SAVE YUKINA...
I'LL FINALLY BE ABLE TO SEE YOU FULL OF ENERGY AND RUNNING AROUND AGAIN...
KI (GLARE)
JUST WAIT FOR ME... YUKINA...!!
NOW, THEN...
KROEL!!
...THE GAME IS OVER!! I THINK IT'S TIME FOR YOU TO SEND US BACK TO THE REAL WORLD IN OUR ORIGINAL BODIES!!

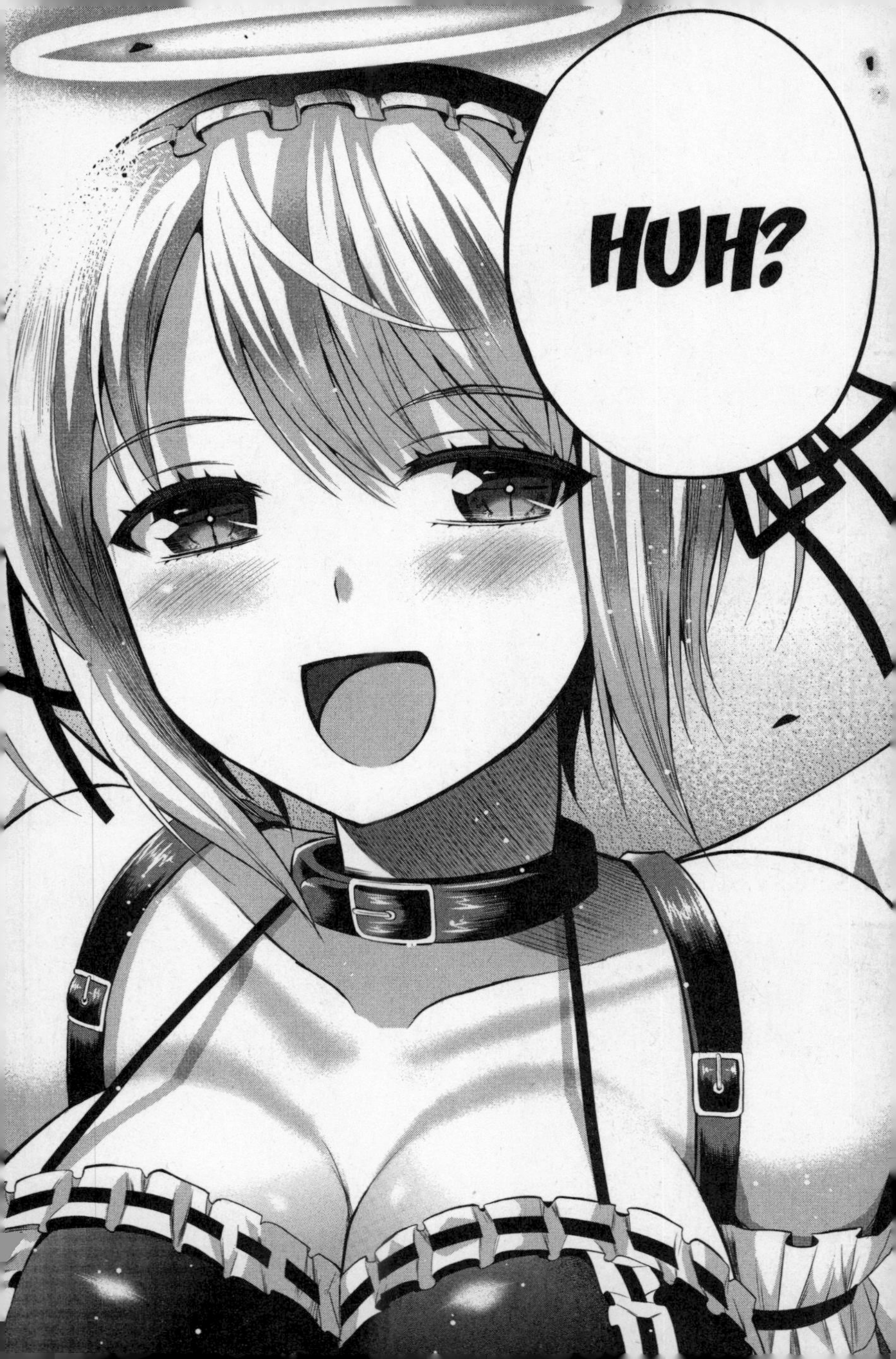
HUH?

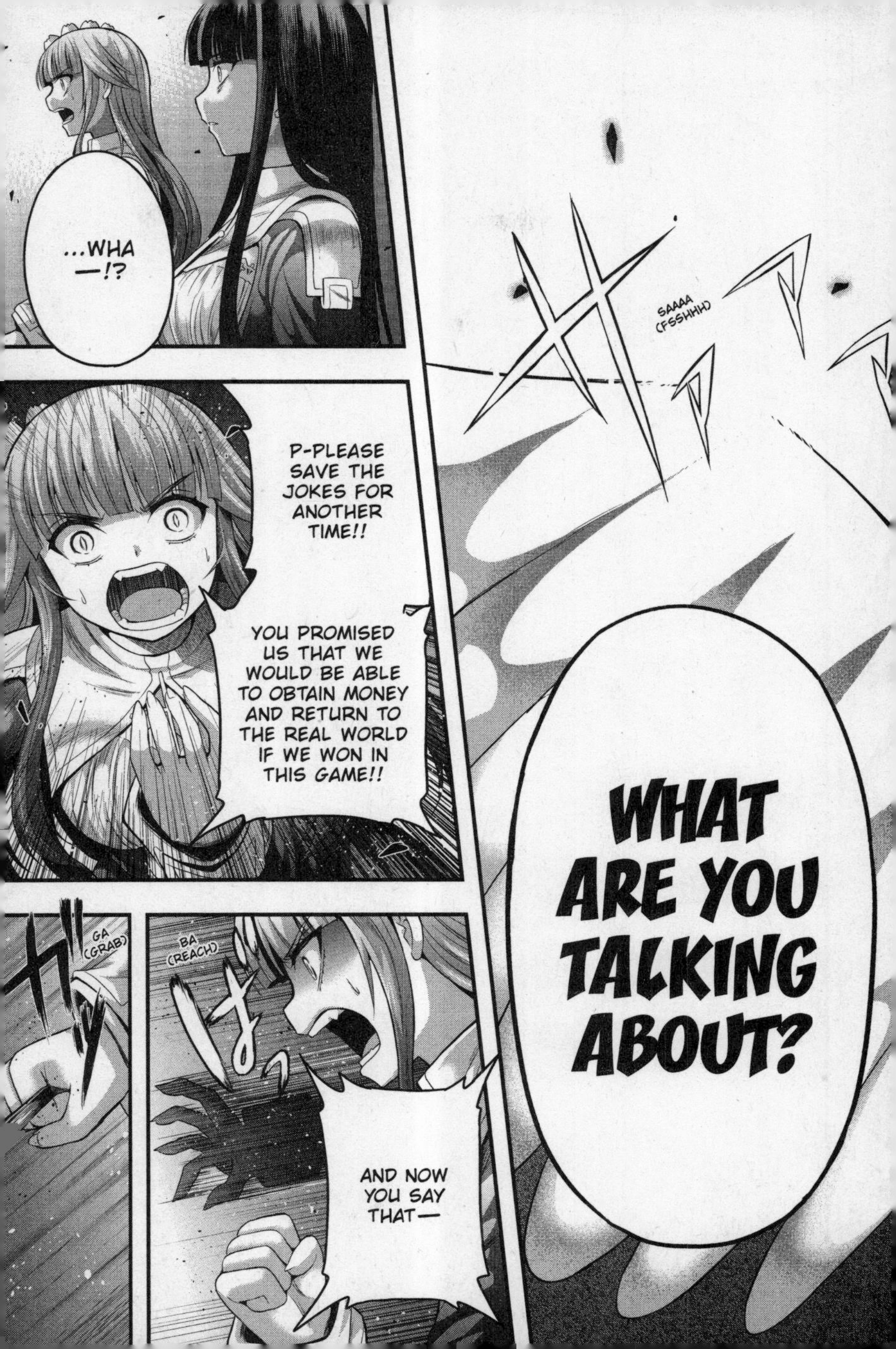
SAAAA (FSSHHH)
WHAT ARE YOU TALKING ABOUT?
...WHA—!?
P-PLEASE SAVE THE JOKES FOR ANOTHER TIME!!
YOU PROMISED US THAT WE WOULD BE ABLE TO OBTAIN MONEY AND RETURN TO THE REAL WORLD IF WE WON IN THIS GAME!!
BA (REACH)
AND NOW YOU SAY THAT—
GA (GRAB)

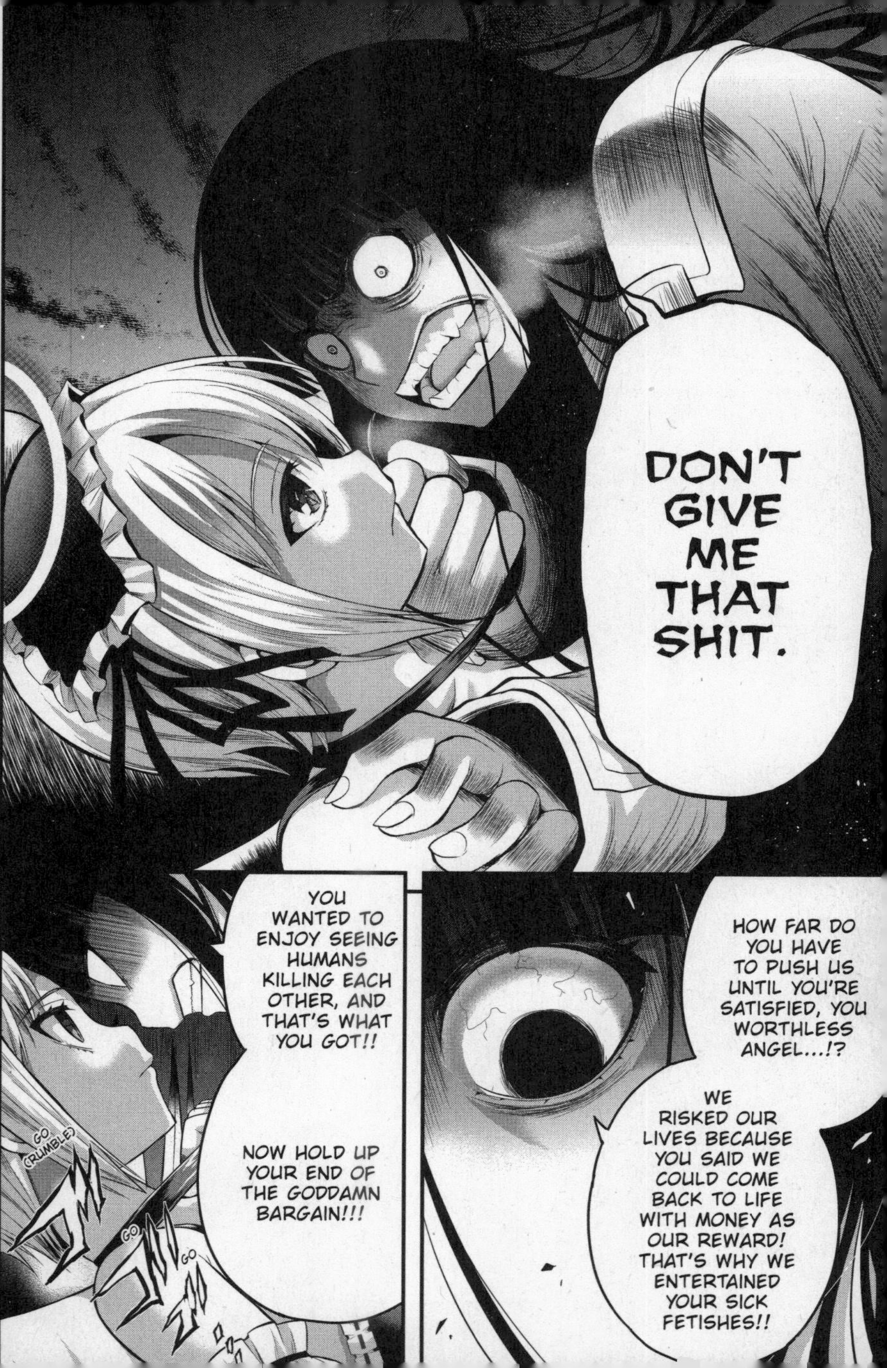
DON'T GIVE ME THAT SHIT.
HOW FAR DO YOU HAVE TO PUSH US UNTIL YOU'RE SATISFIED, YOU WORTHLESS ANGEL...!?
WE RISKED OUR LIVES BECAUSE YOU SAID WE COULD COME BACK TO LIFE WITH MONEY AS OUR REWARD! THAT'S WHY WE ENTERTAINED YOUR SICK FETISHES!!
YOU WANTED TO ENJOY SEEING HUMANS KILLING EACH OTHER, AND THAT'S WHAT YOU GOT!!
NOW HOLD UP YOUR END OF THE GODDAMN BARGAIN!!!
GO (RUMBLE)
GO
GO

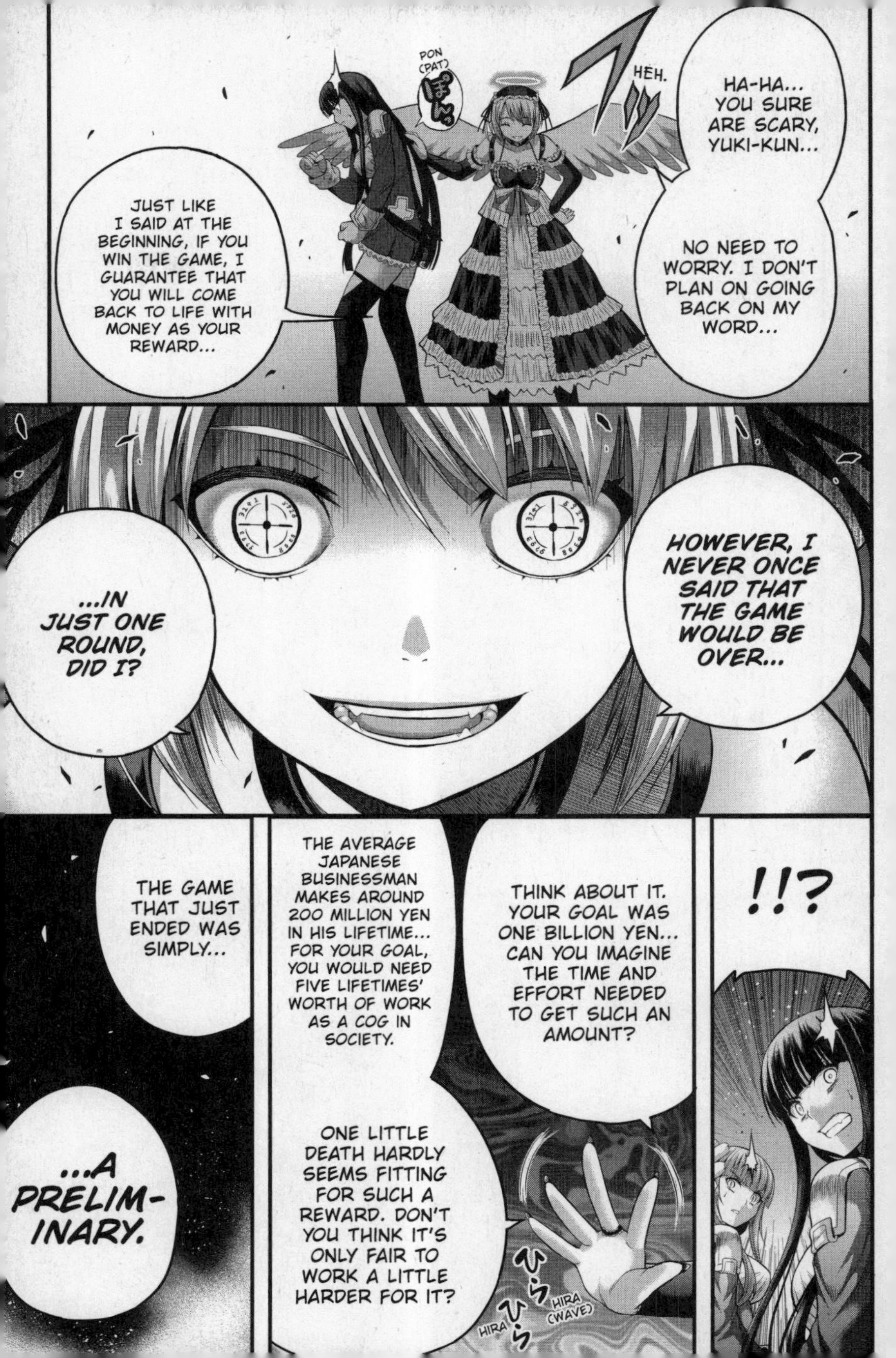
HA-HA... YOU SURE ARE SCARY, YUKI-KUN...
HEH.
NO NEED TO WORRY. I DON'T PLAN ON GOING BACK ON MY WORD...
PON (PAT)
ぽん
JUST LIKE I SAID AT THE BEGINNING, IF YOU WIN THE GAME, I GUARANTEE THAT YOU WILL COME BACK TO LIFE WITH MONEY AS YOUR REWARD...
HOWEVER, I NEVER ONCE SAID THAT THE GAME WOULD BE OVER...
...IN JUST ONE ROUND, DID I?
!!?
THINK ABOUT IT. YOUR GOAL WAS ONE BILLION YEN... CAN YOU IMAGINE THE TIME AND EFFORT NEEDED TO GET SUCH AN AMOUNT?
THE AVERAGE JAPANESE BUSINESSMAN MAKES AROUND 200 MILLION YEN IN HIS LIFETIME... FOR YOUR GOAL, YOU WOULD NEED FIVE LIFETIMES' WORTH OF WORK AS A COG IN SOCIETY.
ONE LITTLE DEATH HARDLY SEEMS FITTING FOR SUCH A REWARD. DON'T YOU THINK IT'S ONLY FAIR TO WORK A LITTLE HARDER FOR IT?
ひら
HIRA (WAVE)
ひら
HIRA
THE GAME THAT JUST ENDED WAS SIMPLY...
...A PRELIMINARY.

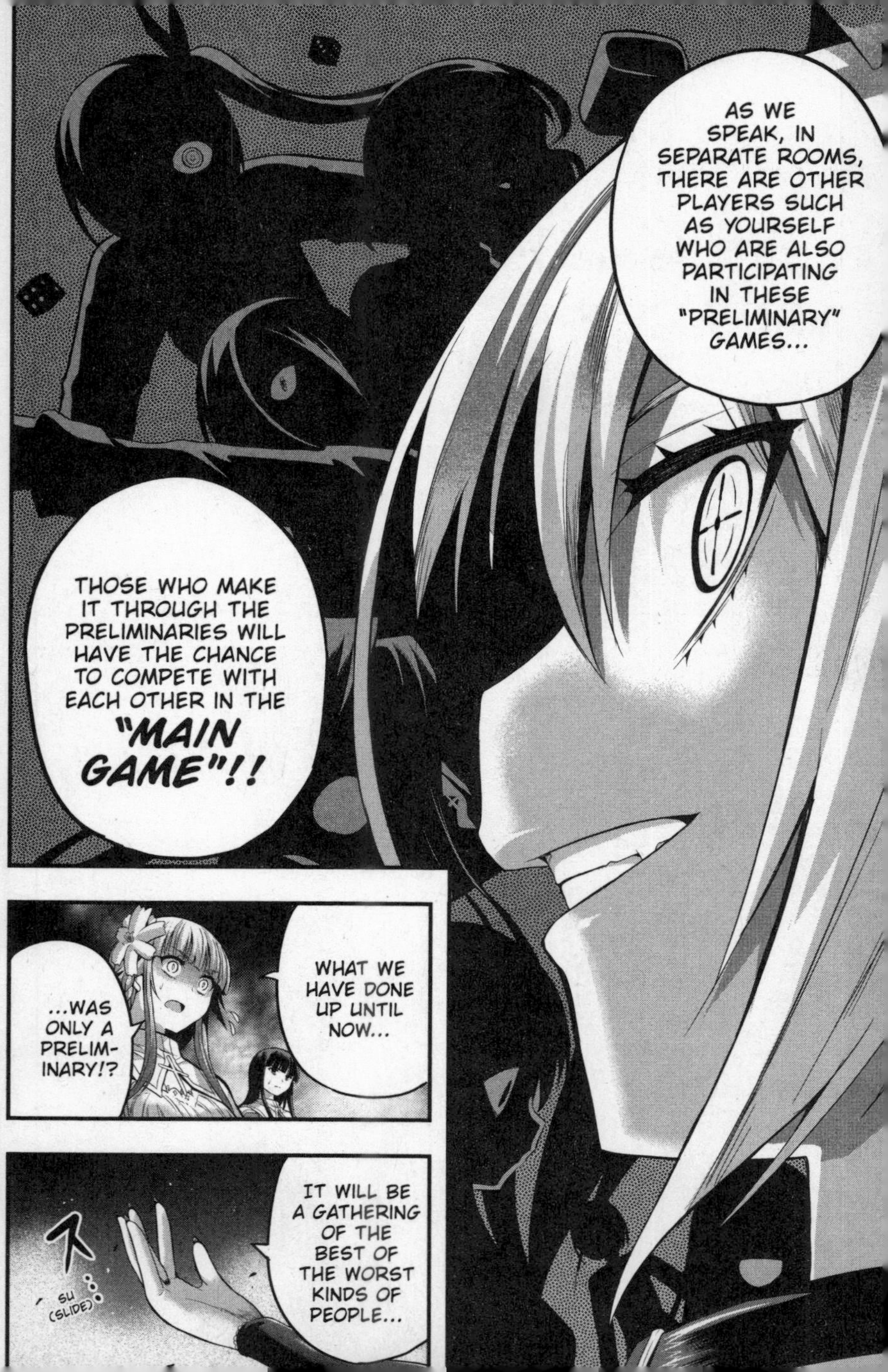
AS WE SPEAK, IN SEPARATE ROOMS, THERE ARE OTHER PLAYERS SUCH AS YOURSELF WHO ARE ALSO PARTICIPATING IN THESE "PRELIMINARY" GAMES...
THOSE WHO MAKE IT THROUGH THE PRELIMINARIES WILL HAVE THE CHANCE TO COMPETE WITH EACH OTHER IN THE "MAIN GAME"!!
WHAT WE HAVE DONE UP UNTIL NOW...
...WAS ONLY A PRELIM-INARY!?
IT WILL BE A GATHERING OF THE BEST OF THE WORST KINDS OF PEOPLE...
SU (SLIDE)

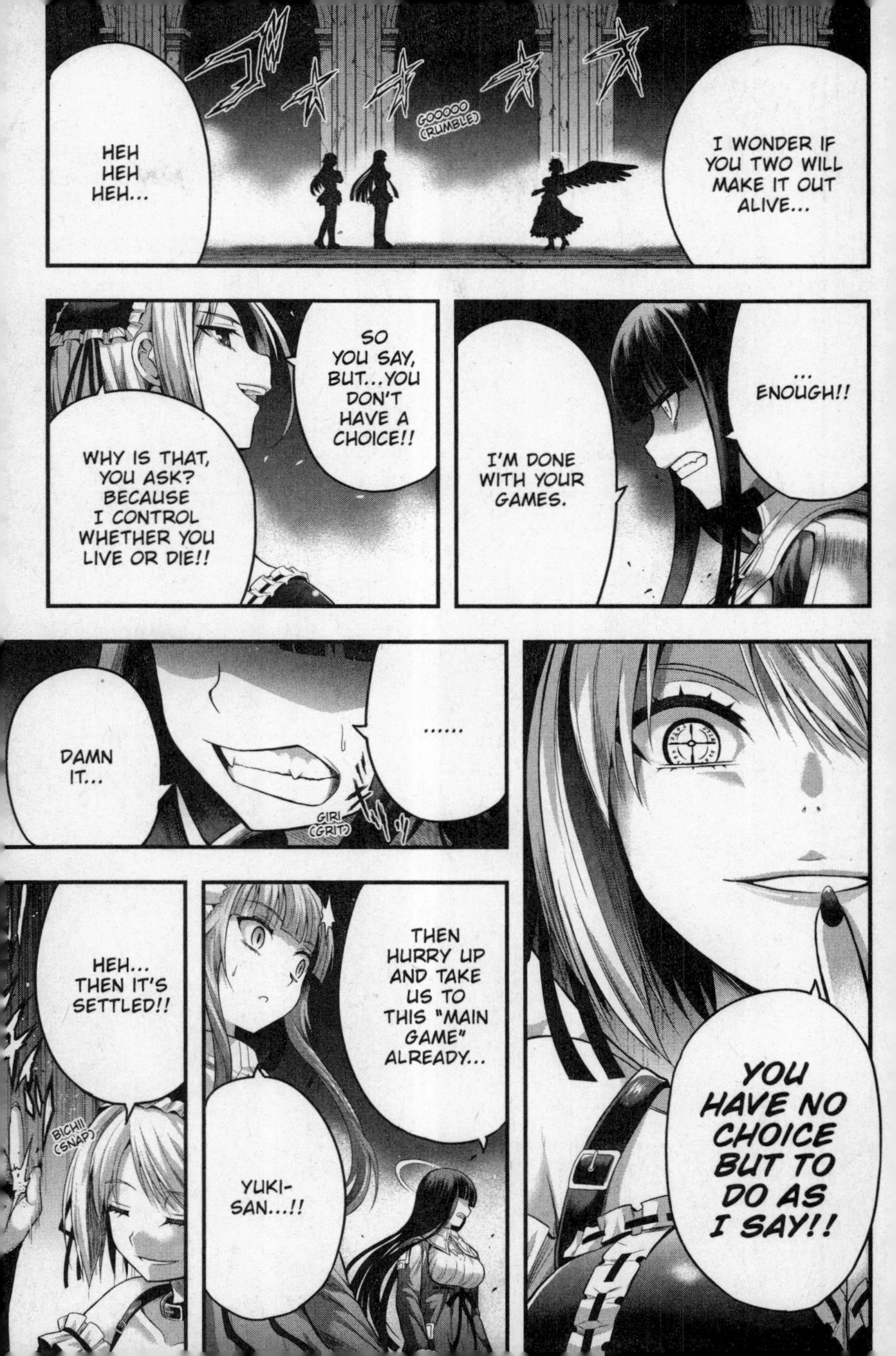
I WONDER IF YOU TWO WILL MAKE IT OUT ALIVE...
GOOOOO (RUMBLE)
HEH HEH HEH...
... ENOUGH!!
I'M DONE WITH YOUR GAMES.
SO YOU SAY, BUT...YOU DON'T HAVE A CHOICE!!
WHY IS THAT, YOU ASK? BECAUSE I CONTROL WHETHER YOU LIVE OR DIE!!
YOU HAVE NO CHOICE BUT TO DO AS I SAY!!
......
DAMN IT...
GIRI (GRIT)
THEN HURRY UP AND TAKE US TO THIS "MAIN GAME" ALREADY...
YUKI-SAN...!!
HEH... THEN IT'S SETTLED!!
BICHI (SNAP)

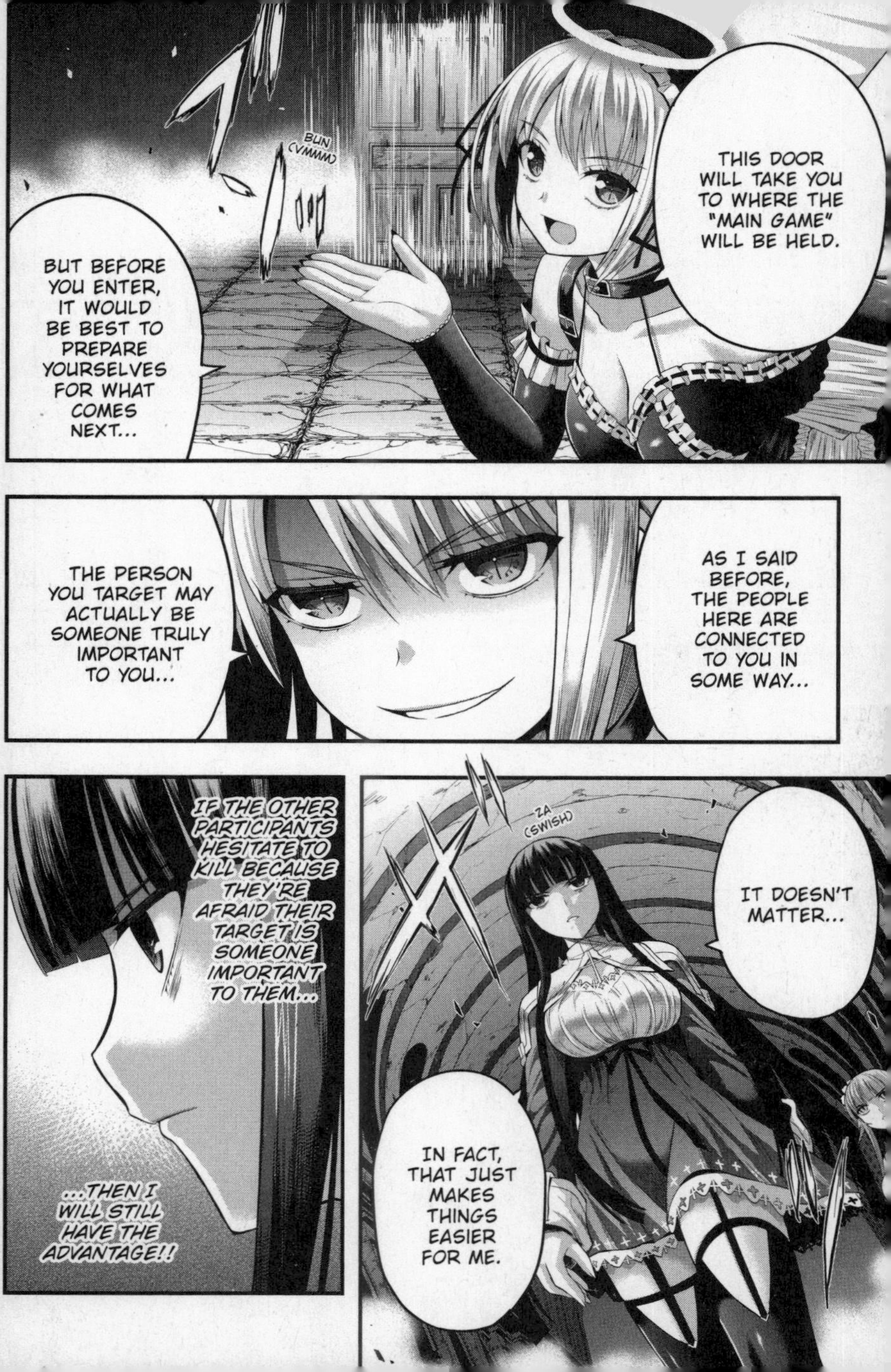
THIS DOOR WILL TAKE YOU TO WHERE THE "MAIN GAME" WILL BE HELD.
BUN (VMMM)
BUT BEFORE YOU ENTER, IT WOULD BE BEST TO PREPARE YOURSELVES FOR WHAT COMES NEXT...
AS I SAID BEFORE, THE PEOPLE HERE ARE CONNECTED TO YOU IN SOME WAY...
THE PERSON YOU TARGET MAY ACTUALLY BE SOMEONE TRULY IMPORTANT TO YOU...
ZA (SWISH)
IT DOESN'T MATTER...
IN FACT, THAT JUST MAKES THINGS EASIER FOR ME.
IF THE OTHER PARTICIPANTS HESITATE TO KILL BECAUSE THEY'RE AFRAID THEIR TARGET IS SOMEONE IMPORTANT TO THEM...
...THEN I WILL STILL HAVE THE ADVANTAGE!!

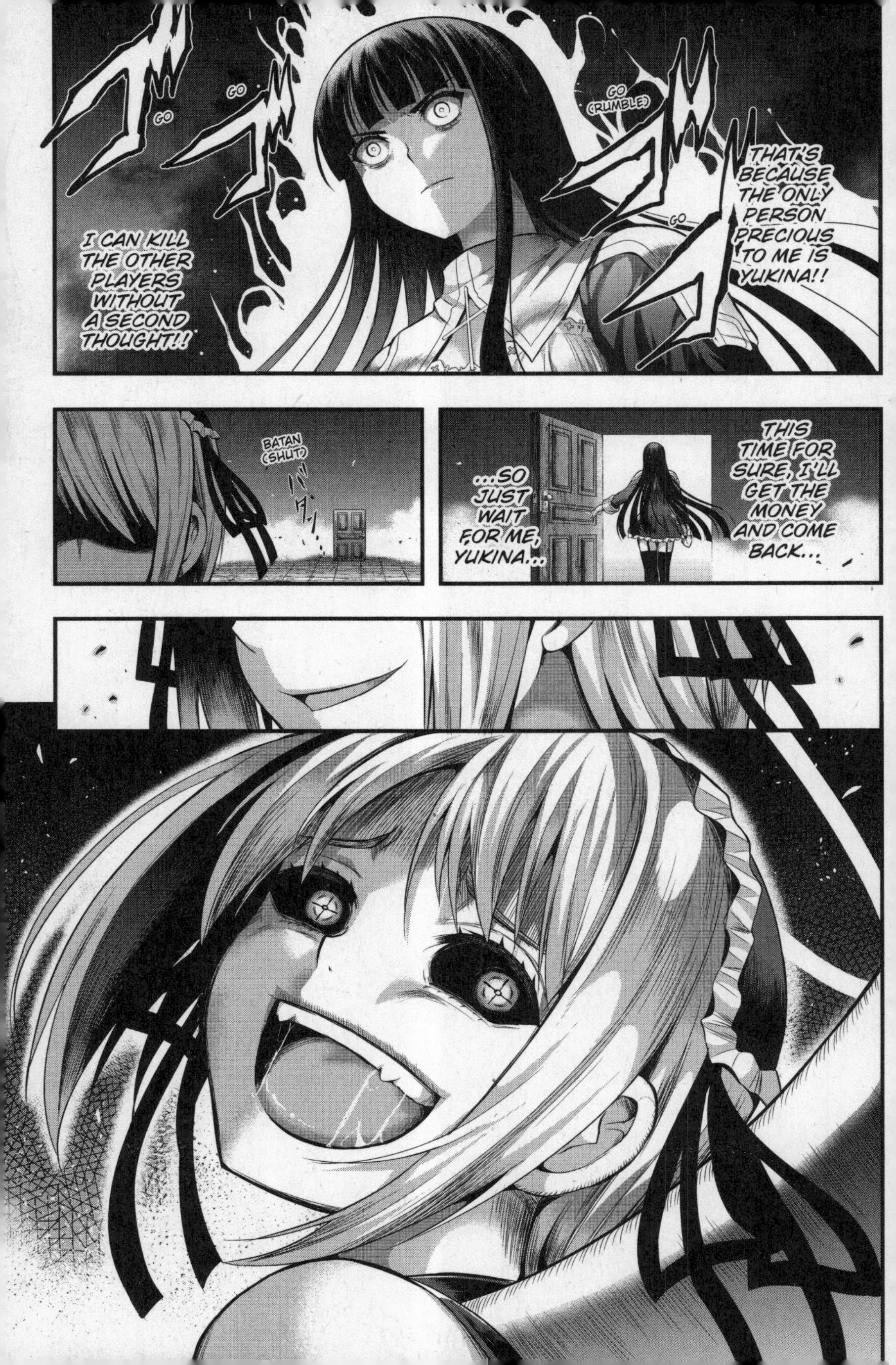

GO (RUMBLE)
GO
GO
THAT'S BECAUSE THE ONLY PERSON PRECIOUS TO ME IS YUKINA!!
GO
I CAN KILL THE OTHER PLAYERS WITHOUT A SECOND THOUGHT!!
THIS TIME FOR SURE, I'LL GET THE MONEY AND COME BACK...
...SO JUST WAIT FOR ME, YUKINA...
BATAN (SHUT)

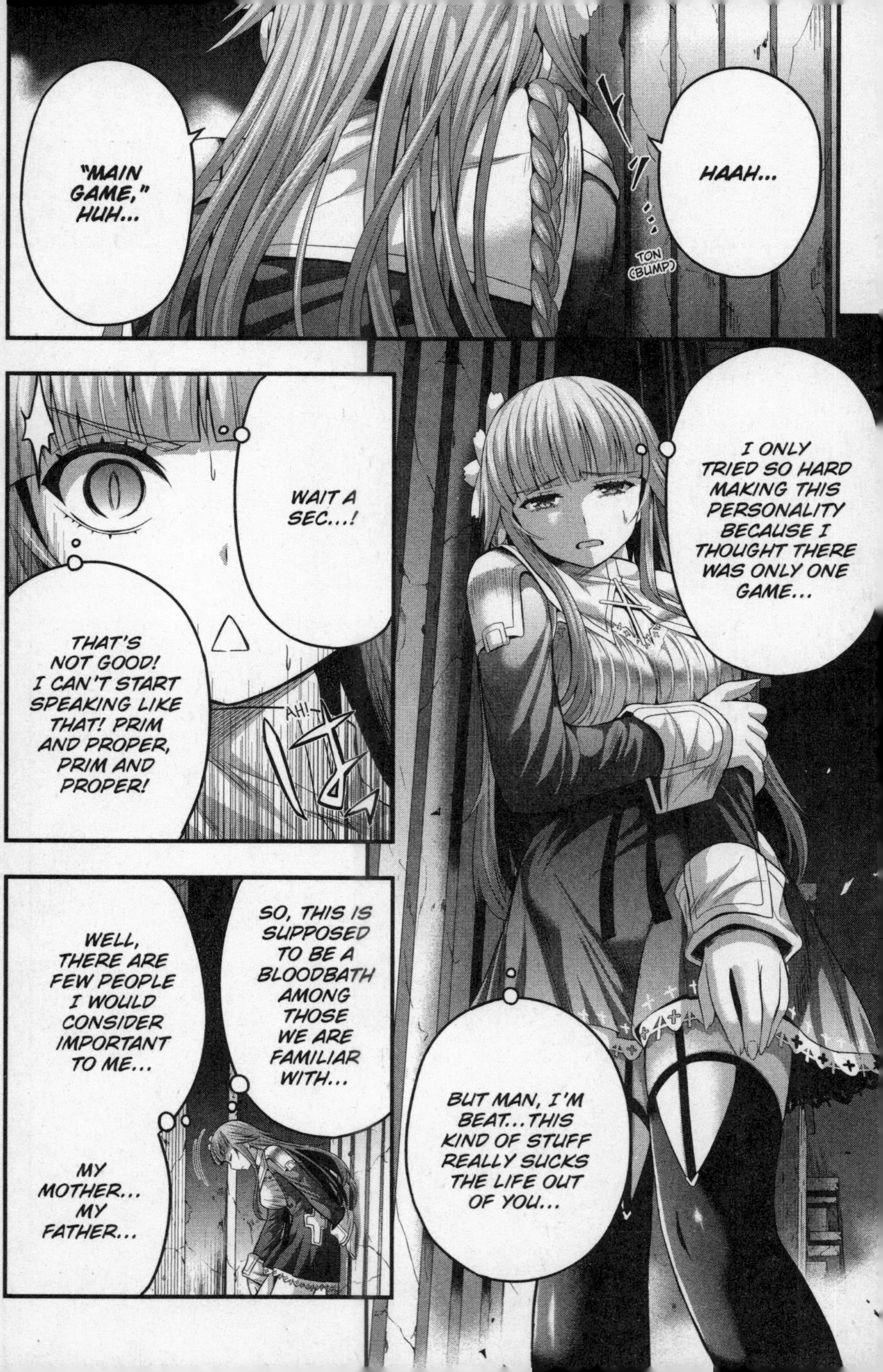
HAAH...
TON (BUMP)
"MAIN GAME," HUH...
I ONLY TRIED SO HARD MAKING THIS PERSONALITY BECAUSE I THOUGHT THERE WAS ONLY ONE GAME...
BUT MAN, I'M BEAT...THIS KIND OF STUFF REALLY SUCKS THE LIFE OUT OF YOU...
WAIT A SEC...!
AH!
THAT'S NOT GOOD! I CAN'T START SPEAKING LIKE THAT! PRIM AND PROPER, PRIM AND PROPER!
SO, THIS IS SUPPOSED TO BE A BLOODBATH AMONG THOSE WE ARE FAMILIAR WITH...
WELL, THERE ARE FEW PEOPLE I WOULD CONSIDER IMPORTANT TO ME...
MY MOTHER... MY FATHER...

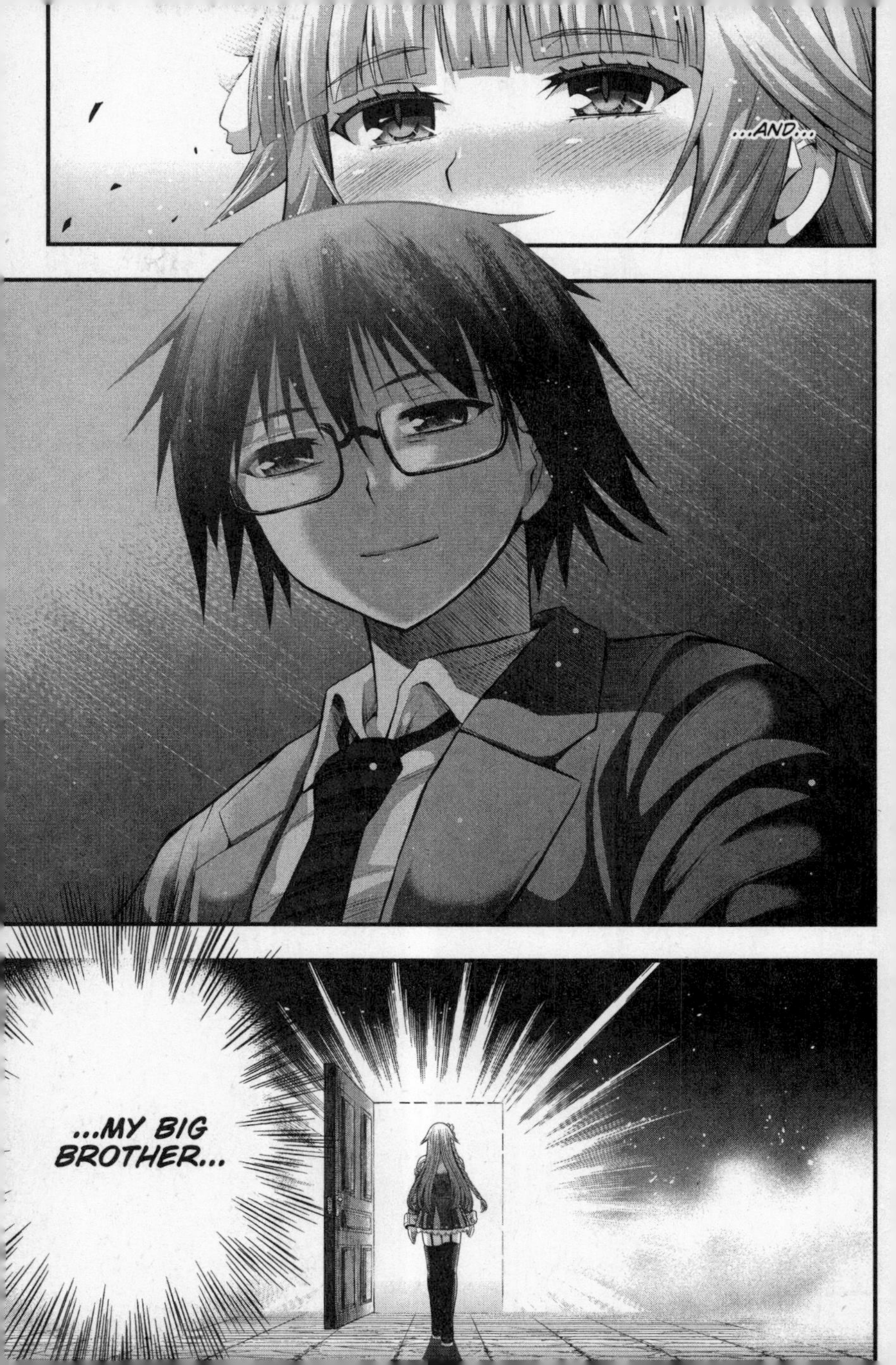
...AND...
...MY BIG BROTHER...

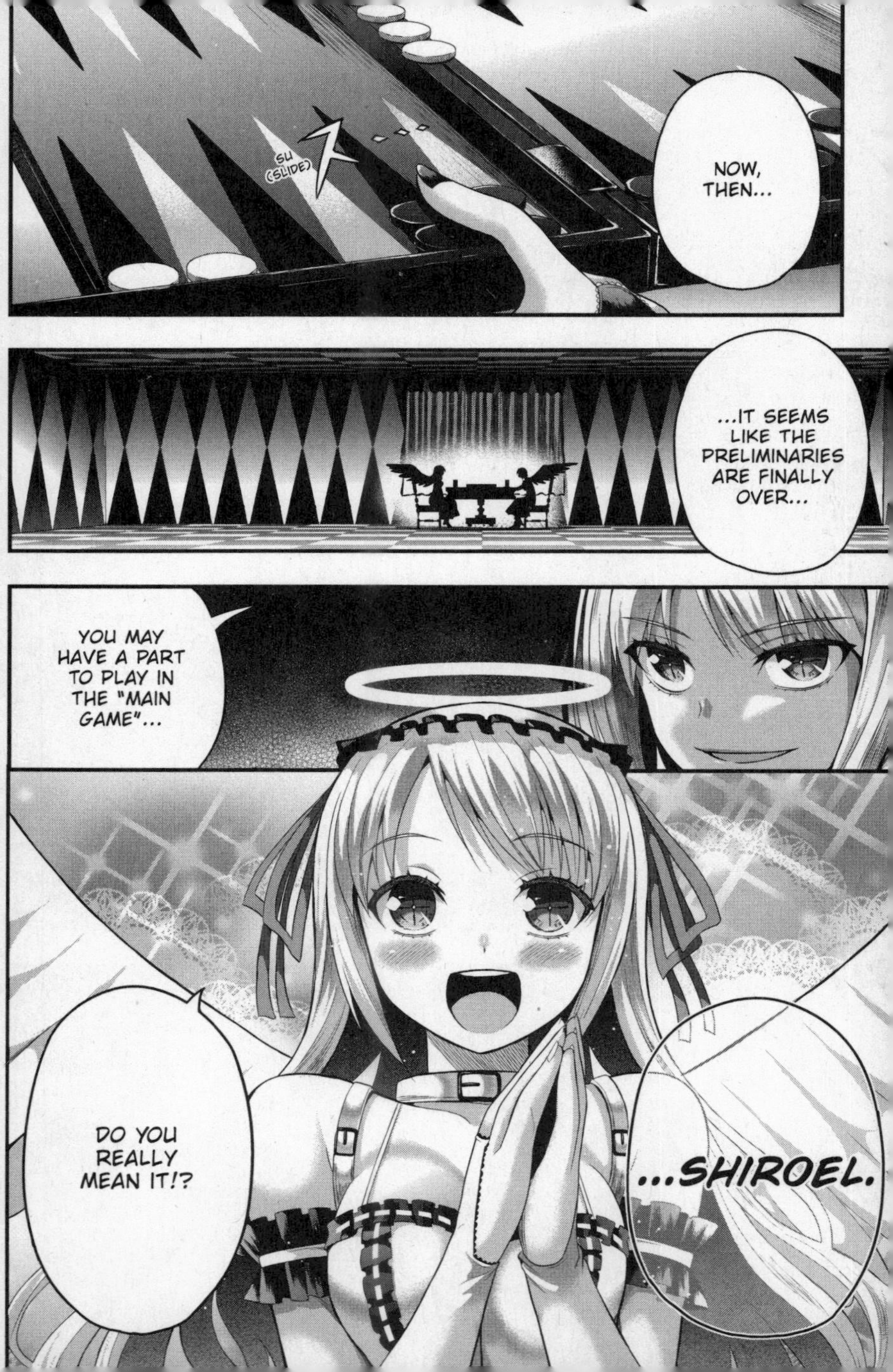
NOW, THEN...
SU (SLIDE)
...IT SEEMS LIKE THE PRELIMINARIES ARE FINALLY OVER...
YOU MAY HAVE A PART TO PLAY IN THE "MAIN GAME"...
...SHIROEL.
DO YOU REALLY MEAN IT!?

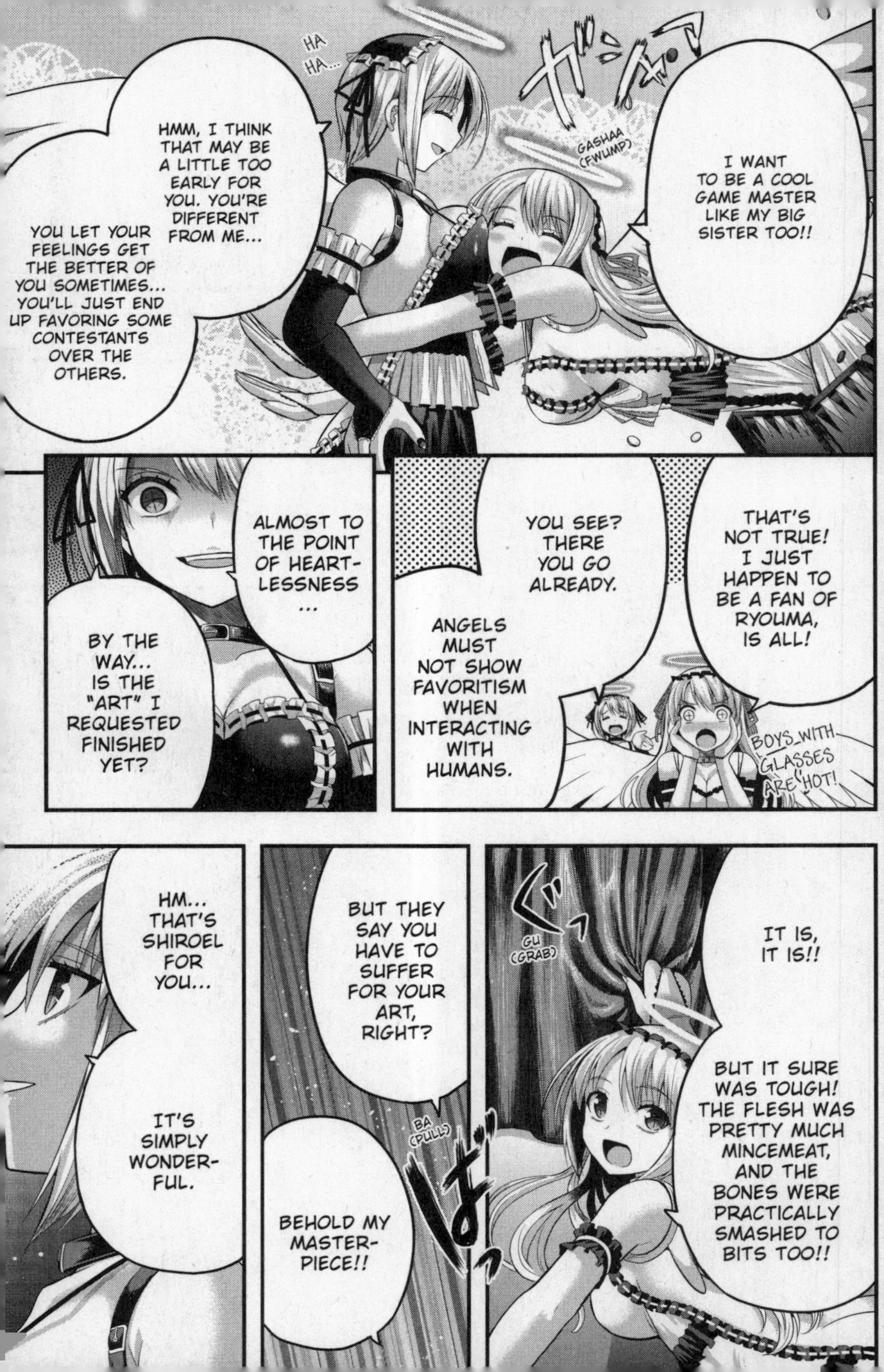
I WANT TO BE A COOL GAME MASTER LIKE MY BIG SISTER TOO!!
GASHAA (FWUMP)
HA HA...
HMM, I THINK THAT MAY BE A LITTLE TOO EARLY FOR YOU. YOU'RE DIFFERENT FROM ME...
YOU LET YOUR FEELINGS GET THE BETTER OF YOU SOMETIMES... YOU'LL JUST END UP FAVORING SOME CONTESTANTS OVER THE OTHERS.
THAT'S NOT TRUE! I JUST HAPPEN TO BE A FAN OF RYOUMA, IS ALL!
YOU SEE? THERE YOU GO ALREADY.
ANGELS MUST NOT SHOW FAVORITISM WHEN INTERACTING WITH HUMANS.
BOYS WITH GLASSES ARE HOT!
ALMOST TO THE POINT OF HEART-LESSNESS...
BY THE WAY... IS THE "ART" I REQUESTED FINISHED YET?
IT IS, IT IS!!
GU (GRAB)
BUT IT SURE WAS TOUGH! THE FLESH WAS PRETTY MUCH MINCEMEAT, AND THE BONES WERE PRACTICALLY SMASHED TO BITS TOO!!
BUT THEY SAY YOU HAVE TO SUFFER FOR YOUR ART, RIGHT?
BA (PULL)
BEHOLD MY MASTER-PIECE!!
HM... THAT'S SHIROEL FOR YOU...
IT'S SIMPLY WONDER-FUL.

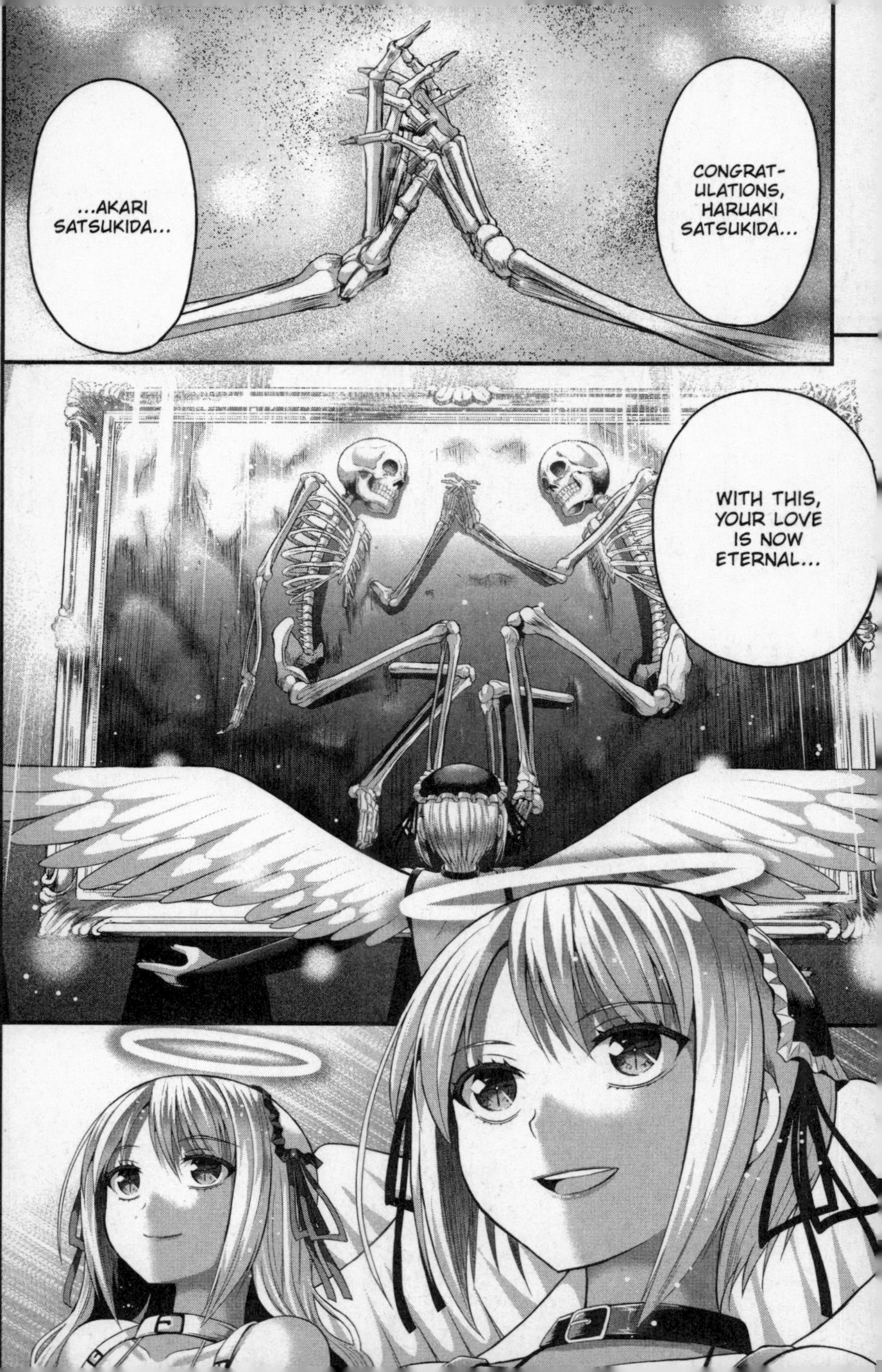
CONGRAT-ULATIONS, HARUAKI SATSUKIDA...
...AKARI SATSUKIDA...
WITH THIS, YOUR LOVE IS NOW ETERNAL...

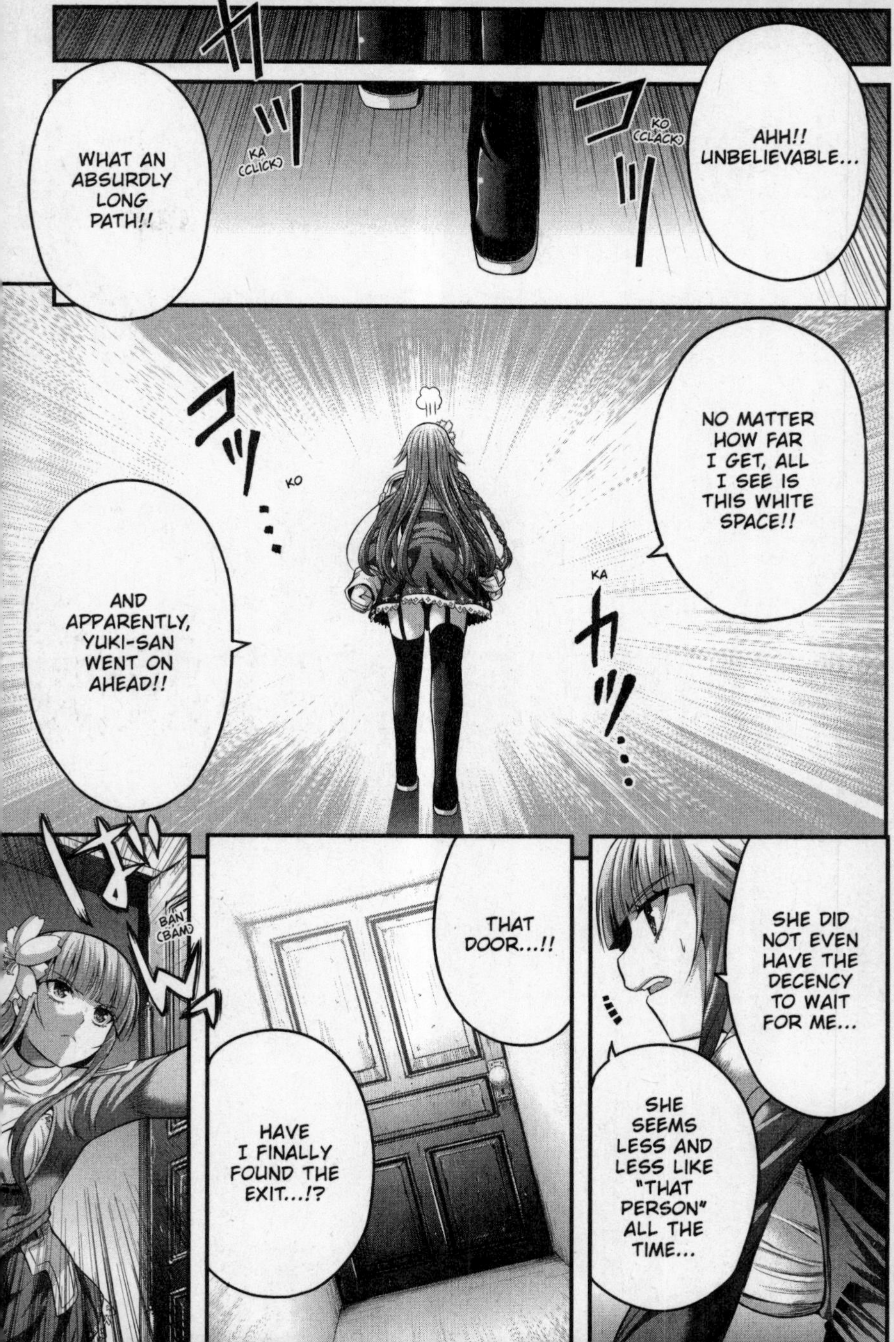
AHH!! UNBELIEVABLE...
KO (CLACK)
KA (CLICK)
WHAT AN ABSURDLY LONG PATH!!
NO MATTER HOW FAR I GET, ALL I SEE IS THIS WHITE SPACE!!
KA
KO
AND APPARENTLY, YUKI-SAN WENT ON AHEAD!!
SHE DID NOT EVEN HAVE THE DECENCY TO WAIT FOR ME...
...
SHE SEEMS LESS AND LESS LIKE "THAT PERSON" ALL THE TIME...
THAT DOOR...!!
HAVE I FINALLY FOUND THE EXIT...!?
BAN (BAM)

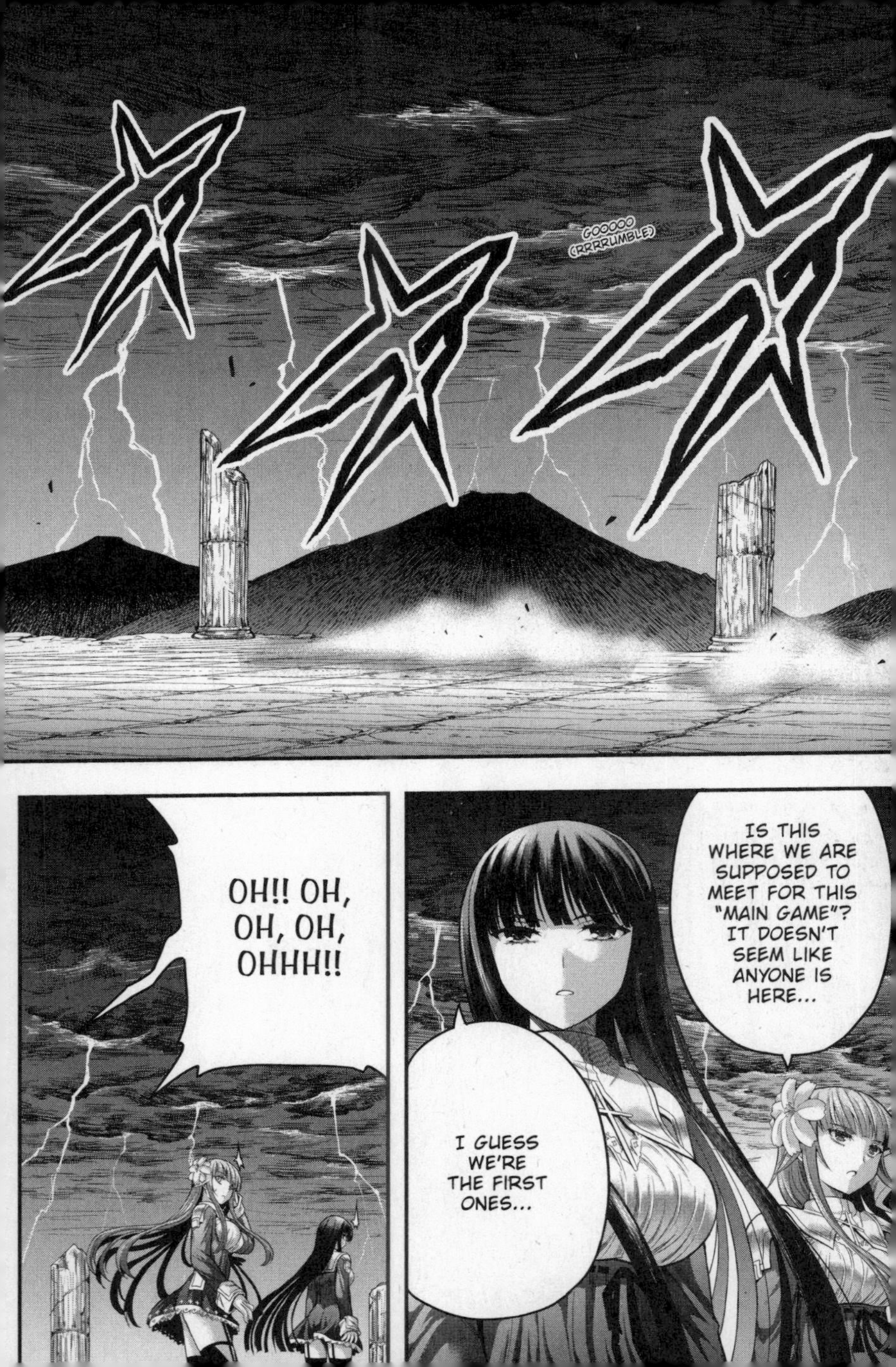
GOOOOO
(RRRRUMBLE)
IS THIS WHERE WE ARE SUPPOSED TO MEET FOR THIS "MAIN GAME"? IT DOESN'T SEEM LIKE ANYONE IS HERE...
I GUESS WE'RE THE FIRST ONES...
OH!! OH, OH, OH, OHHH!!

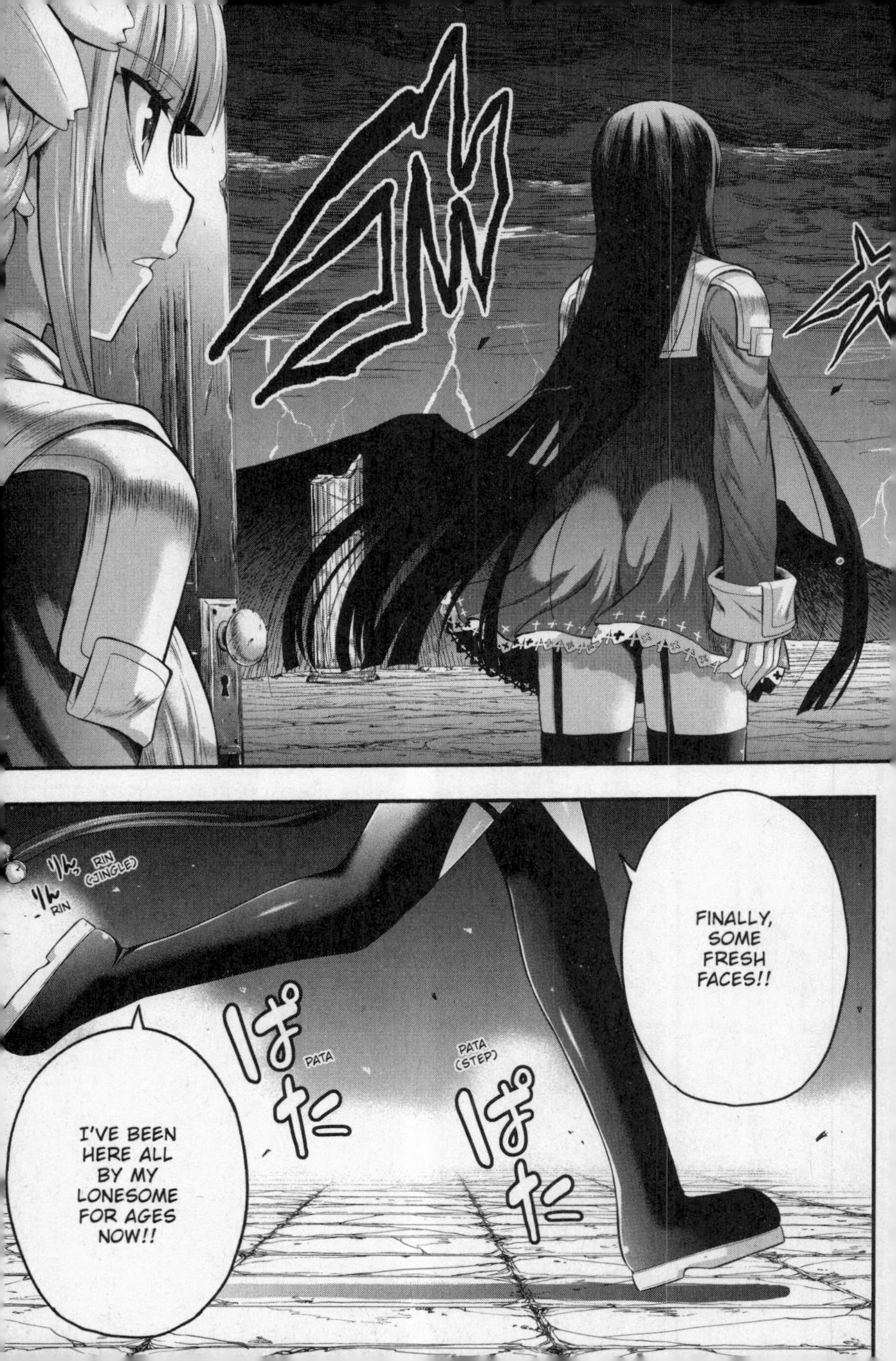
FINALLY, SOME FRESH FACES!!
ぱた
PATA (STEP)
ぱた
PATA
I'VE BEEN HERE ALL BY MY LONESOME FOR AGES NOW!!
りん
RIN (JINGLE)
りん
RIN

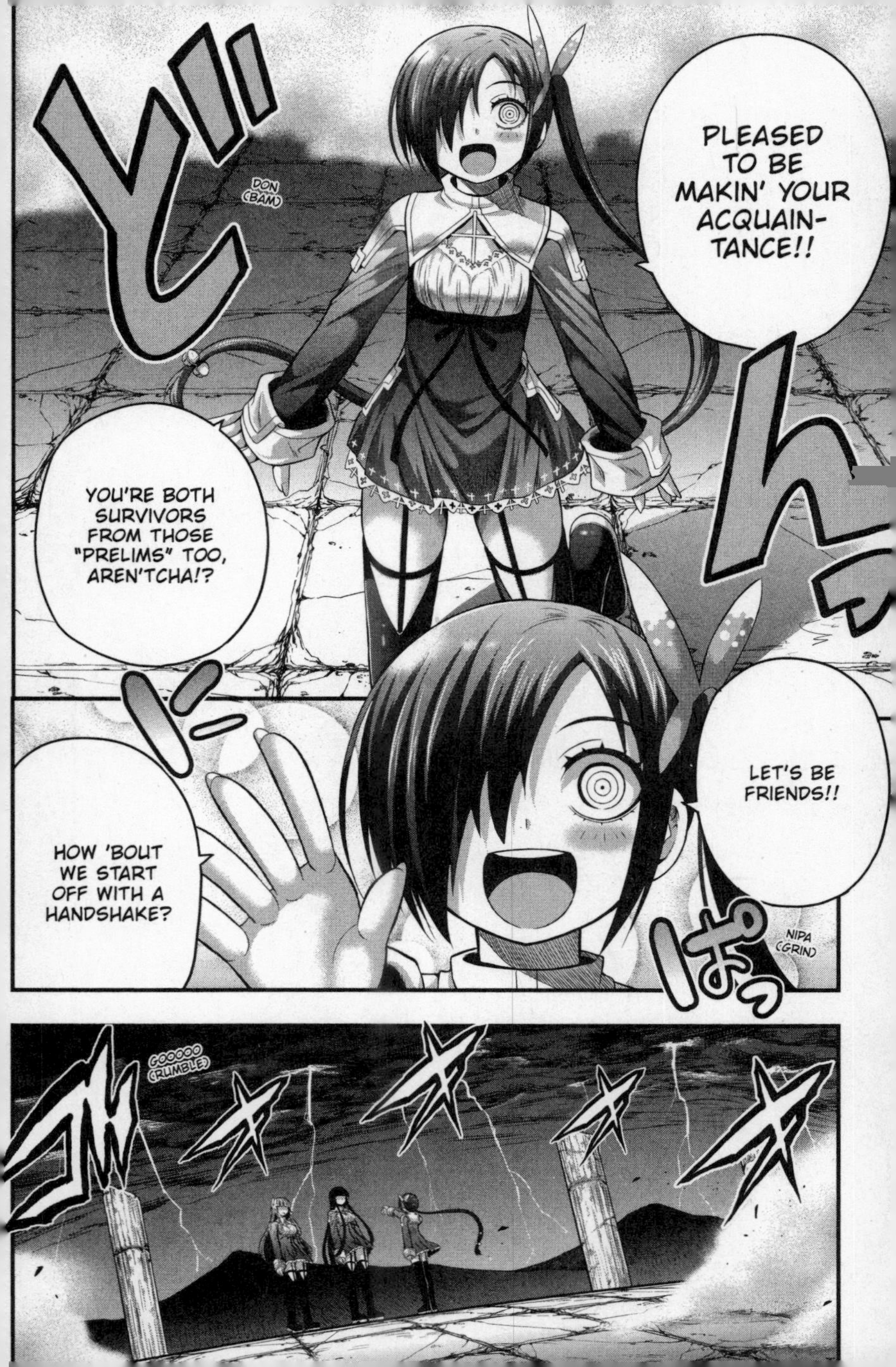
PLEASED TO BE MAKIN' YOUR ACQUAIN-TANCE!!
DON (BAM)
YOU'RE BOTH SURVIVORS FROM THOSE "PRELIMS" TOO, AREN'TCHA!?
LET'S BE FRIENDS!!
NIPA (GRIN)
HOW 'BOUT WE START OFF WITH A HANDSHAKE?
GOOOOO (RUMBLE)

Though You May Burn to Ash

Though You May Burn to Ash

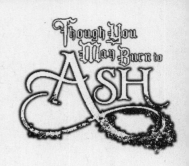

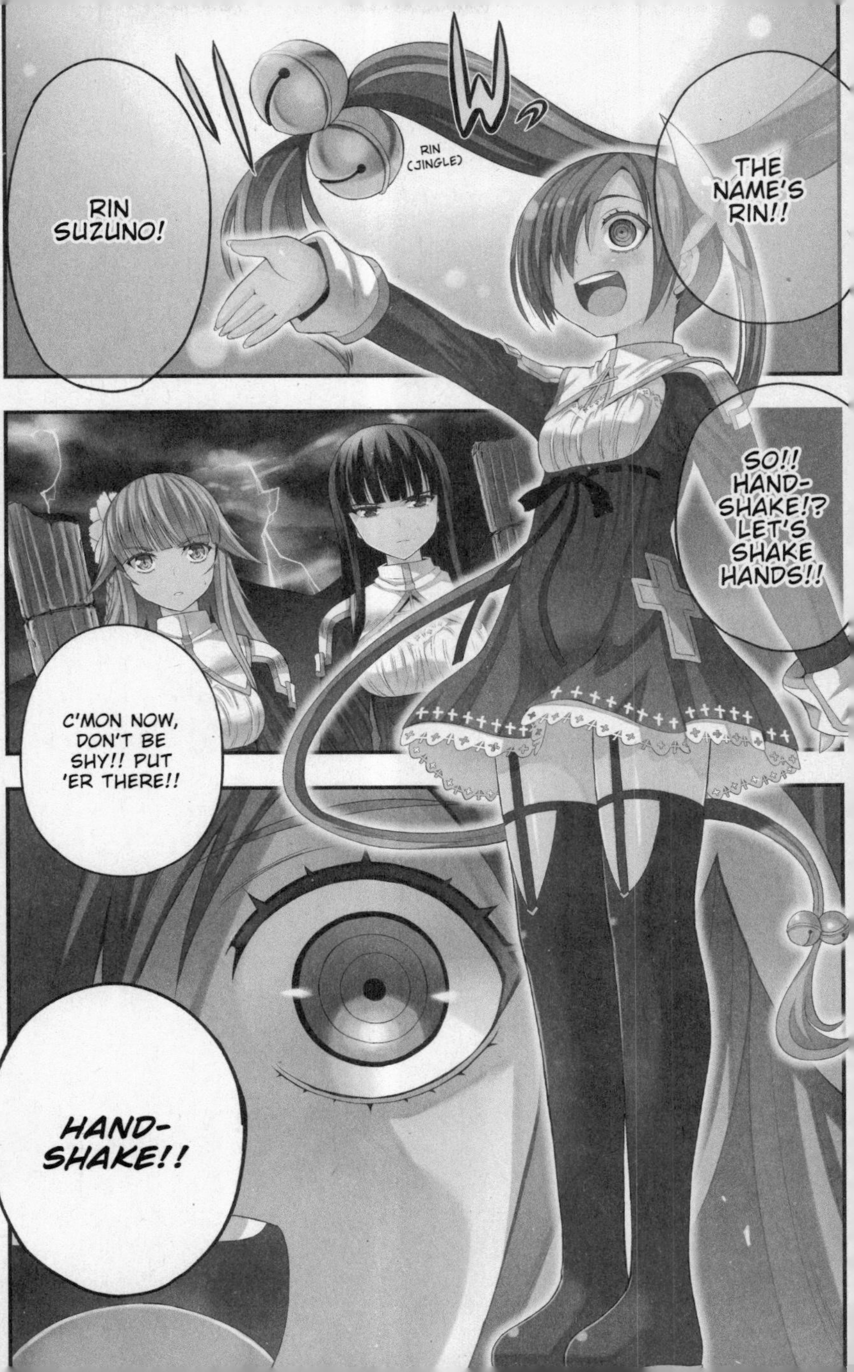
THE NAME'S RIN!!
RIN (JINGLE)
RIN SUZUNO!
SO!! HAND-SHAKE!? LET'S SHAKE HANDS!!
C'MON NOW, DON'T BE SHY!! PUT 'ER THERE!!
HAND-SHAKE!!

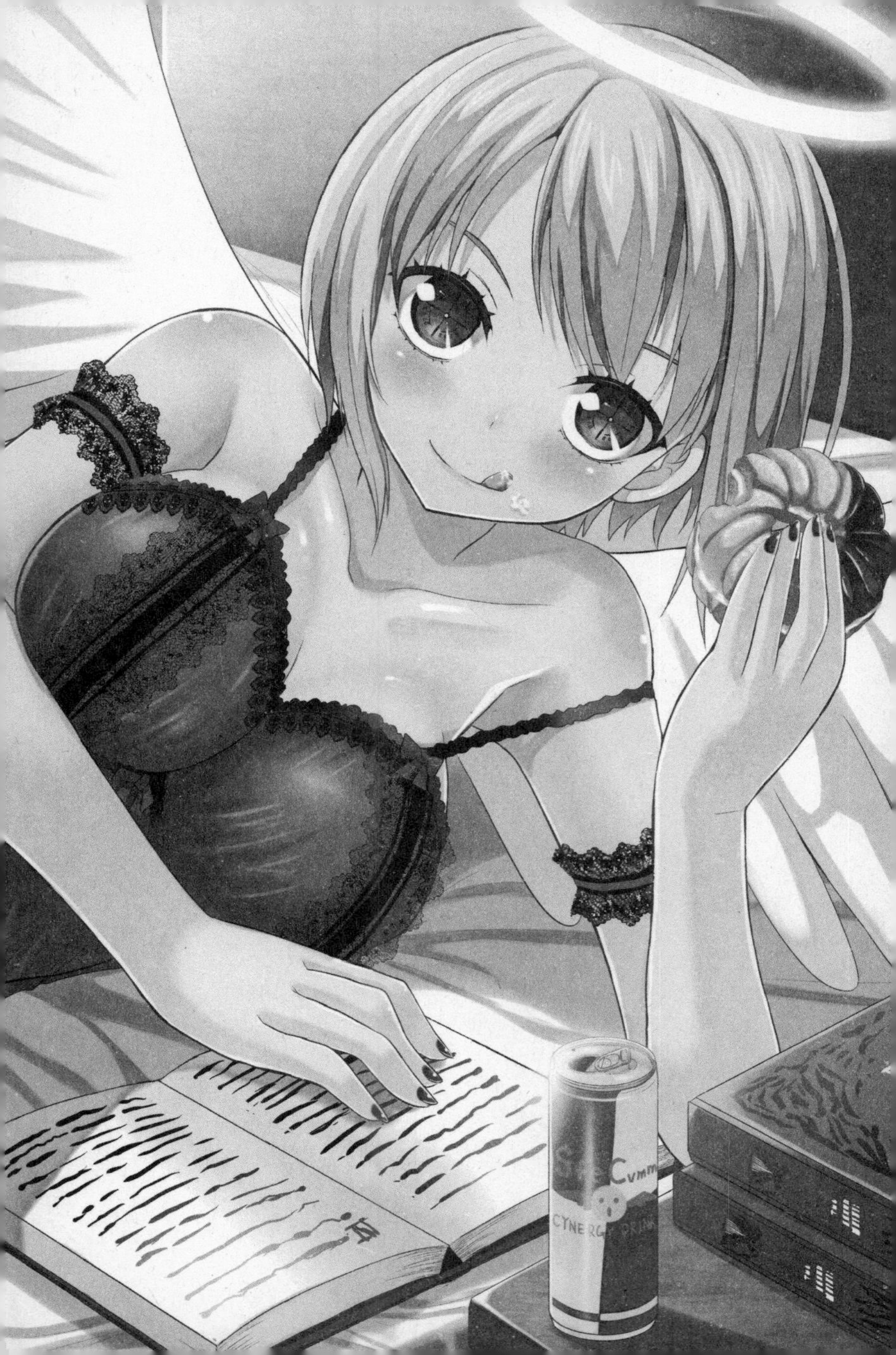

CHAPTER 16: ASSEMBLING THE FOURTEEN

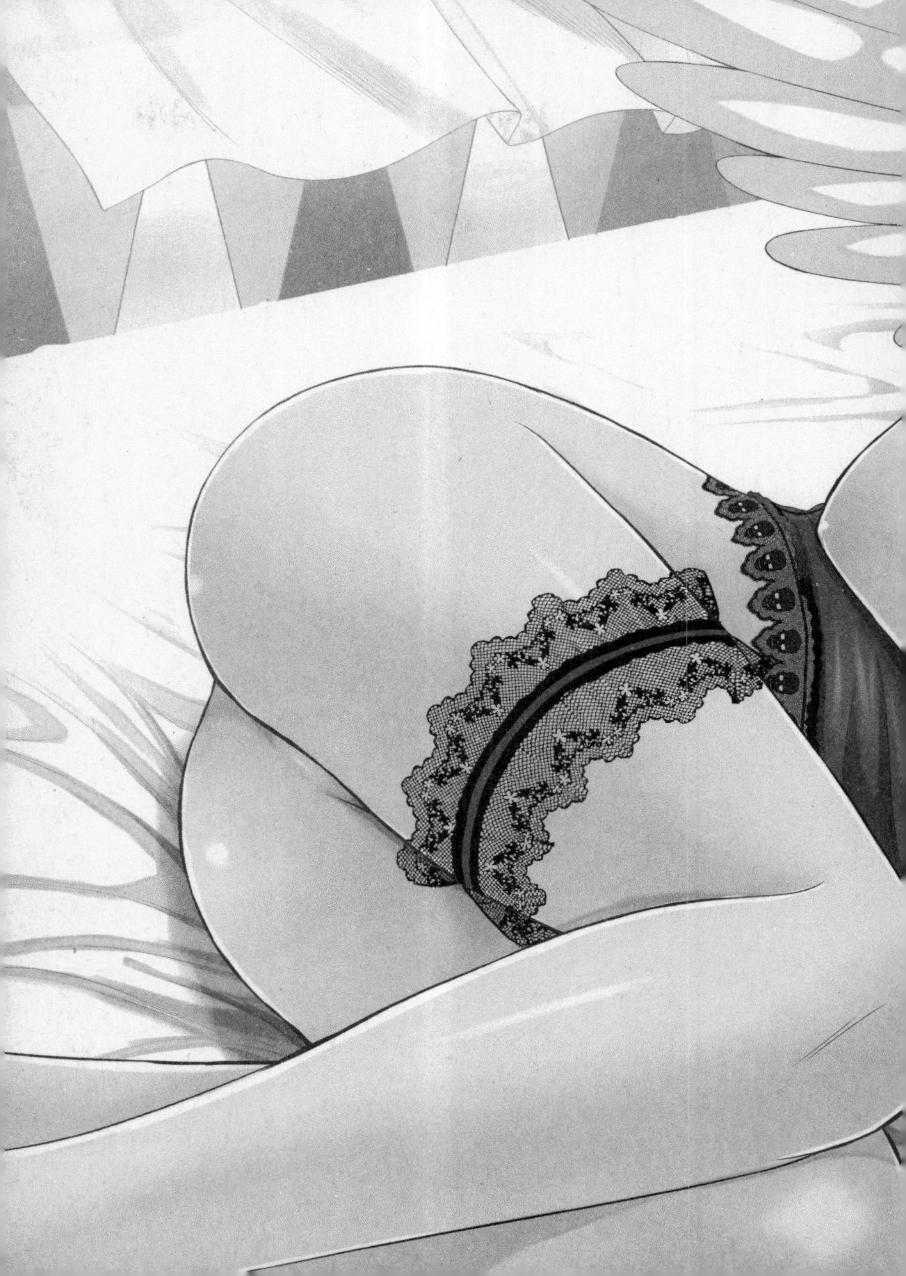

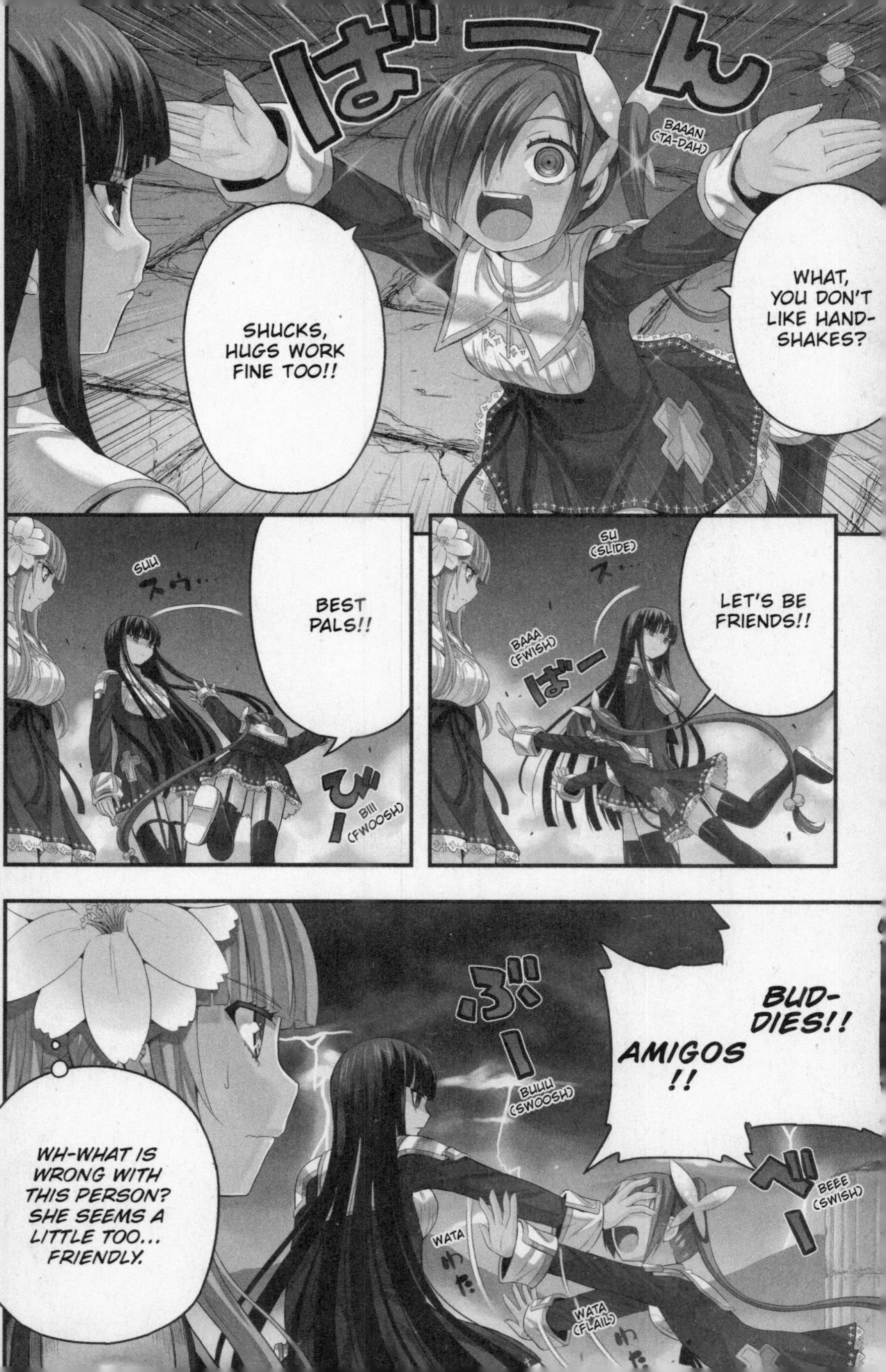
BAAAN (TA-DAH)
WHAT, YOU DON'T LIKE HAND-SHAKES?
SHUCKS, HUGS WORK FINE TOO!!
SU (SLIDE)
LET'S BE FRIENDS!!
BAAA (FWISH)
SUU
BEST PALS!!
BIII (FWOOSH)
BUD-DIES!!
AMIGOS !!
BUUU (SWOOSH)
BEEE (SWISH)
WATA
WATA (FLAIL)
WH-WHAT IS WRONG WITH THIS PERSON? SHE SEEMS A LITTLE TOO... FRIENDLY.

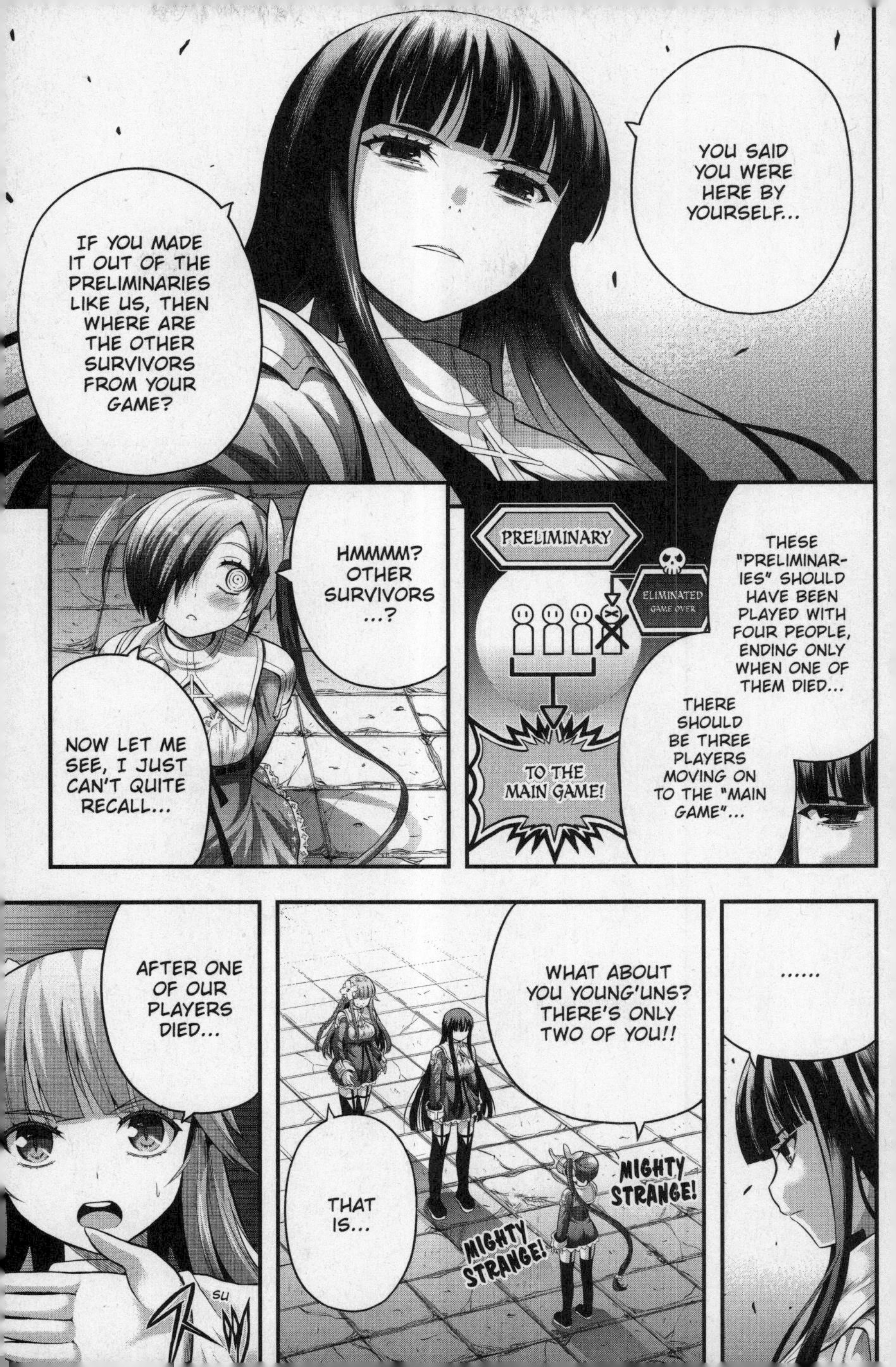
YOU SAID YOU WERE HERE BY YOURSELF...
IF YOU MADE IT OUT OF THE PRELIMINARIES LIKE US, THEN WHERE ARE THE OTHER SURVIVORS FROM YOUR GAME?
THESE "PRELIMINARIES" SHOULD HAVE BEEN PLAYED WITH FOUR PEOPLE, ENDING ONLY WHEN ONE OF THEM DIED...
PRELIMINARY
ELIMINATED
GAME OVER
THERE SHOULD BE THREE PLAYERS MOVING ON TO THE "MAIN GAME"...
TO THE MAIN GAME!
HMMMM? OTHER SURVIVORS ...?
NOW LET ME SEE, I JUST CAN'T QUITE RECALL...
......
WHAT ABOUT YOU YOUNG'UNS? THERE'S ONLY TWO OF YOU!!
MIGHTY STRANGE!
MIGHTY STRANGE!
THAT IS...
AFTER ONE OF OUR PLAYERS DIED...
SU

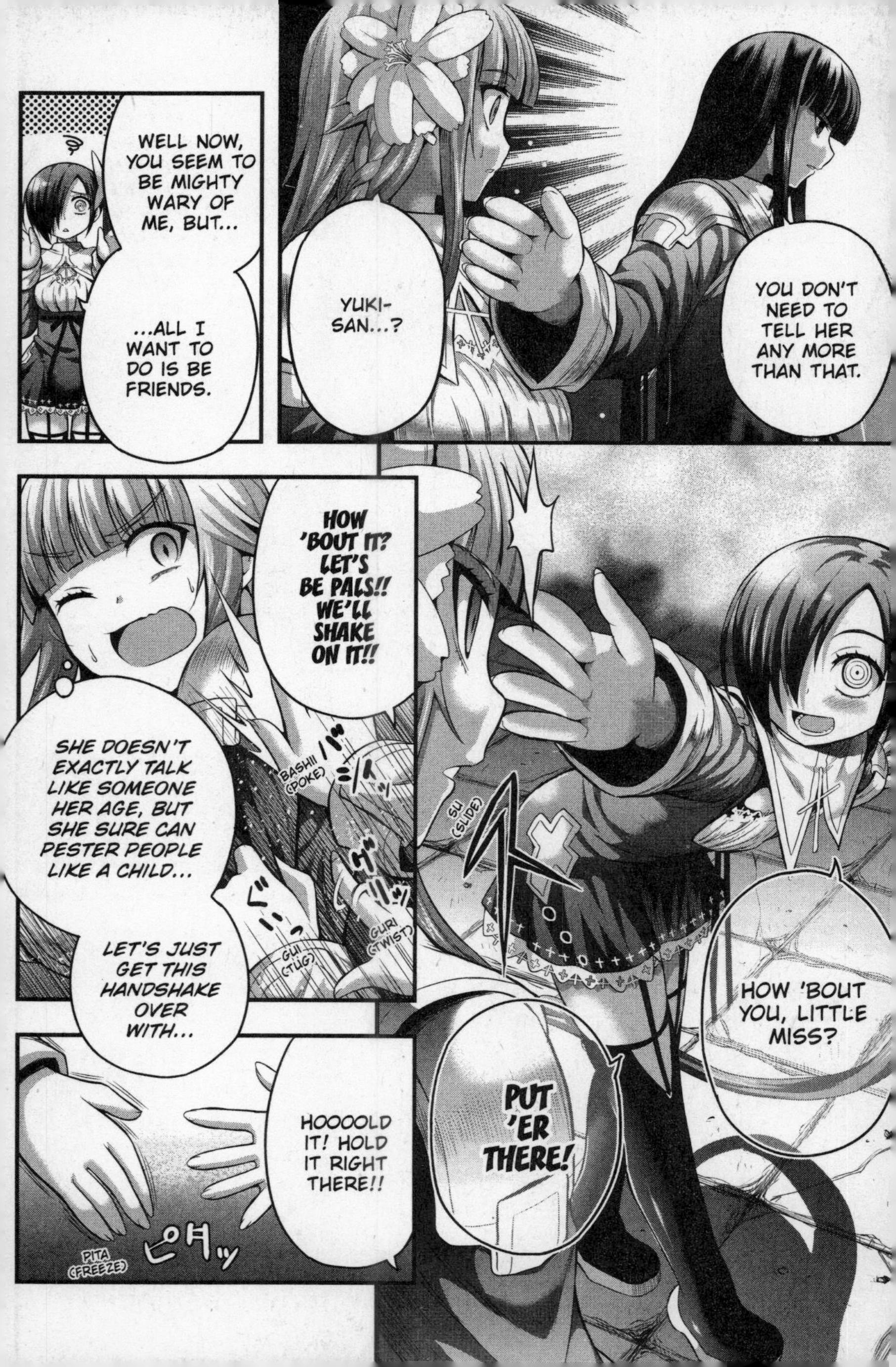
YOU DON'T NEED TO TELL HER ANY MORE THAN THAT.
YUKI-SAN...?
WELL NOW, YOU SEEM TO BE MIGHTY WARY OF ME, BUT...
...ALL I WANT TO DO IS BE FRIENDS.
HOW 'BOUT YOU, LITTLE MISS?
SU (SLIDE)
PUT 'ER THERE!
HOW 'BOUT IT? LET'S BE PALS!! WE'LL SHAKE ON IT!!
SHE DOESN'T EXACTLY TALK LIKE SOMEONE HER AGE, BUT SHE SURE CAN PESTER PEOPLE LIKE A CHILD...
BASHII (POKE)
GURI (TWIST)
GUI (TUG)
LET'S JUST GET THIS HANDSHAKE OVER WITH...
HOOOOLD IT! HOLD IT RIGHT THERE!!
PITA (FREEZE)

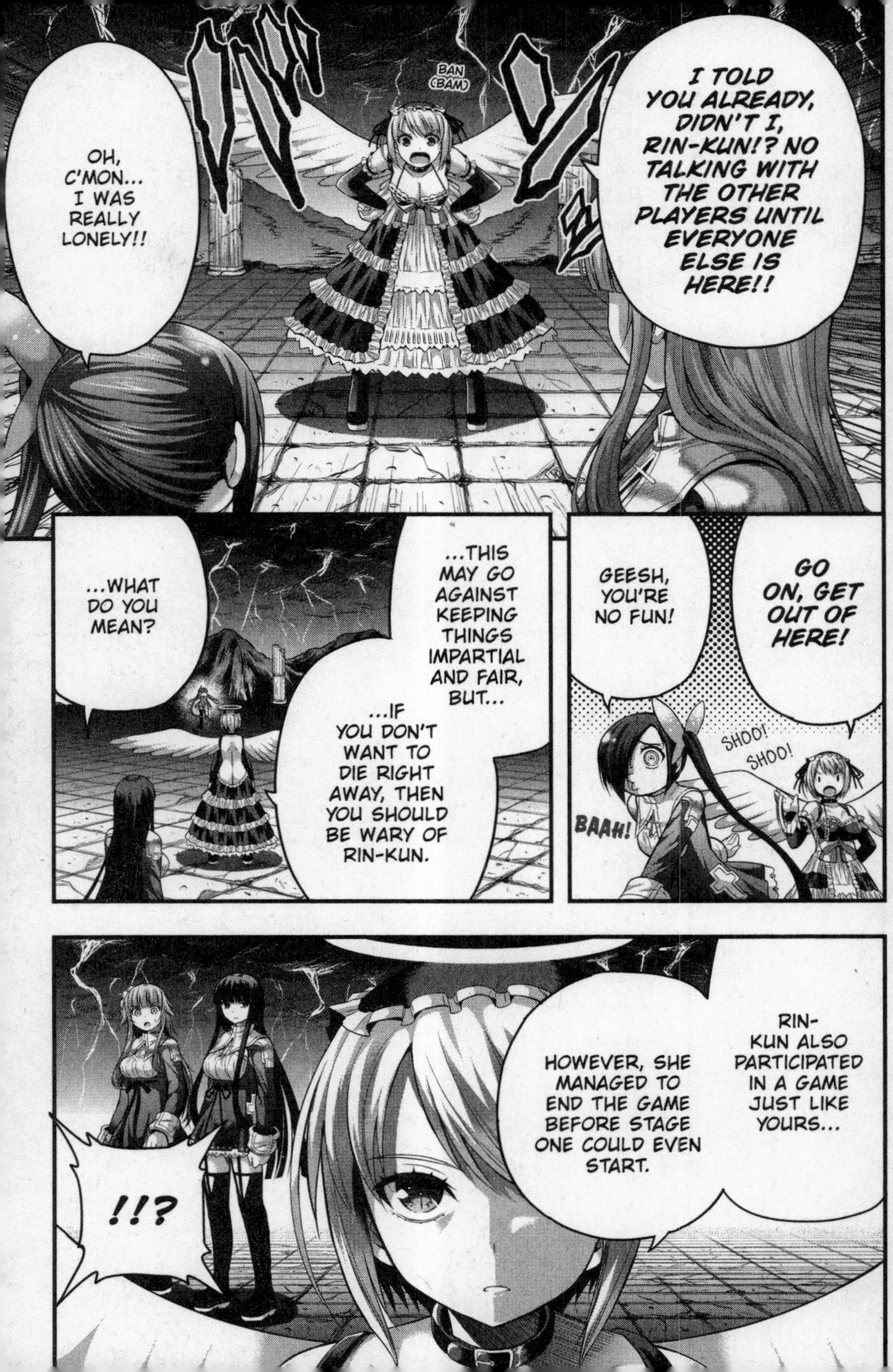
I TOLD YOU ALREADY, DIDN'T I, RIN-KUN!? NO TALKING WITH THE OTHER PLAYERS UNTIL EVERYONE ELSE IS HERE!!
BAN (BAM)
OH, C'MON... I WAS REALLY LONELY!!
GO ON, GET OUT OF HERE!
GEESH, YOU'RE NO FUN!
SHOO! SHOO!
BAAH!
...THIS MAY GO AGAINST KEEPING THINGS IMPARTIAL AND FAIR, BUT...
...WHAT DO YOU MEAN?
...IF YOU DON'T WANT TO DIE RIGHT AWAY, THEN YOU SHOULD BE WARY OF RIN-KUN.
RIN-KUN ALSO PARTICIPATED IN A GAME JUST LIKE YOURS...
HOWEVER, SHE MANAGED TO END THE GAME BEFORE STAGE ONE COULD EVEN START.
!!?

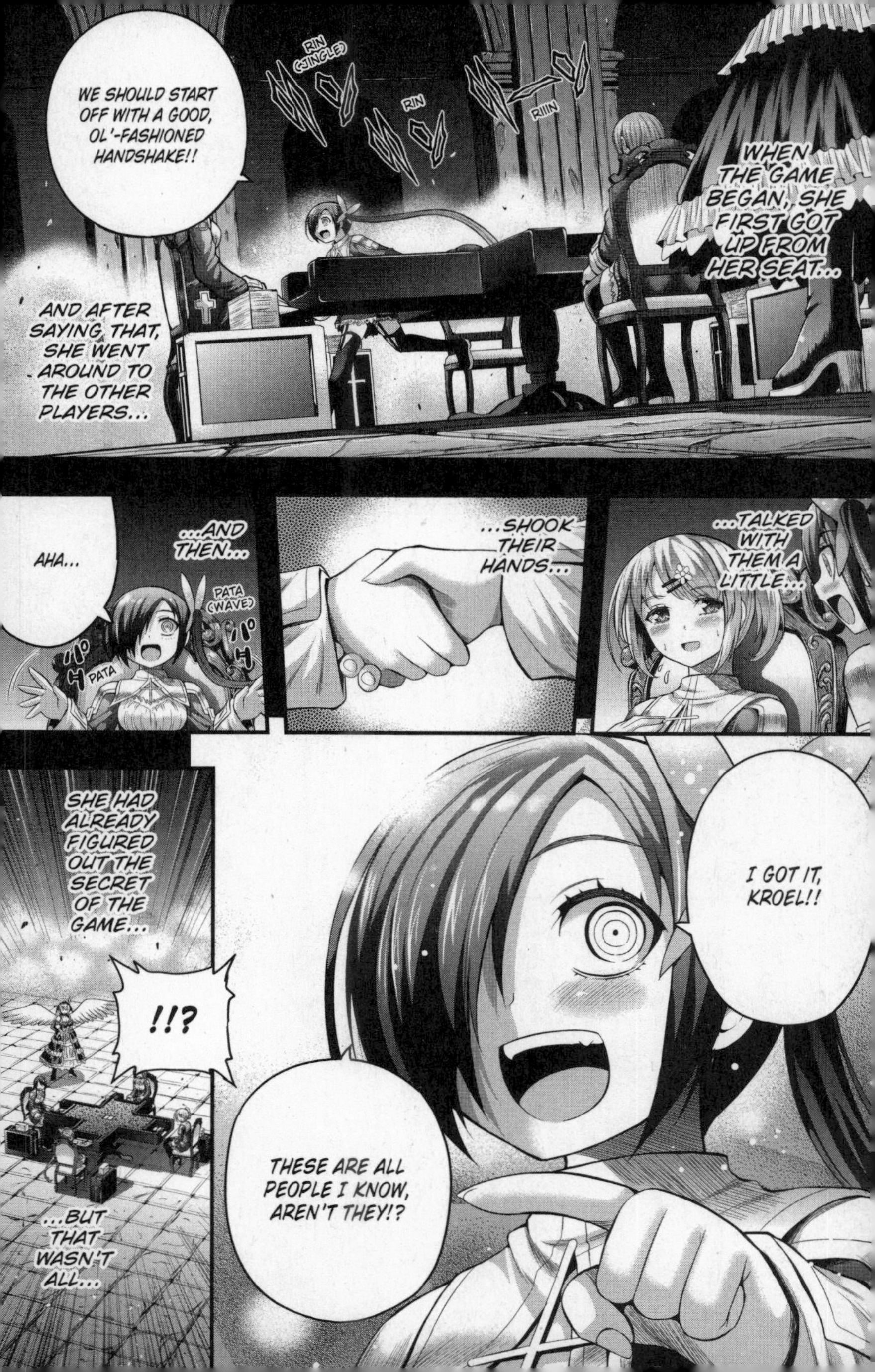
WHEN THE GAME BEGAN, SHE FIRST GOT UP FROM HER SEAT...
RIIIN
RIN
RIN (JINGLE)
WE SHOULD START OFF WITH A GOOD, OL'-FASHIONED HANDSHAKE!!
AND AFTER SAYING THAT, SHE WENT AROUND TO THE OTHER PLAYERS...
...TALKED WITH THEM A LITTLE...
...SHOOK THEIR HANDS...
...AND THEN...
AHA...
PATA (WAVE)
PATA
I GOT IT, KROEL!!
THESE ARE ALL PEOPLE I KNOW, AREN'T THEY!?
SHE HAD ALREADY FIGURED OUT THE SECRET OF THE GAME...
!!?
...BUT THAT WASN'T ALL...

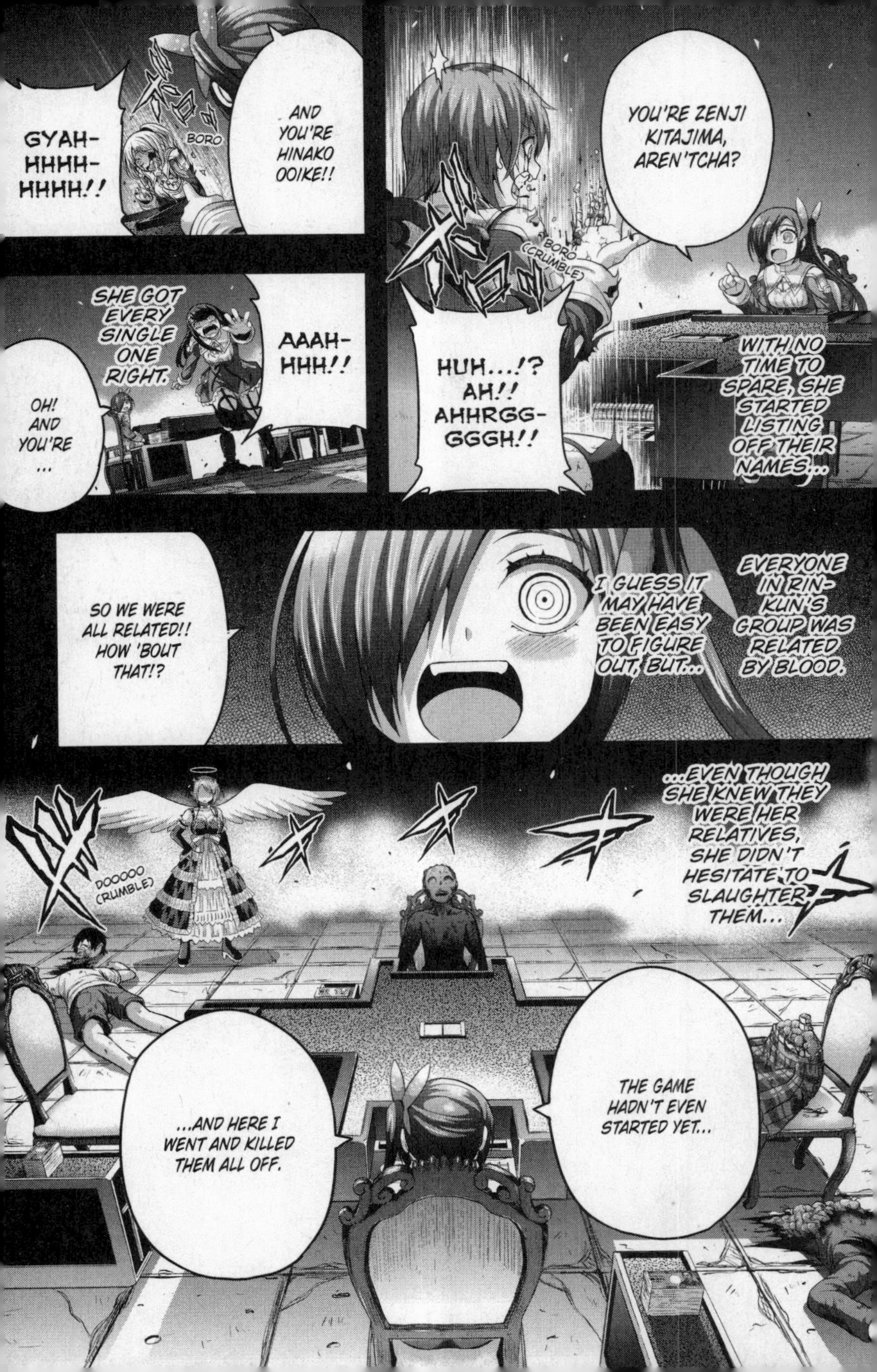
YOU'RE ZENJI KITAJIMA, AREN'TCHA?
BORO (CRUMBLE)
HUH...!? AH!! AHHRGG-GGGH!!
WITH NO TIME TO SPARE, SHE STARTED LISTING OFF THEIR NAMES...
AND YOU'RE HINAKO OOIKE!!
BORO
GYAH-HHHH-HHHH!!
SHE GOT EVERY SINGLE ONE RIGHT.
AAAH-HHH!!
OH! AND YOU'RE ...
EVERYONE IN RIN-KUN'S GROUP WAS RELATED BY BLOOD.
I GUESS IT MAY HAVE BEEN EASY TO FIGURE OUT, BUT...
SO WE WERE ALL RELATED!! HOW 'BOUT THAT!?
...EVEN THOUGH SHE KNEW THEY WERE HER RELATIVES, SHE DIDN'T HESITATE TO SLAUGHTER THEM...
DOOOOO (RUMBLE)
THE GAME HADN'T EVEN STARTED YET...
...AND HERE I WENT AND KILLED THEM ALL OFF.

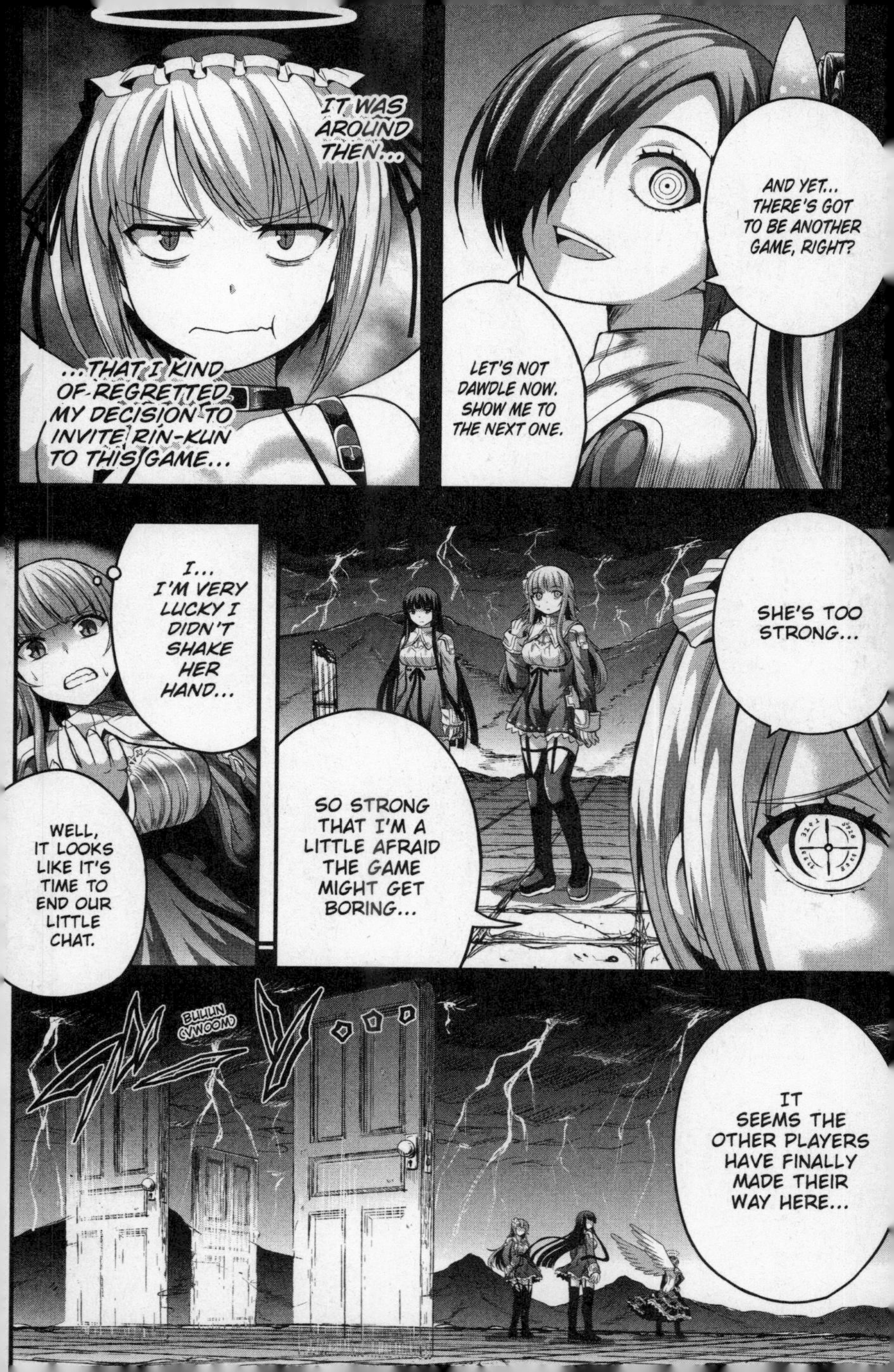
AND YET... THERE'S GOT TO BE ANOTHER GAME, RIGHT?
LET'S NOT DAWDLE NOW. SHOW ME TO THE NEXT ONE.
IT WAS AROUND THEN...
...THAT I KIND OF REGRETTED MY DECISION TO INVITE RIN-KUN TO THIS GAME...
SHE'S TOO STRONG...
SO STRONG THAT I'M A LITTLE AFRAID THE GAME MIGHT GET BORING...
I... I'M VERY LUCKY I DIDN'T SHAKE HER HAND...
WELL, IT LOOKS LIKE IT'S TIME TO END OUR LITTLE CHAT.
IT SEEMS THE OTHER PLAYERS HAVE FINALLY MADE THEIR WAY HERE...
BUHUN (VWOOM)

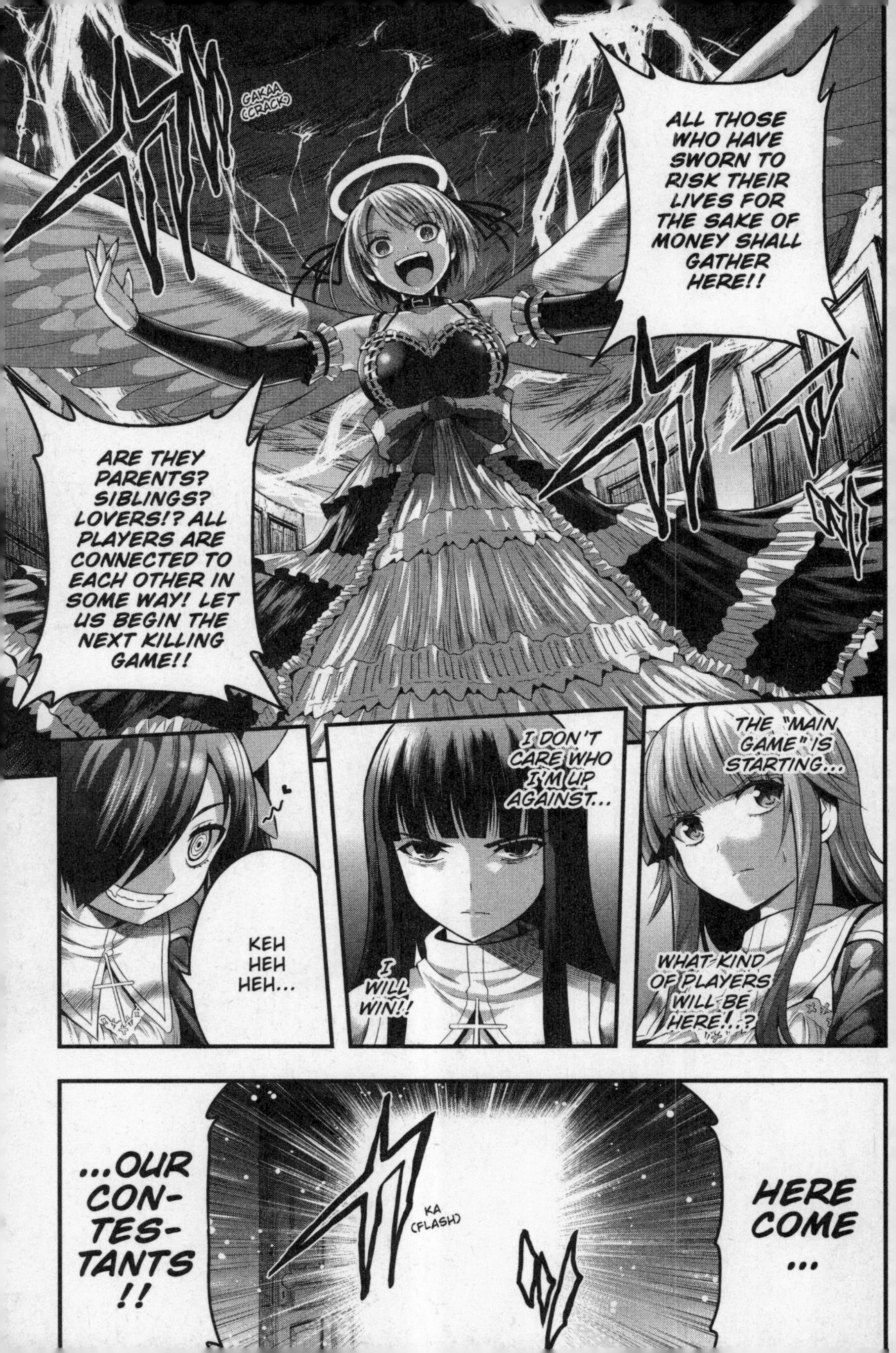
ALL THOSE WHO HAVE SWORN TO RISK THEIR LIVES FOR THE SAKE OF MONEY SHALL GATHER HERE!!
GAKAA (CRACK)
ARE THEY PARENTS? SIBLINGS? LOVERS!? ALL PLAYERS ARE CONNECTED TO EACH OTHER IN SOME WAY! LET US BEGIN THE NEXT KILLING GAME!!
THE "MAIN GAME" IS STARTING...
WHAT KIND OF PLAYERS WILL BE HERE!..?
I DON'T CARE WHO I'M UP AGAINST...
I WILL WIN!!
KEH HEH HEH...
HERE COME...
KA (FLASH)
...OUR CON-TES-TANTS!!

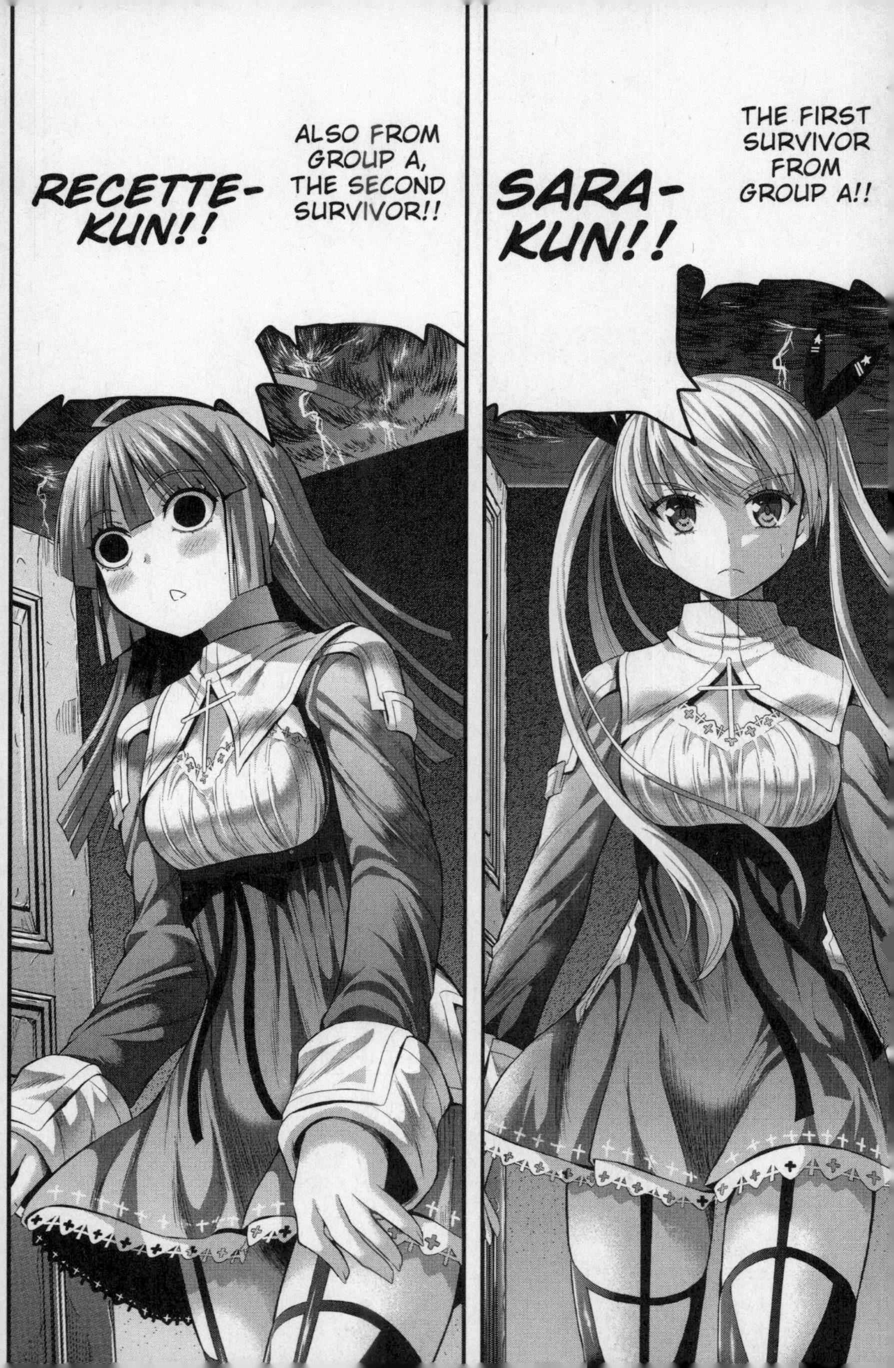
THE FIRST SURVIVOR FROM GROUP A!!
SARA-KUN!!
ALSO FROM GROUP A, THE SECOND SURVIVOR!!
RECETTE-KUN!!

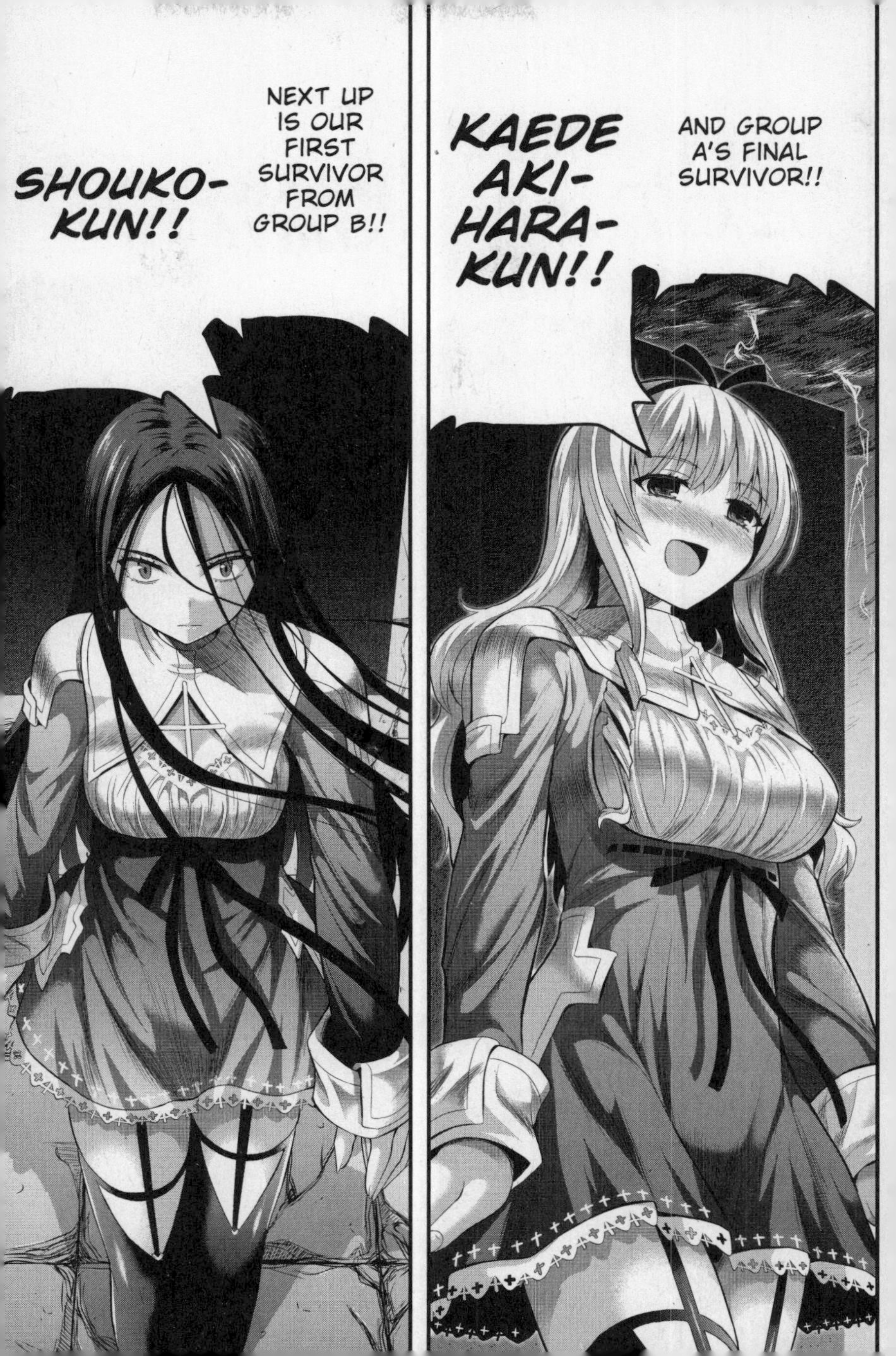
AND GROUP A'S FINAL SURVIVOR!!
KAEDE AKI-HARA-KUN!!
NEXT UP IS OUR FIRST SURVIVOR FROM GROUP B!!
SHOUKO-KUN!!

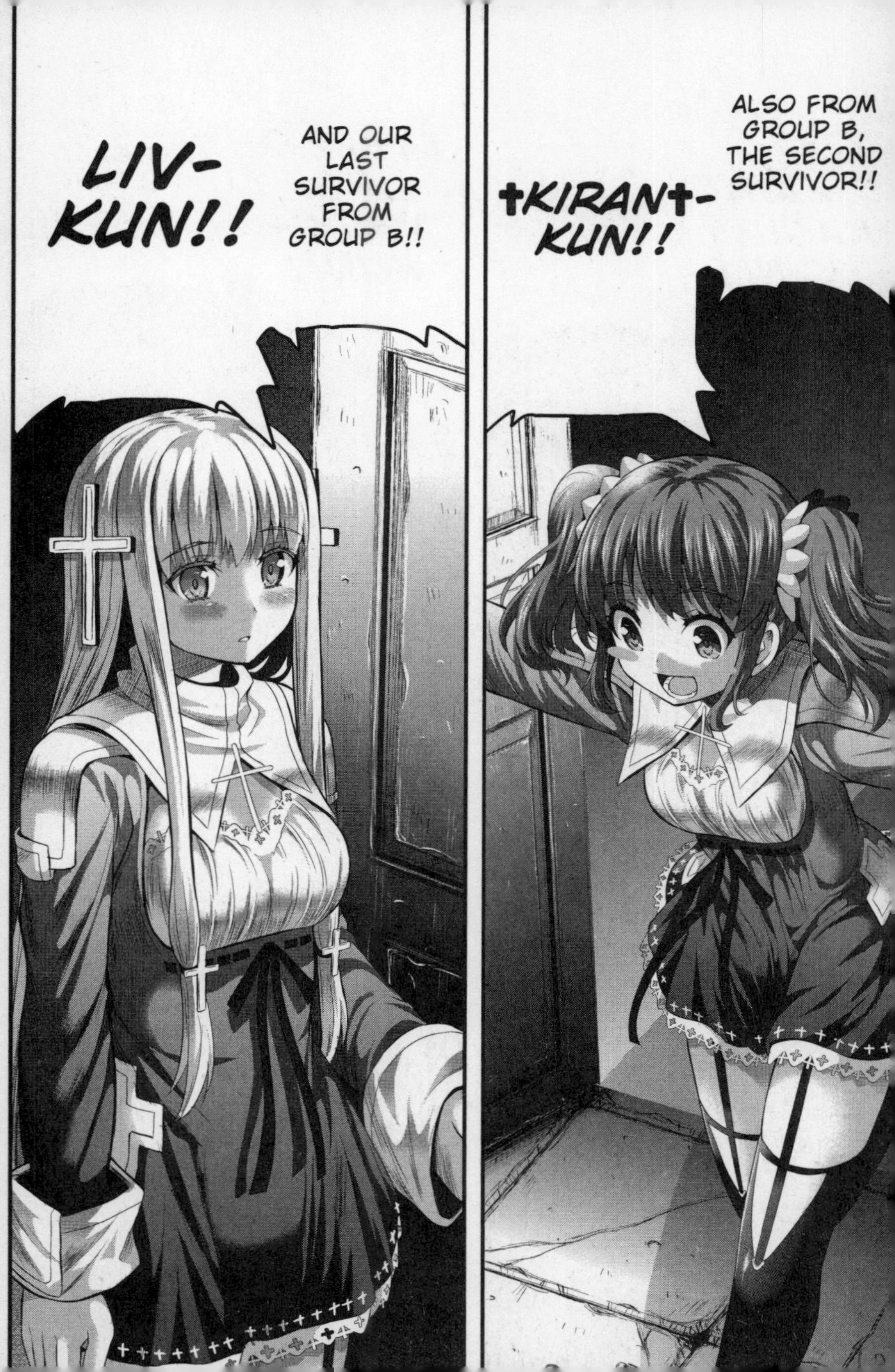
ALSO FROM GROUP B, THE SECOND SURVIVOR!!
†KIRAN†-KUN!!
AND OUR LAST SURVIVOR FROM GROUP B!!
LIV-KUN!!

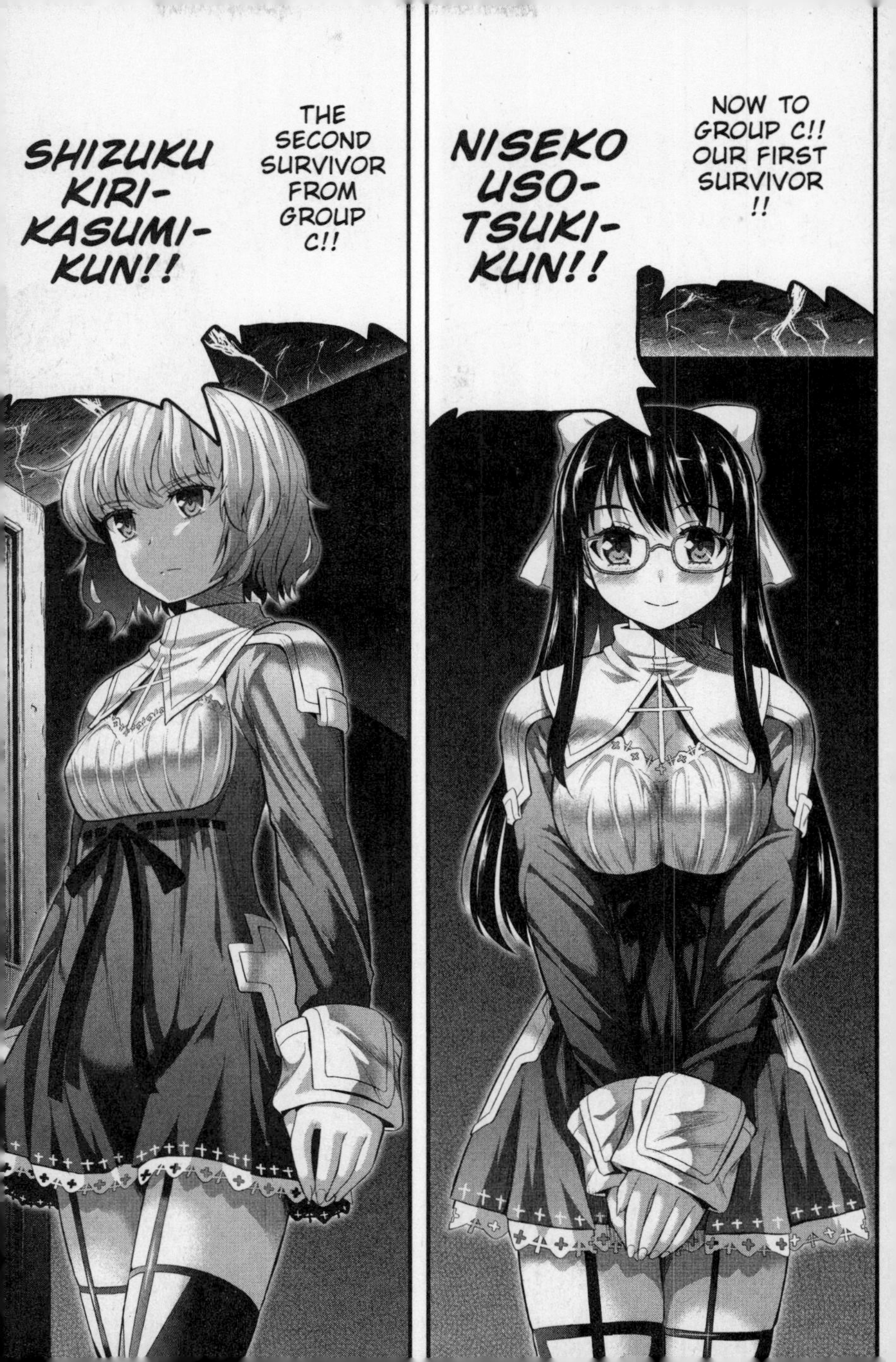
NOW TO GROUP C!! OUR FIRST SURVIVOR !!
NISEKO USO-TSUKI-KUN!!
THE SECOND SURVIVOR FROM GROUP C!!
SHIZUKU KIRI-KASUMI-KUN!!

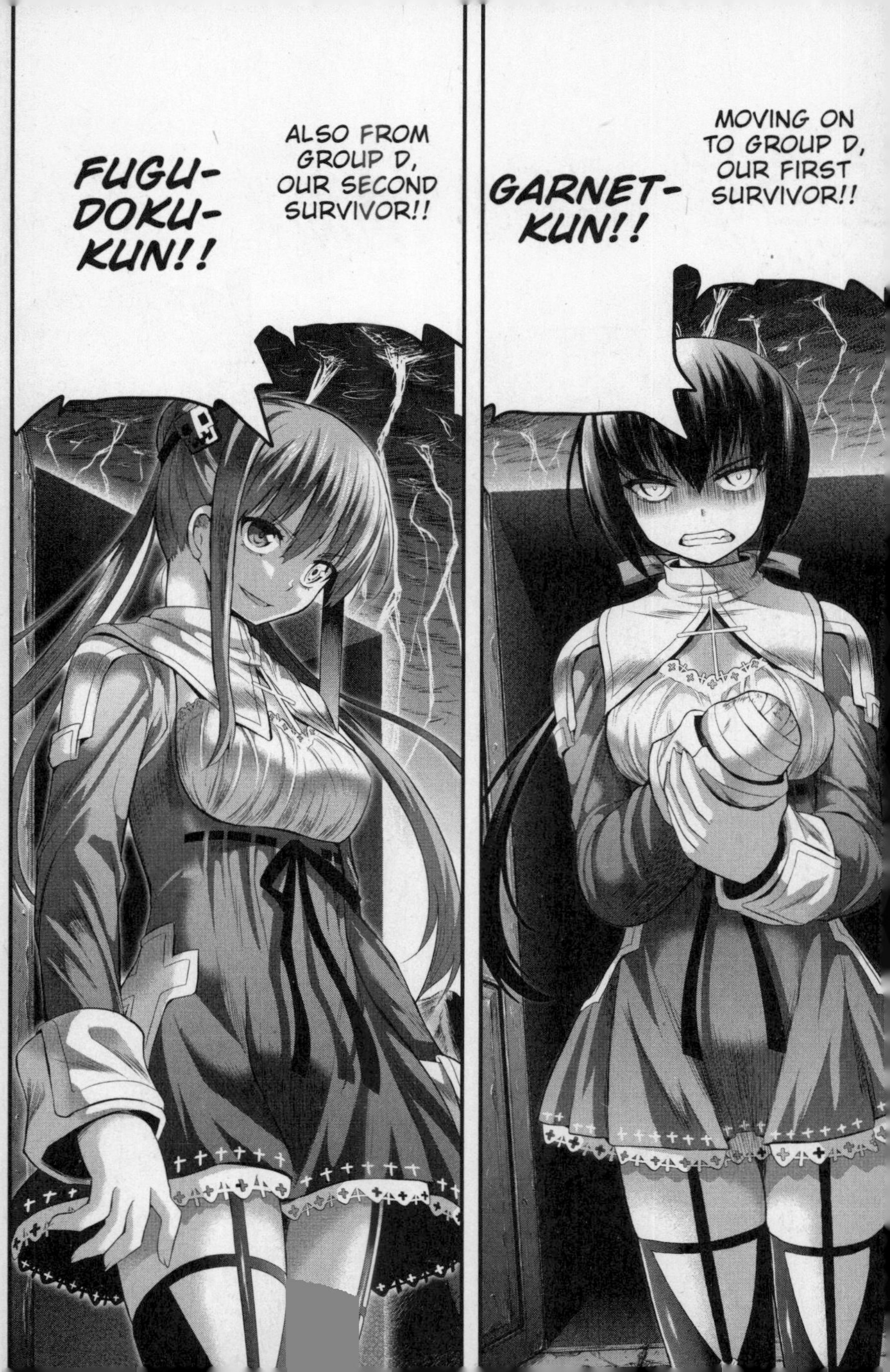
MOVING ON TO GROUP D, OUR FIRST SURVIVOR!!
GARNET-KUN!!
ALSO FROM GROUP D, OUR SECOND SURVIVOR!!
FUGU-DOKU-KUN!!

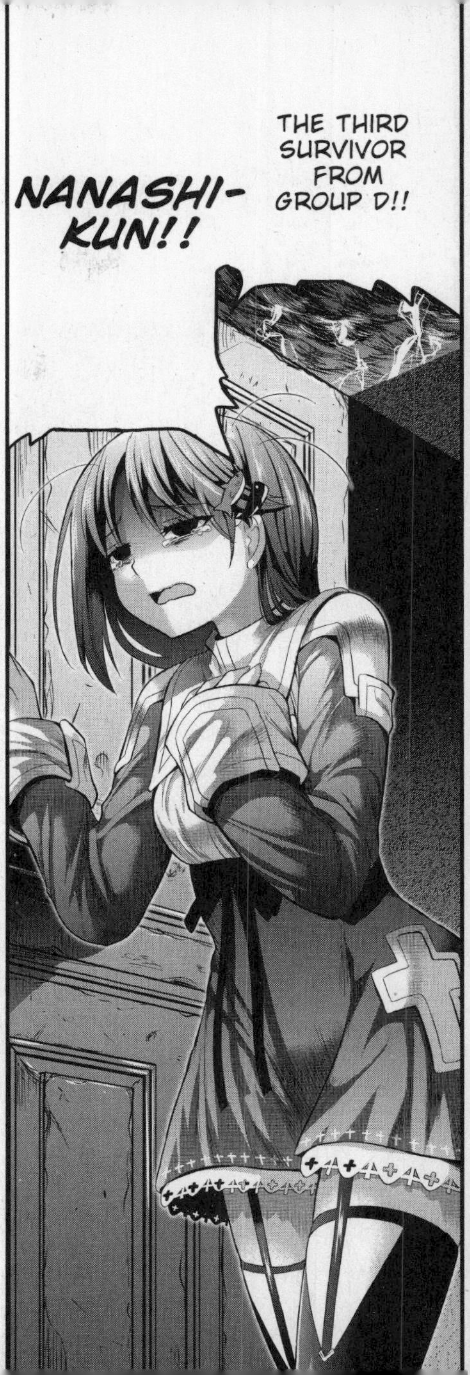
THE THIRD SURVIVOR FROM GROUP D!!
NANASHI-KUN!!
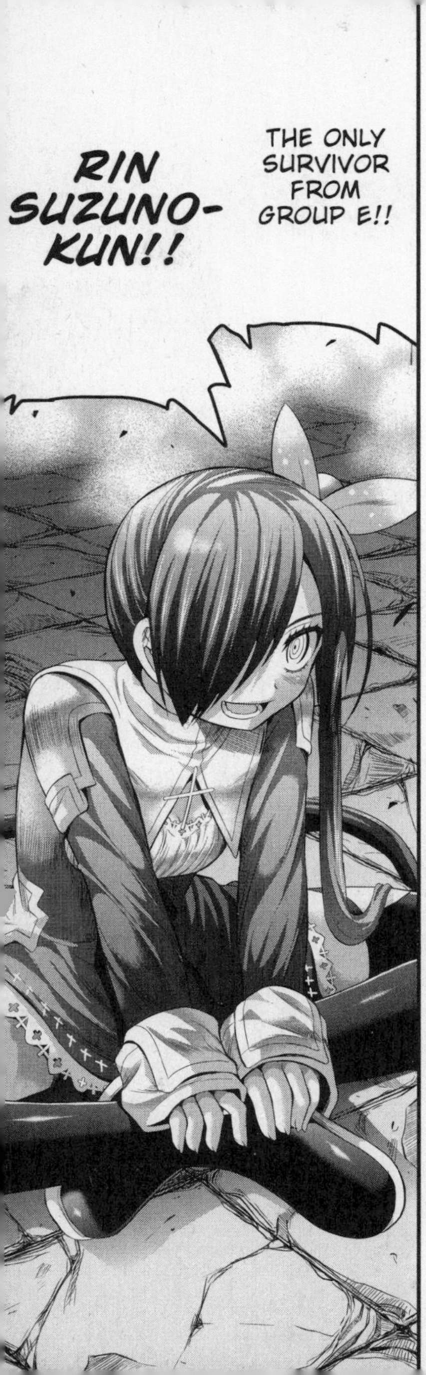
THE ONLY SURVIVOR FROM GROUP E!!
RIN SUZUNO-KUN!!

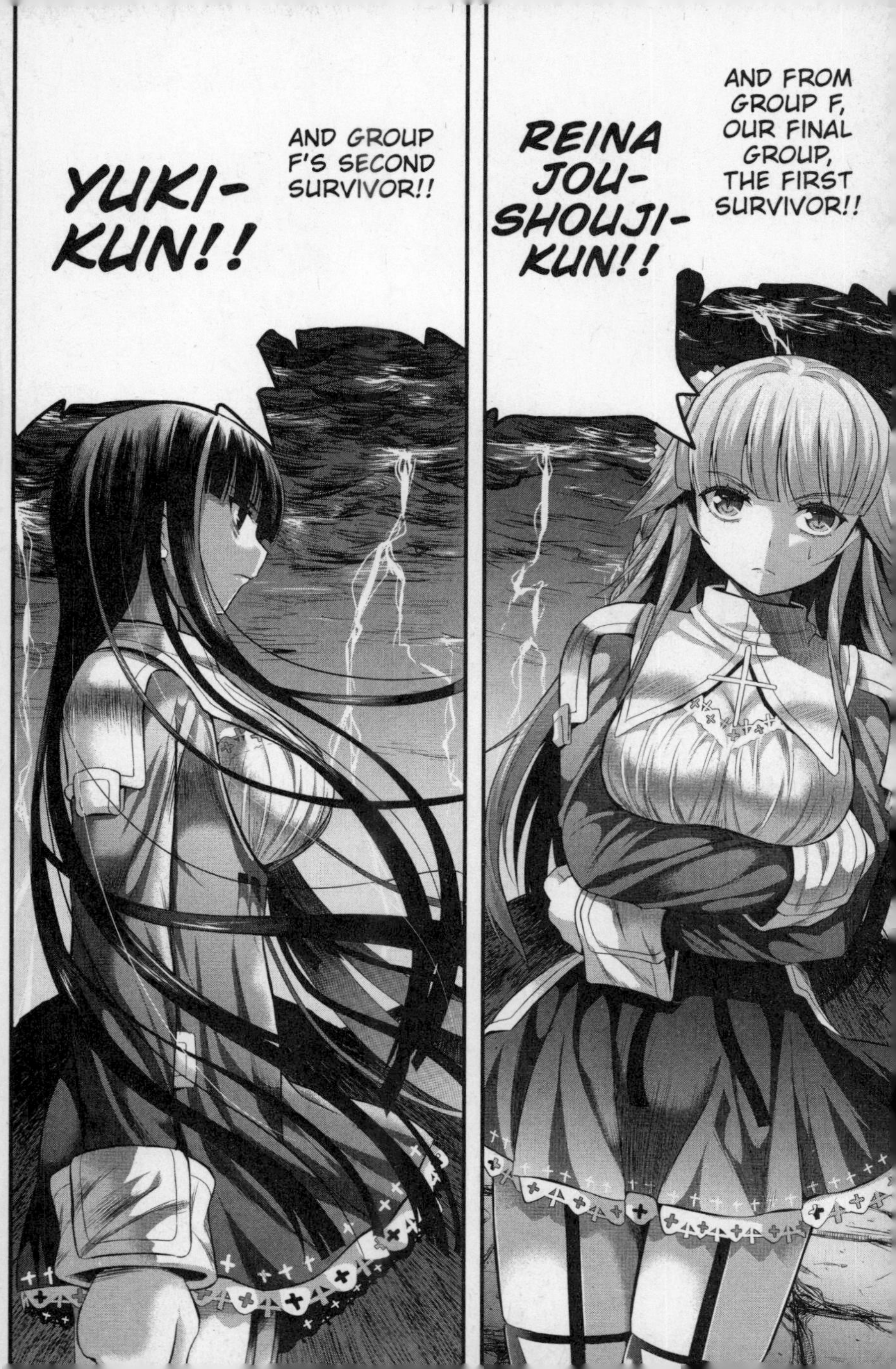
AND FROM GROUP F, OUR FINAL GROUP, THE FIRST SURVIVOR!!
REINA JOU-SHOUJI-KUN!!
AND GROUP F'S SECOND SURVIVOR!!
YUKI-KUN!!

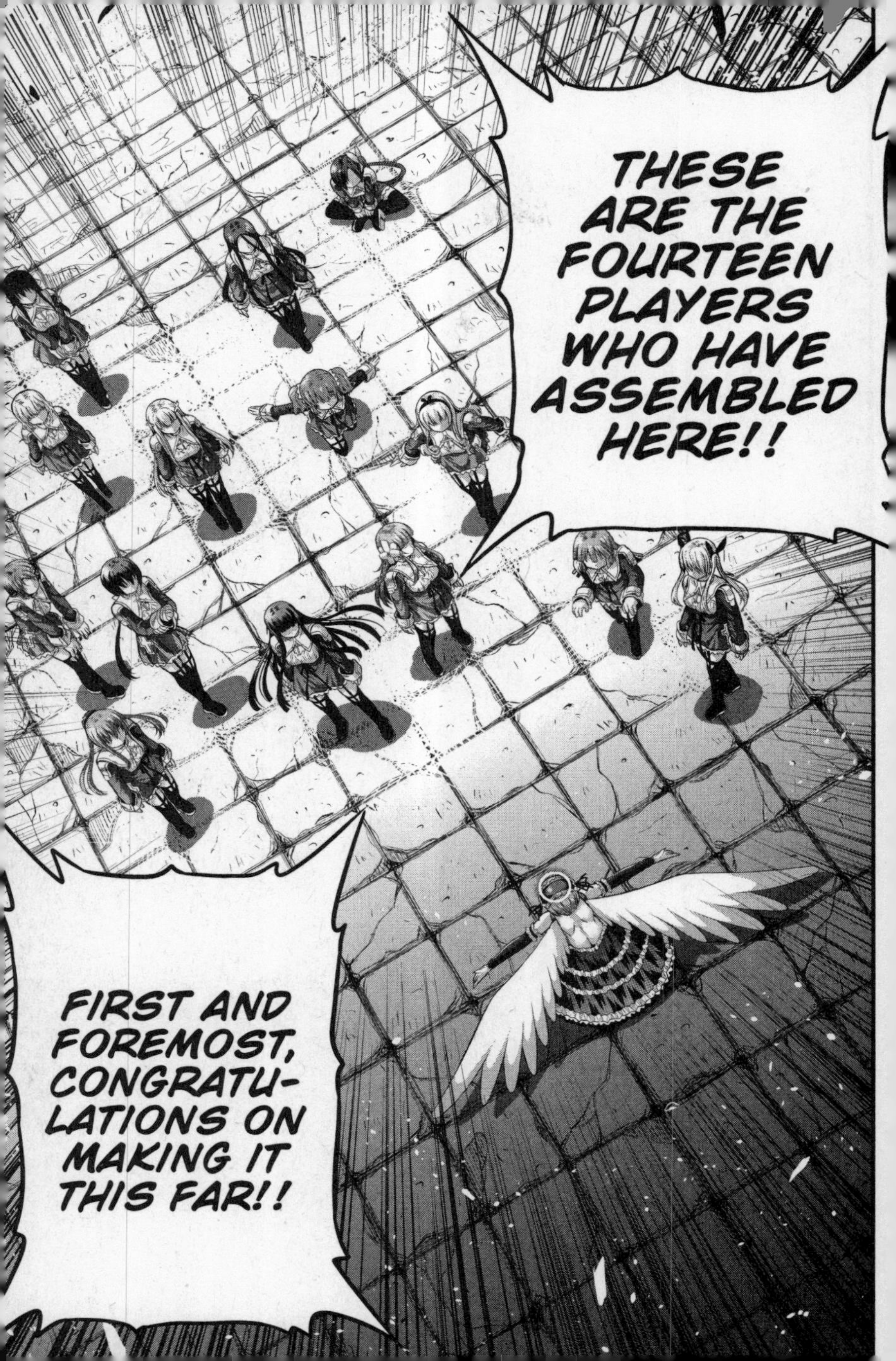
THESE ARE THE FOURTEEN PLAYERS WHO HAVE ASSEMBLED HERE!!
FIRST AND FOREMOST, CONGRATU-LATIONS ON MAKING IT THIS FAR!!

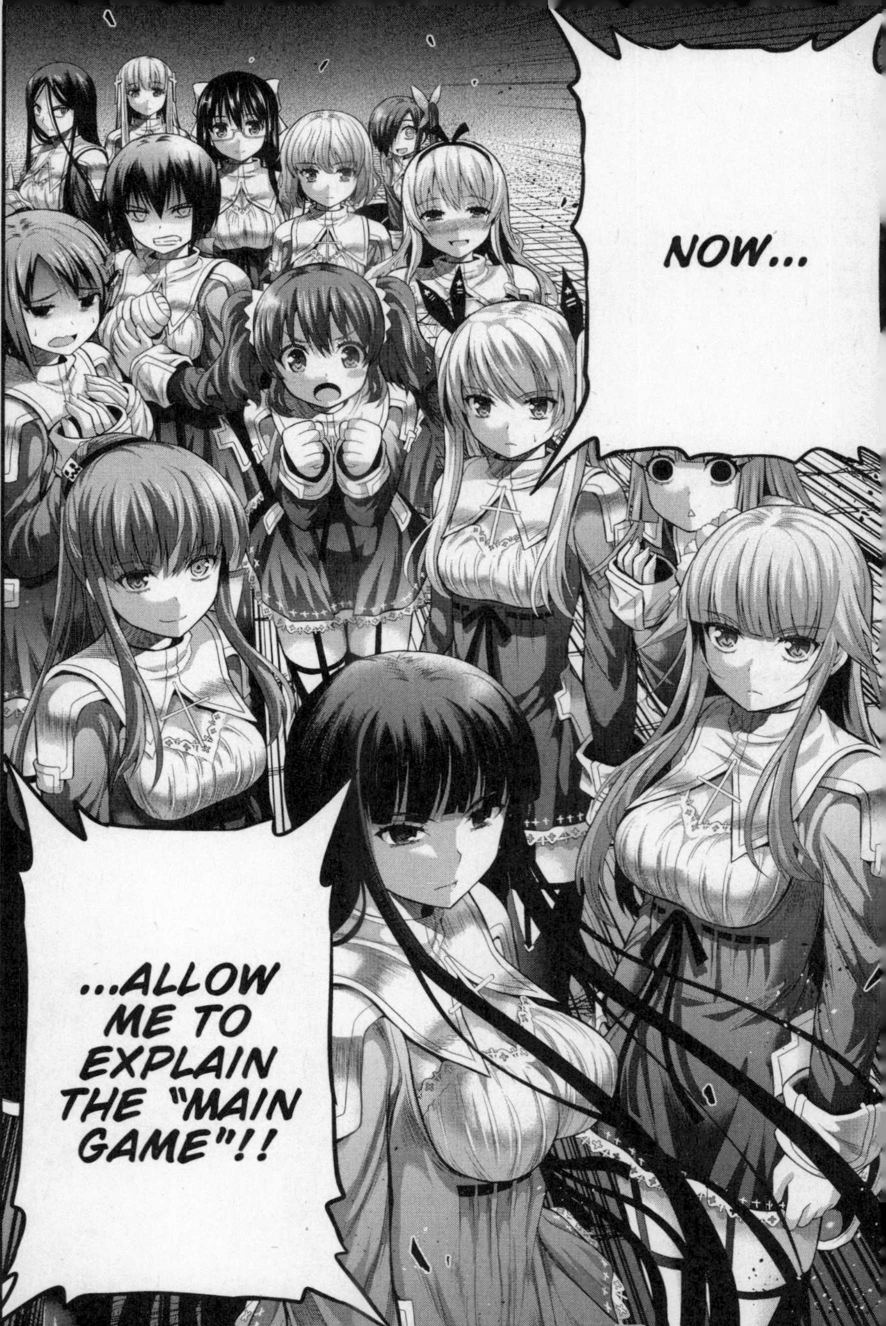
NOW...
...ALLOW ME TO EXPLAIN THE "MAIN GAME"!!

THOUGH YOU MAY BURN TO ASH 2 END

TRANSLATION NOTES

COMMON HONORIFICS
no honorific: Indicates familiarity or closeness; if used without permission or reason, addressing someone in this manner would constitute an insult.
-san: The Japanese equivalent of Mr./Mrs./Miss. If a situation calls for politeness, this is the fail-safe honorific.
-kun: Used most often when referring to boys, this indicates affection or familiarity. Occasionally used by older men among their peers, but it may also be used by anyone referring to a person of lower standing.
-chan: An affectionate honorific indicating familiarity used mostly in reference to girls; also used in reference to cute persons or animals of either gender.
-sensei: A respectful term for teachers, artists, or high-level professionals.

As we heard from Kroel in Volume 1, the contestants cannot divulge their real names, so they need aliases. Many of these aliases have special meanings in Japanese, which will be covered in the following notes.

Page 185
Rin Suzuno means "ring of the bell" in Japanese. Considering the bell in her hair, the alias seems appropriate.

Page 197
Akihara is written with two of the three characters used in "Akihabara," which is Tokyo's anime and manga mecca.

Page 198
Kiran is written with the characters for "orchid" and "princess," and it gives off a cute vibe.

Page 199
Don't trust anyone named ***Niseko Usotsuki***—the name means "fake liar."

Shizuku Kirikasumi is written with the characters for "fog," "haze," and "drop (of liquid)," giving her a mysterious air.

Page 200
Fugudoku means "blowfish poison," and it refers to the extremely lethal tetrodotoxin found in the fish's organs.

Page 201
Nanashi seems to be a bit of an edgy gal—the first two characters of her name mean "deceased," while the last simply means "die," making her name essentially "die, die, die."

Though You May Burn to ASH

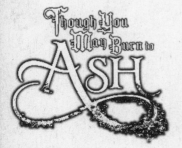

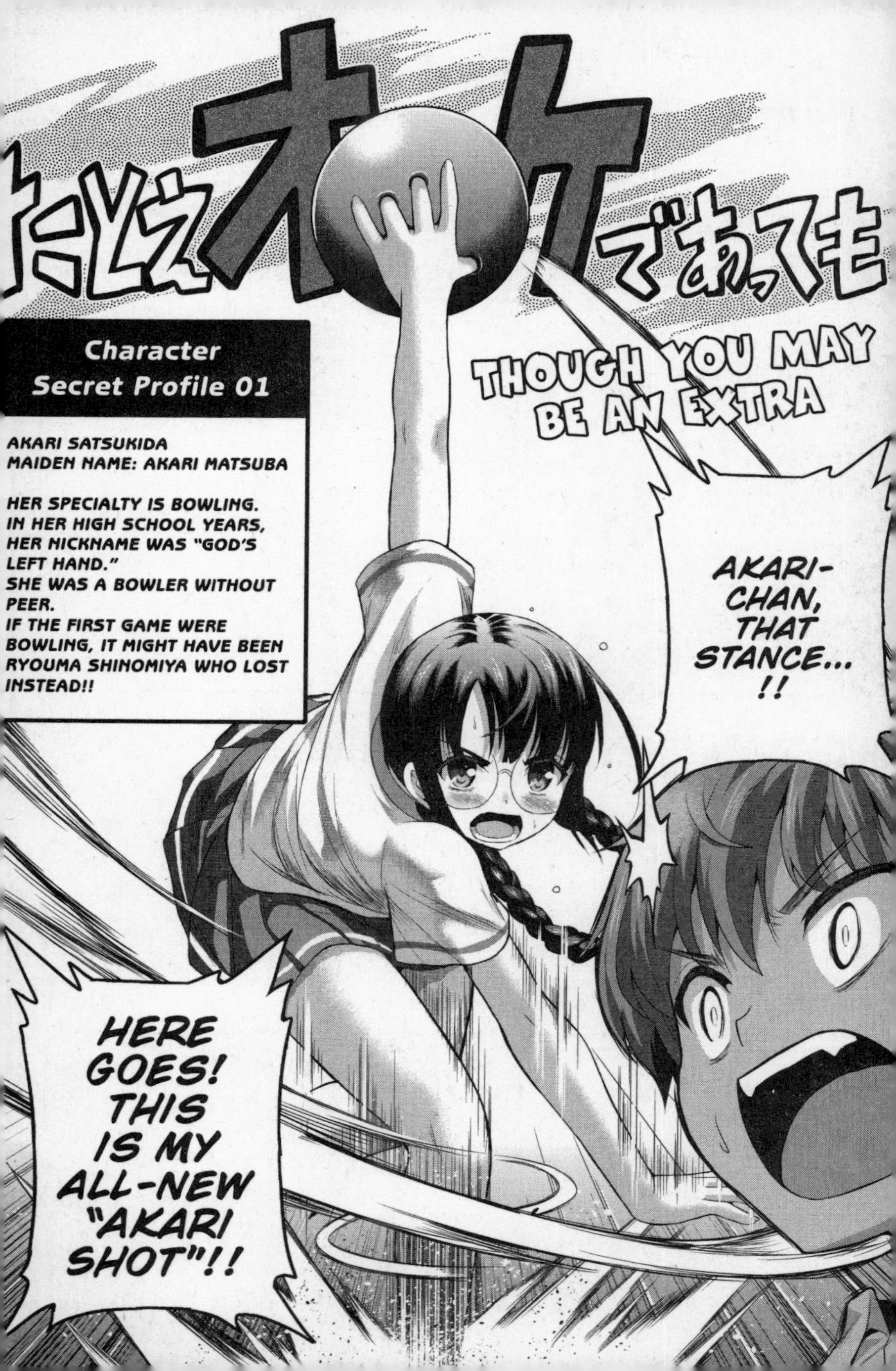
たとえオ●ケであっても
THOUGH YOU MAY BE AN EXTRA
Character Secret Profile 01
AKARI SATSUKIDA
MAIDEN NAME: AKARI MATSUBA
HER SPECIALTY IS BOWLING. IN HER HIGH SCHOOL YEARS, HER NICKNAME WAS "GOD'S LEFT HAND." SHE WAS A BOWLER WITHOUT PEER. IF THE FIRST GAME WERE BOWLING, IT MIGHT HAVE BEEN RYOUMA SHINOMIYA WHO LOST INSTEAD!!
AKARI-CHAN, THAT STANCE...!!
HERE GOES! THIS IS MY ALL-NEW "AKARI SHOT"!!

CHAPTER 9: MONEY IS LIFE, DEBT IS DEATH

Continuing on from what we did in the first volume, let's start the commentary.
I kind of wanted to draw a bonus bit or something here, but I just don't have the time for it.
But you know, according to the laws of physics, even if we didn't have the concept of time, it would still exist.
The concept of time itself is an assumption created from the theory of causality.
Time is an illusion born from the apprehensions of beings with limited perception...
I wonder if it can be thought of that way?

CHAPTER 10: THE COWARD AND THE SNAKE

This is where I start showing off the many faces of Yamada.
I like Yamada the best out of the four players.
No matter how hard she tries, her efforts don't bear fruit.
That part of her seems especially human.

CHAPTER 11: STRAY RABBIT

If this were the magazine, then this would be when you could see Miss Angel's "immodest" pose in all its full-color glory.
However, it's only in black-and-white for the collected volume. Too bad!!
I made sure to use some of the more erotic colors for the magazine, so if you feel like it, head on over to *Young Gangan* to check it out!

CHAPTER 12: A FOUL END

According to my sources, when using Phalaris's brazen bull, people would put herbs or other fragrant-smelling plants in with the person being roasted so they wouldn't have to deal with the smell of a human being cooked alive.
Apparently, Phalaris would hold a banquet with other aristocrats to enjoy the aromas and screams coming from the bull!...

CHAPTER 13: WHEN A WISH COMES TRUE...

This one was traumatic.
If you were to ask to whom, the answer would be me.
Yamada was my favorite character, so after I finished this chapter,
I got super depressed for a while.
What did Yamada do to deserve this!?
How could it end like that for her!?

CHAPTER 14: GRAVITY RESPONSE

Haruaki Satsukida. Age at death: 24 years old.
Akari Satsukida. Age at death: 24 years old.
These two were not only the same age, but also childhood
friends.
When they were in preschool, they made a promise to marry
each other, and they actually did when they got older.
And yet...

CHAPTER 15: THOUGH YOU MAY BURN TO ASH...

Here comes the part where I do a title-drop.
There's actually another part to this phrase, which I'm going to use for the final
chapter of this series.
If I say any more, we'll start getting into spoiler territory, so I'll stop now.
I'll be sure to make it a happy ending.
Let's just put aside who exactly it will be "happy" for.

CHAPTER 16: ASSEMBLING THE FOURTEEN

I'm paw-sitive that fourteen people is going
overboard, meow!
It was mighty difficult shoving fourteen people
into the same picture, that it was!

AFTERWORD

HEYA, IT'S ME.
KAKASHI ONIYAZU.
IT'S BEEN MANY MOONS SINCE VOLUME 1 FIRST WENT ON SALE...
BUT VOLUME 2 IS FINALLY FINISHED! YAY!!

THANK YOU FOR BUYING AND READING THE SECOND VOLUME OF *THOUGH YOU MAY BURN TO ASH.*
A LOT OF STUFF HAS BEEN GOING ON WITH ME SINCE VOLUME 1 WAS RELEASED. IT ALL HAPPENED RIGHT AFTER I FINISHED CHAPTER 15 FOR *YOUNG GANGAN...*

ALL OF A SUDDEN, MY EYES STARTED TO HURT LIKE YOU WOULDN'T BELIEVE. I'M NOT TALKING ABOUT THE "AW CRAP...THAT HURTS" KIND OF PAIN EITHER, OH NO. IT WAS MORE LIKE, "AHRHRHRHHGHHGH!! GYAAAHHHH!! KILL MEEEEE!!" NOT EVEN JOKING. IF THIS WERE AN INTERROGATION, I WOULD HAVE SPILLED MY GUTS THEN AND THERE. I'M GLAD IT WASN'T.

IF I WAS IN THE LIGHT AT ALL, IT WOULD HURT SO BAD THAT I WOULD START TO WRITHE AROUND IN PAIN. SO I WENT TO THE ONLY PLACE IN MY HOUSE THAT THE LIGHT COULDN'T REACH...
AND THAT'S HOW I ENDED UP SPENDING AN ENTIRE DAY IN THE TOILET. I EVEN ATE DINNER AND STUFF IN THERE. WHY THE HELL DID I HAVE TO DO THAT IN MY OWN HOME? I'VE GOTTEN BETTER NOW, BUT MY EYES DO STILL HURT A LITTLE. IT'S APPARENTLY SOMETHING CALLED "SCLERITIS." NOT SURE WHAT CAUSED IT.
MAKE SURE TO TAKE CARE OF YOUR EYES, EVERYONE!

THAT ASIDE, IT'S ALREADY BEEN A YEAR SINCE I GOT SERIALIZED IN *YOUNG GANGAN.* IT'S BEEN QUITE TAXING, ESPECIALLY STAMINA-WISE.
I'M GETTING OLDER TOO. IN THE PAST, I USED TO BE ABLE TO PULL TWO OR THREE ALL-NIGHTERS AND STILL BE FINE, BUT NOW I HAVE TO SLEEP AT LEAST TEN HOURS A DAY, OR MY BODY CAN'T TAKE IT. WHY AM I SLEEPING SO MUCH!?

ANYWAY, THIS HAS BEEN KAKASHI ONIYAZU. SEE YOU ALL AGAIN IN VOLUME 3! OH YEAH!!

✧ SPECIAL THANKS ✧

KAORU NAKAGAWA-SAMA · YUI HINAMORI-SAMA · CHOUNIKU-SAMA

SASAKI-SAN-SAMA · TAKASHI DOMOTO-SAMA · ASAKI NAKAMA-SAMA

HIROSHI ETOU-SAMA · MAKOTO ETOU-SAMA · YAMAGUCHI OPTOMETRY-SAMA

✧ THANK YOU VERY MUCH!

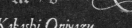

Though You May Burn to ASH 2

Kakashi Oniyazu

TRANSLATION: GARRISON DENIM ☠ LETTERING: ANDWORLDDESIGN

TATOE HAI NI NATTEMO vol. 2
© 2017 Kakashi Oniyazu / SQUARE ENIX CO., LTD.
First published in Japan in 2017 by SQUARE ENIX CO., LTD.
English translation rights arranged with SQUARE ENIX CO., LTD.
and Yen Press, LLC through Tuttle-Mori Agency, Inc.

English translation © 2018 by SQUARE ENIX CO., LTD.

Yen Press
1290 Avenue of the Americas
New York, NY 10104

Visit us at yenpress.com
facebook.com/yenpress
twitter.com/yenpress
yenpress.tumblr.com
instagram.com/yenpress

First Yen Press Edition: June 2018

Yen Press is an imprint of Yen Press, LLC.
The Yen Press name and logo are trademarks of Yen Press, LLC.

The publisher is not responsible for websites (or their content)
that are not owned by the publisher.

Library of Congress Control Number: 2017954641

ISBNs: 978-0-316-44687-7 (paperback)
978-0-316-44688-4 (ebook)

10 9 8 7 6 5 4 3 2 1

WOR

Printed in the United States of America